Sociology: Concepts and Characteristics

Second Edition

Judson R. Landis

**California State University,
Sacramento**

Wadsworth Publishing Company, Inc., Belmont, California

ISBN: 0-534-00344-3

L. C. Cat. Card No.: 73-89889

Printed in the United States of America

3 4 5 6 7 8 9 10—78 77 76 75

Preface

The major function of a beginning class in any field is to describe and illustrate that field's perspective or particular way of looking at phenomena. One way of illustrating a perspective is to provide an encyclopedic analysis of what the discipline is and does—all its tools, techniques, and substantive areas. It seems to me, however, that a *feeling* for an area of study and its unique perspective may be gained by a selective sampling of the concepts of that area of study. An in-depth treatment is more valuable *after* the basic view of the discipline is developed.

This book approaches the task of helping the student develop a general understanding of the sociological perspective by focusing on the *basic concepts* of sociology. How sociologists use these concepts is illustrated by summaries of sociological research and by briefly examining several substantive areas.

Readings have been used to illustrate certain aspects of the concepts, and to clarify the relation of the concepts to the real world. The selections include excerpts from articles, novels, autobiographies, popular magazines, and semi-professional journals that were, more often than not, written for a mass audience rather than for an audience of professional sociologists. The language and precise analysis of the professional sociologist may be missing in these readings, but the clear and direct communication of ideas justifies their presence. It seems to me, for example, that Orwell's description of the police officer facing a wild elephant and a mob and Malcolm X's description of a black growing up in a white community are unique. These writers illustrate aspects of "self" and "socialization." Thus, the concepts of sociology are introduced to give the student an idea of the sociological perspective. The concepts are illustrated by examples from a variety of sources; some are written by sociologists and some by non-sociologists who, intentionally or not, make sociological points very effectively.

In this edition, the chapter on Groups has been revised to include a discussion of primary and small groups. A new chapter on Social Differentiation has been included. Other changes include an expanded discussion of science and of positivism in Chapters 1 and 11, more coverage of socialization and self in Chapter 2, as well as a number of smaller additions to other chapters. Eight of the 31 readings are new to this edition.

Many people have helped me with ideas and criticism: colleagues Louise Kanter, Carole Barnes, Pat McGillivray, Dean Dorn, David Lee, Worth Summers, Ivy Lee, Andres Rendon, and Ayad Al-Qazzaz; reviewers Jeanne G. McKeown, San Jose City College, Nancy Mazanec, University of Missouri, R. C. Stanville, Normandale State Junior College, Dennis C. Scheck, California

State University at San Diego, H. E. Lindgren, North Dakota State University, Barry S. Perlman, Margaret M. Brindley, and Daniel Hebding, Community College of Philadelphia; graduate assistants Joseph Sheley and Jim Spencer; and secretary Lois Hill. This is dedicated to Sheron, who criticized and encouraged, and to young Jeffrey and Brian, who hindered constantly.

Judson R. Landis

Contents

1 Introduction 1

Social Science 1
Science 3
Sociology 5
Design of the Book 8

Part One   Socialization and Culture   9

2 Socialization and Self   11

Socialization—A Social Process 12
Self 14
Definition of the Situation 19
Summary 19
readings
    The Story of My Life
        Helen Keller 21
    A Conversation with Jerome Kagan
        Editors of *Saturday Review* 27
    Mascot
        Malcolm X 32
    Shooting an Elephant
        George Orwell 39

3 Norms, Roles, Culture   45

Norms 46
    Types of Norms 47
    Norm Conflict and Change 48

Status and Role 48
    Achieved and Ascribed Status 50
    Role Strain and Role Conflict 50

Other Cultures, Other Norms 51
    Society and Culture 53
    Culture and Personality 54
    Ethnocentrism and Cultural Relativism 55
    Subculture and Contraculture 55

Summary 57
readings
    The Mysterious Drop in Japan's Birth Rate
        Koya Azumi 58
    Some Conditions of Obedience and Disobedience to Authority
        Stanley Milgram 63
    One Hundred Per Cent American
        Ralph Linton 70

Return to Laughter
    Elenore S. Bowen 73

Part Two   Social Organization 78

4   Groups, Categories, Aggregations 81

Groups and Non-groups 81
    Types of Groups 83
    Primary Groups and Small Groups 84
    Formal Organizations 89

Summary 94

readings
    Friends and Networks
        Elliot Liebow 95
    Inside the New York Telephone Company
        Elinor Langer 99

5   Social Differentiation 111

Social Stratification 112
    Parallel Stratification Systems 112
    Socioeconomic Status 113
    How Many Social Classes? 115
    Determining Social Class 117
    Social Class and Behavior 118
    Social Mobility 120

Race and Ethnicity 122
    Prejudice and Discrimination 124
    Patterns of Interaction 128
    Minority Group Reactions 129

Summary 131

readings
    Making It: The Brutal Bargain
        Norman Podhoretz 132
    Vuitton: Status Never Comes Cheap
        Editors of the New York Times 144
    Black Like Me
        John Howard Griffin 146
    The Womanly Image: Character Assassination Through the Ages
        Paula Stern 154

6   Institutions 163

Family 165
    Structural Variabilities 165
    Functional Uniformities 167
    Family in America 168

Religion 170
    Elements and Functions of Religion 170
    Religious Organizations 173
    Religion in America 173

Summary 177

readings
  Courtship among the Dobu
    Ruth Benedict 178
  Courtship among the Mundugumor
    Margaret Mead 180
  The Family as a People Wrecker
    Snell Putney 182
  The Serpent-Handling Religions of West Virginia
    Nathan L. Gerrard 189

7 Population and Ecology 197

Population 198

Human Ecology 203

Problem Aspects 208

Summary 212

readings
  Can Anyone Run a City?
    Gus Tyler 212
  Overpopulated America
    Wayne H. Davis 221

Part Three   Social Change and Social Deviation 227

8 Social Change and Social Disorganization 229

Factors Related to Social Change 230
  Rates of Change 232
  Planned Social Change and Social Movements 233
  Patterns of Social Change 236

Social Disorganization 237

Summary 239

readings
  Two Tactics for Ethnic Survival—Eskimo and Indian
    Robert J. Dryfoos, Jr. 240
  Steel Axes for Stone Age Australians
    Lauriston Sharp 244
  The Black Muslims in America
    C. Eric Lincoln 252

9 Collective Behavior 259

Crowd 260

Audience, Mob, Riot 261

Panic and Mass Hysteria 262

Rumor 263

Fads, Crazes, Fashions 264

Disaster 264

Publics and Public Opinion 265

Summary 268

readings
Riot: Tampa, Newark, Detroit
U.S. Riot Commission   269
Of Rumor, Myth and a Beatle
Editors of *Time*   277
Maycomb Jail
Harper Lee   280
The English Flood of 1953
John P. Spiegel   285

10   Deviation and Social Control   293

Defining Deviation   293

Categories of Deviation   296

Deviant Behavior and Criminal Behavior   299

Explanations for Deviant Behavior   301

Deviant Behavior in Perspective   302

Social Control   303

Summary   306

readings
Two Delicate Conditions
Robin Zehring   307
The Corporation Prostitute
anonymous   312
How French Children Learn to Drink
Barbara G. Anderson   319
Losers and Outsiders
Hunter S. Thompson   323

11   What Is Sociology?   335

A Sociological Perspective   336

Sociological Perspectives of Sociology   338

What Do Sociologists Do?   341

Sociology and You   342

Annotated Bibliography   345
Glossary   355
Index   361

1

Introduction

Social Science

Social science in general and sociology in particular seem to have developed because of two characteristics that have been noted in the human animal. One is that humans tend to group together and cooperate rather than to remain apart and isolated. The second is that humans tend in similar situations to behave in the same ways time after time. That is, their behavior is predictable. The behavior of humans becomes predictable, however, only after extensive study. And it is basically this study that social scientists undertake. In a variety of ways, social scientists study and record human behavior. The anthropologist traditionally has gone about the task by examining artifacts and remains of long-extinct communities, or by living with and studying preliterate tribes and societies. The concept *culture* is of central importance in anthropological analyses. The historian records an accurate chronology of past events. As events are placed in perspective, analysis of emerging trends may lead the historian to predictions about the future. The political scientist studies the characteristics and patterns of political systems, the principles and conduct of government. His topics include political parties, elections, systems of government, foreign policy, and the comparative structure of governments. The econo-

1

mist is interested in patterns of production, distribution, and consumption of goods and services. He studies such topics as price and market theories, consumer behavior, merchandising and selling practices, money, banking, and credit, and economic growth and development. The psychologist deals with the individual, his adjustment and personality, his patterns of learning, motivation, and perception. The sociologist focuses on groups, on patterns of interaction, on descriptions of the institutions and social organization of society.

In 1963, fifteen or twenty men robbed a mail train in England and got away with more than $7,000,000. The "great train robbery" baffled and amazed the world. If we could imagine for a moment that some social scientists became interested in the event, how might their analyses of it vary? Historians would record all facts and details. Who was involved? How much was taken? When and where did the incident happen? What happened later—who was caught and who remains free? Perhaps they would describe the recent history of the victim, the Royal Mail Train. They might provide an analysis of crime in England in the 1960s to place the event in historical perspective. Psychologists would focus on the personal backgrounds of the individuals involved. They would attempt to describe and explain personalities, motivations for the act, any particular traits that the robbers had. Sociologists would be interested in society's reaction to the event. English courts reacted harshly (thirty years in prison for those caught), yet some Englishmen treated the robbers as folk heroes. (Many recognized the cleverness of the act, and a car manufacturer advertised, in effect, "The train robbers used our vehicles, shouldn't you . . . ?") Sociologists would also be interested in analyzing the train robbers as a group—the organization, the division of labor, the patterns of leadership.

And yet, attempts at distinguishing between the social sciences are difficult, for they are much more similar than they are different. In some areas, anthropologists and sociologists approach their task in the same way. Sociologists frequently make use of cross-cultural analysis and participant observation, techniques that are usually associated with anthropologists. Likewise, many anthropologists are studying aspects of contemporary industrialized societies, which are usually the province of sociologists. In other areas, it is difficult to distinguish between sociological and psychological approaches. A relatively new social science—social psychology—has developed, formally combining aspects of sociology and psychology. Many sociologists use historical analysis, and many historians behave in ways that we are convinced are sociological. In his recent book *Wayward Puritans,* sociologist Kai Erikson applied current theories of deviant behavior to the seventeenth-century Puritans of Massachusetts Bay. His study involved extensive analysis of historical documents and represented a coordination of historical and sociological analyses. In summary, we find some slight differences between respective social sciences in matters of emphasis rather than marked differences in approach.

Science

How do we know what we know? In the past, man has used numerous ways to gain knowledge, and there may remain as yet undiscovered new ways to find "truth." Contrast mysticism, rationalism, and empiricism. Mysticism refers to knowledge gained by intuition, revelation, inspiration, magic, visions, spells. Rationalism refers to knowledge gained through common sense, logic, and reason. Consequently, at one time in history knowledge emerging from a common-sense analysis would tell us that the earth is flat ("Couldn't be round, people on the other side would fall off. . . ."), and that if two metal objects—a heavy one and a light one—were dropped from a height, the heavy object would fall much faster. The major criterion for judgment in common sense, as Whitehead pointed out, is that new ideas shall look like old ones. The lessons of history are important, of course, but not to the extent that they blind us to the present. Empiricism refers to knowledge that is gained by sense observation, and this is the basis of science: Science is a way of gaining knowledge by observing phenomena with the senses. Instead of "arm-chair reasoning" about the heavy and light objects, we will drop them from a tall building and observe whether the heavy one falls faster.

Now, there is more to science than sense observation, although that is at its base. A basic assumption of most scientific endeavors is that phenomena are related causally. Science maintains that a *cause–effect relationship* exists in that each event has a prior cause or causes which theoretically can be discovered. Gravity "causes" the objects to fall (effect) from the building. If the heavy one falls faster or if they fall at the same speed, these effects are also "caused" by something that we can try to discover. The idea of *control* is essential to science. The scientist attempts to control those factors in the environment that he is not studying but that might have an effect on what he is studying. Our friend who is dropping objects from tall buildings may decide to perform his experiment only on calm clear days. He is not studying wind and rain but they might affect how the objects drop, and so he would want to control for them. (Ideally, he would probably want to perform the experiment in a vacuum if that were possible.) Careful *definition of terms* is part of science. These are often called operational or working definitions and they allow others to know precisely what the scientist studied and how he carried out his experiment. The object-dropping experiment would include the following information: the size and weight of the objects being dropped, how far they are to be dropped, method of observation of the drop, pressure and temperature at the time of the drop, and so on. The scientist is assumed to be *objective,* although honest is perhaps a better way of putting it. He is expected to note what he actually sees, not what he hopes to see or wishes he had seen. He doesn't select or choose only those data that will fit or prove the hypothesis on which he is working while ignoring contrary evidence. (One doesn't test the idea that sociology professors are absent-minded by looking for a sociology professor who is so afflicted and then saying I told you so.) If the light object falls faster, or if both objects *rise* when he lets go of them, then that is what the scientist reports. Finally, *replication* and *verification* are important factors and they refer to the necessity for the scientist to repeat his experiment again and again to be sure that the results are consistent.

Generally when the word "scientist" is mentioned one imagines a white-coated figure bending over a microscope surrounded by forty test tubes and a Bunsen burner, or an astronomer peering through a telescope discovering the secrets of the universe. In fact, science encompasses vast and widely differing sets of methods. Look for example at the tremendous variety of techniques used by social scientists. Historians study documents, archives, and other records for evidence about the past. The psychologist gains knowledge by using projective tests such as the Rorschach inkblot test, by experiments on perception involving sensitive laboratory equipment, by running rats through mazes, and by the use of interview rooms with one-way mirrors. Anthropologists developed the technique of participant observation which has been used to study primitive societies, delinquent gangs, and community ethnic and class stratification. Sociologists are much involved in survey research using large numbers of questionnaires and interviews analyzed by computers.

There is much discussion and occasional argument about who "does science" better, and there *are* obvious differences in the effectiveness of different techniques. Some sciences seem to be more objective, some predict with much greater accuracy, and the accumulation of knowledge in some is much greater than in others. These differences may reflect a difference in goals (pure versus applied), a difference in subject matter (people versus elements in possibly more basic forms), or differences in historical development and sophistication of techniques. Let's allow the issue of levels of science to rest, however; the important points for our discussion are that science is a method of gaining knowledge, and that scientists, regardless of the area or subject matter, are guided by a common set of beliefs, assumptions, and principles.

The following brief example may serve to illustrate the link between the general principles of science and a particular social science project. Several students and I worked on a project that centered upon two ideas. First, the women's liberation movement was in full swing and we were interested in the viewpoints college women held on some of the issues of the feminist movement. Second, we were interested in response bias. Will your responses to a questionnaire or interview be the same if you are questioned by a white as compared to a black? By a young person as compared to an older person? By a male as compared to a female? Probably not. Your responses on the questionnaire vary, not so much because of the questions asked (although that is important, too), but because of *who* is asking them. This, of course, greatly affects the accuracy of the questionnaire.

Most research projects center upon a *hypothesis,* which is a statement or proposition that can be subjected to empirical test. From the basic ideas mentioned above an hypothesis was developed for our project: "Response to feminist attitudes will be affected by the sex of the interviewer." A series of items dealing with feminist attitudes were collected and ninety married college women were interviewed. They were asked whether they "strongly agreed," "agreed," were "undecided," "disagreed," or "strongly disagreed" with statements such as "A woman's place is in the home," "Motherhood and a career should not be mixed," "Males have higher I.Q.s and better abilities than females." The subjects were selected randomly and were separated into two groups by the flip of a coin. Half of the subjects (45) were contacted by a male interviewer; the other half were asked the same questions by a female interviewer. When we analyzed their answers, we found that the women responded to the male interviewer much differently from how they did to the female interviewer. I'll return to this later, but which response would you anticipate: a more militantly feminist response to the male interviewer ("the enemy") or to the female interviewer ("she's one of us, she understands"), and why?

Some of the characteristics of science mentioned earlier are illustrated in this study. We were testing a cause–effect relationship. The sex of the interviewer was the *independent variable,* or cause; the women's response on the feminist items was the *dependent variable,* or effect. By selecting the sample randomly we hoped to control for factors we weren't interested in but which might affect the results. Details of the characteristics of subjects and interviewers were noted, as were the questions that were asked as well as the errors or weaknesses of the study. The major weakness, by the way, lies in the area of controls. For example, it was assumed that the interviewer's sex was the cause of the differing responses, but what if it was the personalities of the two interviewers or the clothes they were wearing or something else that had not been controlled for? In other words, because of inadequate controls, *another* "cause" may have produced the "effect" we noted, or perhaps *several* "causes" (of which the interviewer's sex was only one) were operating. The study should be repeated by others to verify the results, and when it is, controlling for the additional factors we missed would be appropriate.[1]

Sociology

This book is about a particular social science called sociology. More specifically, it is about the *concepts* of sociology. Concepts provide a way of generalizing about phenomena; a concept points out an "abstract" similarity in "concrete" events. It is the concept "disaster," for example, that points out a common

[1] For more detail on this study, see "Feminist Attitudes as Related to Sex of the Interviewer," by Judson R. Landis, Daryl Sullivan, and Joseph Sheley, *Pacific Sociological Review,* Vol. 16, No. 3 (July 1973), pp. 305–314.

element in flood, fire, and war; the concept "beauty" that might unify flowers, sunsets, and symphonies.

The concepts we will be examining in this book are the general terms that sociologists have coined to describe significant common phenomena that would not be "apparent" without the use of such concepts. Sociologists use concepts—role, motivation, anticipatory socialization, culture, in-group, cult, institution, mob—to help them organize and understand the events that they are studying. In fact, one could say that the major task of sociology (and probably other disciplines as well) is to build concepts—that is, to isolate certain unifying, abstract qualities that underlie and thus "explain" behavior. This book attempts to gather together some of the major concepts of sociology and define and illustrate them. Not all concepts are included, but the important ones are.

What *is* sociology? The dictionary defines sociology as the "science or study of the origin, development, organization, and functioning of human society." Sociologists study human society and social behavior, and they focus on groups, institutions, and social organization. More than by memorizing this definition, however, I think you will get a feeling for what sociology is from going through the concepts of sociology and some examples of how the concepts are used.

There are several areas of study within the discipline of sociology. For example, sociologists specialize in such areas as small groups, large-scale organizations, race relations, religion, marriage and the family, social problems, collective behavior, criminology and delinquency, social class, urban and rural sociology, population and demography, and the sociology of medicine. Although each area is unique, the same general concepts are important in almost all. It is on these commonly held concepts that this book focuses.

Students of introductory sociology, and many others as well, frequently describe and consequently dismiss sociology as mere common sense. Or worse, they say, "Sociologists describe what we all knew anyway in language that none of us can understand."

Unfortunately, there may be some truth to this statement, especially the indictment of obscure and complicated language. Sociologists might benefit if they learned to use more four-letter words and fewer twenty-four-letter ones. The belief, however, that sociology deals only with common sense is, I think, inaccurate. One reason such a statement is made is that sociologists deal with contemporary human behavior, patterns of interaction between people. Since most of us are humans, we feel quite familiar with the topic. "Atoms and rockets are one thing, but when it comes to understanding people, I'm an expert. . . ." We all are. . . .

In some aspects of human behavior our experiences and our intuition may serve us well. None of us, however, has experienced all situations. Because we live in a particular society, area, social class, and community, at a particular time in history, and because of a number of other biasing factors, our experiences are necessarily limited. We in fact know much less about human behavior than we think. For example, let's return to the study of feminist attitudes described earlier. Which interviewer (male or female) got the more militantly feminist response from the women who were interviewed? Well, it turns out that the women were more militantly feminist to the male interviewer; to the female interviewer asking the same questions, they were much less feminist and less pro-women's liberation. Did you guess right? Perhaps you did and had a logical explanation as well, but a peculiarity of common sense is that it can provide a rationale for almost *any* response. It takes a more sophisticated analysis to accurately predict human behavior and to answer the complex questions of why people do what they do. To further put what we know by means of common sense in perspective, try the "social awareness" questions listed below. How well does your common sense serve you?

"Social Awareness Test"[2]

Are the following true or false?

1. *More thirteen- through fifteen-year-olds are arrested for crimes than twenty-two through twenty-four-year-olds.*
2. *Because of discrimination and depressed living conditions, Negroes commit suicide relatively more often than whites.*
3. *With the exception of movie stars, people who divorce are slow to remarry.*
4. *Land is generally less expensive in the suburbs than in other parts of the city.*
5. *Women, being somewhat more emotional, are more likely to commit suicide than men.*
6. *There are more Hindus in the world than Protestants.*
7. *Cities are where the jobs are; consequently, there are generally more men than women in cities.*
8. *Children from divorced or unhappy homes are usually more careful in selecting a mate and make better marriages.*

---

[2] Gerald Maxwell describes a "Social Awareness" test that he has devised (*The American Sociologist* [November 1966], pp. 253–254). I have used his title as well as one or two of his questions.
   Answers:
   1. True. Thirteen- through seventeen-year-olds lead all ages in arrest statistics. See *Uniform Crime Reports—1972.*
   2. False. See page 299.

9. *Panic is a common response for people confronted by disaster.*
10. *People with some college education are more likely to attend church than are people with only a high-school education.*

Design of the Book

This discussion of sociological concepts is divided into three parts. The first section deals with the development and socialization of the individual, and the concepts of socialization, self, norms, roles, and culture are discussed. The second section examines the social organization of society. The concepts of this section are groups, categories, aggregations, institutions, population, and human ecology. The third section deals with change and deviation in society. This section covers social change, social disorganization, collective behavior, deviation, and social control. A final chapter, "What Is Sociology?" will summarize and conclude. Throughout the book, readings are included to illustrate the concepts discussed, some written by sociologists, some by people from other walks of life, to illustrate the "real" events from which sociological generalizations arise.

3. False. Divorced persons are generally more likely to marry than single persons of the same age. (See Marshall Clinard, *Sociology of Deviant Behavior,* 3rd Ed. [New York: Holt, Rinehart and Winston, 1968], p. 546.)
4. True. See pages 203–204.
5. False. See page 299.
6. True. See page 170.
7. False. See page 199.
8. False. Couples whose parents had unhappy marriages have a greater proneness to divorce. (See Clinard, *Sociology of Deviant Behavior,* 3rd Ed., p. 548.
9. False. See page 265.
10 True. See page 174.

ONE

Socialization and Culture

In this section, we discuss how the infant develops into a social being. The *socialization* process is of major importance. Through this process values are transmitted from one generation to the next, and the infant grows and learns to adapt to his environment. The *self,* the person's conception of what and who he is, slowly emerges from his interaction with others. Through this interaction, the individual is introduced to *norms* and *roles,* behaviors that are expected of him in specific situations and positions. This personal and social development takes place within the context of a specific *culture.* The culture provides a set of behaviors, traditions, customs, habits, and skills that also become a part of the individual. These processes—socialization, development of the self, internalization of norms, roles, and other aspects of the culture—are particularly evident in the young child, although they continue to be important throughout life.

2

Socialization and Self

Few people spend much time thinking about the transformation they went through in the process of becoming mature human beings. Not only are we not concerned with the steps required to carry us from an early "blob" of protoplasm to a complicated, interacting individual, but it is even hard for us to believe that we were ever at the stage of egg and sperm. Beyond a certain idle curiosity as we watch a baby grow up, we take these changes in the developing human for granted. They are like the phases of the moon or the coming of summer—they seem to just happen.

If, however, one decides to analyze the development of the individual in some detail, several approaches are available. A biological approach would emphasize physiological maturation. As a man's hair changes from brown to gray to gone, so does the person grow and mature in other ways. This approach might suggest that maturity is merely a matter of changes in cells, and that given enough time, these changes produce a mature social being.

But if human development is a purely physiological process, how do you explain those cases of humans reared in isolation whose development, as a consequence, is greatly retarded? Studies of isolates—children reared in back rooms or attics by parents attempting to deny their existence—point out that the physiological processes had time to take place, but the result was not a mature social being.[1] Isolation from human interaction in these cases affected the normal growth of the organism in a number of ways. The explanation must be that the development of the individual is, at least in part, a *social* process.

Socialization—A Social Process

The process by which the organism becomes a social being is called socialization. *Socialization* refers to the learning of expectations, habits, skills, values, beliefs, and other requirements necessary for effective participation in social groups. Biological maturity is necessary, hereditary factors may set limits, and the process takes place in a physical environment, but the crucial aspect of socialization is that it is a social process. The individual develops through interaction in the social environment; the social environment "determines" the result. This is not to imply that if baby Willie Mays and baby Leonard Bernstein had been switched in the nursery shortly after birth, Bernstein would have played center field for the New York Mets and Mays would have directed the New York Philharmonic. Other factors are important, too. But by and large (at least according to sociologists) social environment and social interaction are the primary determinants of who we are.

By *social interaction* we mean the process of being aware of others when we act, of modifying our behavior in accordance with others' responses.[2] Social interaction occurs in a variety of ways and its patterns are complex. When a student asks a teacher a question, he speaks differently from when he talks to the student next to him in class. The teacher evaluates the question as fairly sophisticated and this affects his response to the student. If the interaction continues, each response is modified and determined by the response of the other immediately preceding it. The pattern of interaction may be affected by manner, body language, deference, relative status, degree of acquaintance, eye contact, and numerous other factors in addition to the spoken words. Social interaction occurs between two people—husband and wife, strangers on the street—and in groups and even large organizations.

---

[1] Studies of children isolated from other humans are reported by Kingsley Davis, "Final Note on a Case of Extreme Isolation," *American Journal of Sociology*, 52 (1947), pp. 432–437, and Bruno Bettelheim, "Feral Children and Autistic Children," *American Journal of Sociology*, 64 (March 1959), pp. 455–467.

[2] This definition of social interaction follows the discussion presented by Leonard Broom and Phillip Selznick in their book, *Sociology*, 5th Ed. (New York: Harper & Row, 1973), Chapter 2, and by Robert Nisbet in his book, *The Social Bond* (New York: Alfred Knopf, 1970), pp. 57–59.

Socialization is continuous—it takes place throughout life, starting as soon as the infant leaves the womb and continuing until death. It occurs through interaction with other humans. We could call these other humans *agents of socialization*. Who they will be depends on one's place in the life span. For the baby, the socialization agents are his parents, who begin very early to communicate "correct" and expected modes of behavior to the infant. Brothers and sisters also become socialization agents. An aspect of the socialization process can be observed in children as they pretend to be mothers, fathers, airplane pilots, or truck drivers. They are already anticipating and "playing" future roles. Later, peers become socialization agents, and, whether they are school friends or members of a delinquent gang or teammates on the football team, their influence becomes very important. Still later, one's colleagues on the job, one's spouse, and even one's own children become agents of socialization. Also, indirect influences such as vicarious participation or involvement in what we are reading or watching on TV continually play a part in the socialization process.

Socialization may be better understood as occurring at two levels—primary and secondary. According to Berger and Luckmann, *primary socialization* refers to the first socialization an individual undergoes in childhood, through which he becomes a member of society. *Secondary socialization* refers to any subsequent process that inducts an already socialized individual into new sectors of his society.[3] Primary socialization usually takes place in the family. Here, the individual has no choice about the important or significant socializing agents— he almost automatically and inevitably accepts and internalizes their view of the world. As primary socialization proceeds, the child's referents move from specific to general. A progressive abstraction occurs whereby at one stage the child understands that his mother specifically wants him to do certain things (for example, not mess in his food), at a later stage he understands that people in general expect him to behave in certain ways (to use correct manners and not mess in his food). It is through primary socialization that the individual's first world is constructed, and consequently, according to Berger and Luckmann, it is the most important, for the basic structure of all secondary socialization must resemble that of primary socialization. Primary socialization ends when the "generalized other" has been established (see Mead's ideas about the generalized other on page 17).

Secondary socialization takes over where primary socialization leaves off and involves the individual's moving into and internalizing knowledge of new areas or sectors of life. Secondary socialization takes place when the individual decides to learn to read or to type, to take up sky-diving, to become a police officer, or

---

[3] This discussion follows that contained in *The Social Construction of Reality*, by Peter Berger and Thomas Luckmann (Garden City, New York: Doubleday & Company, 1966), especially pp. 129–147.

to raise a family. Secondary socialization does not need an emotionally charged atmosphere to succeed, nor does it presuppose a high degree of identification, and its contents do not possess the quality of inevitability. In secondary socialization, the individual can be more objective than in primary socialization.

A person entering a new profession illustrates adult secondary socialization; an example is the steps in the socialization of the new police officer, outlined by Arthur Niederhoffer. The rookie patrolman proudly accepts the symbols of his new job—uniform, revolver, and badge. At police academy he learns about law, police procedures, human relations, rules and regulations, first aid, and how to fire weapons. He graduates, becomes a patrolman, faces a hostile and unappreciative public, and "reality shock" occurs. The more experienced officers tell him that in order to become a real policeman, he will have to forget everything he learned at the academy. The patrolman learns a new language, he learns to treat people differently in different areas of the city, he learns to react to people's language, attitudes, and dress as well as to their criminal behavior. He learns when to enforce the law and when to look the other way. He learns how to make an arrest effectively and he learns about graft. According to Niederhoffer, his attitudes change the longer he is on the force; if the officer has a college education but is slow to get promoted, he becomes more and more cynical. And generally as officers near retirement they become less cynical.[4]

When a person adopts the values, behavior, or viewpoints of a group he would like to belong to, but does not yet, this is called *anticipatory socialization*. This is a common occurrence and explains the behavior of the lower-class person who develops middle-class values, or the behavior of the gung-ho military recruit who wants to become an officer, or the new behaviors and viewpoints of law or med students who anticipate becoming doctors or lawyers. Anticipatory socialization has the interesting function of easing the transition from one stage in life to another. When individuals "practice for" a new role ahead of time, their assumption of the new role is probably much less difficult. On the other hand, if the new stage in life is never reached, the trauma may be even greater than a sudden, unprepared-for change would have been.

Self

Psychologists talk about personality, sociologists talk about self, and their ideas and the "thing" they are talking about often sound quite similar. In fact, the link between psychology and sociology is closest at this point. A separate discipline—social psychology—has developed to deal with theories of sociali-

---

[4] See *Behind the Shield: The Police in Urban Society,* by Arthur Niederhoffer (Garden City, New York: Doubleday & Company, 1967).

zation and the development of the individual's self and personality. Although our interest here is in how sociologists view the self, a brief summary of some of the psychological perspectives may be helpful.

Generally, psychologists have placed more emphasis on hereditary and biological factors in personality development while sociologists focus on social interaction and the social environment. Psychologists place more emphasis on early childhood than do sociologists. Although there are numerous psychological theories, the most famous ideas are those of Sigmund Freud. Freud (1856–1939) was a Viennese physician and founder of psychoanalysis. According to Freud, the personality is made up of three major components· the id, the ego, and the superego.[5] The *id* is the most primitive aspect of the personality and represents the basic instinctual drives with which the person is born. Sexual and aggressive desires in the id constantly seek expression. The *ego* is the acting self; it is the mediator between the id and the outside world. Whereas the id operates by a pleasure principle—maximizing pleasure for the organism —the ego operates by a reality principle—balancing the instinctual needs of the organism against the conditions in the surrounding environment. The *superego* is an internalized set of rules and regulations that represent the values and ideas of society initially interpreted for the individual by his parents. The superego, commonly referred to as the conscience, is the aspect of personality that controls behavior. Don't think of id, ego, and superego as three little men running around in your head, but rather as three sets of processes whose sometimes conflicting purposes combine to function as personality. Freud believed that the individual passed through a series of psychosexual stages and that personality was fixed very early in life, around the age of six. Unlike Freud, sociologists believe that although the early years are extremely important, socialization and development of self are lifelong processes. Since Freud was a psychoanalyst and was working with people who were mentally ill, he emphasized the restricting nature of parents and society, and the conflict aspects of group life. Sociologists have focused more on the positive roles played by parents and groups in socialization and development of self.

With this brief view of Freud as introduction, let's turn to sociological theories of the self. Sociologists believe that self-development is rooted in social behavior, and not in biological, hereditary, or instinctual factors. Through the socialization process the self is developed. The *self* may be defined as one's awareness of and ideas and attitudes about his own personal and social identity. Through interaction and association with others, the individual develops an image of *what he is*. This involves one's perception of his role requirements and his position and behavioral expectations in the various social groupings with which he identifies. As C. H. Cooley put it, the word "self" means simply that

---

[5] For more detail, see *Theories of Personality*, by Calvin Hall and Gardner Lindzey (New York: John Wiley & Sons, 1957).

which is designated in common speech by the pronouns of the first person singular, "I," "me," "mine," and "myself."[6] Aspects of one's self might include: I am male, I am a college student, I am of medium height, I am athletic, I am usually happy, I am intelligent. The self might include as well: I can never do anything right, I am not worth much, nobody listens to me, I am inadequate, I am unloved, I am not as capable as my older brother.

The individual develops these images or viewpoints about himself from the way others react to him. More specifically, he develops them from the way *he thinks* others are reacting to him. Development of the self is a two-way interactive process which takes place throughout the period of socialization, the entire life span. Development of the self is an extremely subjective process involving interpretations of others' evaluations. Current evaluations are based on past evaluations, so that earlier mistakes become additive. A mother may continually tell her son that he is extremely intelligent. This becomes part of his self, one of the ways he views himself, and he behaves and has certain expectations because of it. If he flunks bonehead English as a college freshman, contradictory information comes in. What happened? He makes excuses and rationalizes his failure in order to support the view of self that he had held. He will probably seek reinforcement from other sources (mother, girl friend, I.Q. test scores) to support his self view. If evidence is lacking or reinforcement becomes harder to find (other bad grades, low I.Q. test scores) this part of his self conception will probably begin to change.

Aspects of self constantly undergo change. Often these changes occur slowly. Occasionally changes may be more rapid, sudden, and dramatic, as might be found, for example, with inmates of prisons and concentration camps, or, to a lesser extent, with recruits in military basic training. All these changes are a result of our evaluations of others' evaluations of us.

Charles H. Cooley described the development of the self in his concept the *looking-glass self*. The looking-glass self contains three elements: the imagination of our appearance to the other person, the imagination of his judgment of that appearance, and some sort of self-feeling, such as pride or mortification. Suppose, for example, a person eating in a crowded restaurant accidentally knocks his plate off the table. It makes a huge crash, and the food spills all over him. According to Cooley, he first "steps outside himself" and observes himself from the viewpoint of others in the room (". . . a well-dressed fellow with spaghetti all over him. . ."). Next, still examining himself as object, he imagines that others are evaluating his behavior (". . . must be a rather clumsy and awkward person. . ."). Finally, the individual as subject develops feelings and reactions to these imaginary evaluations of himself as object. He gets embar-

---

[6] Charles Horton Cooley's books are *Human Nature and the Social Order* (New York: Charles Scribner's, 1902) and *Social Organization* (New York: Charles Scribner's, 1909).

rassed, his face reddens, and he tries unsuccessfully to pretend it didn't happen. The process is made more interesting when we note that probably the same things would have happened if the room had been totally empty. We are "carrying" our judges around with us, and they are constantly "evaluating" our behavior.

George Herbert Mead[7] described the development of the self this way: An individual will conceive of himself as he believes significant others conceive of him. He will then tend to act in accordance with expectations he imputes to these significant others concerning the way "people like him" should act. As the child develops the ability to examine and control his behavior in accordance with others' views and attitudes about his behavior, he is learning to "take the role of the other." At this first stage of development (called primary socialization by Berger and Luckmann), the child does not cooperate with others and relates only to specific individuals such as parents and perhaps an older brother or sister or a teacher—persons whom Mead describes as "significant others." Later, as the individual develops he is less likely to continue to react to individual others and learns instead to react more to a less personalized grouping of others. This grouping of others, which Mead called the "generalized other," represents the sum of the viewpoints of the social group or community of people to which one belongs. The second stage of development (secondary

[7] George Herbert Mead's writings include *Mind, Self, and Society* (Chicago: University of Chicago Press, 1934) and "The Genesis of the Self and Social Control," from *International Journal of Ethics,* 35 (April 1925), pp. 251–273. Also see Broom and Selznick's short summary of Mead in *Sociology,* 5th Ed., Chapter 4.

socialization) begins, then, when the child is mature enough to cooperate with others in joint activities and to be able to react to the idea of people in general rather than to specific others.

Although our internalized attitudes of others are crucial, they do not determine all behavior. Mead made a distinction between two aspects of the self, the "I" and the "me." The "I" represents the subjective, acting self which may initiate spontaneous and original behavior. The "me" sees self as object and represents a conception of others' attitudes and viewpoints toward self. The "I" is freer, more innovative; the "me" is more conventional. "I" behaves, "me" judges and evaluates. "I" is in part governed by "me" but not completely. The abstract scrawling on the wall or in the dirt by the young child might represent "I" behavior; the same child's in-school drawing of the houses or trees that seem to please the teacher so much would be closer to "me" behavior. The driver involved in an auto accident who leaps out of his car and punches the other driver, swears at his wife, and kicks a passing dog is probably showing us the "I" aspect of self, while his passenger who goes to the nearest phone to call the highway patrol illustrates the "me."

It was also Mead who first emphasized that socialization and development of the self could not occur without *language*. Indeed, it is argued that it is largely language that distinguishes man from other animals. The essential factor in language and symbolic communication is that a symbol arouses in one's self the same meaning it arouses in another. Primitive communication begins with a conversation of gestures, such as the mating dance of birds, the snarl of dogs, the roar of lions, or the cry of an infant. At this level, meanings of gestures are not shared. To be sure, the gestures may bring forth a response in some observer (another dog or lion, the infant's mother) but the important fact, according to Mead, is that the gesture does not arouse in the actor the same response it arouses in the observer. For example, a very young baby feels discomfort and cries. His mother interprets this as hunger and feeds him. If the mother is right, this is communication of a sort, but for the baby, the act of crying had no communicative intent; it was merely a biological response. This represents primitive communication because the meanings were not shared by both parties.

As the child matures, he learns to use symbols and words. The words are poorly formed at first, and probably only a mother could understand them, but they are the beginnings of language—something beyond primitive communication. As his use of language improves, the child learns that what he says and does elicits responses from others. Language allows him to replace behavior with ideas—he can now say "I'm hungry," rather than acting it out—crying or pointing at food. Language allows him to think, makes possible the internalization of attitudes of others, and allows the individual to control his responses to others. We can imagine an internal conversation in the child: "I would really like to have ice cream and cake, but mother seems to like me better if I eat that other stuff she puts out . . . ." Mead suggests that the use of symbolic communication continues to develop, and through language man is able to think, to develop shared social meanings, to take the self as object and evaluate his own behavior as he thinks others do. In sum, then, language makes possible the development of mind and self.

Definition of the Situation

The phrase "definition of the situation" introduces another important idea. Sociologist W. I. Thomas once wrote, "If men define situations as real, they are real in their consequences." The point he was making is that man constructs his own reality, that man responds as much or more to the meaning a situation has for him as to the objective features of a situation. If a student defines passing a certain exam as the most important thing in the world, then for him it is, and he goes to great extremes to insure that he makes it. People define certain races as inferior and certain cultural beliefs or practices (cannibalism, polygamy) as peculiar, regardless of the objective reality of the situation.

The self-fulfilling prophecy provides another illustration of how a definition of the situation operates. A self-fulfilling prophecy occurs when a *false* definition of a situation evokes a new behavior which makes the originally false conception come *true*.[8] A student is worried that he will flunk an exam. This makes him so nervous and anxious that he is unable to study effectively, and he flunks the exam. Or police believe Gorples to be very criminal types. Consequently, more police patrols and surveillance are concentrated in those sections of the city where the Gorples live. Increased police surveillance leads to greater visibility and reporting of crime and the crime rate of Gorples increases. Merton puts it this way: "confident error generates its own spurious confirmation," and if one looks carefully, this phenomenon can be seen to occur frequently in everyday situations. Again, the point is that our reality is subjective and socially structured. Men create their reality through shared interaction and communication.

Summary

Our study of sociology starts with the understanding that man is a group or a social animal. The obvious question is, how does he become that way? In this chapter we have discussed some of the processes that sociologists feel are important and essential if we are to understand how one changes from a blob of matter into a complex, interacting, social being.

---

[8] This discussion of definition of the situation and self-fulfilling prophecy follows that of Robert Merton in *Social Theory and Social Structure,* 2nd Ed. (New York: The Free Press, 1957), pp. 421–436.

The process through which this transformation occurs is called socialization. During socialization, the self is developed. The self is the individual's set of images about *what he is*. The development of the self is a social process; it arises out of our interpretations of others' reactions to us. Several theories were examined which describe in detail how the self is developed. Cooley's explanation involves the *looking-glass self,* while Mead describes self growth through *significant others,* the *generalized other,* and *taking the role of the other*. Language, a complex method of symbolic communication, is something that man has that other animals seem to lack. In Mead's view, language is essential in socialization and in development of the self.

Although the individual is a combination of biological, hereditary, and social factors, the sociologist focuses his studies on interaction in the social environment. The social environment is the stage or setting in which socialization and self development take place. The emphasis throughout this chapter has been on interaction and on interpretation and internalization of others' reactions to us. The effect of the social environment on the individual is also a very subjective process. There are substantial variations in how individuals perceive, interpret, and react to their social environment. Suppose twenty people observe an automobile accident at a busy intersection, and then each writes a description of what happened. How many different descriptions might we get? Probably at least ten. or fifteen, maybe even twenty (or more, if we have a few schizophrenics in the group). Or observe how different students react to a good or bad grade on an exam—again, there is great variation. The effect of the social environment, then, is a very subjective and interpretive phenomenon; no two people react in the same way. Differences multiply because future perceptions and interpretations are based on past perceptions and interpretations. In like manner, socialization and development of the self are building processes which take place throughout the life span.

Four readings follow which will help illustrate some of the concepts we have discussed in this chapter. In an excerpt from her book *The Story of My Life,* Helen Keller, who was deaf and blind from early childhood, recalls meeting her new teacher and beginning her "education." This article illustrates how important language and symbolic communication are in the processes of socialization and self development. An interview with Jerome Kagan provides some cross-cultural viewpoints on child development and continues the debate on the importance of the early years of life. In an excerpt from his autobiography, Malcolm X describes some events that occurred during his early teens that seemed to have a great and lasting impact. Here we see that socialization is a continuing process. In this chapter, we have emphasized the importance of social interaction. Our interpretation of how others see us strongly determines how we actually behave. In his essay "Shooting an Elephant," George Orwell describes the dilemma of a police officer who wants to do one thing but is confronted by a crowd that seems to want him to do something else.

The Story of My Life

Helen Keller

Socialization is defined as the process by which the organism becomes a social being—the learning of habits, skills, and other requirements for effective participation in social groups. Socialization is a continuing process and occurs through interaction with other humans—parents, teachers, friends.

Helen Keller was deaf and blind from early childhood. In this excerpt from one of her books, she describes the period when her new teacher first arrived and a new form of learning began to take place.

The most important day I remember in all my life is the one on which my teacher, Anne Mansfield Sullivan, came to me. I am filled with wonder when I consider the immeasurable contrasts between the two lives which it connects. It was the third of March, 1887, three months before I was seven years old.

On the afternoon of that eventful day, I stood on the porch, dumb, expectant. I guessed vaguely from my mother's signs and from the hurrying to and fro in the house that something unusual was about to happen, so I went to the door and waited on the steps. The afternoon sun penetrated the mass of honeysuckle that covered the porch, and fell on my upturned face. My fingers lingered almost unconsciously on the familiar leaves and blossoms which had just come forth to greet the sweet southern spring. I did not know what the future held of marvel or surprise for me. Anger and bitterness had preyed upon me continually for weeks and a deep languor had succeeded this passionate struggle.

Have you ever been at sea in a dense fog, when it seemed as if a tangible white darkness shut you in, and the great ship, tense and anxious, groped her way toward the shore with plummet and sounding-line, and you waited with beating heart for something to happen? I was like that ship before my education began, only I was without compass or sounding-line, and had no way of knowing how near the harbour was. "Light! give me light!" was the wordless cry of my soul, and the light of love shone on me in that very hour.

I felt approaching footsteps. I stretched out my hand, as I supposed to my mother. Someone took it, and I was caught up and held close in the arms of her who had come to reveal all things to me, and, more than all things else, to love me.

From *The Story of My Life* by Helen Keller. Reprinted by permission of Doubleday & Company, Inc.

The morning after my teacher came she led me into her room and gave me a doll. The little blind children at the Perkins Institution had sent it and Laura Bridgman had dressed it; but I did not know this until afterward. When I had played with it a little while, Miss Sullivan slowly spelled into my hand the word "d-o-l-l." I was at once interested in this finger play and tried to imitate it. When I finally succeeded in making the letters correctly I was flushed with childish pleasure and pride. Running downstairs to my mother I held up my hand and made the letters for doll. I did not know that I was spelling a word or even that words existed; I was simply making my fingers go in monkey-like imitation. In the days that followed I learned to spell in this uncomprehending way a great many words, among them pin, hat, cup and a few verbs like sit, stand and walk. But my teacher had been with me several weeks before I understood that everything has a name.

One day, while I was playing with my new doll, Miss Sullivan put my big rag doll into my lap also, spelled "d-o-l-l" and tried to make me understand that "d-o-l-l" applied to both. Earlier in the day we had had a tussle over the words "m-u-g" and "w-a-t-e-r." Miss Sullivan had tried to impress it upon me that "m-u-g" is mug and that "w-a-t-e-r" is water, but I persisted in confounding the two. In despair she had dropped the subject for the time, only to renew it at the first opportunity. I became impatient at her repeated attempts and, seizing the new doll, I dashed it upon the floor. I was keenly delighted when I felt the fragments of the broken doll at my feet. Neither sorrow nor regret followed my passionate outburst. I had not loved the doll. In the still, dark world in which I lived there was no strong sentiment of tenderness. I felt my teacher sweep the fragments to one side of the hearth, and I had a sense of satisfaction that the cause of my discomfort was removed. She brought me my hat, and I knew I was going out into the warm sunshine. This thought, if a wordless sensation may be called a thought, made me hop and skip with pleasure.

We walked down the path to the well-house, attracted by the fragrance of the honeysuckle with which it was covered. Some one was drawing water and my teacher placed my hand under the spout. As the cool stream gushed over one hand she spelled into the other the word water, first slowly, then rapidly. I stood still, my whole attention fixed upon the motions of her fingers. Suddenly I felt a misty consciousness as of something forgotten—a thrill of returning thought; and somehow the mystery of language was revealed to me. I knew then that "w-a-t-e-r" meant the wonderful cool something that was flowing over my hand. That living word awakened my soul, gave it light, hope, joy, set it free! There were barriers still, it is true, but barriers that could in time be swept away.

I left the well-house eager to learn. Everything had a name, and each name gave birth to a new thought. As we returned to the house every object which I touched seemed to quiver with life. That was because I saw everything with the strange, new sight that had come to me. On entering the door I remembered the doll I had broken. I felt my way to the hearth and picked up the pieces. I tried vainly to put them together. Then my eyes filled with tears; for I realized what

I had done, and for the first time I felt repentance and sorrow.

I learned a great many new words that day. I do not remember what they all were; but I do know that mother, father, sister, teacher were among them— words that were to make the world blossom for me, "like Aaron's rod, with flowers." It would have been difficult to find a happier child than I was as I lay in my crib at the close of that eventful day and lived over the joys it had brought me, and for the first time longed for a new day to come.

I recall many incidents of the summer of 1887 that followed my soul's sudden awakening. I did nothing but explore with my hands and learn the name of every object that I touched; and the more I handled things and learned their names and uses, the more joyous and confident grew my sense of kinship with the rest of the world.

When the time of daisies and buttercups came Miss Sullivan took me by the hand across the fields, where men were preparing the earth for the seed, to the banks of the Tennessee River, and there, sitting on the warm grass, I had my first lessons in the beneficence of nature. I learned how the sun and the rain make to grow out of the ground every tree that is pleasant to the sight and good for food, how birds build their nests and live and thrive from land to land, how the squirrel, the deer, the lion and every other creature finds food and shelter. As my knowledge of things grew I felt more and more the delight of the world I was in. Long before I learned to do a sum in arithmetic or describe the shape of the earth, Miss Sullivan had taught me to find beauty in the fragrant woods, in every blade of grass, and in the curves and dimples of my baby sister's hand. She linked my earliest thoughts with nature, and made me feel that "birds and flowers and I were happy peers."

I had now the key to all language, and I was eager to learn to use it. Children who hear acquire language without any particular effort; the words that fall from others' lips they catch on the wing, as it were, delightedly, while the little deaf child must trap them by a slow and often painful process. But whatever the process, the result is wonderful. Gradually from naming an object we advance step by step until we have traversed the vast distance between our first stammered syllable and the sweep of thought in a line of Shakespeare.

At first, when my teacher told me about a new thing I asked very few questions. My ideas were vague, and my vocabulary was inadequate; but as my knowledge of things grew, and I learned more and more words, my field of inquiry broadened, and I would return again and again to the same subject, eager for further information. Sometimes a new word revived an image that some earlier experience had engraved on my brain.

I remember the morning that I first asked the meaning of the word, "love." This was before I knew many words. I had found a few early violets in the garden and brought them to my teacher. She tried to kiss me: but at that time I did not like to have any one kiss me except my mother. Miss Sullivan put her arm gently round me and spelled into my hand, "I love Helen."

"What is love?" I asked.

She drew me closer to her and said, "It is here," pointing to my heart, whose beats I was conscious of for the first time. Her words puzzled me very much because I did not then understand anything unless I touched it.

I smelt the violets in her hand and asked, half in words, half in signs, a question which meant, "Is love the sweetness of flowers?"

"No," said my teacher.

Again I thought. The warm sun was shining on us.

"Is this not love?" I asked, pointing in the direction from which the heat came. "Is this not love?"

It seemed to me that there could be nothing more beautiful than the sun, whose warmth makes all things grow. But Miss Sullivan shook her head, and I was greatly puzzled and disappointed. I thought it strange that my teacher could not show me love.

A day or two afterward I was stringing beads of different sizes in symmetrical groups—two large beads, three small ones, and so on. I had made many mistakes, and Miss Sullivan had pointed them out again and again with gentle patience. Finally I noticed a very obvious error in the sequence and for an instant I concentrated my attention on the lesson and tried to think how I should have arranged the beads. Miss Sullivan touched my forehead and spelled with decided emphasis, "Think."

In a flash I knew that the word was the name of the process that was going on in my head. This was my first conscious perception of an abstract idea.

For a long time I was still—I was not thinking of the beads in my lap, but trying to find a meaning for "love" in the light of this new idea. The sun had been under a cloud all day, and there had been brief showers; but suddenly the sun broke forth in all its southern splendour.

Again I asked my teacher, "Is this not love?"

"Love is something like the clouds that were in the sky before the sun came out," she replied. Then in simpler words than these, which at that time I could not have understood, she explained: "You cannot touch the clouds, you know; but you feel the rain and know how glad the flowers and the thirsty earth are to have it after a hot day. You cannot touch love either; but you feel the sweetness that it pours into everything. Without love you would not be happy or want to play."

The beautiful truth burst upon my mind—I felt that there were invisible lines stretched between my spirit and the spirits of others.

From the beginning of my education Miss Sullivan made it a practice to speak to me as she would speak to any hearing child; the only difference was that she spelled the sentences into my hand instead of speaking them. If I did not know the words and idioms necessary to express my thoughts she supplied them, even suggesting conversation when I was unable to keep up my end of the dialogue.

This process was continued for several years; for the deaf child does not learn in a month, or even in two or three years, the numberless idioms and expressions used in the simplest daily intercourse. The little hearing child learns these from constant repetition and imitation. The conversation he hears in his home stimulates his mind and suggests topics and calls forth the spontaneous expression of his own thoughts. This natural exchange of ideas is denied to the deaf child. My teacher, realizing this, determined to supply the kinds of stimulus I lacked. This she did by repeating to me as far as possible, verbatim, what she heard, and by showing me how I could take part in the conversation. But it was a long time before I ventured to take the initiative, and still longer before I could find something appropriate to say at the right time.

The deaf and the blind find it very difficult to acquire the amenities of conversation. How much more this difficulty must be augmented in the case of those who are both deaf and blind. They cannot distinguish the tone of the voice or, without assistance, go up and down the gamut of tones that give significance to words; nor can they watch the expression of the speaker's face, and a look is often the very soul of what one says.

The next important step in my education was learning to read.

As soon as I could spell a few words my teacher gave me slips of cardboard on which were printed words in raised letters. I quickly learned that each printed word stood for an object, an act, or a quality. I had a frame in which I could arrange the words in little sentences; but before I ever put sentences in the frame I used to make them in objects. I found the slips of paper which represented, for example, "doll," "is," "on," "bed" and placed each name on its object; then I put my doll on the bed with the words *is, on, bed* arranged beside the doll, thus making a sentence of the words, and at the same time carrying out the idea of the sentence with the things themselves.

One day, Miss Sullivan tells me, I pinned the word *girl* on my pinafore and stood in the wardrobe. On the shelf I arranged the words, *is, in, wardrobe*. Nothing delighted me so much as this game. My teacher and I played it for hours at a time. Often everything in the room was arranged in object sentences.

From the printed slip it was but a step to the printed book. I took my "Reader for Beginners" and hunted for the words I knew; when I found them my joy was like that of a game of hide-and-seek. Thus I began to read. Of the time when I began to read connected stories I shall speak later.

For a long time I had no regular lessons. Even when I studied most earnestly it seemed more like play than work. Everything Miss Sullivan taught me she illustrated by a beautiful story or a poem. Whenever anything delighted or interested me she talked it over with me just as if she were a little girl herself. What many children think of with dread, as a painful plodding through grammar, hard sums and harder definitions, is to-day one of my most precious memories.

I cannot explain the peculiar sympathy Miss Sullivan had with my pleasures and desires. Perhaps it was the result of long association with the blind. Added to this she had a wonderful faculty for description. She went quickly over uninteresting details, and never nagged me with questions to see if I remembered the day-before-yesterday's lesson. She introduced dry technicalities of science little by little, making every subject so real that I could not help remembering what she taught.

Once there were eleven tadpoles in a glass globe set in a window full of plants. I remember the eagerness with which I made discoveries about them. It was great fun to plunge my hand into the bowl and feel the tadpoles frisk about, and to let them slip and slide between my fingers. One day a more ambitious fellow leaped beyond the edge of the bowl and fell on the floor, where I found him to all appearance more dead than alive. The only sign of life was a slight wriggling of his tail. But no sooner had he returned to his element than he darted to the bottom, swimming round and round in joyous activity. He made his leap, he had seen the great world, and was content to stay in his pretty glass house under the big fuchsia tree until he attained the dignity of froghood. Then he went to live in the leafy pool at the end of the garden, where he made the summer nights musical with his quaint love-song.

Thus I learned from life itself. At the beginning I was only a little mass of possibilities. It was my teacher who unfolded and developed them. When she came, everything about me breathed of love and joy and was full of meaning. She has never since let pass an opportunity to point out the beauty that is in everything, nor has she ceased trying in thought and action and example to make my life sweet and useful.

It was my teacher's genius, her quick sympathy, her loving tact which made the first years of my education so beautiful. It was because she seized the right moment to impart knowledge that made it so pleasant and acceptable to me. She realized that a child's mind is like a shallow brook which ripples and dances merrily over the stony course of its education and reflects here a flower, there a bush, yonder a fleecy cloud; and she attempted to guide my mind on its way, knowing that like a brook it should be fed by mountain streams and hidden springs, until it broadened out into a deep river, capable of reflecting in its placid surface billowy hills, the luminous shadows of trees and the blue heavens, as well as the sweet face of a little flower.

Any teacher can take a child to the classroom, but not every teacher can make him learn. He will not work joyously unless he feels that liberty is his, whether he is busy or at rest; he must feel the flush of victory and the heart-sinking of disappointment before he takes with a will the tasks distasteful to him and resolves to dance his way bravely through a dull routine of textbooks.

My teacher is so near to me that I scarcely think of myself apart from her. How much of my delight in all beautiful things is innate, and how much is due to her influence, I can never tell. I feel that her being is inseparable from my own, and that the footsteps of my life are in hers. All the best of me belongs to her—there is not a talent, or an aspiration or a joy in me that has not been awakened by her loving touch.

Questions

1. *Without language and communication, socialization cannot take place. Discuss.*
2. *What natural skills were developed by Helen Keller during the period discussed in this article? Could she have learned these skills without the help of others? Is the same true for a person who doesn't have the handicaps that Helen Keller had?*

A Conversation with Jerome Kagan

Saturday Review

The importance of the first year or two of life in determining intelligence and learning capacity is emphasized by numerous experts including Freud, Piaget, and many learning theorists. Jerome Kagan believed it, too, until he discovered a village in Guatemala in which the children broke all the rules of development. What follows is an interview with Kagan by the editors of *Saturday Review* on his research. Jerome Kagan is a professor of human development at Harvard University.

SR: *What happened in Guatemala to make you reverse your thinking?*

Kagan: I found myself in a thirteenth-century, pre-Columbian village, located on the shores of Lake Atitlan. I saw 850 Indians, poor, exploited, alienated, bitter, sick. I saw infants in the first years of their lives completely isolated in their homes, because parents believe that sun and dust and air or the gazes of either pregnant women or men fresh with perspiration from the field will cause illness. It's the evil-eye belief. So the infants are kept in the hut. Now these are bamboo huts, and there are no windows, so the light level in this hut at high noon in a perfectly azure sky is what it should be at dusk. Very dark. Although parents love their children—mothers nurse on demand and hold their infants close to their bodies—they don't talk or interact with them. And there are no toys. So at one and one-half years of age, you have a very retarded child.

SR: *What are the children like?*

Kagan: Not only are they quiet, somber, motorically passive, and extremely fearful, but on tests of maturational and intellectual development, they are four or five months behind American children.

SR: *What kinds of tests do you use?*

Kagan: Here's an example of a maturational test. Take a child nine months of age, cover an object with a cloth, and then, through sleight of hand, remove the object. We know from Piaget's work that if he pulls off the cloth and the object's not there, he shows surprise, indicating that he knows the object should be there. That ability should occur somewhere in the last third of the first year. None of the Guatemalan babies showed this until 18 months of age. We also know that babies in the Western world become frightened of strangers at about eight months. It's called "stranger anxiety." You won't get that [in Guatemala] until the middle of the second year. In the Western world children begin to talk between 12 and 18 months. The Guatemalan kids don't talk until about two and a half to three years. If I had seen infants like the Guatemalans in America prior to my experience, I would have gotten very upset, called the police, had the children removed, and begun to make gloomy statements about the fact that it was all over for these children.

SR: *But they do recover.*

Kagan: That's the paradox. The 11-year-olds in this Guatemalan village are beautiful. They're gay, alert, active, affective, just like 11-year-olds in the United States. They're *more* impressive than Americans in a set of "culture-fair" tests—where the words and the materials are familiar. For example, we asked them, "What is brown, hard, and found near the shore of the lake?" And they'd say, "a wharf." They have no problem with this. In reasoning, memory, inference, deduction, and perception, these children at 11—who, we must assume, were "ghosts" as infants—had recovered. Therefore, one must conclude that the first two years of life do not inexorably doom you to retardation and that there's much more potential for recovery than Western psychologists have surmised, including me. I didn't go to Guatemala to prove this; I found it a complete surprise.

SR: *Don't the experiments that Harry Harlow [a psychologist at the University of Wisconsin] conducted with monkeys contradict that conclusion?*

Kagan: They did until last year, when Harlow published a very important report. He took monkeys and put them in isolation for six months, and they emerged with the expected bizarre, abnormal, crazy behavior. But this time he placed them with normal infant female monkeys three months younger than themselves for 26 weeks (seven months). He reports that after seven months they could not be distinguished from normal monkeys. If we can do this in seven months with a creature less complex than we, then certainly it does not require an enormous stretch of imagination to believe that in nine years a human infant, treated less bizarrely, can recover.

SR: *Any human studies to support your findings?*

Kagan: Freda Rebelsky spent several years in eastern Holland, where there is a middle-class, stable, nuclear family arrangement. In this small part of this very small country, it's local custom to isolate a child for the first ten months. He's put in a room outside the house; he's tightly bound—no mobiles, no toys, and minimal interaction. Like our Guatemalan children. He emerges at one year absolutely retarded, but at five years of age he's fully recovered.

SR: *But what about René Spitz's [a professor of psychiatry at the University of Colorado] observations?*

Kagan: Spitz made his observations on South American children in an orphanage. He saw ghostlike (what he called "marasmic") children much like the ones I saw. They lacked both stimulation and affection, so he made the same mistake many analysts have made and concluded their retardation was due to lack of affection. It's not affection, because my infants in San Marcos are on their mother's bodies three-quarters of the day, and they get lots of physical holding, lots of skin contact. So it's not the love, but the input, that's important.

SR: *If you kept the infant or the monkey deprived for a longer period of time, would there be permanent effects?*

Kagan: We don't know. I am not saying that there is no treatment you can give a child from which he cannot recover. That is obviously too strong. We do have extreme case-history reports: for instance, a mother locked her kid up in a closet for six years. He emerged mute but still managed to learn language later. But I'm trying to be a reasonably cautious person. What I can say with confidence—and had I not had this experience, I would have resisted it—is that an abnormal experience in the first two years of life in no way affects basic intellectual functions or the ability to be affectively normal—to experience gaiety and sadness, guilt and shame.

SR: *What implications do you see for American schools?*

Kagan: I think my work suggests we've got to stop the very early, and I think, premature rank-ordering of children in grades one, two, and three. We decide too soon. Poor children enter the school system (a) with less motivation, because they see less value in intellectual activity, and (b) one or two years behind in the emergence of what I call executive-cognitive functions (what Piaget would call concrete operational thinking). They are going to get there, but they are a year or two behind. We arbitrarily decide that age seven is when the race starts, so you have a larger proportion of poor than of privileged children who are not yet ready for school instruction. And then we classify them, prematurely. Let's use the example of puberty. Suppose we decided that fertility was important in our society and that fertility should occur at age 13. Then if you're not fertile at 13, we conclude that you are never going to be fertile, and we give you a different kind of life. It's illogical, because that 13-year-old who is not fertile now will be next year.

SR: *In other words, learning does not follow the same pattern in every child.*

Kagan: Yes. We used to think that all learning was continuous—like a "freight train." There is a series of closely connected cars: you start at car one and do certain things; then you jump to car two, and you carry your baggage with you. But now let me substitute an analogy that makes more sense: development as a series of lily pads. I choose that because lily pads are farther apart, because each child dumps a lot of baggage in traversing the lily pads (he doesn't have to carry everything with him), and because he can skip some of the lily pads. American psychologists have surmised that you could never walk unless you crawled. Now we know that is false. I could prevent a child from crawling —bind him up until he was two and then unbind him—and we know he would walk. He wouldn't have to crawl. Now maybe that analogy holds for a lot more in mental development than we have surmised.

SR: *How has the public reacted to your rather optimistic conclusions?*

Kagan: What I say is often misunderstood. When I say kids can catch up, people say that can't be right, because they know that a poor child always remains retarded relative to a middle-class child in the school system. But these people—most Americans—are confusing relative and absolute standards. Absolute retardation refers to a lack of certain fundamental motor, affective, and intellectual skills that are basic to our species. They include crawling, walking, standing, speaking, inference, and reasoning. Now if a child isn't walking by three, he is absolutely retarded. If a child cannot remember four numbers when he is ten years old, he is absolutely retarded.

SR: *Then what is "relative retardation"?*

Kagan: If kids don't have certain culturally arbitrary skills—like being able to read—they are retarded relative to some other reference group. When we say a Mexican-American child from a ghetto is retarded, we mean relative to that arbitrary reference which is the middle-class child. The analogy of physical development should make that distinction clearer. There are natural skills like walking or running which you get better at each year; if a child of ten cannot run as fast as a three-year-old, we worry about it. So it makes sense to say that this ten-year-old is physically retarded. But would we ever say that a ten-year-old who can't play hockey is retarded? Well, when it comes to intellectual skills, that's exactly what we do; we say if this child can't multiply, he is retarded. But multiplication is like hockey; no child's going to know how to multiply unless you teach him how to multiply. See the mistake we make? In the physical area we never confuse relative with absolute retardation. But in the mental area we do.

SR: *Given the vast implications of your study, where do you plan to go from here?*

Kagan: I want to see schools begin to serve the needs of society. Ancient Sparta needed warriors, Athens needed a sense of the hero, the ancient Hebrews needed knowledge of the Testament, nineteenth-century Americans needed managers and technicians—and the schools responded beautifully in each case by providing the kind of people the society needed. What do we need now? I believe that we need to restore faith, honesty, humanity. And I am suggesting in deep seriousness that we must, in the school, begin to reward these traits as the Spartans rewarded physical fitness. I want children rank-ordered on the basis of humanism as we rank-order on the basis of reading and mathematics. I'm dead serious. When I was a kid, deportment was always a grade. In a funny way, I want that, but instead of deportment, I want him graded on humanism: How kind is he? How nurturant is he?

SR: *But aren't we getting back then to the same problem of sorting?*

Kagan: Every society must sort its children according to the traits it values. We will never get away from that. A society needs a set of people whom it can trust in and give responsibility to for the management of its capital and resources, for the health of its people, the legal prerogatives of its people, the wars of its people. The function of the school system is in fact to prepare this class.

Questions

1. *Isolation in the early years of life leads to retardation. Discuss.*
2. *Can socialization occur without interaction, or is some kind of social interaction actually occurring between the Guatemalan infants and their parents?*
3. *Different socialization patterns in different societies still result in normal, nonretarded children. Discuss.*
4. *If it is true that learning does not follow the same pattern in every child, what implications does this have for our school systems?*

Mascot

Malcolm X

Socialization involves many things. Part of it is learning that you are male or female, short or tall, black or white; a major part is learning how people react to you *because* you are male or female, short or tall, black or white. These reactions and interpretations become an important part of the self. Many people probably do not recall the stage in the socialization process when they became aware of their sex or race. In order to remember, one must be very perceptive, and the new learning must be so unique or unexpected that it creates a lasting impression. In this excerpt from his autobiography, Malcolm X recalls learning what it means to be black in America.

. . . They told me I was going to go to a reform school. I was still thirteen years old.

But first I was going to the detention home. It was in Mason, Michigan, about twelve miles from Lansing. The detention home was where all the "bad" boys and girls from Ingham County were held, on their way to reform school —waiting for their hearings.

The white state man was a Mr. Maynard Allen. He was nicer to me than most of the state Welfare people had been. He even had consoling words for the Gohannas and Mrs. Adcock and Big Boy; all of them were crying. But I wasn't. With the few clothes I owned stuffed into a box, we rode in his car to Mason. He talked as he drove along, saying that my school marks showed that if I would just straighten up, I could make something of myself. He said that reform school had the wrong reputation; he talked about what the word "reform" meant—to change and become better. He said the school was really a place where boys like me could have time to see their mistakes and start a new life and become somebody everyone would be proud of. And he told me that the lady in charge of the detention home, a Mrs. Swerlin, and her husband were very good people.

They were good people. Mrs. Swerlin was bigger than her husband, I remember, a big, buxom, robust, laughing woman, and Mr. Swerlin was thin, with black hair, and a black mustache and a red face, quiet and polite, even to me.

They liked me right away, too. Mrs. Swerlin showed me to my room, my own room—the first in my life. It was in one of those huge dormitory-like buildings where kids in detention were kept in those days—and still are in most places. I discovered next, with surprise, that I was allowed to eat with the Swerlins. It was the first time I'd eaten with white people—at least with grown white people—since the Seventh Day Adventist country meetings. It wasn't my own exclusive privilege, of course. Except for the very troublesome boys and girls at the detention home, who were kept locked up—those who had run away and been caught and brought back, or something like that—all of us ate with the Swerlins sitting at the head of the long tables.

They had a white cook-helper, I recall—Lucille Lathrop. (It amazes me how these names come back, from a time I haven't thought about for more than twenty years.) Lucille treated me well, too. Her husband's name was Duane Lathrop. He worked somewhere else, but he stayed there at the detention home on the weekends with Lucille.

I noticed again how white people smelled different from us, and how their food tasted different, not seasoned like Negro cooking. I began to sweep and mop and dust around in the Swerlins' house, as I had done with Big Boy at the Gohannas'.

They all liked my attitude, and it was out of their liking for me that I soon became accepted by them—as a mascot, I know now. They would talk about anything and everything with me standing right there hearing them, the same way people would talk freely in front of a pet canary. They would even talk about me, or about "niggers," as though I wasn't there, as if I wouldn't understand what the word meant. A hundred times a day, they used the word "nigger." I suppose that in their own minds, they meant no harm; in fact they probably meant well. It was the same with the cook, Lucille, and her husband, Duane. I remember one day when Mr. Swerlin, as nice as he was, came in from Lansing, where he had been through the Negro section, and said to Mrs. Swerlin right in front of me, "I just can't see how those niggers can be so happy and be so poor." He talked about how they lived in shacks, but had those big, shining cars out front.

And Mrs. Swerlin said, me standing right there, "Niggers are just that way. . . ." That scene always stayed with me.

It was the same with the other white people, most of them local politicians, when they would come visiting the Swerlins. One of their favorite parlor topics was "niggers." One of them was the judge who was in charge of me in Lansing. He was a close friend of the Swerlins. He would ask about me when he came, and they would call me in, and he would look me up and down, his expression approving, like he was examining a fine colt, or a pedigreed pup. I knew they must have told him how I acted and how I worked.

What I am trying to say is that it just never dawned upon them that I could understand, that I wasn't a pet, but a human being. They didn't give me credit for having the same sensitivity, intellect, and understanding that they would have been ready and willing to recognize in a white boy in my position. But it has historically been the case with white people, in their regard for black people, that even though we might be *with* them, we weren't considered *of* them. Even though they appeared to have opened the door, it was still closed. Thus they never did really see *me*.

This is the sort of kindly condescension which I try to clarify today, to these integration-hungry Negroes, about their "liberal" white friends, these so-called "good white people"—most of them anyway. I don't care how nice one is to you; the thing you must always remember is that almost never does he really see you as he sees himself, as he sees his own kind. He may stand with you through thin, but not thick; when the chips are down, you'll find that as fixed in him as his bone structure is his sometimes subconscious conviction that he's better than anybody black.

But I was no more than vaguely aware of anything like that in my detention-home years. I did my little chores around the house, and everything was fine. And each week-end, they didn't mind my catching a ride over to Lansing for the afternoon or evening. If I wasn't old enough, I sure was big enough by then, and nobody ever questioned my hanging out, even at night, in the streets of the Negro section.

I was growing up to be even bigger than Wilfred and Philbert, who had begun to meet girls at the school dances, and other places, and introduced me to a few. But the ones who seemed to like me, I didn't go for—and vice versa. I couldn't dance a lick, anyway, and I couldn't see squandering my few dimes on girls. So mostly I pleasured myself these Saturday nights by gawking around the Negro bars and restaurants. The jukeboxes were wailing Erskine Hawkins' "Tuxedo Junction," Slim and Slam's "Flatfoot Floogie," things like that. Sometimes, big bands from New York, out touring the one-night stands in the sticks, would play for big dances in Lansing. Everybody with legs would come out to see any performer who bore the magic name "New York." Which is how I first heard Lucky Thompson and Milt Jackson, both of whom I later got to know well in Harlem.

Many youngsters from the detention home, when their dates came up, went off to the reform school. But when mine came up—two or three times—it was always ignored. I saw new youngsters arrive and leave. I was glad and grateful. I knew it was Mrs. Swerlin's doing. I didn't want to leave.

She finally told me one day that I was going to be entered in Mason Junior High School. It was the only school in town. No ward of the detention home had ever gone to school there, at least while still a ward. So I entered their seventh grade. The only other Negroes there were some of the Lyons children, younger than I was, in the lower grades. The Lyons and I, as it happened, were the town's only Negroes. They were, as Negroes, very much respected. Mr. Lyons was a smart, hardworking man, and Mrs. Lyons was a very good woman. She and my mother, I had heard my mother say, were two of the four West Indians in that whole section of Michigan.

Some of the white kids at school, I found, were even friendlier than some of those in Lansing had been. Though some, including the teachers, called me "nigger," it was easy to see that they didn't mean any more harm by it than the Swerlins. As the "nigger" of my class, I was in fact extremely popular—I suppose partly because I was kind of a novelty. I was in demand, I had top priority. But I also benefited from the special prestige of having the seal of approval from that Very Important Woman about the town of Mason, Mrs. Swerlin. Nobody in Mason would have dreamed of getting on the wrong side of her. It became hard for me to get through a school day without someone after me to join this or head up that—the debating society, the Junior High basketball team, or some other extracurricular activity. I never turned them down.

And I hadn't been in the school long when Mrs. Swerlin, knowing I could use spending money of my own, got me a job after school washing the dishes in a local restaurant. My boss there was the father of a white classmate whom I spent a lot of time with. His family lived over the restaurant. It was fine working there. Every Friday night when I got paid, I'd feel at least ten feet tall. I forget how much I made, but it seemed like a lot. It was the first time I'd ever had any money to speak of, all my own, in my whole life. As soon as I could afford it, I bought a green suit and some shoes, and at school I'd buy treats for the others in my class—at least as much as any of them did for me.

English and history were the subjects I liked most. My English teacher, I recall—a Mr. Ostrowski—was always giving advice about how to become something in life. The one thing I didn't like about history class was that the teacher, Mr. Williams, was a great one for "nigger" jokes. One day during my first week at school, I walked into the room and he started singing to the class, as a joke, " 'Way down yonder in the cotton field, some folks say that a nigger won't steal." Very funny. I liked history, but I never thereafter had much liking for Mr. Williams. Later, I remember, we came to the textbook section on Negro history. It was exactly one paragraph long. Mr. Williams laughed through it practically in a single breath, reading aloud how the Negroes had been slaves and then were freed, and how they were usually lazy and dumb and shiftless. He added, I remember, an anthropological footnote on his own, telling us between laughs how Negroes' feet were "so big that when they walk, they don't leave tracks, they leave a hole in the ground.". . .

Then, in the second semester of the seventh grade, I was elected class president. It surprised me even more than other people. But I can see now why the class might have done it. My grades were among the highest in the school. I was unique in my class, like a pink poodle. And I was proud; I'm not going to say I wasn't. In fact, by then, I didn't really have much feeling about being a Negro, because I was trying so hard, in every way I could, to be white. Which is why I am spending much of my life today telling the American black man that he's wasting his time straining to "integrate." I know from personal experience. I tried hard enough. . . .

That summer of 1940, in Lansing, I caught the Greyhound bus for Boston with my cardboard suitcase, and wearing my green suit. If someone had hung a sign, *"hick,"* around my neck, I couldn't have looked much more obvious. They didn't have the turnpikes then; the bus stopped at what seemed every corner and cowpatch. From my seat in—you guessed it—the back of the bus, I gawked out of the window at white man's America rolling past for what seemed a month, but must have been only a day and a half.

When we finally arrived, Ella met me at the terminal and took me home. The house was on Waumbeck Street in the Sugar Hill section of Roxbury, the Harlem of Boston. I met Ella's second husband, Frank, who was now a soldier; and her brother Earl, the singer who called himself Jimmy Carleton; and Mary, who was very different from her older sister. It's funny how I seemed to think of Mary as Ella's sister, instead of her being, just as Ella is, my own half-sister. It's probably because Ella and I always were much closer as basic types; we're dominant people, and Mary has always been mild and quiet, almost shy.

Ella was busily involved in dozens of things. She belonged to I don't know how many different clubs; she was a leading light of local so-called "black society." I saw and met a hundred black people there whose big-city talk and ways left my mouth hanging open.

I couldn't have feigned indifference if I had tried to. People talked casually about Chicago, Detroit, New York. I didn't know the world contained as many Negroes as I saw thronging downtown Roxbury at night, especially on Saturdays. Neon lights, nightclubs, poolhalls, bars, the cars they drove! Restaurants made the streets smell—rich, greasy, down-home black cooking! Jukeboxes blared Erskine Hawkins, Duke Ellington, Cootie Williams, dozens of others. If somebody had told me then that some day I'd know them all personally, I'd have found it hard to believe. The biggest bands, like these, played at the Roseland State Ballroom, on Boston's Massachusetts Avenue—one night for Negroes, the next night for whites.

I saw for the first time occasional black-white couples strolling around arm in arm. And on Sundays, when Ella, Mary, or somebody took me to church, I saw churches for black people such as I had never seen. They were many times finer than the white church I had attended back in Mason, Michigan. There, the white people just sat and worshiped with words; but the Boston Negroes, like all other Negroes I had ever seen at church, threw their souls and bodies wholly into worship.

Two or three times, I wrote letters to Wilfred intended for everybody back in Lansing. I said I'd try to describe it when I got back.

But I found I couldn't.

My restlessness with Mason—and for the first time in my life a restlessness with being around white people—began as soon as I got back home and entered eighth grade.

I continued to think constantly about all that I had seen in Boston, and about the way I had felt there. I know now that it was the sense of being a real part of a mass of my own kind for the first time.

The white people—classmates, the Swerlins, the people at the restaurant where I worked—noticed the change. They said, "You're acting so strange. You don't seem like yourself, Malcolm. What's the matter?"

I kept close to the top of the class, though. The top-most scholastic standing, I remember, kept shifting between me, a girl named Audrey Slaugh, and a boy named Jimmy Cotton.

It went on that way, as I became increasingly restless and disturbed through the first semester. And then one day, just about when those of us who had passed were about to move up to 8-A, from which we would enter high school the next year something happened which was to become the first major turning point of my life.

Somehow, I happened to be alone in the classroom with Mr. Ostrowski, my English teacher. He was a tall, rather reddish white man and he had a thick mustache. I had gotten some of my best marks under him, and he had always made me feel that he liked me. He was, as I have mentioned, a natural-born "advisor," about what you ought to read, to do, or think—about any and everything. We used to make unkind jokes about him: why was he teaching in Mason instead of somewhere else, getting for himself some of the "success in life" that he kept telling us how to get?

I know that he probably meant well in what he happened to advise me that day. I doubt that he meant any harm. It was just in his nature as an American white man. I was one of his top students, one of the school's top students—but all he could see for me was the kind of future "in your place" that almost all white people see for black people.

He told me, "Malcolm, you ought to be thinking about a career. Have you been giving it thought?"

The truth is, I hadn't. I never have figured out why I told him, "Well, yes, sir, I've been thinking I'd like to be a lawyer." Lansing certainly had no Negro lawyers—or doctors either—in those days, to hold up an image I might have aspired to. All I really knew for certain was that a lawyer didn't wash dishes, as I was doing.

Mr. Ostrowski looked surprised, I remember, and leaned back in his chair and clasped his hands behind his head. He kind of half-smiled and said, "Malcolm, one of life's first needs is for us to be realistic. Don't misunderstand me, now. We all here like you, you know that. But you've got to be realistic about being a nigger. A lawyer—that's no realistic goal for a nigger. You need to think about something you *can* be. You're good with your hands—making things. Everybody admires your carpentry shop work. Why don't you plan on carpentry? People like you as a person—you'd get all kinds of work."

The more I thought afterwards about what he said, the more uneasy it made me. It just kept treading around in my mind.

What made it really begin to disturb me was Mr. Ostrowski's advice to others in my class—all of them white. Most of them told him they were planning to become farmers. But those who wanted to strike out on their own, to try something new, he had encouraged. Some, mostly girls, wanted to be teachers. A few wanted other professions, such as one boy who wanted to become a county agent; another, a veterinarian; and one girl wanted to be a nurse. They all reported that Mr. Ostrowski had encouraged what they had wanted. Yet nearly none of them had earned marks equal to mine.

It was a surprising thing that I had never thought of it that way before, but I realized that whatever I wasn't, I *was* smarter than nearly all of those white kids. But apparently I was still not intelligent enough, in their eyes, to become whatever *I* wanted to be.

It was then that I began to change—inside.

I drew away from white people. I came to class, and I answered when called upon. It became a physical strain simply to sit in Mr. Ostrowski's class.

Where "nigger" had slipped off my back before, wherever I heard it now, I stopped and looked at whoever said it. And they looked surprised that I did.

I quit hearing so much "nigger" and "What's wrong?"—which was the way I wanted it. Nobody, including the teachers, could decide what had come over me. I knew I was being discussed.

In a few more weeks, it was that way, too, at the restaurant where I worked washing dishes, and at the Swerlins'. . . .

Questions

1. *Using examples from Malcolm X, illustrate development of the self, using Cooley's and Mead's theories.*
2. *Describe aspects of the self that Malcolm X seemed to develop during the period discussed in this essay.*
3. *Malcolm X believes he was treated as a "mascot." Why? Discuss.*
4. *Attempts were made to socialize Malcolm X one way, but it turned out differently. Explain how or why this could happen, using theories discussed in this chapter.*

Shooting an Elephant

George Orwell

The self is a product of social interaction. The way we think others are evaluating us has much to do with how we see ourselves. What others expect of us determines to a large extent how we will behave. These points are illustrated in George Orwell's description of a British police officer's problems with an unruly Burmese elephant.
Orwell's other works include *1984* and *Animal Farm*.

In Moulmein, in Lower Burma, I was hated by large numbers of people— the only time in my life that I have been important enough for this to happen to me. I was sub-divisional police officer of the town, and in an aimless, petty kind of way anti-European feeling was very bitter. No one had the guts to raise a riot, but if a European woman went through the bazaars alone somebody would probably spit betel juice over her dress. As a police officer I was an obvious target and was baited whenever it seemed safe to do so. When a nimble Burman tripped me up on the football field and the referee (another Burman) looked the other way, the crowd yelled with hideous laughter. This happened more than once. In the end the sneering yellow faces of young men that met me everywhere, the insults hooted after me when I was a safe distance, got badly on my nerves. The young Buddhist priests were the worst of all. There were several thousand of them in the town and none of them seemed to have anything to do except stand on street corners and jeer at Europeans.

All this was perplexing and upsetting. For at that time I had already made up my mind that imperialism was an evil thing and the sooner I chucked up my job and got out of it the better. Theoretically—and secretly, of course—I was all for the Burmese and all against their oppressors, the British. As for the job I was doing, I hated it more bitterly than I can perhaps make clear. In a job like that you see the dirty work of Empire at close quarters. The wretched prisoners huddling in the stinking cages of the lock-ups, the grey, cowed faces of the long-term convicts, the scarred buttocks of the men who had been flogged with bamboos—all these oppressed me with an intolerable sense of guilt. But I could get nothing into perspective. I was young and ill-educated and I had had to think out my problems in the utter silence that is imposed on every Englishman in the East. I did not even know that the British Empire is dying, still less did I know that it is a great deal better than the younger empires that are going to supplant it. All I knew was that I was stuck between my hatred of the empire I served and my rage against the evil-spirited little beasts who tried to make my job impossible. With one part of my mind I thought of the British Raj as an unbreakable tyranny, as something clamped down, in *saecula saeculorum,* upon the will of prostrate peoples; with another part I thought that the greatest joy in the world would be to drive a bayonet into a Buddhist priest's guts. Feelings like these are the normal by-products of imperialism; ask any Anglo-Indian official, if you can catch him off duty.

One day something happened which in a roundabout way was enlightening. It was a tiny incident in itself, but it gave me a better glimpse than I had had before of the real nature of imperialism—the real motives for which despotic governments act. Early one morning the sub-inspector at a police station the other end of the town rang me up on the phone and said that an elephant was ravaging the bazaar. Would I please come and do something about it? I did not know what I could do, but I wanted to see what was happening and I got on to a pony and started out. I took my rifle, an old .44 Winchester and much too small to kill an elephant, but I thought the noise might be useful *in terrorem.* Various Burmans stopped me on the way and told me about the elephant's doings. It was not, of course, a wild elephant, but a tame one which had gone "must." It had been chained up, as tame elephants always are when their attack of "must" is due, but on the previous night it had broken its chain and escaped. Its mahout, the only person who could manage it when it was in that state, had set out in pursuit, but had taken the wrong direction and was now twelve hours' journey away, and in the morning the elephant had suddenly reappeared in the town. The Burmese population had no weapons and were quite helpless against it. It had already destroyed somebody's bamboo hut, killed a cow and raided some fruit-stalls and devoured the stock; also it had met the municipal rubbish van and, when the driver jumped out and took to his heels, had turned the van over and inflicted violences upon it.

The Burmese sub-inspector and some Indian constables were waiting for me in the quarter where the elephant had been seen. It was a very poor quarter, a labyrinth of squalid bamboo huts, thatched with palm-leaf, winding all over a steep hillside. I remember that it was a cloudy, stuffy morning at the beginning of the rains. We began questioning the people as to where the elephant had gone and, as usual, failed to get any definite information. That is invariably the case in the East; a story always sounds clear enough at a distance, but the nearer you get to the scene of events the vaguer it becomes. Some of the people said that the elephant had gone in one direction, some said that he had gone in another, some professed not even to have heard of any elephant. I had almost made up my mind that the whole story was a pack of lies, when we heard yells a little distance away. There was a loud, scandalized cry of "Go away, child! Go away this instant!" and an old woman with a switch in her hand came round the corner of the hut, violently shooing away a crowd of naked children. Some more women followed, clicking their tongues and exclaiming; evidently there was something that the children ought not to have seen. I rounded the hut and saw a man's dead body sprawling in the mud. He was an Indian, a black Dravidian coolie, almost naked, and he could not have been dead many minutes. The people said that the elephant had come suddenly upon him round the corner of the hut, caught him with its trunk, put its foot on his back and ground him into the earth. This was the rainy season and the ground was soft, and his face had scored a trench a foot deep and a couple of yards long. He was lying on his belly with arms crucified and head sharply twisted to one side. His face was coated with mud, the eyes wide open, the teeth bared and grinning with an expression of unendurable agony. (Never tell me, by the way, that the dead look peaceful. Most of the corpses I have seen looked devilish.) The friction of the great beast's foot had stripped the skin from his back as neatly as one skins a rabbit. As soon as I saw the dead man I sent an orderly to a friend's house nearby to borrow an elephant rifle. I had already sent back the pony, not wanting it to go mad with fright and throw me if it smelt the elephant.

The orderly came back in a few minutes with a rifle and five cartridges and meanwhile some Burmans had arrived and told us that the elephant was in the paddy fields below, only a few hundred yards away. As I started forward practically the whole population of the quarter flocked out of the houses and followed me. They had seen the rifle and were all shouting excitedly that I was going to shoot the elephant. They had not shown much interest in the elephant when he was merely ravaging their homes, but it was different now that he was going to be shot. It was a bit of fun to them, as it would be to an English crowd; besides they wanted the meat. It made me vaguely uneasy. I had no intention of shooting the elephant—I had merely sent for the rifle to defend myself if necessary—and it is always unnerving to have a crowd following you. I marched down the hill, looking and feeling a fool, with the rifle over my shoulder and an ever-growing army of people jostling at my heels. At the bottom, when you got away from the huts, there was a metalled road and beyond that a miry waste of paddy fields a thousand yards across, not yet ploughed but soggy from the first rains and dotted with coarse grass. The elephant was standing eight yards from the road, his left side towards us. He took not the slightest notice of the crowd's approach. He was tearing up bunches of grass, beating them against his knees to clean them and stuffing them into his mouth.

I had halted on the road. As soon as I saw the elephant I knew with perfect certainty that I ought not to shoot him. It is a serious matter to shoot a working elephant—it is comparable to destroying a huge and costly piece of machinery—and obviously one ought not to do it if it can possibly be avoided. And at that distance, peacefully eating, the elephant looked no more dangerous than a cow. I thought then and I think now that his attack of "must" was already passing off; in which case he would merely wander harmlessly about until the mahout

came back and caught him. Moreover, I did not in the least want to shoot him.
I decided that I would watch him for a little while to make sure that he did not
turn savage again, and then go home.

But at that moment I glanced round at the crowd that had followed me. It
was an immense crowd, two thousand at the least and growing every minute. It
blocked the road for a long distance on either side. I looked at the sea of yellow
faces all happy and excited over this bit of fun, all certain that the elephant
was going to be shot. They were watching me as they would watch a conjurer
about to perform a trick. They did not like me, but with the magical rifle in my
hands I was momentarily worth watching.

And suddenly I realized that I should have to shoot the elephant after all.
The people expected it of me and I had got to do it; I could feel their two thousand wills pressing me forward, irresistibly. And it was at this moment, as I stood
there with the rifle in my hands, that I first grasped the hollowness, the futility of
the white man's dominion in the East. Here was I, the white man with his gun,
standing in front of the unarmed native crowd—seemingly the leading actor of
the piece; but in reality I was only an absurd puppet pushed to and fro by the
will of those yellow faces behind. I perceived in this moment that when the
white man turns tyrant it is his own freedom that he destroys. He becomes a sort
of hollow, posing dummy, the conventionalized figure of a sahib. For it is the
condition of his rule that he shall spend his life in trying to impress the "natives,"
and so in every crisis he has got to do what the "natives" expect of him. He wears
a mask, and his face grows to fit it. I had got to shoot the elephant. I had committed myself to doing it when I sent for the rifle. A sahib has got to act like a
sahib; he has got to appear resolute, to know his own mind and do definite
things. To come all that way, rifle in hand, with two thousand people marching
at my heels, and then to trail feebly away, having done nothing—no, that was
impossible. The crowd would laugh at me. And my whole life, every white
man's life in the East, was one long struggle not to be laughed at.

But I did not want to shoot the elephant. I watched him beating his bunch of
grass against his knees, with that preoccupied grandmotherly air that elephants
have. It seemed to me that it would be murder to shoot him. At that age I was
not squeamish about killing animals, but I had never shot an elephant and never
wanted to. (Somehow it always seems worse to kill a *large* animal.) Besides,
there was the beast's owner to be considered. Alive, the elephant was worth at
least a hundred pounds; dead he would only be worth the value of his tusks, five
pounds, possibly. But I had got to act quickly. I turned to some experienced-
looking Burmans who had been there when we arrived, and asked them how the
elephant had been behaving. They all said the same thing: he took no notice of
you if you left him alone, but he might charge if you went too close to him.

It was perfectly clear to me what I ought to do. I ought to walk up to within,
say, twenty-five yards of the elephant and test his behavior. If he charged, I
could shoot; if he took no notice of me, it would be safe to leave him until the
mahout came back. But also I knew that I was going to do no such thing. I

was a poor shot with a rifle and the ground was soft mud into which one would sink at every step. If the elephant charged and I missed him, I should have about as much chance as a toad under a steam-roller. But even then I was not thinking particularly of my own skin, only of the watchful yellow faces behind. For at that moment, with the crowd watching me, I was not afraid in the ordinary sense, as I would have been if I had been alone. A white man mustn't be frightened in front of "natives;" and so, in general, he isn't frightened. The sole thought in my mind was that if anything went wrong those two thousand Burmans would see me pursued, caught, trampled on and reduced to a grinning corpse like that Indian up the hill. And if that happened it was quite possible that some of them would laugh. That would never do. There was only one alternative. I shoved the cartridges into the magazine and lay down on the road to get a better aim.

The crowd grew very still, and a deep, low, happy sigh, as of people who see the theatre curtain go up at last, breathed from innumerable throats. They were going to have their bit of fun after all. The rifle was a beautiful German thing with cross-hair sights. I did not then know that in shooting an elephant one would shoot to cut an imaginary bar running from ear-hole to ear-hole. I ought, therefore, as the elephant was sideways on, to have aimed straight at his ear-hole; actually I aimed several inches in front of this, thinking the brain would be further forward.

When I pulled the trigger I did not hear the bang or feel the kick—one never does when a shot goes home—but I heard the devilish roar of glee that went up from the crowd. In that instant, in too short a time, one would have thought, even for the bullet to get there, a mysterious, terrible change had come over the elephant. He neither stirred nor fell, but every line of his body had altered. He looked suddenly stricken, shrunken, immensely old, as though the frightful impact of the bullet had paralysed him without knocking him down. At last, after what seemed a long time—it might have been five seconds, I dare say—he sagged flabbily to his knees. His mouth slobbered. An enormous senility seemed to have settled upon him. One could have imagined him thousands of years old. I fired again into the same spot. At the second shot he did not collapse but climbed with desperate slowness to his feet and stood weakly upright, with legs sagging and head drooping. I fired a third time. That was the shot that did for him. You could see the agony of it jolt his whole body and knock the last remnant of strength from his legs. But in falling he seemed for a moment to rise, for as his hind legs collapsed beneath him he seemed to tower upward like a huge rock toppling, his trunk reaching skywards like a tree. He trumpeted, for the first and only time. And then down he came, his belly towards me, with a crash that seemed to shake the ground even where I lay.

I got up. The Burmans were already racing past me across the mud. It was obvious that the elephant would never rise again, but he was not dead. He was breathing very rhythmically with long rattling gasps, his great mound of a side painfully rising and falling. His mouth was wide open—I could see far down into caverns of pale pink throat. I waited a long time for him to die, but his breathing did not weaken. Finally I fired my two remaining shots into the spot where I thought his heart must be. The thick blood welled out of him like red velvet, but still he did not die. His body did not even jerk when the shots hit him, the tortured breathing continued without a pause. He was dying, very slowly and in great agony, but in some world remote from me where not even a bullet could damage him further. I felt that I had got to put an end to that dreadful noise. It seemed dreadful to see the great beast lying there, powerless to move and yet powerless to die, and not even to be able to finish him. I sent back for my small rifle and poured shot after shot into his heart and down his throat. They seemed to make no impression. The tortured gasps continued as steadily as the ticking of a clock.

In the end I could not stand it any longer and went away. I heard later that it took him half an hour to die. Burmans were bringing dahs and baskets even before I left, and I was told they had stripped his body almost to the bones by the afternoon.

Afterwards, of course, there were endless discussions about the shooting of the elephant. The owner was furious, but he was only an Indian and could do nothing. Besides, legally I had done the right thing, for a mad elephant has to be killed, like a mad dog, if its owner fails to control it. Among the Europeans opinion was divided. The older men said I was right, the younger men said it was a damn shame to shoot an elephant for killing a coolie, because an elephant was worth more than any damn Coringhee coolie. And afterwards I was very glad that the coolie had been killed; it put me legally in the right and it gave me a sufficient pretext for shooting the elephant. I often wondered whether any of the others grasped that I had done it solely to avoid looking a fool.

Questions

1. Use Cooley's concept of the looking-glass self to describe and explain the police officer's behavior.
2. How could Mead's concepts dealing with the self be used to explain the behavior of the police officer?
3. Use Mead's concepts of "I" and "me" to analyze the police officer's behavior.
4. Is it possible to predict how the police officer would have behaved had no one been watching? If so, how would you do it?

3

Norms, Roles, Culture

A sociology instructor is lecturing to a class of college freshmen and sophomores. At one point in his lecture, he asks a student to help him illustrate a point by standing up. The student he asks is belligerent and upset at being interrupted in his reading of the school newspaper. The student replies that he would rather not help, and that the teacher should ask someone else. The teacher asks the student once more to please help him with the experiment and to stand up. The student replies in a louder voice that he doesn't think much of this stupid class or the teacher, and he is not about to participate in some silly experiment. The now angry teacher responds, "Either stand up or get out of this classroom!!!" The student replies, "I'm not standing up—and if you want me out of here you'll have to throw me out!!!" The two then glare at each other for what seems like a year.

If we were watching the scene and could take our eyes off the principal characters, we would notice that the rest of the class is behaving strangely. Nearly all appear to be very uncomfortable, many are obviously embarrassed. They are twisting and squirming and are avoiding meeting the eyes of the instructor. At the beginning of the confrontation some may have laughed nervously; now all are quiet. They act as if they are trying to deny that what is happening is actually happening. . . . Why?

Norms

All societies have rules that specify what people should do in specific situations. Sociologists call these shared standards for behavior *norms*. Norms describe the accepted or required behavior for a person in a particular situation. When a person gets into his car, he unconsciously begins to behave according to a whole set of norms relating to driving procedure. In America he knows that he should drive on the right side of the road, pass on the left, signal before turning, and so on. The norms vary from place to place, but they always exist. These shared standards for behavior allow us to predict what other people will do. Without even thinking about it or knowing him, I know how the driver of the car approaching me will behave. The system of norms allows us to predict what other people will do in specific situations and to pattern our own behavior accordingly.

It is disturbing when the normative system breaks down and predictability of behavior vanishes. Norm breakdown occurs when there are conflicting sets of norms and when groups and societies change. We see norm breakdown most vividly during periods of rapid social change, such as wars or disasters. When norms cease to be effective at controlling people's behavior, we say that a state of normlessness or *anomie* is present. (We will return to these terms in the chapter on social disorganization.) One tends to lose all sense of stability, security, and orderliness when norms break down. Imagine the consternation if we did not know what to expect of that oncoming driver—if we had *no* idea what he was going to do.

This may explain the "strange behavior" of the students in the classroom. There are norms that govern the student-teacher relationship. These norms are so obvious and ingrained that we do not even think about them. Characteristically, norms do not become apparent until they are violated. According to norms dealing with student-teacher relationships, the student will show respect for the teacher, will laugh at his jokes, and will generally obey the authority that the teacher represents. That is, students will respect any reasonable demands made by the teacher without resorting to mutiny. When, as in our example above, behavior is contrary to the norms, the situation becomes uncomfortable for others. Instructors who have tried this "stand up" experiment on classes (with the aid of a willing "villain"), report that the experience is almost as hard on the two of them (instructor and "villain"), who know it's a fake, as it is for the rest of the class, who don't know that it has been set up. Thus even planned and legitimate norm violation may be hard on individuals when done in the context of a group that is unaware of the new definitions.

Other experiments in norm violation have been devised.[1] For example, get somebody you don't know very well in a game of ticktacktoe. Invite the other

---

[1] These and other examples are contained in *Studies in Ethnomethodology* by Harold Garfinkel (Englewood Cliffs, New Jersey: Prentice-Hall, 1967).

person to make the first move. After he or she makes a mark, you erase it, move it to another square, and make your own mark. Act as if nothing unusual has happened. Or select a person (not a family member or very close friend) and during the course of an ordinary conversation, and without indicating that anything unusual is happening, bring your face closer to the other person's until your noses are almost touching. The first experiment deals with norms concerning game playing, and the second with norms concerning "spatial invasion" or the appropriate distance between people who are interacting. In each case, the subject will react noticeably (and possibly unpredictably) because common norms that ordinarily one doesn't even think about are suddenly being violated.

Types of Norms

Norm strength varies greatly. One way of determining the relative strength of norms is by the sanctions that the norms carry. A *sanction* is the punishment one receives for violation of a norm or the reward one receives for correct norm performance. Sanctions take a variety of forms: a look on someone's face, an "A" on an exam, a sharp word from the wife or boss, a kind word from a parent, a traffic ticket from a police officer, a life sentence in a penitentiary. Some norms are obligatory, and the sanctions are harsh if these are violated. Sociologists use the term *mores* to describe norms that fit into this category. Norms regulating which side of the road one can drive on and prohibiting the taking of another's life are mores. Mores may be translated into written law. Whether written or unwritten, the emotional force of mores is strong—they still represent the "musts" of behavior.

There are also norms dealing with what we *should* do rather than what we *must* do. These norms are less obligatory than mores, and the sanctions for violation are milder in degree. People may look at us rather strangely if we violate these norms, but they probably will not lock us up or banish us. These norms are called *folkways.*[2] Practices like shaking hands when meeting someone or norms regulating the type of clothes one wears would be considered folkways. A student coming to class in a bikini and golf shoes would probably be allowed to stay in spite of the obvious violation of the folkways. At the same time there would likely be ample private discussion of her character and intelligence.

A further distinction should be made between ideal norms and statistical norms. *Ideal norms* refer to what people agree *should* be done. *Statistical norms* refer to what they *actually* do. Ideal norms indicate that cheating on tests, premarital sexual intercourse, and falsifying one's income tax are wrong. However, statistical norms—what people are actually doing—would indicate that

[2] These terms ("folkways" and "mores") were introduced by William Graham Sumner in his book *Folkways* (Boston: Ginn and Company, 1907). (Later and paperback editions have appeared.)

a substantial number of people are performing these activities, often, amazingly enough, the same people who previously told us these things were wrong. It shouldn't surprise us that there may be quite a discrepancy between talk and action—or, "Do as I say, not as I do. . . ."

Norm Conflict and Change

Norms exist at different levels. Some norms are society-wide, and many times these, if they are of an obligatory nature, are made into written laws. Norms also exist at the group level when specific clubs, organizations, or categories of people develop norms governing their behavior. Sometimes the norms of a particular group come in conflict with norms of another group or with the norms of society. Use of marijuana is governed by different norms at different levels in our society. Drug laws in the United States currently prohibit sale and possession of marijuana. However, norms prevalent among numbers of teenagers and young adults suggest just the opposite—use of marijuana is not only accepted, but expected.

Society's laws usually reflect its mores, but sometimes they do not. It is natural for different segments of society to disagree on norms. Occasionally, however, a minority or special interest group gains enough power to manipulate laws. Or sometimes change in norms is rapid, and change in laws does not keep pace. When either of these situations occurs, laws may not reflect the mores of society. It is usually predicted that, when laws and mores are in conflict, in the long run mores will win out. The prohibition laws apparently did not reflect the mores of the country, and the laws were flagrantly violated until rescinded. We may have a similar situation today concerning marijuana use.

Norms constantly change in any society. What is accepted at one time may be rejected at another. For example, change in fashion norms—clothes, hair, speech—is rapid. Although there is undoubtedly more frequent change in folkways than in mores, the more obligatory norms also change.

Status and Role

When students and an instructor walk into class the first day of the semester, they know without thinking what to expect of each other and how each will behave. These things are known even though they have not seen each other before. The students know that the instructor will stand in front of the class behind a lectern, probably call roll, assign reading, and dismiss them early the first day. The instructor knows that, unless the class is required, students will be shopping around. They will be trying to decide whether to take this class, and their decision will be based on course content, the viewpoint and personality of the instructor, the amount and type of work required, or how the instructor is known to grade.

We know these things about each other partly because of the system of norms discussed previously. The concepts of status and role are closely related to norms, and they play a major part in the situation described above. By *status* we mean a position in society or in a group. There are innumerable positions that one may occupy—teacher, student, police officer, president, football player, father, wife, convict. Furthermore, each of us may occupy several positions at once—teacher, handball player, father, husband, and so on. By *role* we mean the behavior of one who occupies a particular status. As Bierstedt puts it, a role is what an individual *does* in the status he occupies; statuses are occupied, roles are played.[3]

A set of norms surrounds each status and role. These norms, called *role requirements,* describe the behavior expected of persons holding a particular position in society. Recalling our earlier example, the behavior of the student who refused to stand up was disturbing because it was unpredictable. He was occupying the status or position of student, but the role he played—his behavior—was contrary to the expected behavior of a person in that status. His behavior was outside the limits set by the norms or role requirements.

Within the boundaries set by the role requirements, there is often extensive variation in how a role is played. On a football team, status would refer to the positions, role to the behavior of the incumbent of the position. One status would be quarterback. Role requirements of quarterbacks are generally that they call the plays, direct the team, and try to move the ball down the field. But now look at the actual performance of several quarterbacks. One passes frequently, another seldom passes but runs with the ball often, and a third does neither but usually blocks. Compare four or five of your instructors in their role behavior. Although all occupy the status of college professor, no doubt their behavior varies markedly. One paces the floor, another stays behind the podium while lecturing. One demands class discussion, the next dislikes having his lectures interrupted. One has beautifully organized and prepared lectures, and another has a disorganized, stream-of-consciousness presentation that he put together on the way to class. Or, compare the behavior of the last three Presidents of the United States. Again we see marked differences in role within a given status. These differences in behavior obviously occur because people holding the same status define the role differently. They also have different skills, interests, abilities, and personalities. Therefore, although each status carries with it certain role requirements, there is still variation and flexibility in actual behavior.

Role—behavior that is suited to a particular status—varies not only because of the style of a particular quarterback, college professor, or president. Roles must be seen in an *interaction* setting. While behaving, people are always socially

---

[3] Robert Bierstedt, *The Social Order*, 3rd Ed. (New York: McGraw-Hill Book Co., 1970), Chapter 9.

interacting with others and consequently their behavior adjusts to and is modified by the responses of others. This continues the viewpoint introduced in the previous chapter in which we pointed out that socialization and self-development occur through the process of social interaction. Roles we play are shaped by others' reactions to us: After comments and complaints from an unhappy class, the unprepared, stream-of-consciousness professor mentioned above may modify his performance. It is a common occurrence to go into a situation prepared for one sort of role only to find that in the process of the interaction, another sort of behavior is necessary.

Achieved and Ascribed Status

How do we happen to occupy the statuses that we do? Some, probably most, statuses are earned or achieved in some way, and hence these are called *achieved* statuses. Astronaut, policeman, college professor, and truck driver represent achieved statuses. Some statuses are automatically conferred on us with no effort or choice on our part. These are *ascribed* statuses. One's sex, race, and nationality are ascribed (although occasionally some changes can be made). Sometimes it is difficult to tell whether a status is ascribed or achieved. Take the fellow who is "forced" to go to college because of the wishes of his parents—is his status of student ascribed or achieved? Or how about statuses that a child "inherits" from his parents, such as political and religious affiliations—are they ascribed or achieved?

Statuses are stratified or ranked at a number of levels. Some statuses are of high rank and bring much prestige to the occupant. Doctor, board chairman of a large corporation, college president, author, artist, scientist, and movie star are statuses that have high value and prestige in our society. Evaluation of positions is usually determined by the requirements that one must have to fill that status—extensive education, wealth, beauty, skill, or some other extraordinary characteristic. Sometimes this ranking is based on a societal tradition that "automatically" ranks certain characteristics above others, like being male, of a particular race or religion, or born in a particular "royal" family. In the United States, we are said to be very status- or rank-conscious. We will return to this topic when we discuss social stratification.

Role Strain and Role Conflict

Problems may occur when a person must play several roles simultaneously, or when one role requires a person to perform in several different ways. These situations are called role conflict and role strain and they may lead to personal stress and discomfort. *Role strain* refers to the situation in which there are differing and conflicting expectations regarding one's status or position. A student may experience role strain when he compares the expectations of his parents (study, get As, prepare for a vocation, practice frugality in all things) with the expectations of his fraternity brothers (be social, be active in fraternity affairs, be athletic). The police officer who is trained to arrest people who have committed crimes probably feels role strain when he is ordered by superiors who do not want to make a bad situation worse to stand by and watch looting take place during a riot.

Role conflict occurs when a person occupies several statuses or positions that have contradictory role requirements. Here there is not the confusion or disagreement about the requirements of a single role we saw in the first case. The requirements of the roles are clearly understood—the problem is that the requirements of two or more roles are contradictory. The young woman who is a graduate student and wife of a professor may experience role conflict. As a college professor's wife, she interacts socially with other professors. At the same time, as a student, she takes classes from many of these same people. In this case the role requirements of student (deference for and a degree of social distance from teachers) and wife (interact socially with husband's friends and colleagues) are contradictory. Doctors seldom treat members of their own families because of the role conflict that may occur. Similarly, the football coach whose son is trying out for the team experiences conflict between the contradictory requirements of two different roles—coach and father. And finally, if we have ever marvelled at the phenomenon of the champion woman tennis player beating everyone in the world except her future husband, we should have recognized and sympathized with her attempt to resolve her role conflict.

Other Cultures, Other Norms

Normative behavior varies from one place to another. Actions that are correct and expected in one part of the world are wrong and peculiar in another part of the world. Appropriate role performance in one country is inappropriate in another. Social scientists use the concept *culture* to understand and explain these phenomena. Before defining society and culture, it might be well to illustrate some aspects of culturally related behavior. There are a multitude of examples, but the following come to mind.

Every four years, writers from England and Europe flock to the U.S. to observe a very peculiar ritual the like of which is unknown throughout the rest of the civilized world. These strange ceremonies are written up and read about by disbelieving audiences everywhere. The tribal celebrations being enacted are called locally the "American Political Conventions." Strange indeed. . . .

Imagine you are dropped onto a small South Sea island, and your only possession is a golf club—a #2 iron. To avoid being eaten alive you have to explain the function and purpose of the golf club to the natives. Where do you start?

Anthropologists describe a society in which very fat women are highly valued. Women in this society spend weeks in "fattening sheds" where they eat starchy, fatty foods and have their bodies greased to make them more attractive. On festival day they are paraded before the king, who chooses the fattest and heaviest as his mate. Very peculiar people. But imagine for a moment that you have to explain to a member of that society the popularity in America of the various dieting and health spas where men and women spend great sums of money to get slimmer bodies.

Some Indian tribes living along the Amazon have an interesting reaction to pregnancy. The woman breaks off from work in the fields and returns home for only two or three hours to give birth to the child. Meanwhile, her husband has been lying at home in a hammock, tossing about and groaning as if in great pain. Even after the birth when the woman has returned to the fields, the husband remains in bed with the baby to recuperate from his "ordeal." It appears that pain is determined by something more than the nature of the wound.

Anthropologist Margaret Mead visited three primitive tribes in New Guinea and wrote about them in her book *Sex and Temperament*. First, Mead describes the mountain-dwelling Arapesh, among whom both the men and the women behave in a way that Americans would describe as maternal or feminine. Both parents devote their lives to raising the children. The men are gentle, and there is complete cooperation between both sexes at all times. Next, Mead describes a cannibalistic tribe living on a river, the Mundugumor. Here both the men and the women behave in a way that Americans would describe as masculine. Men and women work in the fields together and are aggressive individualists. Finally, Margaret Mead describes the lake-dwelling Tchambuli. In this society the men behave in a manner that Americans define as feminine or maternal, and the women are masculine by our standards. The women spend the days fishing and weaving, and they have all the power. The men spend their time dancing in ceremonies, dressing and making themselves up, and in artistic endeavors. The men gossip, quarrel, and get very jealous of each other over the affections of a woman. The women's attitude toward the men is one of kindly tolerance and appreciation—they watch the shows that the men put on.

We tend to believe that certain patterns of behavior and temperament are automatically, necessarily related to sex. We may believe that to be male is to behave a certain way "naturally," and that female behavior is innate as well. The point of Mead's research is that the relationship between sex and the corresponding behavior and temperament is determined by the society in which one lives—as are body shape and size preference, taste in food or art, belief in a supreme being, nature of recreational activity, and many other characteristics.

Society and Culture

A *society* is defined as a number of people who have lived together long enough to become organized to some degree and who share a common culture. The emphasis in defining society is on "a number of people." By *culture* we mean that complex set of learned and shared beliefs, customs, skills, habits, traditions, and knowledge common to the members of a society. Culture is viewed as the "social heritage" of a society. According to Kluckhohn, culture represents the distinctive way of life of a group of people, their complete design for living.[4] So, if in discussing society the emphasis is on "a number of people," in discussing culture the emphasis is on the "learned, shared patterns of behavior" common to that people.

For social scientists, the concept of culture is very important. The culture is shared by the members of a society. It is learned through the socialization process. In fact, the socialization process might be viewed as the process whereby one learns and internalizes the norms and roles of the culture in which he lives. The culture determines for us what we will want to eat, whom we will like or hate, what we will fear (snakes and mice, but not evil spirits), how we will express our emotions, how we will dress (levis and bikinis but not turbans or saris), our manners, and how we will celebrate New Year's Eve. In other words, culture determines who we are and how we will live.

The distinction is frequently made between the material and non-material aspects of a culture. *Material* culture refers to the concrete things that a society creates and uses—screwdriver, house, classroom, desk, car, plane, telephone. *Non-material* culture refers to the more abstract creations of a society such as customs, laws, ideas, values, and beliefs. The non-material culture would include beliefs about religion and courtship, ideas about democracy and communism, definitions of good manners, and rules for driving a car.

Certain aspects of any given culture are unique to that culture. Some striking contrasts in cultures were shown earlier in this chapter. However, many aspects are shared with other cultures. General patterns recur frequently—a family system, the incest taboo, a system of religion. Variation in culture traits and patterns is more likely to occur in certain specific practices than in general patterns. Cultures constantly change as old traits and patterns die out and new ones are introduced through invention from within or diffusion from some other culture. Some cultures change rapidly, others slowly, but change is inevitable.

---

[4] This follows Broom and Selznick's definition of culture. See also Clyde Kluckhohn, "The Study of Culture," *The Policy Sciences,* edited by Daniel Lerner and Harold D. Lasswell (Stanford, Calif: Stanford University Press, 1951), p. 86, and quoted in Leonard Broom and Phillip Selznick, *Sociology,* 5th Ed. (New York: Harper & Row, 1973), p. 57.

Personality and temperament vary from one culture to another. As we noted, Margaret Mead described a variety of relationships between sex and temperament in three primitive societies. Ruth Benedict in her book *Patterns of Culture* describes two distinct character traits she observed in her comparison of primitive societies in North America. The Zuni are described as "Apollonian" in that they are extremely self-controlled. They emphasize formality, sobriety, and inoffensiveness, they are not individualistic, and they are traditional, frowning on anything new or different. The Kwakiutl, on the other hand, are described as "Dionysian" in that they emphasize self-gratification to excess. They are wildly ceremonious and strive for ecstasy, which is achieved through complete loss of self-control. Benedict reports that dancers were sometimes tethered by four ropes so that they might not do irreparable damage to themselves in their frenzy.

David Riesman in *The Lonely Crowd* describes the effect of culture on personality in a somewhat different manner. His subject is American character, and he describes how character and personality change as other aspects within the culture change. According to Riesman, three types of social characters have been dominant in American society. In earlier years the dominant type of character was *tradition-directed*. In a tradition-directed culture, behavior is carefully controlled. Routine orients and occupies the lives of everyone. Ritual, religion, and custom are dominant. New solutions are not sought, and change is very slow. Later, the *inner-directed* type of character appeared. The inner-directed person is taught early in life to have an inward focus, with emphasis on the self and its needs and gratifications. Other persons are not of crucial importance. The individual may be internally driven toward such ideals as power and wealth; he is encouraged to set his own goals and to be on his own. His life is concerned with self-mastery and accomplishment. change is very slow. Later, the *other-directed* type of character appeared. The chief interest for the other-directed person is to be liked by other people. According to Riesman, the other-directed person has a built-in radar system which searches out the reactions and feelings of others so that he may adapt himself to them. The person is more concerned with conformity, is shallower, friendlier, more unsure of himself, and more demanding of approval from others. The peer group is all-important, as is the "front" which one puts up. Riesman believes that these types of character result from other changes within the culture, such as population growth or change, along with changes in economic, industrial, and agricultural techniques, and urbanization. Again the major point for us is that the culture one lives in determines who he is and how he behaves, including patterns of personality and character.

Ethnocentrism and Cultural Relativism

Ethnocentrism describes a type of prejudice that says simply, my culture's ways are right and other cultures' ways that are not like mine are wrong. The ethnocentric person says that the familiar is good and the unfamiliar or foreign is bad. An ethnocentric person in the United States might maintain, among other things, that non-Christians are barbarians, that Eskimo tribes practicing sexual hospitality are totally lacking in moral fiber, that anybody who eats dogmeat, horsemeat, or people is not civilized, that democracy is the only way of government, and generally that we are doing other cultures a favor when we go in and "Americanize" them.

Being ethnocentric to some degree is difficult to avoid. Informally, in interacting with family and friends, and formally through a kind of indoctrination in the educational system, we are frequently taught that our ways are best and, at least by implication, others' ways are less good. The mass media encourage ethnocentrism by treating the foreign and unfamiliar in terms of easily recognized stereotypes. It is probably true that ethnocentrism is impossible to escape, as it is encouraged in one way or another by most of the institutions (family, church, schools, government) in any society. Even social scientists (who should know better) sometimes run into difficulty when studying other cultures. Since most social scientists are white middle-class representatives of the dominant culture, they may have a tendency to describe phenomena that are different—Amish, Eskimos, delinquent gangs—from the viewpoint of their own value system rather than from the viewpoint of the people they are studying.

Related to ethnocentrism but opposite in meaning is the concept of *cultural relativism*. Cultural relativism suggests that each culture be judged from its own viewpoint without imposing outside standards of judgment. Behaviors, values, and beliefs are relative to the culture in which they appear. The cultural relativist believes that what is right in one society may be wrong in another and what is considered civilized in one society may be seen as barbaric in another, but basically judgments should not be made about the "goodness" or "badness" of traits in cultures other than one's own. A multitude of anthropological studies comparing societies in various stages of development have substantiated the contention that, when looked at from the viewpoint of a given culture, there are probably no absolutes, no universal rights and wrongs. All aspects of culture are relative only to the particular society in which they appear.

Subculture and Contraculture

Most societies, especially large complex societies like the United States, have groups that, by their traits, beliefs, or interests, are somewhat separated and distinct from the rest of society. Members of such a group may share many of the characteristics of the dominant culture, but they have some of their own specific customs or ways as well. We generally refer to such groups as *subcultures*. The line of distinction between culture and subculture is not always clear. Some have argued, for example, that in a melting-pot society like the United States, the idea of a dominant culture is a myth and that what we really have is a mass of somewhat similar, somewhat different subcultures all mixed together. However, sociologists generally use the term "subculture" to refer to smaller groups that appear to have some values and customs different from the rest of society.

Some religious groups, the Amish for example, seem to qualify as subcultures. A major problem for the Amish, as for many subcultures, is to maintain their identity, even their existence, in the face of a dominant culture frequently hostile to their beliefs. The opposition of the Amish to electricity (which meant no lights at night on their horse-drawn carriages) and their opposition to any formal education beyond the eighth grade brought well-publicized confrontations with the authorities in several Midwestern states.

Urban lower-class youth who band together in gangs have been described by the term "delinquent subculture." Albert Cohen, Walter Miller, and other sociologists have studied these gangs and have described them as subcultures distinct from the dominant culture. The delinquent subculture has its own set of values and beliefs, and frequently these are in conflict with the rest of society. Often, acts that youth feel are acceptable are not viewed that way by the authorities representing the dominant society. The frequent result is that individuals following the subculture's norms find themselves locked up in the culture's jails.

This element of conflict in some "subcultural" behavior led Milton Yinger to propose the term *contraculture*. The central element in a contraculture is the idea of opposition to or conflict with the norms and values of the dominant culture. Subculture describes the group that has some separate customs, some differing beliefs and behaviors, from the dominant society, whereas contraculture describes the group whose behavior is disintegrative and destructive to the dominant society. Examples of contracultures could include delinquent gangs and revolutionary groups whose opposition to society is expressed through use of violence to bring about social change. Examples of subcultures could include college students, the Amish, Chicanos, the Hutterites, and sociologists.[5]

---

[5] J. Milton Yinger, "Contraculture and Subculture," *American Sociological Review,* 25 (October 1960), pp. 625–635. Also see an analysis by Ruth Shonle Cavan, "The Concepts of Tolerance and Contraculture as Applied to Delinquency," *Sociological Quarterly,* 2 (1961), pp. 243–258, and an empirical test by Dean S. Dorn, "A Partial Test of the Delinquency Continuum Typology: Contracultures and Subcultures," *Social Forces,* 47 (March 1969), pp. 305–314.

Summary

In the first chapter in this section on socialization and culture, we focused on how the individual develops into a social being. In this chapter, we have turned our attention from the individual and the processes of socialization and self-development to the stage or setting where these processes take place. This setting is called the social environment, and we have introduced concepts which can be used to examine the social environment in more detail. The individual exists in a specific society and culture. Further, the individual will occupy numerous positions, be governed by rules, and behave in a variety of ways that are sometimes appropriate, sometimes inappropriate, but seldom unusual. The basic fact in this chapter is that the individual's membership in a given society and culture, whose patterns and customs developed long before him and will probably long outlive him, affect and explain much of his behavior.

Norms are the "rules of society." We operate effectively and behavior becomes predictable because of them. Norm breakdown occasionally occurs, and when it does it may produce crises both for society and for the individual. Norms vary in strength—"shoulds" are called folkways, "musts" are called mores. There are group norms and societal norms, and sometimes these contrasting sets of norms are in conflict. When this happens it produces problems for people who are influenced by the conflicting sets of norms. A status is a position in society, and role describes the behavior of one who occupies a status. Norms define the boundaries for role requirements, but within these boundaries there is variation in how the role is actually performed. Statuses, which may be either achieved or ascribed, are ranked in value or prestige. When a person occupies several statuses with contradictory role requirements, role conflict may occur. Role strain may result for one who tries to play a role having conflicting expectations.

Society is defined as a number of people who have lived together long enough to become organized. Culture is made up of the learned, shared patterns of behavior and knowledge common to a society. There are material and non-material aspects to a culture. Subcultures refer to groups that share many of the traits of the dominant culture but have some unique customs and traits as well. Our cultural and subcultural affiliations are of crucial importance in determining who we are and what we do. The concepts of ethnocentrism and cultural relativism help us to understand the familiar tendency to assume that the world everywhere is the same as it is here, and that if by some chance it's not, it should be.

The first of four readings which follow illustrates several characteristics of norms. Norms come in a variety of types—written laws, unwritten customs, myths, and legends. Norms are "culture-bound"—they are tied to a given culture, and there is often great variation from one culture to another. In "The Mysterious Drop in Japan's Birth Rate," Koya Azumi describes how a superstition or myth exerts normative power. The second article also deals with norms. Stanley Milgram describes what happens in an experimental situation when subjects are faced with conflicting norms: Should they follow orders and hurt someone, or should they respond to the cries of pain and disobey orders? New elements of a culture are introduced from within through invention or are adapted from other cultures through the process of diffusion. In his classic article, "One Hundred Per Cent American," Ralph Linton discusses the origins of parts of the American culture. The final article in this section is an excerpt from a novel by an anthropologist in which she describes some of the cultural patterns of the Tiv of Northern Nigeria, and her reactions to them.

The Mysterious Drop
in Japan's Birth Rate

Koya Azumi

Norms and roles exist in a cultural context. What is "normative"—the expected behavior —in one culture will not be in another. Norms come in a variety of forms, from written laws to informal agreements. Even superstitions and myths may represent values that act as norms when they suggest or require that people behave in specific ways at certain times or under certain conditions.

Sociologist Koya Azumi describes how in Japan in the mid-twentieth century, an ancient superstition exerts the normative power to change population rates.

In 1966, the birth rate in Japan suddenly plunged to a record low of 13.7 per thousand—down almost half a million births from the preceding year. This decline in births—26 percent in one year—was extraordinary. Such a birth-rate plunge would have exceeded the wildest hopes of the countries that are frantically trying to limit their populations. But in Japan, a prosperous and heavily industrialized country that is *not* trying to limit its population, the drop seemed to make no sense.

None of the usual explanations for a rapid birth decline seemed to work. A quick survey of the country showed that Japan in 1966 was no different from Japan in 1965 or 1967—and the number of births in 1967 increased by 50 percent over 1966. The year 1966 was marked by no war, no sudden shifts in prosperity, and no change in the legal codes that might have influenced reproductive behavior.

Furthermore, the decline could not be ascribed to any sudden lack of sexual activity. In fact, during the last half of 1965 the number of induced abortions rose sharply. This suggests that people were still engaging in their usual sexual activities but that, for some reason, they were determined not to have children.

This determination first became evident in the birth statistics for January 1966. In December 1965 the birth rate stood at a steady 17.3; by the end of January it had fallen to 14.6. In a single month, the Japanese made their birth rate fall by a spectacular 16 percent. True, with modern contraceptive methods (and, as a last resort, modern abortion methods), people have greater control over their reproductive lives. But under no normal circumstances do they choose to exercise this control to the extent that the Japanese did in the last nine months of 1965 and the first three months of 1966.

This was not the first time that the Japanese birth rate had fallen sharply. But this was the first time it had done so without apparent reason. The birth rate took a sharp plunge in the 1950s, for example, but that was in response to deliberate government policy. Such a policy was necessary because by 1947, two years after the end of World War II, the Japanese rate had risen to 34.4 per thousand—a figure comparable to the current high rates in countries like Taiwan, Cuba, and Ceylon. The Japanese government was alarmed. To stop this dangerous trend toward overpopulation, the government launched a massive birth-control campaign. It adopted family planning as national policy and began to spread birth-control information and materials throughout the country. Legal restrictions against abortion were eased—so much so that abortion became available to almost any woman who wanted it.

The desire to limit family size was apparently there, for contraception soon became accepted and widespread. Within 10 years, the birth rate had actually halved—a decline unprecedented in Japan or anywhere else. If it had continued at this pace, within a few decades there would have been no births at all. But by 1957, the rate stabilized at between 17 and 18 live births per thousand per year.

On the basis of that sustained low rate, demographers predicted that by the 1980s the Japanese population would hit a ceiling of about 110 million. Then a cycle of depopulation would begin.

The nationalistic Japanese, faced with the declining vigor of an increasing older population and the long-term threat of possible depopulation, might have been expected to respond to this prospect by starting to plan larger families. But instead, in 1966, they reduced their birth rate even beyond the sustained low figure that had prevailed for the past nine years.

A Bad Year for Girls

Why then, against all logical expectations to the contrary, did the Japanese apparently declare a moratorium on child-bearing in 1966? The answer lies in an ancient superstition.

The superstition is rooted in the ancient lunar-solar calendar of Chinese origin. This old calendar, although abandoned by the Japanese in 1872 in favor of the Gregorian calendar used in the West, is still very much a part of Japanese thinking. It is composed of two circular systems—one a decimal system of 10 "trunks" and the other a duodecimal system of 12 "twigs." The trunks carry the names of natural objects or elements, and the twigs carry the names of animals. Every 60 years, when the "fire" period of the first system coincides with the "horse" period of the second, a new cycle of history begins. The first year of each new cycle is called a year of Hinoeuma.

What explains Japan's sudden birth-rate decline in 1966 is the fact that 1966 was a year of Hinoeuma. For according to the superstition, any girl born in such a year will be of harsh temperament and invite misfortune—in other words, she will have great difficulty finding a husband The Japanese just weren't taking that chance. Rather than conceiving children on the chance that they would be boys and thus immune to the misfortunes of Hinoeuma, many Japanese decided to wait till next year. During 1965 and early 1966, they practiced rigorous birth control. And failing that, they were quite prepared to resort to abortion to make certain that they brought no unlucky daughters into the world.

Recurrent Declines

Plainly, the Hinoeuma superstition has withstood industrialization, mass education, and the growth of science and technology, as well as the passage of time. But how can we be sure that it was responsible for the birth decline of 1966? The answer is that the persistence of the superstition and its link to the birth rate can be shown statistically. For example, government figures indicate that the 1966 decline was greatest in the traditional, rural areas.

Since the phenomenon is also a recurrent one, the case for superstition becomes even stronger. The last time a year of Hinoeuma came around was in 1906. Predictably, the birth rate declined—from 31.1 per thousand in 1905 down to 29.6 in 1906. The next year, it rose rapidly to about 34. Something else very peculiar happened in 1906: The sex ratio at birth became noticeably unbalanced. Normally, each year there are slightly more boys than girls born, but in 1906 the number of boys so far exceeded the number of girls that the usual ratio was definitely upset. In 1905, the sex ratio of boys to girls was 102.7

to 100. In 1906, the year of Hinouema, the ratio jumped to 108.7 to 100. Then in 1907, it returned to 102.7 to 100—a normal figure.

The explanation circulated at the time laid the sudden increase in boys to a mysterious force of nature that compensates for the loss of men during war. And Japan had concluded a war against Russia the year before. But there is some reason to doubt that such an increase in male births really occurs after a war. For example, the American demographer C. T. McMahan tested this expectation against actual birth statistics in the United States following both world wars and found no such increase.

McMahan's findings suggest that Japan's apparent proportionate increase in male births following the Russo-Japanese War may need a skeptical second look. How can we be sure that such an increase occurred? In other words, how reliable are Japan's birth statistics for 1906?

False Statistics

It turns out that in 1906, like today, the responsibility for registering the vital events of birth, marriage, and death rested with Japan's heads of household. This fact, plus the fact that 1906 was a year of Hinouema, may help explain the peculiar activity of the 1906 birth rate. Household heads may simply have responded to the Hinouema superstition by failing to register the births of girls born in 1906. Since there was no vigorously enforced time requirement for registration, these household heads could easily have registered these girl children as having been born in 1905 or in 1907. If this had happened, we would expect the over-registration of girls in those years to depress the sex ratio—and the 102.7-to-100 figure that prevailed during both these years *was,* although within the normal range, slightly below average. (The figures for 1904 and 1908 give male rates of 105.1 and 104.6 respectively.) By this very rational method of accommodating to an irrational belief, then, Japanese parents—in their effort to shield their newborn daughters from the stigma of Hinouema—likely falsified the birth statistics for 1906.

By 1966, the next unlucky year, the Japanese no longer needed to falsify the birth statistics. Modernization had brought family planning within the reach of almost everyone. But in the 60 years since 1906, Japan had also undergone other radical changes: Illiteracy had been wiped out, the agricultural population had dwindled from about two-thirds to less than one-fourth of the labor force, and a modern industrial economy had evolved. In addition, most of the women who were of child-bearing age in 1966 were modern women, born after 1930. All of this should have helped quash the Hinouema superstition. If, as sociologists believe, modernization means demystification, secularization, and rationalization, then the Japanese of 1966 should have been free of the idea that a woman's year of birth can determine her personality and even her life chances.

But the birth-rate plunge of 1966 showed that the superstition was still very much alive. Modernization, it appears, served only to provide the Japanese with more efficient ways to propitiate the same old deities. The Japanese of 1906 concealed female births, and the Japanese of 1966 *prevented* them. But the motivation—to avoid the year of Hinouema—was still the same.

Of course, it is not fair to conclude that *all* the Japanese who avoided having children in 1966 because it was the year of Hinouema were themselves superstitious. Perhaps they merely felt that *others* believed in the superstition and that this might be enough to hinder the chances of girls born in that year. But whether the potential parents of 1966 themselves believed in the superstition, or whether they merely thought that others believed in it, they acted *as if* they believed it by postponing many of the births that normally would have occurred that year.

Despite the plunging birth rate, there were still a great many girls born in 1966. Perhaps Hinouema's 1966 children will have sufficiently fortunate lives to dilute the superstition, or to dispel it completely. In any case, most of them will still be around to see what happens the next time a new cycle begins, in the year 2026. It will be interesting to watch the birth rate then, and to see whether Japan's Hinouema superstition can survive the turn of still another century.

Questions

1. What types of norms are described here—folkways, mores or both? What are the sanctions for norm violation?
2. What conditions in society seem to be more conducive to maintaining traditional beliefs and norms? What conditions seem more conducive to dropping traditional beliefs and norms?
3. Make a list of situations in the United States that are similar to that in Japan described by Azumi. That is, list those superstitions, myths, and customs that exert normative power to the extent that they change behavior (birth rates, crime rates, drinking rates, buying rates, etc.) under certain conditions (time of the year, phase of the moon, etc.).

Some Conditions of
Obedience and Disobedience
to Authority

Stanley Milgram

Stanley Milgram is a social psychologist and professor at City University of New York. In this excerpt from one of his research papers he describes what happens when people are faced with conflicting norms. Milgram's research question is this: If a person tells another to hurt a third person, under what conditions will he refuse to obey?

The situation in which one agent commands another to hurt a third turns up time and again as a significant theme in human relations. It is powerfully expressed in the story of Abraham, who is commanded by God to kill his son. It is no accident that Kierkegaard, seeking to orient his thought to the central themes of human experience, chose Abraham's conflict as the springboard to his philosophy.

War too moves forward on the triad of an authority which commands a person to destroy the enemy, and perhaps all organized hostility may be viewed as a theme and variation on the three elements of authority, executant, and victim. We describe an experimental program, recently concluded at Yale University, in which a particular expression of this conflict is studied by experimental means.

In its most general form the problem may be defined thus: if X tells Y to hurt Z, under what conditions will Y carry out the command of X and under what conditions will he refuse. In the more limited form possible in laboratory research, the question becomes: if an experimenter tells a subject to hurt another person, under what conditions will he refuse to obey. The laboratory problem is not so much a dilution of the general statement as one concrete expression of the many particular forms this question may assume.

From *Human Relations,* February 1965, pp. 57–76. Reprinted by permission of the author. A more thoroughgoing analysis of the experiments described in this article may be found in Stanley Milgram's *Obedience to Authority,* published by Harper & Row, 1974. A 45 minute film depicting the experiments is available to educational groups. It is entitled *Obedience* and is distributed by the New York University Film Library, 41 Press Annex, Washington Square, New York, N.Y. 10003.

One aim of the research was to study behavior in a strong situation of deep consequence to the participants, for the psychological forces operative in powerful and lifelike forms of the conflict may not be brought into play under diluted conditions.

This approach meant, first, that we had a special obligation to protect the welfare and dignity of the persons who took part in the study; subjects were, of necessity, placed in a difficult predicament, and steps had to be taken to ensure their wellbeing before they were discharged from the laboratory. Toward this end, a careful, post-experimental treatment was devised and has been carried through for subjects in all conditions.

The subjects used in all experimental conditions were male adults, residing in the greater New Haven and Bridgeport areas, aged 20 to 50 years, and engaged in a wide variety of occupations. Each experimental condition described in this report employed 40 fresh subjects and was carefully balanced for age and occupational types. The occupational composition for each experiment was: workers, skilled and unskilled: 40 percent; white collar, sales, business: 40 percent; professionals: 20 percent. The occupations were intersected with three age categories (subjects in 20s, 30s, and 40s, assigned to each condition in the proportions of 20, 40, and 40 percent respectively).

The focus of the study concerns the amount of electric shock a subject is willing to administer to another person when ordered by an experimenter to give the "victim" increasingly more severe punishment. The act of administering shock is set in the context of a learning experiment, ostensibly designed to study the effect of punishment on memory. Aside from the experimenter, one naive subject and one accomplice perform in each session. On arrival each subject is paid $4.50. After a general talk by the experimenter, telling how little scientists know about the effect of punishment on memory, subjects are informed that one member of the pair will serve as teacher and one as learner. A rigged drawing is held so that the naive subject is always the teacher, and the accomplice becomes the learner. The learner is taken to an adjacent room and strapped into an "electric chair."

The naive subject is told that it is his task to teach the learner a list of paired associates, to test him on the list, and to administer punishment whenever the learner errs in the test. Punishment takes the form of electric shock, delivered to the learner by means of a shock generator controlled by the naive subject. The teacher is instructed to increase the intensity of electric shock one step on the generator on each error. The learner, according to plan, provides many wrong answers, so that before long the naive subject must give him the strongest shock on the generator. Increases in shock level are met by increasingly insistent demands from the learner that the experiment be stopped because of the growing discomfort to him. However, in clear terms the experimenter orders the teacher to continue with the procedure in disregard of the learner's protests. *Thus, the naive subject must resolve a conflict between two mutually incompatible demands from the social field. He may continue to follow the orders of the experimenter and shock the learner with increasing severity, or he may refuse to follow the orders of the experimenter and heed the learner's pleas. The experimenter's authority operates not in a free field, but against evermounting countervailing pressures from the person being punished.*

A few technical points need to be considered before the findings of the study are described. For the purpose of delivering shock, a simulated shock generator is used, with 30 clearly marked voltage levels that range from 15 to 450 volts (and each activated by one of 30 individual lever switches set in a horizontal line). The naive subject is given a sample shock of 45 volts to convince him of the authenticity of the instrument. The generator bears verbal designations that range from "Slight Shock" to "Danger: Severe Shock."

The responses of the victim are standardized on tape, and each protest is coordinated to a particular voltage level on the shock generator. Starting with 75 volts the learner begins to grunt and moan. At 150 volts he demands to be let out of the experiment. At 180 volts he cries out that he can no longer stand the pain. At 300 volts he refuses to provide any more answers to the memory test, insisting that he is no longer a participant in the experiment and must be freed. In response to this last tactic, the experimenter instructs the naive subject to treat the absence of an answer as equivalent to a wrong answer, and to follow the usual shock procedure. The experimenter reinforces his demand with the statement: "You have no other choice, you must go on!" (This imperative is used whenever the naive subject tries to break off the experiment.) If the subject refuses to give the next higher level of shock, the experiment is considered at an end. A quantitative value is assigned to the subject's performance based on the maximum intensity shock he administered before breaking off. Thus any subject's score may range from zero (for a subject unwilling to administer the first shock level) to 30 (for a subject who proceeds to the highest voltage level on the board). For any particular subject and for any particular experimental condition the degree to which participants have followed the experimenter's orders may be specified with a numerical value, corresponding to the metric on the shock generator.

This laboratory situation gives us a framework in which to study the subject's reactions to the principal conflict of the experiment. Again, this conflict is between the experimenter's demands that he continue to administer the electric shock, and the learner's demands, which become increasingly more insistent, that the experiment be stopped. The crux of the study is to vary systematically the factors believed to alter the degree of obedience to the experimental commands, to learn under what conditions submission to authority is most probable, and under what conditions defiance is brought to the fore.

This series consisted of four experimental conditions. In each condition the victim was brought "psychologically" closer to the subject giving him shocks.

In the first condition (Remote Feedback) the victim was placed in another room and could not be heard or seen by the subject, except that, at 300 volts, he pounded on the wall in protest. After 315 volts he no longer answered or was heard from.

The second condition (Voice Feedback) was identical to the first except that voice protests were introduced. As in the first condition the victim was placed in an adjacent room, but his complaints could be heard through a door left slightly ajar, and through the walls of the laboratory. It is difficult to convey on the printed page the full tenor of the victim's responses, for we have no adequate notation for vocal intensity, timing, and general qualities of delivery. Yet these features are crucial to producing the effect of an increasingly severe reaction to mounting voltage levels. In general terms, however, the victim indicates no discomfort until the 75-volt shock is administered, at which time there is a light grunt in response to the punishment. Similar reactions follow the 90- and 105-volt shocks, and at 120 volts the victim shouts to the experimenter that the shocks are becoming painful. Painful groans are heard on administration of the 135-volt shock, and at 150 volts the victim cries out, "Experimenter, get me out of here! I won't be in the experiment any more! I refuse to go on!" Cries of this type continue with generally rising intensity, so that at 180 volts the victim cries out, "I can't stand the pain," and by 270 volts his response to the shock is definitely an agonized scream. Throughout, he insists that he be let out of the experiment. At 300 volts the victim shouts in desperation that he will no longer provide answers to the memory test; and at 315 volts, after a violent scream, he reaffirms with vehemence that he is no longer a participant. From this point on, he provides no answers, but shrieks in agony whenever a shock is administered; this continues through 450 volts. Of course, many subjects will have broken off before this point.

The third experimental condition (Proximity) was similar to the second, except that the victim was now placed in the same room as the subject, and

1½ feet from him. Thus he was visible as well as audible, and voice cues were provided.

The fourth, and final, condition of this series (Touch-Proximity) was identical to the third, with this exception: the victim received a shock only when his hand rested on a shockplate. At the 150-volt level the victim again demanded to be let free and, in this condition, refused to place his hand on the shockplate. The experimenter ordered the naive subject to force the victim's hand onto the plate. Thus obedience in this condition required that the subject have physical contact with the victim in order to give him punishment beyond the 150-volt level.

Forty adult subjects were studied in each condition. The data revealed that obedience was significantly reduced as the victim was rendered more immediate to the subject.

Expressed in terms of the proportion of obedient to defiant subjects, the findings are that 34 percent of the subjects defied the experimenter in the Remote condition, 37.5 percent in Voice Feedback, 60 percent in Proximity, and 70 percent in Touch-Proximity.

If the spatial relationship of the subject and victim is relevant to the degree of obedience, would not the relationship of subject to experimenter also play a part? There are reasons to feel that, on arrival, the subject is oriented primarily to the experimenter rather than to the victim. He has come to the laboratory to fit into the structure that the experimenter—not the victim—would provide. He has come less to understand his behavior than to *reveal* that behavior to a competent scientist, and he is willing to display himself as the scientist's purposes require. Most subjects seem quite concerned about the appearance they are making before the experimenter, and one could argue that this preoccupation in a relatively new and strange setting makes the subject somewhat insensitive to the triadic nature of the social situation. In other words, the subject is so concerned about the show he is putting on for the experimenter that influences from other parts of the social field do not receive as much weight as they ordinarily would. This overdetermined orientation to the experimenter would account for the relative insensitivity of the subject to the victim, and would also lead us to believe that alterations in the relationship between subject and experimenter would have important consequences for obedience.

In a series of experiments we varied the physical closeness and degree of surveillance of the experimenter. In one condition the experimenter sat just a few feet away from the subject. In a second condition, after giving initial instructions, the experimenter left the laboratory and gave his orders by telephone; in still a third condition the experimenter was never seen, providing instructions by means of a tape recording activated when the subjects entered the laboratory.

Obedience dropped sharply as the experimenter was physically removed from the laboratory. The number of obedient subjects in the first condition (Experimenter Present) was almost three times as great as in the second, where the experimenter gave his orders by telephone. Twenty-six subjects were fully obedient in the first condition, and only 9 in the second. Subjects seemed able to take a far stronger stand against the experimenter when they did not have to encounter him face to face, and the experimenter's power over the subject was severely curtailed.

Moreover, when the experimenter was absent, subjects displayed an interesting form of behavior that had not occurred under his surveillance. Though continuing with the experiment, several subjects administered lower shocks than were required and never informed the experimenter of their deviation from the correct procedure. (Unknown to the subjects, shock levels were automatically recorded by an Esterline-Angus event recorder wired directly into the shock generator; the instrument provided us with an objective record of the subjects' performance.) Indeed, in telephone conversations some subjects specifically assured the experimenter that they were raising the shock level according to instruction, whereas in fact they were repeatedly using the lowest shock on the board. This form of behavior is particularly interesting: although these subjects acted in a way that clearly undermined the avowed purposes of the experiment, they found it easier to handle the conflict in this manner than to precipitate an open break with authority.

Experiments in this series show that the physical *presence* of an authority is an important force contributing to the subject's obedience or defiance. Taken together with the first experimental series on the proximity of the victim, it would appear that something akin to fields of force, diminishing in effectiveness with increasing psychological distance from their source, have a controlling effect on the subject's performance. As the victim is brought closer, the subject finds it harder to administer shocks to him. When the victim's position is held constant relative to the subject, and the authority is made more remote, the subject finds it easier to break off the experiment. This effect is substantial in both cases, but manipulation of the experimenter's position yielded the more powerful results. Obedience to destructive commands is highly dependent on the proximal relations between authority and subject.

One general finding that merits attention is the high level of obedience manifested in the experimental situation. Subjects often expressed deep disapproval of shocking a man in the face of his objections, and others denounced it as senseless and stupid. Yet many subjects complied even while they protested. The proportion of obedient subjects greatly exceeded the expectations of the experimenter and his colleagues. At the outset, we had conjectured that subjects would not, in general, go above the level of "Strong Shock." In practice, many subjects were willing to administer the most extreme shocks available when commanded by the experimenter. For some subjects the experiment provides an occasion for aggressive release. And for others it demonstrates the extent to which obedient dispositions are deeply ingrained, and are engaged irrespective of their consequences for others. Yet this is not the whole story. Somehow, the subject becomes implicated in a situation from which he cannot disengage himself.

The departure of the experimental results from intelligent expectation, to some extent, has been formalized. The procedure was to describe the experimental situation in concrete detail to a group of competent persons, and to ask them to predict the performance of 100 hypothetical subjects. For purposes of indicating the distribution of break-off points judges were provided with a diagram of the shock generator, and recorded their predictions before being informed of the actual results. Judges typically underestimated the amount of obedience demonstrated by subjects.

What is the limit of such obedience? At many points we attempted to establish a boundary. Cries from the victim were inserted; not good enough. The victim claimed heart trouble; subjects still shocked him on command. The victim pleaded that he be let free, and his answers no longer registered on the signal box; subjects continued to shock him. At the outset we had not conceived that such drastic procedures would be needed to generate disobedience, and each step was added only as the ineffectiveness of the earlier techniques became clear. The final effort to establish a limit was the Touch-Proximity condition. But the very first subject in this condition subdued the victim on command, and proceeded to the highest shock level. A quarter of the subjects in this condition performed similarly.

The results, as seen and felt in the laboratory, are to this author disturbing. They raise the possibility that human nature, or—more specifically—the kind of character produced in American democratic society, cannot be counted on to insulate its citizens from brutality and inhumane treatment at the direction of malevolent authority. A substantial proportion of people do what they are told to do, irrespective of the content of the act and without limitations of conscience, so long as they perceive that the command comes from a legitimate authority.

Questions

1. *How is role strain illustrated in this article?*
2. *What conflicting norms did the subjects face? How did they resolve the conflicts?*
3. *Under what conditions were subjects most likely to comply with the experimenter's instructions? Why?*
4. *A number of the principles or characteristics of scientific inquiry are outlined in Chapter 1. Show how these principles are illustrated in Milgram's research.*

One Hundred Per Cent
American

Ralph Linton

The content of a culture—skills, customs, material objects, and non-material ideas—comes from several sources. Some aspects of culture appear spontaneously and are developed from within the culture through the process of invention. Much more, however, is borrowed from other cultures through the usually unconscious process of diffusion. Anthropologist Ralph Linton wrote this passage some years ago. It is often quoted and still remains a classic at demonstrating the importance of diffusion. Much of what we thought was "one hundred percent American" actually came long ago from societies we never heard of.

There can be no question about the average American's Americanism or his desire to preserve this precious heritage at all costs. Nevertheless, some insidious foreign ideas have already wormed their way into his civilization without his realizing what was going on. Thus dawn finds the unsuspecting patriot garbed in pajamas, a garment of East Indian origin; and lying in a bed built on a pattern which originated in either Persia or Asia Minor. He is muffled to the ears in un-American materials; cotton, first domesticated in India; linen, domesticated in the Near East; wool from an animal native to Asia Minor; or silk, whose uses were first discovered by the Chinese. All these substances have been transformed into cloth by a method invented in Southwestern Asia. If the weather is cold enough he may even be sleeping under an eiderdown quilt invented in Scandinavia.

On awakening he glances at the clock, a medieval European invention, uses one potent Latin word in abbreviated form, rises in haste, and goes to the bathroom. Here, if he stops to think about it, he must feel himself in the presence of a great American institution; he will have heard stories of both the quality and frequency of foreign plumbing and will know that in no other country does the average man perform his ablutions in the midst of such splendor. But the insidious foreign influence pursues him even here. Glass was invented by the ancient Egyptians, the use of glazed tiles for floors and walls in the Near East, porcelain in China, and the art of enameling on metal by Mediterranean artisans of the Bronze Age. Even his bathtub and toilet are but

From *The American Mercury,* April 1937, pp. 427–429. Reprinted by permission of the publisher.

slightly modified copies of Roman originals. The only purely American contribution to the ensemble is the steam radiator.

In this bathroom the American washes with soap invented by the ancient Gauls. Next he cleans his teeth, a subversive European practice which did not invade America until the latter part of the eighteenth century. He then shaves, a masochistic rite first developed by the heathen priests of ancient Egypt and Sumer. The process is made less of a penance by the fact that his razor is of steel, an iron-carbon alloy discovered in either India or Turkestan. Lastly, he dries himself on a Turkish towel.

Returning to the bedroom, the unconscious victim of un-American practices removes his clothes from a chair, invented in the Near East, and proceeds to dress. He puts on close-fitting tailored garments whose form derives from the skin clothing of the ancient nomads of the Asiatic steppes and fastens them with buttons whose prototypes appeared in Europe at the close of the Stone Age. This costume is appropriate enough for outdoor exercise in a cold climate, but is quite unsuited to American summers, steam-heated houses, and Pullmans. Nevertheless, foreign ideas and habits hold the unfortunate man in thrall even when common sense tells him that the authentically American costume of gee string and moccasins would be far more comfortable. He puts on his feet stiff coverings made from hide prepared by a process invented in ancient Egypt and cut to a pattern which can be traced to ancient Greece, and makes sure they are properly polished, also a Greek idea. Lastly, he ties about his neck a strip of bright-colored cloth which is a vestigial survival of the shoulder shawls worn by seventeenth-century Croats. He gives himself a final appraisal in the mirror, an old Mediterranean invention, and goes downstairs to breakfast.

Here a whole new series of foreign things confront him. His food and drink are placed before him in pottery vessels, the popular name of which—china—is sufficient evidence of their origin. His fork is a medieval Italian invention and his spoon a copy of a Roman original. He will usually begin the meal with coffee, an Abyssinian plant first discovered by the Arabs. The American is quite likely to need it to dispel the morning-after effects of over-indulgence in fermented drinks, invented in the Near East; or distilled ones, invented by the alchemists of medieval Europe. Whereas the Arabs took their coffee straight, he will probably sweeten it with sugar, discovered in India, and dilute it with cream, both the domestication of cattle and the technique of milking having originated in Asia Minor.

If our patriot is old-fashioned enough to adhere to the so-called American breakfast, his coffee will be accompanied by an orange, domesticated in the Mediterranean region, a cantaloupe domesticated in Persia, or grapes, domesticated in Asia Minor. He will follow this with a bowl of cereal made from grain domesticated in the Near East and prepared by methods also invented there. From this he will go on to waffles, a Scandinavian invention, with plenty of butter, originally a Near-Eastern cosmetic. As a side dish he may have the egg of a bird domesticated in Southeastern Asia or strips of the flesh of an animal domesticated in the same region, which have been salted and smoked by a process invented in Northern Europe.

Breakfast over, he places upon his head a molded piece of felt, invented by the nomads of Eastern Asia, and, if it looks like rain, puts on outer shoes of rubber, discovered by the ancient Mexicans, and takes an umbrella, invented in India. He then sprints for his train—the train, not the sprinting, being an English invention. At the station he pauses for a moment to buy a newspaper, paying for it with coins invented in ancient Lydia. Once on board he settles back to inhale the fumes of a cigarette invented in Mexico, or a cigar invented in Brazil. Meanwhile, he reads the news of the day, imprinted in characters invented by the ancient Semites by a process invented in Germany upon a material invented in China. As he scans the latest editorial pointing out the dire results to our institutions of accepting foreign ideas, he will not fail to thank a Hebrew God in an Indo-European language that he is a one hundred per cent (decimal system invented by the Greeks) American (from Americus Vespucci, Italian geographer).

Questions

1. *While it is true that many material objects have come to us through diffusion, most of the non-material aspects of American culture are original and the products of invention. Discuss.*
2. *This article was written in 1930—the same sort of statements could not be made today. Discuss. To prove the point, draw up a list of aspects of American culture developed through invention.*
3. *Analyze Linton's article, using the terms "ethnocentrism" and "cultural relativism."*

Return to Laughter

Elenore S. Bowen

This excerpt from the book *Return to Laughter* describes the patterns of kinship and marriage—in this case, polygamy—of an African society. Patterns of culture that are quite different from our own are illustrated as well as the concepts ethnocentrism and cultural relativism. Elenore Bowen is the pen name of anthropologist Laura Bohannan who wrote the novel *Return to Laughter* after working among the Tiv of Northern Nigeria.

"You feed Ihugh, therefore you *are* his mother." Udama corrected me firmly but quite patiently now that she saw I meant no insult. "Listen, Redwoman, if a woman dies, do her children become motherless? Is not the woman who feeds them and cares for them their mother? Therefore these are not merely matters of birth. They are matters of deed as well. You and I, we are both Ihugh's mother; therefore his children are *our* grandchildren. But there is more. Kako has put some of his youngest wives in my hut, for me to watch and care for; therefore they are my wives as well. Ihugh's wife I treat as I treat them; therefore she is my wife and she is your wife, and her children are our children."

Dazed, but convinced I was struggling along the right track, I ventured a deduction. "Then, if Rogo calls me 'my mother,' it is because I feed him. But if he calls me 'my mother-in-law,' it is because . . ."

"Because he respects you, but must nevertheless say to you things you will not like."

"I sat on a teak root." In my own ears this did not sound very coherent, but Udama followed with the same facility Rogo had used in the original connection. "And some young man told you you must not," she finished. "Therefore of course he called you 'mother-in-law,' or it would have been rude."

Udama meditated into her pipe. I wrestled with the implications of this dual aspect of kinship, by birth and by deed. She was the first to rouse herself. "You must learn more of these matters, Redwoman, or you will be like a child among us, a child who knows nothing of life, nor of death, nor of birth." She scrabbled among the ashes looking for a coal to relight her pipe. "You know Ava and her wives?"

I nodded. Everyone knew Ava and her wives. They were the model household of the community, one every husband cited when his wives disagreed. Ava was a tall, rather light-skinned woman who was one of the leading dancers and song-leaders at all successful wedding parties. She was also the senior of five wives who lived with their husband and children alone in a homestead not very far from Kako's. The women were fast friends. Indeed, it was Ava who had picked out all the others. She saved up forty or fifty shillings every few years, searched out an industrious girl of congenial character, then brought her home and presented her to her husband: "Here is your new wife."

Ava's husband always welcomed her additions to his household and he always set to work to pay the rest of the bridewealth, for he knew perfectly well that Ava always picked hardworking, healthy, handsome, steady women who wouldn't run away. Many men envied him. Thanks to Ava he had peace and quiet in his home and did not, like so many others, have to spend time and money chasing after truant wives. My feelings were more mixed. If, before I came out here, I had expected to feel sorry for anyone in a polygamous household, it was the women. But these women did very well. It was their husband I felt sorry for. We tend to think of the henpecked husband as a rather weak character. But what man can stand up against five united women? If Ava's husband raised his voice to any one of his wives, all of them refused to cook for him. If he bought one of them a cloth, he had to buy four other identical cloths. Discipline of the wives was in Ava's hands, and stayed there. When the poor man got drunk one day and struck one wife for nagging—well, until he had given many and expensive presents to all his wives, the five of them slept barricaded in one hut. Yes, I knew Ava.

"One of Ava's wives," Udama went on, "will soon bear a child. I will be the midwife, and I shall call you, for I would have you see for yourself what it means to have co-wives to help you and to know that if you die in labour there are those who will care for your children."

A few days later, Ava herself stuck her head into my reception hut and called me without ceremony. "Come, Redwoman, my wife is in labour. Udama told me to fetch you while she banked her fire." The three of us walked to Ava's homestead. Her husband was sitting in his reception hut, whittling aimlessly away at a stick and pretending not to be anxious. It was his twelfth child, he told me, but this wife's first. He greeted Udama with relief.

We went inside the hut. The mother-to-be was sitting on a very low reclining chair, looking quite composed while all her co-wives bustled about her. Udama, after a brief and expert examination, announced that there was plenty of time. She and Ava began to lecture me on the benefits of being one of many wives.

"When an only wife has a child, who will help her so she may rest? Who will feed her husband and her other children? Who will tend her farm and bring her firewood so she may be warm? Who will comfort her in labour and who will stop her cries?"

No adult should be so weakminded as to cry out with pain. The two times when people will yell out, circumcision and childbirth, someone stands behind to clap a hand over the mouth at the first scream. Hard, perhaps, but certainly easier on their relatives and neighbours. I could not, however, even for sake of argument protest that any of the other services they mentioned could be performed by any other relatives. I had been there long enough to know that no kinsman will take over the duties of another; it would be considered wrong, and these were the duties of no one but a co-wife.

"Never," said Ava severely, "let your husband rest with one wife. Men are lazy. If they have one woman to cook for them, they are content. If you leave it to your husband, you'll never get another wife to help you carry the firewood and the water or to look after you when you are ill. And if you do nag him into it, he'll pick up the first good-looking wench he sees. You can't trust a man to inquire into a woman's character and industry. Let a man pick his own mistresses; he knows what he wants there. But they're all bunglers when it comes to choosing wives."

"That," Udama interpolated, "is why a man's father selects his first wife."

"And the first wife," Ava continued, "should get the rest herself, like me."

I replied mildly that men in our country generally couldn't afford more than one wife at a time. "Earn the money yourself by going to market," Ava advised. "It only takes a small chicken to start with, if you're a good trader." I explained that we had a law against it as well. Udama stopped Ava's incredulity. "Indeed, I think it must be so. Rogo told Ihugh that very few Europeans have even one wife because the bridewealth is very high and anyhow they don't have enough women to go around."

There was a stifled cry from the chair and conversation stopped. Two of the wives held her back in her chair, a third pressing back her head and holding a hand over her mouth. Ava and Udama were busy for a long time, mixing herbs, massaging, giving encouragement. Finally, at sunset, Udama called out to the father, "A boy." He flapped happily in the background while the new mother was led outside to be washed, and the baby made uncomplimentary noises about the hot water in which Udama washed him. An elder appeared. Ava told me he had come to 'remove the blood' from all of us who had been inside the hut during the birth. I found myself lined up with the other women and having my legs brushed with a wet and squawking chicken while the elder mumbled his incantation. It was a unique sensation.

Ava gave Udama the salt, palm oil and camwood that are the midwife's due and we went home.

"A very easy birth," she commented as we parted. I had not thought it so, nor, by the looks of her, had the mother. Perhaps it was easier if one didn't know there were such things as anaesthetics. One must make shift to endure unavoidable pain. But it wasn't just a matter of suffering. I remembered what the government and mission doctors had told me about deliveries gone wrong and about the damage caused by native midwifery even when there were no complications.

I also remembered that my great-grandmother had her first child alone with her husband on the frontier; in her diary she had longed for another woman then. I tried to imagine her surrounded by four co-wives, and could not. More generally, though, I could see that where we multiply specialists and services, these people multiplied personal relationships and perhaps in this way were closer to my great-grandmother than I was. But not in detail, not my great-grandmother with co-wives. What she wanted of her husband wasn't readily shareable.

Here people looked for little in marriage. A man would turn to his sixteenth cousin twice removed before he turned to his wife. Here the important ties were between blood relatives. Again I remembered Ihugh's pessimistic lecture by the roadside: women bring trouble between friends and relatives and age mates. Perhaps it was woman's only remedy against such an attitude—to club together, as co-wives, when they were far from their own relatives. Certainly a woman in trouble turned to her guardian or her brother and not to her husband.

I was beginning to understand what they did. I could not understand what they felt. I could admire the way co-wives got on together and still know that I, born and reared as I had been, could never take such a relationship. I would have all the wrong emotions.

Questions

1. *Compare the role expectations of the Tiv wife, as described in this article, and the American wife of the 1970s.*

2. *What examples of ethnocentrism can be found in this article? Why are people ethnocentric? What functions does ethnocentrism perform in societies?*
3. *Outline the positive aspects of the Tiv family patterns from both male and female viewpoints.*

TWO

Social Organization

In preceding chapters we have looked at basic units of analysis used by sociologists to understand, describe, and explain human behavior. In this section our view becomes more general. If we combine these basic units and move to a higher level of abstraction, we come to the concept of social organization. If, in a like manner, we were analyzing football, we could first look at the basic elements—players, a ball, a marked-off field, and maybe some spectators. But our description is helped a great deal if we move to the next level and describe a football *game,* because it is now necessary to look beyond the elements and deal with the combination of the setting, the rules, shared expectations and interaction patterns of participants—in other words, the social organization present that allows twenty-two players, six officials, and 20,000 observers to mutually participate in and get something out of the same event.

As there is an extensive degree of organization to a football game, so there is to society. The basic elements of a society are a number of people and an inhabitable geographical area. But no understanding of a society is obtained until we study the patterns of interaction and organization that are characteristic of the people. We see that cities exist (why do they?), that highways link cities, that educational facilities are developed, that some individuals are more highly valued than others, that governments run the cities. These things don't just happen by accident; they are evidences that there is organization to society. People cooperate, interact, and share expectations and mutual interests, and there is a structure or system to society much as there is to a building or a machine or a football game—parts link together to form a complex whole. The social organization of society is frequently referred to as a "social fabric," an integrated net of norms, roles, cultural values, and beliefs through which people interact with each other, individually and through groups.

Studying various aspects of this social organization is the central task of sociology. We undertake this analysis in a variety of ways. It is as if we were looking at a subject, society in this case, through a number of windows. Each window is of a different shape, size, thickness, and color of glass. So, though we are looking at the same subject, each approach gives a somewhat different viewpoint, emphasizing certain aspects and ignoring others. The following chapters will analyze the social organization of society through several "windows." Chapter 4 will introduce the concepts *group, category,* and *aggregation,* and deal with several types of groups in detail. Chapter 5 will cover two types of categories, social class and race/ethnicity. In Chapter 6 we will discuss *institutions* as the sociologist sees them. And Chapter 7 will cover *population* and *ecology.*

Group members have common loyalties

4

Groups, Categories, Aggregations

The group is a major unit of analysis for sociologists. A group, simply defined, is a collection of people. Not all collections of people, however, are defined as groups. Are the people on a bus a group? How about red-haired people between the ages of thirty and forty-five? Or what about the students at a large university? At the same time, collectivities that *are* defined as groups may vary tremendously in some characteristics. Your family, my sociology department, a college's football team or a sorority, and the President's Cabinet could probably be defined as groups, but they are quite different in many dimensions—size, complexity, type of interaction, division of labor. Much of the study of social organization, therefore, could be described as centering around two questions: What constitutes a group, and how is the group developed? What are the different types of groups?

Groups and Non-groups

Sociologists say that a *group* exists when you have a number of people who (1) have shared or patterned interaction; and (2) feel bound together by a "consciousness of kind" or a "we" feeling. By "consciousness of kind" or "we" feeling, we mean that group members will have common loyalties, share at least some similar values, and see themselves as set apart from the rest of the world because of their membership in this particular group. Groups may be of tremendous varieties, sizes, and shapes. A group may be as small as two people or almost infinitely large. Groups may be simple in structure or exceedingly complex; they may involve close, intimate relationships between members or more distant and infrequent personal contacts. In other words, the definition of group—patterned interaction and "we" feeling—may fit an enormous variety of situations: a family, a basketball team, a sociology class, IBM or General Motors.

This definition of groups, imprecise as it may seem, allows us to distinguish groups from other types of collectivities of people which we could call "non-groups." One type of non-group, which we will call an *aggregate* (or aggregation), consists of a number of people clustered together in one place.[1] Examples of aggregates might be all the people in New York City, or the pedestrians at a busy intersection waiting for the light to change to "walk," or all the people in North America, or the passengers on a jet from New York to San Francisco. A second useful non-group, called a *category,* consists of a number of people who have a particular characteristic in common. Examples of categories would be all females, or all red-haired people, or all pilots, or all teenagers, or all blacks.

Although we have called them non-groups, aggregates and categories may be transformed into groups should they develop patterned interaction among members and consciousness of kind. For example, let's examine our aggregate of ten people waiting at the intersection for the light to change to "walk." Then suppose it *doesn't* change—for five, ten, even fifteen minutes the light refuses to budge from "wait." The pedestrians, strangers until now, begin talking to each other about the impossible situation. Should they race across through traffic against the light? Where's the cop—you can never find one when you really need one. . . . A kind of interaction develops and a consciousness of kind—a group of good people being victimized by a lousy, mechanical light. Or, take the passengers on the jet from New York to San Francisco, another aggregate. Somewhere over Pennsylvania the pilot says to himself, "I'm sick and tired of flying to San Francisco all the time, I guess I'll go to the North Pole. . . ." The passengers, who did not know each other up to now, begin

---

[1] This use of aggregate is general (see, for example, introductory texts by Lundberg, Schrag, and Larsen, by Horton and Hunt, or by Cuber) but not universal (Chinoy's use of "statistical aggregate" is more similar to our use of category than aggregate; Nisbet uses the term "social aggregate" which, to a certain extent, seems to cut across the concepts group, category, and aggregation, as we are using them here. See Ely Chinoy, *Society* [New York: Random House, 1961], pp. 82–83, and Robert Nisbet, *The Social Bond* [New York: Alfred Knopf, 1970], pp. 80–83).

to interact, possibly in a rather agitated manner, and by the time they reach the Arctic Circle there would probably be quite highly developed group interaction.

Categories may also become groups. All the red-haired people between the ages of thirty and forty-five would constitute a category, as would all carpenters of Irish ancestry. But suppose the middle-aged redheads decided to get together and put out a journal telling of their common problems and aspirations. Or suppose the Carpenters of Irish Ancestry decide it's time to start an organization (CIA?), have a convention, and elect officers. In each case we might have a category developing into a group. These sound far-fetched, but the point is that sociologists study both groups and non-groups (categories and aggregates), and the lines between these collectivities are somewhat fluid and easily crossed.

Sociologists study groups and non-groups for several reasons. For one thing, the study of human behavior is a huge task. Use of categories and aggregates helps us to break the whole down into more basic parts. If we divide a society into categories (males, upper-class whites, teenage Negro females) or aggregates (a crowd, a city), our analysis is easier (smaller units) and more precise (the units now have some characteristics in common). Sociologists study groups because they feel that, to a certain extent, a person *is* the sum of the groups he belongs to. Socialization, transmission of culture, values, attitudes, ways of behaving and believing are mainly a product of the groups to which one belongs. For these reasons, groups and non-groups are of tremendous importance to sociologists in their analysis of the social organization of society. For the remainder of this chapter we will focus on types of groups that have been of special interest to sociologists.

Types of Groups

As we have noted, the criteria that determine a group are sufficiently broad to allow many types of collectivities to be included. In an effort to refine the concept of groups, attempts have been made to label some of the general categories into which groups might fit. In some groups membership is automatic and the participant has no choice; in others the option is open and the individual may join or not as he wishes. These two types are labeled involuntary and voluntary groups. *Involuntary* groups might include the family one is born into or the army platoon one is drafted into. *Voluntary* groups would include any of a vast number which the member may exercise some choice in joining—lodges, fraternities, bridge clubs, student governments, black power organizations. *In-groups* and *out-groups* are labels applied on the one hand to groups that *I* belong to, that *I* identify with, that are *my* groups, as opposed to groups that I do not belong to or identify with and which may even be alien to me. Again the examples are numerous and could involve the dimensions of family, race, religion, occupation, age, sex, political viewpoint, and many others.

Reference groups are groups that serve as models for our behavior, groups whose perspectives we assume and mold our behavior after. A reference group may be made up of people one associates with or knows personally, or it may be an abstract collectivity of individuals who represent models for our behavior. Each individual will "belong" to many reference groups. As a teacher I would have one reference group, as a sociologist another, as a husband another, and as a tennis or hand-ball player still others. One's *peer group* is made up of people of relatively the same age, interests, and social position with whom one has reasonably close association and contact. A peer group may consist of a class at school, a street gang, or an occupational group such as the members of a college sociology department or a group of lawyers in a law firm. Not all the members of a peer group are necessarily friends, but the peer group exercises a major role in the socialization process. During adolescence, it may be *the* major socializing agent.

Groups whose members come predominantly from one social-class level are called *horizontal* groups. Examples of horizontal groups would include almost any organization formed along occupational lines—an association of doctors, carpenters, or prostitutes. If a group includes members from a variety of social classes it could be called a *vertical* group. Vertical groups are more difficult to find in American society, since many divisions are made along social-class lines. A church congregation might constitute a vertical group, and in some cases an army platoon made up of draftees would include members from a variety of social classes. Groups are also categorized according to their longevity. A group brought together to perform a single, short-term task could be called a *temporary* group, whereas a longer-lasting collectivity like a family could be called a *permanent* group. Groups are defined as open or closed according to the ease of gaining membership. A white fraternity is often a *closed* group as far as a black male is concerned, but the U.S. Army is probably a very *open* group for the same individual.

Primary Groups and Small Groups

Most of the socialization process—learning society's norms and roles, development of the self—takes place in small groups, especially primary groups. The *primary* group was first described by C. H. Cooley as referring to groups in which contacts between members are intimate, personal, and face-to-face. A great part of the individual's total life experience is bound up in the group and is known to other group members. The primary type of relationship is one which involves both the whole person and deep and personal interaction and communication. This interaction is an end in itself—primary groups often exist because of the value of the primary relationship rather than because of other specific goals or tasks. People conform in primary groups because of strong informal norms—fear of being ostracized, scorned, ridiculed—rather than because of any formal written rules. A *secondary* group, on the other hand, is more impersonal. Interaction is more superficial and probably based on utilitarian goals. That is, the whole person is less important than a particular skill he may offer the group. Interaction and communication are based on the value of his particular skill rather than on interest in his general personal qualities. It is probably most helpful to see the concepts "primary" and "secondary" as opposite ends of a continuum. The completely primary or completely secondary group may seldom be found. Rather, groups vary in their degree of "primariness" or "secondariness." Moving from primary to secondary along the continuum we might see these groups: a married couple, an extended family including parents and grandparents, a basketball team, a fraternity or civil rights organization, a professional organization or labor union, the employees of a large corporation

Small groups are a popular topic today. They are used as vehicles for treatment—group therapy has proven to be a useful mechanism for change in prisons, mental hospitals, and organizations dealing with alcoholism and drug usage. T-groups, sensitivity training groups, and encounter groups have become popular on college campuses and with large organizations as techniques for improving communication, interaction, and self-understanding. The small class is believed to "work" better than the large class in the educational process. Small groups, as we are describing them here, combine a primary type of interaction with a task orientation. Achievement of the task—better education, self-understanding, improved communication and management skills—is facilitated by the primary group atmosphere. Social scientists have done extensive research on small groups, and in the following paragraphs we will discuss ways of studying small groups, and some of the characteristics of small group behavior.[2]

Small groups are studied in a variety of ways and each method focuses on a different perspective of small group interaction. Robert Bales assigns tasks to small groups placed in rooms with one-way windows. The interaction patterns of the individuals in the group are broken down into bits or small parts and placed in categories that Bales has constructed. This technique is called interaction process analysis (IPA) and it focuses on four main problems with which groups are confronted: adaptation to outside factors that influence the group, management and control of group tasks, expression and management of group members' feelings, and maintenance of the integration of the group. Bales has developed twelve observation categories in order to classify each bit of group interaction.

[2] My major sources for the following paragraphs are *Small Groups* by Clovis Shepard (San Francisco: Chandler, 1964), *Order and Change* by Gerald Leslie, Richard Larson, and Benjamin Gorman (New York: Oxford, 1973) and *Sociology: Man in Society* by Melvin DeFleur, William D'Antonio, and Lois DeFleur (Glenview, Ill.: Scott, Foresman and Co., 1971). Especially, see Leslie, Chapter 10, and Shepard, pp. 1–2, 27–36.

Try observing a group in action and see if each interaction between group members will fit into one of these categories: 1, shows solidarity (gives help, rewards others); 2, shows tension release; 3, shows agreement; 4, gives suggestion; 5, gives opinion; 6, gives information; 7, asks for information; 8, asks for opinion; 9, asks for suggestion; 10, shows disagreement; 11, shows tension; 12, shows antagonism. Bales has found that generally, 56 percent of group responses are answers (categories 4, 5, and 6 above), 25 percent are positive reactions (categories 1, 2, 3), 7 percent are questions (categories 7, 8, 9), and 12 percent are negative reactions (categories 10, 11, 12). Satisfied and dissatisfied groups differ somewhat in their responses, and there is probably an optimum pattern for most effective group performance. If the percentage of "answers" drops too low, the group may be seen as "a waste of time." Too many "negative reactions" and the group turns into a name-calling session; too many "positive reactions" and it becomes a mutual admiration society. Critics of this type of research on small groups are dubious about the "created-in-the-laboratory" nature of these experiments—they suggest that in real life small groups may behave differently from how they do in small group labs.

J. L. Moreno developed a technique called sociometry that provides a quite different way of studying small groups. Here the focus is more on the *who* of interaction rather than on the *what*. Sociometry looks not at the nature or type of interaction, as Bales' IPA does, but at the direction of interaction—who interacts with whom. Members of the group being studied are asked questions like "Who is your best friend in the group?" or "Who would you most like to work with on an important project?" The patterns and directions of interaction are then graphed as in the figure on page 87. This figure represents a sociogram of the members of a volunteer fire department. Each member of the group was asked three questions: "Who would you most prefer to have help you fight a fire?" "Who would you most prefer to have help you plan a social function?" and "Who is your best friend on the department?" The lines and arrows in the sociogram represent the resulting choices. For example, fireman thirteen chose fireman eleven, firemen one and seven named each other, and so on. Not all the selections are shown in this sociogram in order to keep it from getting too complicated. Those near the center of the sociogram were chosen more often— fireman eleven was named 28 times, fireman nine 14 times, fireman four not at all. Several typical sociometric patterns appear in this figure. Four was not chosen and is called an "isolate." Five, ten, and thirteen were named only once each and are near-isolates or "neglectees." Eleven was chosen by nearly everybody and is termed a "star." Rank in the department and political preference are shown in the sociogram to see if these explain patterns of selection. One of the assistant chiefs was more "popular" than the chief, and the three captains were all near the center of the sociogram. Hosemen, the lowest rank, are consistently around the edge. More detail on fireman eleven indicates that aside from being a Republican and a captain, he is one of two men in the department with a college degree, he is the third oldest member, he is one of five Catholics, he has the highest social-class standing in the department, and he participates actively in departmental activities.

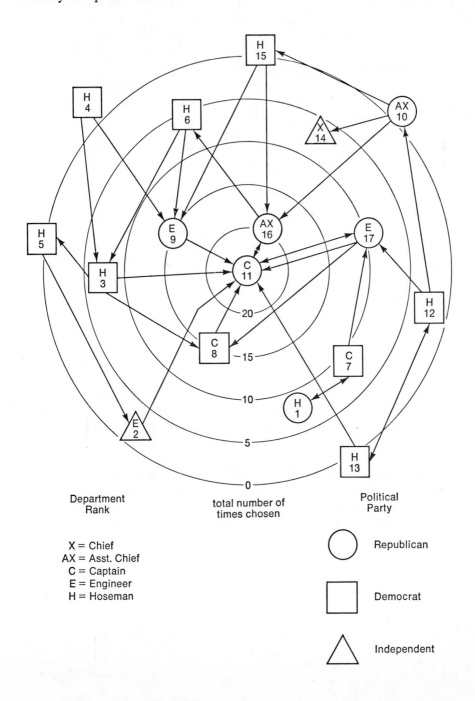

Department
Rank

total number of
times chosen

Political
Party

X = Chief
AX = Asst. Chief
C = Captain
E = Engineer
H = Hoseman

◯ Republican

▢ Democrat

△ Independent

As a technique for the study of groups, sociometry presents both advantages and disadvantages. On the positive side, it helps uncover informal interaction and friendship patterns, and helps to identify variables associated with leadership and social isolation. On the negative side, sociometry is somewhat static and, unless repeated often, does not take into account the fluid and rapidly changing nature of group structure. It is an effective technique for mapping interaction but does not provide an in-depth analysis of that interaction.

A third way of studying small groups is by means of participant observation. Here, the researcher joins the group he is studying and becomes involved in their activities—he learns about the group by becoming part of it. This type of observation is more casual and less controlled, and consequently its scientific credentials are sometimes questioned. When used by a talented observer, however, participant observation provides useful insights about delinquent gangs, primitive tribes, and even such large organizations as the telephone company (see Elinor Langer's article at the end of this chapter).

There is much information on the characteristics of small groups, and I have found the following most interesting. A number of studies have illustrated the effects of group pressure on individual judgment. A stationary light in a dark room appears to move—this is called the "autokinetic effect." Muzafer Sherif asked subjects to judge how far the light moved. When small groups were tested, they quickly arrived at agreement on the light's movement—a group norm. When the members were tested individually, they stuck to the earlier established group norm. When other subjects were tested individually *first* (no group norm available), their judgments of the light's movement were more variable and erratic. In other studies, Solomon Asch asked small groups of people to compare the length of lines. Some members of the group were "stooges," or confederates of the researcher. The stooges were instructed to make obviously wrong selections—two lines which were of different lengths were said to be the same. In studies involving eight stooges and one subject, the subject was faced with the choice of going along with the majority or making an independent judgment. Many avoided stress and simply went along with the majority.[3]

There is variation in how small groups handle deviants. Laboratory experiments indicate that if one person continues to disagree with or block a position on which the rest of the group agrees, there is a tendency to reject the deviant. In another study of Quaker work groups and army basic training squads, however, another pattern emerged. Dentler and Erikson found that in some groups, deviant behavior helps maintain group equilibrium, and attempts to alienate a member whose behavior was deviant were resisted. Mentally ill (schizophrenic) members of basic-training squads were taken care of by the other recruits. Others performed the deviant's duties, they became very protective of him, and

[3] These studies are summarized from DeFleur, D'Antonio, and DeFleur, pp. 150 and 152.

when he was finally hospitalized, other squad members became disturbed and angry at his removal.

Leadership and other roles in small groups follow certain predictable patterns. Two types of leaders generally appear: the task leader and the social-emotional leader. The *task leader* possesses skills or characteristics that the group values highly, but he is not highly approachable. The *social-emotional* leader is highly approachable—he is the one to whom other group members can complain, show affection, or in other ways express feelings. The social-emotional leader may have some influence on the task leader. Other group roles are described by the terms nice guys, ignored, and rejected. *Nice guys* are approachable—not as much as the social-emotional leader but enough that their membership and contributions are valued. Those *ignored* are members who are usually in-active—they are an unknown quantity to the rest of the group. Those *rejected* are members perceived as unapproachable because they have no skills or characteristics valued by the group or because of hostile or confusing behavior on their part.[4]

Some of the effects and constraints that small groups have on behavior can be seen in the actions of people on juries. The jury usually quickly selects a person of high status (wealth, education) as foreman. People of high status are more active on the jury—they talk more, have more influence, and are seen as more competent. Low status people tend to defer to the higher status members. Men are more active on juries, but women are better jurors—they take more care in considering testimony. Jurors are very reluctant to come back without a verdict. The self-confidence of a witness often has more effect on the jury than the logic or soundness of what he says. Juries often "try" the lawyer rather than the man he is representing. Finally, the mere fact of a person's being brought to trial makes him suspect in the eyes of the jury, in spite of the presumption of innocence in our court system.[5]

Formal Organizations

Large-scale formal organizations are an essential part of modern society. These organizations, often called bureaucracies, arise as societies' activities become increasingly planned rather than spontaneous. Men discovered long ago that if several people got together and planned an activity—building a car, educating a student—they often got the job done more rapidly and efficiently than if each pursued the task in his own way, spontaneously and haphazardly.

---

[4] The studies cited in these two paragraphs are summarized from Shepard, pp. 69, 74–79.

[5] For more detail on these and other studies of jury behavior, see *Legal and Criminal Psychology*, Hans Toch, ed. (New York: Holt, Rinehart and Winston, 1961).

Arthur Stinchcombe defines a formal organization as any social arrangement in which the activities of some people are systematically planned by other people in order to achieve some special purpose. Those who plan the activities automatically have authority over the others. Formal organizations seem to arise in societies with a money economy that are pursuing complex tasks requiring the coordinated efforts of a number of people. As the size of the organization increases, administrative tasks multiply, and this encourages further bureaucratization. There is an enduring quality about these organizations—people leave, but like the building they worked in their jobs and the organization remain, seemingly forever.[6]

Some years ago, sociologist Max Weber identified the characteristics of an abstract or "pure" form of bureaucracy: (1) There is a precise division of labor, so that each individual in the organization is a specialist—he is an expert in performing a specific task. (2) There is a hierarchy of authority, a chain of command in which each individual is clearly in control of some and clearly responsible to others. (3) There is an exhaustive and consistent system of rules designed to assure uniformity in the performance of every task. (4) Social relationships between individuals in the organization, especially between a superior and his subordinates, are formal and impersonal. (5) The bureaucracy is technically highly efficient, much like a machine. (6) Employees are highly trained for their task; they are, in turn, protected from arbitrary dismissal—their job constitutes a career with possibilities for advancement according to seniority and/or achievement.

Weber was talking about how bureaucracies in an abstract sense might operate. Formal organizations in fact do not necessarily resemble Weber's description on all or even most points. In any organization, much that is unplanned occurs. The chain of command is often circumvented. Shortcuts reduce bureaucratic red tape in a variety of ways. Relationships between individuals are often personal and informal. Organizations occasionally are grossly inefficient. In fact, to counteract the somewhat negative view that many people have of the huge bureaucracy, organizations often consciously attempt to look and act less formal, less bureaucratic. Nevertheless, Weber's description provides us with a useful abstraction of the general characteristics of large organizations.

Weber also distinguished between several different types of organizations, of which we will mention three: the charismatic retinue, the modern bureaucracy, and the modern professional organization. The *charismatic retinue* is an organization made up of followers or disciples of a charismatic leader. Charisma refers to a certain superior quality an individual may have that sets him apart

---

[6] These paragraphs on formal organizations cite ideas presented by Arthur Stinchcombe in his paper "Formal Organizations," in Neil Smelser's book, *Sociology: An Introduction*, 2nd Ed. (New York: John Wiley, 1973). I have also used Peter Blau and Marshall Meyer's book *Bureaucracy in Modern Society*, 2nd Ed. (New York: Random House, 1971), and H. H. Gerth and C. W. Mills, *From Max Weber: Essays in Sociology* (New York: Oxford University Press, 1958).

from others. He is viewed as super-human, capable of exceptional acts. The followers of a civil rights leader like Martin Luther King, Jr., or the followers of a black nationalist leader like Malcolm X would constitute a charismatic retinue. Charismatic retinues are probably frequently found in religious organizations. The *modern bureaucracy* comes closest to Weber's characteristics of bureaucracy. Specialization, a system of rules, formality, and a hierarchy of authority are highly developed. Large public utilities, government agencies, and military organizations probably provide the best examples today of the modern bureaucracy. In the *modern professional organization,* individuals are granted wide leeway and responsibility once their qualifications have been evaluated and their competence certified. Extreme decentralization of responsibility is the major characteristic here; Stinchcombe suggests that a university and a hospital provide the best examples of a modern professional organization.

A proliferation in society of large organizations and the bureaucratic values of efficiency and rationality will have consequences, some obvious, some less so. Large organizations allow the performance of tasks that could not otherwise be accomplished. There is undoubtedly greater efficiency in producing products. At the same time, alienation may result when the worker sees himself as a small cog in a huge, impersonal machine. Stinchcombe states that in societies dominated by formal organizations, people tend to become specialists in particular activities. Educational institutions respond by encouraging students to concentrate on learning a specific technique or skill rather than attaining a broader, more general education. In societies dominated by formal organizations, a larger percentage of a person's social relationships become planned instead of spontaneous. Interaction is more superficial, and emotions play less of a part in social relationships of this type. A person is judged more by what he *does* (actions) than by what he *is* (his more permanent qualities). To put it another way, interaction of all types, on the job or off, is more secondary, less primary. Some analysts of modern society have commented with concern on the decline in the number of primary groups with which one can affiliate. They argue that groups and contacts are becoming increasingly secondary in modern industrialized countries like the United States.

Long ago, sociologist Ferdinand Tonnies described two contrasting types of societies.[7] The *Gemeinschaft* is a more primary and closely-knit society in which relationships are personal and informal and there is a commitment or identification with the community. The *Gesellschaft* is a more secondary society based on contractual arrangements, bargaining, a well-developed division of labor, and on rational thought rather than emotion. Relationships between people are impersonal and utilitarian. Many, who feel as Cooley did that primary group

---

[7] Ferdinand Tonnies, *Community and Society,* translated and edited by Charles A. Loomis (East Lansing, Mich.: Michigan State University Press, 1957). Tonnies's book *Gemeinschaft und Gesellschaft* first appeared in 1887.

relationships are of great importance in the socialization process and the development of the self and personality, are concerned that the increasing secondariness or *Gesellschaft*-like nature of modern societies will have serious effects on the developmental processes. Some would no doubt point to high rates of divorce and marital breakup, rising crime and delinquency, increased mental illness, and other individual and group pathologies as consequences of restricted primary-group contacts. Others would argue that these conditions are merely the consequences of any modern, complex society. Moreover, the huge, complicated, multi-layered bureaucracies that perform tasks for us today are highly efficient even though somewhat impersonal. To idealize the *Gemeinschaft* society, they would argue, is unrealistic and shows a lack of understanding of the positive aspects of the large organizations of today. They would conclude that there is not really more pathology (crime, marital breakup, mental illness); our efficient bureaucracies just do a better job of ferreting it out and letting us know about it.

In sometimes interesting ways, formal organizations modify their forms and structures, and change their philosophies. For example, bureaucracies have long had a basic belief in specialization—the simpler the task, the better and more efficiently it can be performed. (See Weber's first characteristic of bureaucracy.) Break the job down into its basic parts. Make it simple, precise, and repetitive and the worker can't possibly mess it up. Well, this sort of approach to tasks— three turns on the same nut with the same wrench 3,000 times a day—may *be* more efficient, but people don't like it. They get bored, job satisfaction goes down, and absenteeism goes up. The new fad in management is to reverse the cherished specialization ethic and *enrich* jobs, make them more interesting, more varied, not so repetitive. This view has been widely picked up by industry and by business graduate schools. The new pitch is that jobs should be meaningful, self-fulfillment is a worthwhile goal, and work groups are important for improving job satisfaction. The worker will take more pride in the product if he can follow it all the way through performing a variety of tasks toward its completion.

They may be right, and it certainly sounds like a more enlightened approach to the work situation. But a skeptic might inquire as to management's reasons for this new approach. Companies like to feel they are progressive. And, of course, it's good for the image—current ads portray the happy Swedish automobile workers who get to follow a car to complete construction. You just *know* that's a better car. Industry can be humanistic after all. But the clincher for the organization is the economic pay-off. Improved worker morale means less absenteeism, employee turnover, and sabotage, and improved quality of product. The best of all possible worlds exists if organizations can improve their image and cut costs at the same time. Imagine the company's dilemma, however, if the new program increases worker morale, happiness, and self-fulfillment—but efficiency and output are unchanged or reduced. . . .

Bureaucratic formal organizations are dominant today—every year more and more people work for them. But what of the future? Will the classic bureaucratic structure described by Max Weber continue to be the prevailing mode of social organization? A number of experts, including Alvin Toffler and Warren Bennis, think not. Toffler predicts that in the future we will witness not the triumph, but the breakdown of bureaucracy.[8] He calls the organization of the future the "ad-hocracy" (from the Latin, "ad hoc": meant for a particular purpose or goal). A number of factors are leading to the demise of old-style bureaucracy. Mergers, organizational upheavals, and internal reorganizations are occurring at rapidly increasing rates and this is disrupting once-stable bureaucratic rules and structures. The individual's place in the organization is less stable—he is shifted from one task to another. There is a rapid increase in "project" or "task-force" management. Teams are put together to perform specific short-term tasks, and when finished the teams are disassembled and the people are reassigned, "exactly like mobile playgrounds." It is this particular characteristic that Toffler means by his term "ad-hocracy." Weber's hierarchy of authority is collapsing also and the chain of command is altered. The rapidity of events and the need for quick actions mean that decisions are being made at all levels without waiting for higher-ups to approve.

[8] The ideas of Toffler and Bennis in this and the following paragraphs are summarized from *Future Shock* by Alvin Toffler (New York: Random House, 1970), Chapter 7.

Warren Bennis believes, like Toffler, that bureaucracies worked well in stable societies for routine tasks. But with the rapid change of today, those characteristics—routine, stability—are disappearing. The future will see adaptive, short-term, rapidly changing, temporary systems—task forces that solve specific problems. Gone will be permanence and enduring relationships between man and the organization. Gone will be the powerful hierarchies of authority that kept the individual in line. Loyalties will be to one's profession rather than to the organization. All of this, according to Toffler, is caused basically by the rapidity of change. To keep pace, organizations will adapt and change their structure and hence, ad-hocracy. But what's the price? Much is unforeseen, but Toffler and Bennis suggest that there will be strains on the adaptability of men. We should anticipate substantial social strains and psychological tensions, and many will experience "future shock" as the future arrives too soon.

Several factors might be remembered as we consider Bennis and Toffler's speculations about the formal organization of the future. Weber's general characteristics of bureaucracy should not blind us to the fact that individual differences in organizations (as in people) are vast. Some are more affected by change and more responsive to it than others. For example, educational institutions are probably more likely to react to demands for change than are military organizations. Bureaucracies may be responsive to change in one area but resist it in another. The auto industry changes styles yearly but their responses to suggestions of environmentalists come more slowly. Some organizations generate member loyalty more easily than others. Compare turnover rates in several organizations with which you are familiar. Short-term task groups probably do work well in some situations, but to generalize is risky. And finally, organizations traditionally have been very slow to change. Problems inherent in industrial bureaucracies have been discussed for well over 100 years and little has changed. Today we are more bureaucratized than ever—large formal organizations are the handmaidens of mass society. Under these conditions it is hard to imagine that the changes predicted by Toffler and Bennis will take place—but time will tell.

Summary

The social organization or *social fabric* of a society is woven of cultural norms, values, beliefs, and patterns of behavior through which people interact with each other. The analysis and description of this social organization is a major area of study for sociologists. The analysis of the social organization of a society can be approached from a number of viewpoints. The viewpoint we have taken in this chapter introduces the concepts of group, category, and aggregation. A group exists when a number of people have shared or patterned interaction and feel bound together by a consciousness of kind. A collectivity of people lacking these traits is called a category (if they have a particular characteristic in common) or an aggregate (if they are located in a specific area).

Sociologists categorize groups in a variety of ways. Of special importance are primary groups, small groups, secondary groups, and formal organizations. Ways of studying small groups were described as well as some of the effects small groups have on their members. Characteristics of past, present, and future bureaucracies were compared. By categorizing and analyzing specific types of groups we are better able to understand and explain the variety, importance, and effect of the group affiliations which individuals have. With the number of different types of groups we have discussed here, it is probably obvious that a given group will cut across types and carry several labels. I work for a large formal organization in which I am a member of a sociology department which could be described as a reference group, a peer group, an in-group, a voluntary group, a horizontal group, a permanent group, a closed group (depending on the job market and how many professors are seeking the California climate), and sometimes more a primary group, sometimes more a secondary group.

Two readings follow. The first is an excerpt from the book *Tally's Corner* by Elliot Liebow. This is a study of Negro streetcorner men, and the selection here describes a particular pattern of primary relationships and small group life. The second reading by Elinor Langer describes a large, formal organization. Her article on the New York Telephone Company illustrates many of the characteristics of bureaucracy that we have discussed.

Friends and Networks

Elliot Liebow

Primary relationships take a variety of forms—a couple dating, a family, maybe an athletic team, or a work group in a large organization. In this excerpt from *Tally's Corner,* Elliot Liebow describes the primary relationships existing among lower class Negro streetcorner men in Washington, D.C.

More than most social worlds, perhaps, the streetcorner world takes its shape and color from the structure and character of the face-to-face relationships of the people who live in it. Unlike other areas in our society, where a large portion of the individual's energies, concerns and time are invested in self-improvement, career and job development, family and community activities, religious and cultural pursuits, or even in broad, impersonal social and political issues, these resources in the streetcorner world are almost entirely given over to the construction and maintenance of personal relationships.

On the streetcorner, each man has his own network of these personal relationships and each man's network defines for him the members of his personal community. His personal community, then, is not a bounded area but rather a web-like arrangement of man-man and man-woman relationships in which he is selectively attached in a particular way to a definite number of discrete persons. In like fashion, each of these persons has his own personal network.

At the edges of this network are those persons with whom his relationship is affectively neutral, such as area residents whom he has "seen around" but does not know except to nod or say "hi" to as they pass on the street. These relationships are limited to simple recognition. Also at the edges are those men and women, including former friends and acquaintances, whom he dislikes or fears or who dislike or fear him. These relationships are frequently characterized by avoidance but the incumbents remain highly visible and relevant to one another.

In toward the center are those persons he knows and likes best, those with whom he is "up tight": his "walking buddies," "good" or "best" friends, girl friends, and sometimes real or putative kinsmen. These are the people with whom he is in more or less daily, face-to-face contact, and whom he turns to for emergency aid, comfort or support in time of need or crisis. He gives them and receives from them goods and services in the name of friendship, ostensibly keeping no reckoning. Routinely, he seeks them out and is sought out by them. They serve his need to be with others of his kind, and to be recognized as a discrete, distinctive personality, and he, in turn, serves them the same way. They are both his audience and his fellow actors.

It is with these men and women that he spends his waking, nonworking hours, drinking, dancing, engaging in sex, playing the fool or the wise man, passing the time at the Carry-out or on the streetcorner, talking about nothing and everything, about epistemology or Cassius Clay, about the nature of numbers or how he would "have it made" if he could have a steady job that paid him $60 a week with no layoffs.

So important a part of daily life are these relationships that it seems like no life at all without them. Old Mr. Jenkins climbed out of his sickbed to take up a seat on the Coca-Cola case at the Carry-out for a couple of hours. "I can't stay home and play dead," he explained, "I got to get out and see my friends."

In general, close friendships tend to develop out of associations with those who are already in one's network of personal relationships: relatives, men and women who live in the area and spend much of their time on the street or in public places, and co-workers. The result is that the streetcorner man, perhaps more than others in our society, tends to use the same individuals over and over again: he may make a friend, neighbor and co-worker of his kinsman, or a friend, co-worker and kinsman of his neighbor. A look at some of the personal relationships can illustrate the many-stranded aspects of friendship and the bi-directional character of friendship on the one hand, and kinship, neighbor, co-worker and other relationships on the other.

When Tonk and Pearl got married and took an apartment near the Carry-out, Pearl's brother, Boley, moved in with them. Later, Pearl's nephew, J. R., came up from their hometown in North Carolina and he, too, moved in with them. J. R. joined Tonk and Boley on the streetcorner and when Earl told Tonk of some job openings where he worked, Tonk took J. R. with him. These three, then, were kinsmen, shared the same residence, hung out together on the streetcorner, and two of them—for a time at least—were co-workers.

Preston was Clarence's uncle. They lived within a block of each other and within two blocks of the Carry-out. Clarence worked on a construction job and later got Preston a job at the same place. Tally, Wee Tom and Budder also worked at the same construction site. The five men regularly walked back from the job to the streetcorner together, usually sharing a bottle along the way. On Friday afternoons, they continued drinking together for an hour or so after returning to the streetcorner. Tally referred to the other four men as his "drinking buddies."

Tally had met Wee Tom on the job. Through Tally, Wee Tom joined them on the walk home, began to hang around the Carry-out and finally moved into the neighborhood as well. Budder had been the last to join the group at the construction site. He had known Preston and Clarence all along, but not well. He first knew Tally as a neighbor. They came to be friends through Tally's visits to the girl who lived with Budder, his common-law wife, and his wife's children. When Tally took Budder onto the job with him, Budder became a co-worker and drinking buddy, too. Thus, in Tally's network, Wee Tom began as co-worker, moved up to drinking buddy, neighbor and finally close friend; Budder from neighbor and friend to co-worker. Importantly, and irrespective of the direction in which the relationships developed, the confluence of the co-worker and especially the neighbor relationship with friendship deepened the friend relationship.

One of the most striking aspects of these overlapping relationships is the use of kinship as a model for the friend relationship. Most of the men and women on the streetcorners are unrelated to one another and only a few have kinsmen in the immediate area. Nevertheless, kinship ties are frequently manufactured to explain, account for, or even to validate friend relationships. In this manner, one could move from friendship to kinship in either direction. One could start with kinship, say, as did Preston and Clarence or Boley and Tonk and build on this, or conversely, one could start with friendship and build a kin relationship.

The most common form of the pseudo-kin relationship between two men is known as "going for brothers." This means, simply, that two men agree to present themselves as brothers to the outside world and to deal with one another on the same basis. Going for brothers appears as a special case of friendship in which the usual claims, obligations, expectations, and loyalties of the friend relationship are publicly declared to be at their maximum.

Sea Cat and Arthur went for brothers. Sea Cat's room was Arthur's home so far as he had one anywhere. It was there that he kept his few clothes and other belongings, and it was on Sea Cat's dresser that he placed the pictures of his girl friends (sent "with love" or "love and kisses"). Sea Cat and Arthur wore one another's clothes and, whenever possible or practical, were in one another's company. Even when not together, each usually had a good idea of where the other was or had been or when he would return. Generally, they seem to prefer going with women who were themselves friends; for a period of a month or so, they went out with two sisters.

Sea Cat worked regularly; Arthur only sporadically or for long periods not at all. His own credit of little value, Arthur sometimes tried to borrow money from the men on the corner, saying that the lender could look to his "brother" for payment. And when Sea Cat found a "good thing" in Gloria, who set him up with a car and his own apartment, Arthur shared in his friend's good fortune. On the streetcorner or in Sea Cat's room, they laughed and horsed around together, obviously enjoying one another's company. They cursed each other and called each other names in mock anger or battle, taking liberties that were reserved for and tolerated in close friends alone.

The social reality of the pseudo-kinship tie between those who are "going for brothers" is clearly evident in the case of Richard and Leroy. Richard and Leroy had been going for brothers for three months or so when Leroy got in a fight with a group of teenagers and young adults. Leroy suffered serious internal injuries and was hospitalized for more than a month. One week after the fight, Richard and one of the teenagers who had beaten up Leroy, and with whom both he and Leroy had been on friendly terms, got into a fight over a private matter having nothing to do with Leroy, and Richard killed the teenager. Richard was immediately arrested and the police, acting on information from the dead boy's friends, relatives, and others in the community, charged him with first degree murder for the premeditated revenge killing of one who had beaten up "his brother." But when it was established that Leroy and Richard were not related in any way the charge was dropped to murder in the second degree. The dead boy's friends and relatives were outraged and bewildered. To them, it was clearly a premeditated and deliberate killing. Hadn't Richard and Leroy been going for brothers? And hadn't Leroy been badly beaten by this same boy just eight days earlier?

Questions

1 What is meant by "going for brothers?"
2 Why would the relationships described in this reading be referred to as primary rather than secondary?
3 Give examples of peer group, reference group, and primary group from this reading.
4 What methods did Liebow apparently use to study the relationships on Tally's corner? What other methods could have been used and what are the advantages and disadvantages of each?

Inside the New York Telephone Company

Elinor Langer

Formal organizations are everywhere in modern industrialized societies. It has been estimated that more than ninety percent of the work force in the U.S. is employed in formal organizations. In Max Weber's typology, the New York Telephone Company is a good example of a *modern bureaucracy*. Journalist Elinor Langer worked for the phone company, and here she describes how a large bureaucratic organization works.

From October to December 1969 I worked for the New York Telephone Company as a Customer's Service Representative in the Commercial Department. My office was one of several in the Broadway-City Hall area of lower Manhattan, a flattened, blue-windowed commercial building in which the telephone company occupies three floors. The room was big and brightly lit—like the city room of a large newspaper—with perhaps one hundred desks arranged in groups of five or six around the desk of a Supervisor. The job consists of taking orders for new equipment and services and pacifying customers who complain, on the eleven exchanges (although not the more complex business accounts) in the area between the Lower East Side and 23rd Street on the North and bounded by Sixth Avenue on the West.

My Supervisor is the supervisor of five women. She reports to a Manager who manages four supervisors (about twenty women) and he reports to the District Supervisor along with two other managers. The offices of the managers are on the outer edge of the main room separated from the floor by glass partitions. The District Supervisor is down the hall in an executive suite. A job identical in rank to that of the district supervisor is held by four other men in Southern Manhattan alone. They report to the Chief of the Southern Division, himself a soldier in an army of division chiefs whose territories are the five boroughs, Long Island, Westchester, and the vast hinterlands vaguely referred to as "Upstate." The executives at _____ Street were only dozens among the thousands in New York Tel alone.

Authority in their hierarchy is parceled out in bits. A Representative, for example, may issue credit to customers up to, say, $10.00; her supervisor, $25.00; her manager, $100.00; his supervisor, $300.00; and so forth.

. . . Securing the position was not without hurdles. I was "overqualified," having confessed to college; I performed better on personnel tests than I intended to do; and I was inspected for symptoms of militance by a shrewd but friendly interviewer who noticed the several years' gap in my record of employment. "What have you been doing lately?" she asked me. "Protesting?" I said: "Oh, no, I've been married," as if that condition itself explained one's neglect of social problems. She seemed to agree that it did.

. . . I was welcomed at length by both the District Supervisor and the man who was to be my Manager, and given a set of fluffy feminist speeches about "opportunities for women" at New York Tel. I was told in a variety of ways that I would be smarter than the other people in my class; "management" would be keeping an eye on me. Then the Manager led me personally to the back classroom where my training program was scheduled to begin.

The Representative's course is "programmed." It is apparent that the phone company has spent millions of dollars for high-class management consultation on the best way to train new employees. The two principal criteria are easily deduced. First, the course should be made so routine that any employee can teach it. The teacher's material—the remarks she makes, the examples she uses —are all printed in a loose-leaf notebook that she follows. Anyone can start where anyone else leaves off. I felt that I could teach the course myself, simply by following the program. The second criterion is to assure the reproducibility of results, to guarantee that every part turned out by the system will be inter-changeable with every other part. The system is to bureaucracy what Taylor was to the factory: it consists of breaking down every operation into discrete parts, then making verbal the discretions that are made.

Soon acting out the right way to deal with customers became more important than self-instruction. The days were organized into Lesson Plans, a typical early one being: How to Respond to a Customer if You Haven't Already Been Trained to Answer His Question, or a slightly more bureaucratic rendering of that notion. Sally explained the idea, which is that you are supposed to refer the call to a more experienced Representative or to the Supervisor. But somehow they manage to complicate this situation to the point where it becomes confus-ing even for an intelligent person to handle it. You mustn't say: "Gosh, that's tough, I don't know anything about that, let me give the phone to someone who does," though that in effect is what you do. Instead when the phone rings, you say: "Hello. This is Miss Langer. May I help you?" (The Rule is, get im-mediate "control of the contact" and hold it lest anything unexpected happen, like, for instance, a human transaction between you and the customer.)

He says: "This is Mr. Smith and I'd like to have an additional wall telephone installed in my kitchen."

You say: "I'll be very glad to help you, Mr. Smith (Rule the Second: Always express interest in the Case and indicate willingness to help), but I'll need more information. What is your telephone number?"

He tells you, then you confess: "Well, Mr. Smith, I'm afraid I haven't been trained in new installations yet because I'm a new representative, but let me give you someone else who can help you." (Rule the Third: You must get his consent to this arrangement. That is, you must say: *May* I get someone else who can help you? *May* I put you on hold for a moment?)

The details are absurd but they are all prescribed. What you would do natu-rally becomes unnatural when it is codified, and the rigidity of the rules makes the Representatives in training feel they are stupid when they make mistakes. Another lesson, for example, was: What to Do if a Customer Calls and Asks for a Specific Person, such as Miss Smith, another Representative, or the Mana-ger. Whatever the facts, you are to say "Oh, Miss Smith is busy but I have access to your records, may I help you?" A customer is never allowed to iden-tify his interests with any particular employee. During one lesson, however, Sally said to Angela: "Hello, I'd like immediately to speak to Mrs. Brown," and Angela said, naturally, "Hold the line a minute, please. I'll put her on." A cardinal sin, for which she was immediately rebuked. Angela felt terrible.

Company rhetoric asserts that this rigidity does not exist, that Representatives are supposed to use "initiative" and "judgment," to develop their own language. What that means is that instead of using the precise words "Of course I'll be glad to help you but I'll need more information," you are allowed to "create" some individual variant. But you must always (1) express willingness to help and (2) indicate the need for further investigation. In addition, while you are doing this, you must always write down the information taken from the customer, coded, on a yellow form called a CF-1, in such a way as to make it possible for a Representative in Florida to read and translate it. "That's the point," Sally told us. "You are doing it the same way a rep in Illinois or Alaska does it. We're one big monopoly."

The logic of training is to transform the trainees from humans into machines. The basic method is to handle any customer request by extracting "bits" of information: by translating the human problem he might have into bureaucratic language so that it can be processed by the right department. For instance, if a customer calls and says: "My wife is dying and she's coming home from the hospital today and I'd like to have a phone installed in her bedroom right away," you *say*, "Oh, I'm very sorry to hear that sir, I'm sure I can help you, would you be interested in our Princess model? It has a dial that lights up at night," meanwhile *writing* on your ever-present CF-1: "Csr wnts Prn inst bdrm immed," issuing the order, and placing it in the right-hand side of your work-file where it gets picked up every fifteen minutes by a little clerk.

The knowledge that one is under constant observation (of which more later) I think helps to ensure that contacts are handled in this uniform and wooden manner. If you varied it, and said something spontaneous, you might well be overheard; moreover, it is probably not possible to be especially human when you are concentrating so hard on extracting the bits, and when you have to deal with so many bits in one day.

Sometimes the bits can be extraordinarily complicated. A customer (that is, CSR) calls and says rapidly, "This is Mrs. Smith and I'm moving from 23rd Street to 68th Street, and I'd like to keep my green Princess phone and add two white Trimlines and get another phone in a metallic finish and my husband wants a new desk phone in his study." You are supposed to have taken that all down as she says it. Naturally you have no time to listen to how she says it, to strike up a conversation, or be friendly. You are desperate to get straight the details.

The dehumanization and the surprising degree of complication are closely related: the number of variables is large, each variable has a code which must be learned and manipulated, and each situation has one-and only one-correct answer. The kind of problem we were taught to handle, in its own language, looks like this:

A CSR has: IMRCV EX CV GRN BCHM IV

He wants: IMRCV WHT EX CV WHT BCHM IV

This case, very simplified, means only that the customer has regular residential phone service with a black phone, a green one, and an ivory bell chime, and that he wants new service with two white phones and a bell chime. Nonetheless, all these items are charged at differing monthly rates which the Representative must learn where to find and how to calculate; each has a separate installation charge which varies in a number of ways; and, most important, they represent only a few of the dozens of items or services a customer could possibly want (each of which, naturally, has its own rates and variables, its own codes).

He could want a long cord or a short one, a green one or a white one, a new party listed on his line, a special headset for a problem with deafness, a touch-tone phone, and on and on and on. For each of the things he could possibly want there would be one and only one correct charge to quote to him, one and only one right way to handle the situation.

Observers at the phone company. They are everywhere. I became aware of a new layer of Observation every day. The system works like this. For every five or six women there is, as I have said, a Supervisor who can at any moment listen in from the phone set on her desk to any of her Representatives' contacts with a customer. For an hour every day, the Supervisor goes to a private room off the main floor where she can listen (herself unobserved) to the conversations of any of her "girls" she chooses. The women know, naturally, *when* she is doing this but not *whose* contact she is observing.

Further off the main floor is a still more secret Observing Room staffed by women whose title and function is, specifically, Observer. These women "jack in" at random to any contact between any Representative and a customer:

their job is basically to make sure that the Representatives are giving out correct information. Furthermore, these observers are themselves observed from a central telephone company location elsewhere in the city to make sure that they are not reporting as incorrect information which is actually correct. In addition the Observers make "access calls" by which they check to see that the telephone lines are open for the customers to make their connections. This entire structure of observation is, of course, apart from the formal representative-supervisor-manager-district-supervisor-division-head chain of managerial command. They are, in effect, parallel hierarchical structures.

One result of the constant observation (the technology being unbounded) is that one can never be certain where the observation stops. It is company policy to stress its finite character, but no one ever knows for sure. Officials of the Communications Workers of America have testified, for instance, that the company over-indulged in the wired-Martini stage of technology, bugging the pen sets of many of its top personnel. At _____ Street there were TV cameras in the lobby and on the elevators. This system coexists with the most righteous official attitude toward wiretapping. Only supervisors and managers can deal with wiretap complaints; Federal regulations about the sanctity of communications are posted; and the overt position toward taps, in the lower managerial echelons, is that they are simply illegal and, if they exist, must be the result of private entrepreneurship (businesses bugging one another) rather than Government policy.

"If someone complains about a tap," Sally said, "I just ask them: Why would anyone be tapping your phone?" Consciousness of the Government's "internal security" net is simply blacked out. Nonetheless, the constant awareness of the company's ability to observe creates unease: Are the lounge phones wired into the Observing structure? Does the company tap the phones of new or suspicious personnel? Is union activity monitored? No one can say with confidence.

The system of Observers is linked with the telephone company's ultimate weapon, the Service Index by which Errors are charted and separate units of the company rated against each other. Throughout training—in class and in our days on the floor—hints of the monumental importance of the Index in the psychic life of the employees continually emerged. "Do you know how many Errors you're allowed?" Sally would ask us. "No Errors"—proud that the standard was so high. Or: "I can't afford an Error"—from my supervisor, Laura, on the floor, explaining why she was keeping me roped in on my first days on the job. But the system was not revealed in all its parts until the very end of training when as a *pièce de résistance* the manager, Y, came in to give a little talk billed as a discussion of "Service" but in fact an attempt to persuade the class of the logic of observation.

Y was a brooding, reserved man in his mid-twenties, a kind of Ivy League leftover who looked as if he'd accidentally got caught in the wrong decade. His talk was very much like Sally's. "We need some way to measure Service. If a customer doesn't like Thom McCann shoes he can go out and buy Buster Brown. Thom McCann will know something is wrong. But the phone company is a monopoly, people can't escape it, they have no other choice. How can we tell if our product, Service, is good?" He said that observation was begun in 1924 and that, although the Company had tried other methods of measuring service, none had proved equally satisfactory. Specifically, he said, other methods failed to provide an accurate measure of the work performance of one unit as opposed to another.

Y's was a particularly subtle little speech. He used the Socratic method, always asking us to give the answers or formulate the rationales, always asking is it right? Is it fair? (I'm certain that if we did not agree it was right and fair, he wanted to know.) He stressed the limited character of observation. His units (twenty "girls"), he said, took about 10,000 calls per month; of these only about 100 were observed, or about five observations per woman per month. He emphasized that these checks were random and anonymous.

For every contact with a customer, the amount of paperwork is huge: a single contact can require the completion of three, four, or even five separate forms. No problems can be dispensed with handily. Even if, for example, you merely transfer a customer to Traffic or Repair you must still fill out and file a CF-1. At the end of the day you must tally up and categorize all the services you have performed on a little slip of paper and hand it in to the Supervisor, who completes a tally for the unit: it is part of the process of "taking credit" for services rendered by one unit vis-à-vis the others.

As Daniel Bell points out in his extraordinary essay, "Work and Its Discontents," the rhythm of the job controls the time spent off the job as well: the breaks, the lunches, the holidays; even the weekends are scarcely long enough to reestablish a more congenial or natural path. The work rhythm controls human relationships and attitudes as well. For instance: there was a Puerto Rican worker in the Schrafft's downstairs whose job was to sell coffee-to-go to the customers: he spent his day doing nothing but filling paper cups with coffee, fitting on the lids, and writing out the checks. He was very surly and very slow and it looked to me as if the thoughts swirling in his head were those of an incipient murderer, not an incipient revolutionary. His slowness was very inconvenient to the thousands of workers in the building who had to get their coffee, take it upstairs, and drink it according to a precise timetable. We never had more than fifteen minutes to get there and back, and buying coffee generally took longer. The women resented him and called him "Speedy Gonzales," in tones of snobbery and hate. I know he hated us.

. . . The company gave every woman a Christmas present: a little wooden doll, about four inches tall, with the sick-humor look that was popular a few years ago and still appears on greeting cards. On the outside the doll says "Joy

is . . ." and when you press down the springs a little stick pops up that says
"Extensions in Color" (referring to the telephone extensions we were trying
to sell). Under that label is another sticker, the original one, which says "Knowing I wuv you." The doll is typical of the presents the company distributes periodically: a plastic shopping bag inscribed with the motto "Colorful Extensions
Lighten the Load"; a keychain with a plastic Princess telephone saying "It's Little, It's Lovely, It Lights"; plastic rain bonnets with the telephone company emblem, and so forth.

There were also free chocolates at Thanksgiving and, when the vending machine companies were on strike, free coffee for a while in the cafeteria. The
women are disgusted by the company's gift-giving policies. Last year, I was
told, the Christmas present was a little gold-plated basket filled with velour fruit
and adorned with a flag containing a company motto of the "Extensions in
Color" type. They think it is a cheap trick—better not done at all—and cite
instances of other companies which give money bonuses at Christmas.

It is obvious that the gifts are all programmed, down to the last cherry-filled
chocolate, in some manual of Personnel Administration that is the source of
all wisdom and policy; it is clear from their frequency that a whole agency of
the company is devoted to devising these gimmicks and passing them out. In
fact, apart from a standard assortment of insurance and pension plans, the
only company policy I could discover which offers genuine advantage to the
employees and which is not an attempt at manipulation is a tuition support
program in which the company pays $1000 out of $1400 of the costs of continuing education.

Another characteristic of the telephone company is a kind of programmed
"niceness" which starts from the top down but which the women internalize and
mimic. For management the strategy is clear (the Hawthorne experiments, after all, were carried out at Western Electric): it is, simply, make the employees
feel important. For trainees this was accomplished by a generous induction
ceremony complete with flowers, films, a fancy buffet, and addresses by top division representatives, all of which stressed the theme: the company cares
about you.

The ceremonies had another purpose and effect: to instill in the minds of
new employees the image the company would like the public to have of it, that
it is a goodhearted service organization with modest and regulated profits. A deliberate effort was made to fend off any free-floating negative ideas by explaining carefully, for instance, why AT&T's monopolistic relationship with Western
Electric was a good thing. The ideology of Service, embraced without much
cynicism by the low-level managers who are so abundant, is in that way—and
others—passed along.

The paternalism, the "niceness," filters down and is real. Employees are on
a first-name basis, even the women with the managers. The women are very

close to one another, sharing endless gossip, going on excursions together, and continually engaging in ceremonial celebration of one another's births, engagements, promotions. The generosity even extends to difficult situations on the job. I have, for example, seen women voluntarily sharing their precious closed time when one of them was overcommitted and the other slightly more free. Their attitude toward new employees was uniformly friendly and helpful. When I first went out on the floor my presence was a constant harassment to the other women in my unit: I didn't know what to do, had to ask a lot of questions, filed incorrectly. As a newcomer, I made their already tense lives far more difficult. Nonetheless I was made to feel welcome, encouraged. "Don't feel bad," one or another would say at a particularly stupid error. "We were all new once. We've all been through it. Don't worry. You'll catch on." In the same way I found them invariably trying to be helpful in modest personal crises: solicitous about my health when I faked a few days of illness, comforting in my depression when a pair of gloves was stolen, always friendly, cheering me (and each other) on.

This "niceness" is carefully preserved by the women as a protection against the stress of the work and the hostility of customers. "We have to be nice to each other," Sally told me once. "If we yelled at each other the way the customers yell at us, we'd go crazy." At the same time it is a triumph of their spirit as well. There is some level on which they are too proud to let the dehumanization overtake them; too decent to let the rat race get them down.

On the job, at least, the women's sense of identification with the company is absolute. On several occasions I tried to bring up issues on which their interest—and the public's—diverged from that of the company, and always I failed to make my point. It happened, for example, on the issue of selling, where I told my class frankly that I couldn't oversell, thought it was wrong, and that people needed far fewer telephones than we were giving them. Instead of noticing that I was advocating a position of principle, my class thought that, because I was so poor myself (as measured by having only one black telephone) I just somehow couldn't grasp the concept of the "well-telephoned home," but that I would catch on when I became convinced that the goods and services in question were truly valuable and desirable.

The women have a strangely dissociated attitude toward company operations that aren't working well. What company *policy* is—that is the way they learn things are supposed to be—gets pressed into their heads so much that they get a little confused by their simultaneous understanding that it isn't really working that way at all. I pointed that out a lot to see what would happen. For instance our lesson books say: "Customers always get Manhattan directories delivered with their regular installations." I said, in class: "Gee, that's funny, Sally, I had a telephone installed recently and I didn't get any phone books at all." Sally would make sure not to lose control and merely repeat: "Phone books are delivered with the regular installations."

It was the same with installation dates, which, in the company's time of troubles, are lagging behind. Company *policy* is that installations are made two days from the date they are requested. In reality we were making appointments for two, three, or even four weeks in advance. There are explanations for these lapses—everyone knows that things go wrong all the time—but there are no reasonable explanations which do not undermine the basic assumption that the company has everything "scientifically" under control. Thus the "policy" is that they are not happening at all.

Perhaps the best way to think about the women of the telephone company is to ask the question: what reinforces company-minded behavior and what works against it? It is a difficult question. The reinforcement comes not from the work but from the externals of the job: the warmth of friendships, the mutual support, the opportunities for sharing and for gossip, the general atmosphere of company benevolence and paternalism: not to mention the need for money and the very human desire to do a good job.

I never heard any of the women mouth the company rhetoric about "service to the customer" but it was obvious to me that a well-handled contact could be satisfying in some way. You are the only person who has access to what the customer needs—namely, telephones, and if you can provide him with what he wants, on time and efficiently, you might reasonably feel satisfied about it. The mutual support—the sharing of closed time, helping one another out on commitments—is also very real. The continual raffles, sales contests, gimmicks, and parties are part of it, too. They simply make you feel part of a natural stream.

Working in that job one does not see oneself as a victim of "Capitalism." One is simply part of a busy little world which has its own pleasures and satisfactions as well as its own frustrations but, most important, it is a world with a shape and an integrity all its own. The pattern of co-optation, in other words, rests on details: hundreds of trivial, but human, details.

What is on the other side? Everyone's consciousness of the iron fist, though what they usually see is the velvet glove: the deadening nature of the work; the low pay; what is going on in the outside world (to the extent that they are aware of it); the malfunctioning of the company; the pressure of supervision and observation. There was a sign that sat on the desk of one of the women while I was there, a Coney Island joke-machine sign: "Due to Lack of Interest, Tomorrow Will be Postponed." For a time I took it as an emblem and believed that was how the woman really felt. But now I am not sure.

Questions

1. *Illustrate Weber's characteristics of bureaucracy with examples from the description of the phone company.*

2. What are the disadvantages and advantages—to em
   ployees, to the general public—of the bureaucratic cha
   acteristics of the phone company?
3. Illustrate different types of groups (voluntary-involuntary
   in-out, reference, etc.) with examples from the description
   of the phone company.
4. "Organizations consciously make attempts to look and
   act less formal, less bureaucratic. . ." Does the New
   York Telephone Company do this? If so, how?
5. Draw a comparison between the phone company and a
   formal organization that you are familiar with, like the college or university you are attending. How are they similar
   and how different? Would your formal organization
   "work" better or worse if it was more like the phone company?

5

Social Differentiation

Sociologists study groups and non-groups in order to understand the social organization of society. The previous chapter dealt with groups—specifically, small primary groups and large formal organizations. In this chapter our attention turns to non-groups. Many sociologists spend much of their time specializing in the study of *categories* of people—people who have a particular characteristic in common but who do not constitute a group. Those who specialize in the study of older people, an age category, are called gerontologists. Others study race, ethnic, religious, social-class, and sex categories.

The process of defining, describing, and distinguishing between different categories of people is called social differentiation. People differ across a range of variables, and some of these categories we find ourselves in automatically—age, sex, race. Other categories have a greater degree of flexibility and to a certain extent one's position can be changed—social class, religion. (Recall the discussion of ascribed and achieved status in Chapter 3.)

As we pointed out in the previous chapter, members of a category may become a group if they become involved in shared or patterned interaction and feel bound together by a "consciousness of kind." People belonging to categories—race, religion, age, sex—obviously share common values and interests and the formation of smaller groups along these lines naturally follows. This chapter, however, focuses on categories in the larger sense, and we will examine what sociologists know about the general characteristics of social class, race, and ethnic categories.

Social Stratification

The study of social stratification arises out of the recognition that in United States society and probably in all societies people are ranked or evaluated at a number of levels. As the geologist finds layers in the earth when he looks at a cross-section, so the sociologist finds layers in the social world. We generally call these categories "social classes."

People are *unequal*—they are constantly evaluated and ranked by their fellow men on a number of criteria. The idea exists that we are all created equal, but what is really meant is that we all have an equal chance to become unequal, and even that is not true because some people have an obvious head start and others are blocked from the time they are born.

Parallel Stratification Systems

Most societies have more than one system of stratification. These several or parallel stratification systems are based on different factors. The system we usually use when discussing social class is based on occupation, wealth, power, and prestige. We could refer to this as socioeconomic status. Another stratification system might be based on race—individuals are ranked high or low purely on the basis of racial characteristics. We see this kind of stratification in South Africa and to a lesser extent in the United States. Age, sex, and religion may be the bases for other stratification systems. In some societies, older people automatically have higher status than younger people. Or, males have higher status than females in many countries. In Northern Ireland in the late 1960s and early 1970s, the battles between the Protestants and Catholics frequently made news. Northern Ireland is religiously stratified: Protestants have higher status than Catholics.

When there are a number of parallel stratification systems, an individual will be ranked in several different systems at the same time. He may be ranked in terms of race, then in terms of socioeconomic factors, then in terms of age, and so on. And though the stratification systems are parallel, they are not necessarily equal. The status of an American Negro who is upper-class in terms of wealth and occupation may be roughly equivalent to the status of a white who is middle-class in wealth and occupation. The discrepancy is explained by the existence of two stratification systems—one which ranks a person according to his socioeconomic status, a second according to his race.

Socioeconomic Status

Status based on socioeconomic factors represents one of the major systems of stratification. Following from the ideas of Max Weber, socioeconomic status is usually determined by wealth, power, and prestige.[1] Generally, when comparing and evaluating people we rank those higher who have the greater *wealth* and store of material possessions—type and size of house, area of residence, make and number of cars, quality of clothes, and so on. In a society that places value on wealth and material possessions, it becomes important to allow others to find out how well-off one really is, and so we have "status symbols." These are visible symbols of having "made it." If a person drives a Rolls Royce, Lincoln Continental, or exotic foreign car with a low-numbered license plate, lives in Beverly Hills or on Park Avenue, is mentioned in the society pages, winters in Palm Springs and summers in Switzerland, then we have a pretty good idea of where he belongs on the social-class ladder. The game gets complicated, however, when status symbols change or become generally available. Then it becomes more difficult to tell who ranks where. Only the tax man knows for sure.

Wealth is strongly correlated with education, income, and occupation, and when socioeconomic status is measured, these other factors are usually included. Income refers to current earning capacity, whereas wealth refers more to an accumulation of money and property over time.

People are also ranked according to the amount of *power* we think they have. Individuals who run things, who make the important decisions in our cities or at a national level, whether they are formally elected or informally appointed, are accorded high status by those who know of the power they exercise. Elected government officials, advisers to presidents, consultants in high, mysterious-sounding positions are automatically given high status because we know that they are at or near the centers of power.

Power is a fascinating variable that stimulates numerous questions—Who has it? How did they get it? How is it used? Some critiques of American society have focused on the amount of power concentrated in the hands of a few people who are not directly responsible to others. For example, C. Wright Mills saw classes or layers of power in society. At the top, power lies in the hands of "the warlords, the corporation chieftains, and the political directorate," who tend to work together to form a power elite in America.[2] According to Mills, what decisions are made in this country are made by a few people, and they govern a fragmented mass of people which is impotent in any power sense. Between the elite and the mass is a group whose power is a semi-organized stalemate. The middle is visible but neither represents the mass nor has any real effect on the elite. The

---

[1] H. H. Gerth and C. W. Mills, *From Max Weber: Essays in Sociology* (New York: Oxford University Press, 1958), Chapter 7.

[2] See *The Power Elite* by C. Wright Mills (New York: Oxford University Press, 1959).

elite is highly organized and made up of military leaders (admirals and generals), politicians, and business leaders. Mills suggests that a system in which so much power is held by a few who are not responsible to anyone but themselves is both immoral and irresponsible.

Some students of social class suggest that it is basically wealth (education, occupation) that establishes one's position in society and that power follows rather than determines status. It does seem that of the two possibilities, it is more often the case that wealth leads to power than power to wealth, although there are numerous (sometimes spectacular) instances where the latter has occurred. At the same time, all three variables—wealth, power, prestige—are woven together in complex patterns.

Prestige means distinction or reputation and refers to how we subjectively evaluate others. It is usually connected to a position that one holds in society. Some positions have high prestige (doctor, Supreme Court justice), others carry lower prestige (shoe shiner, garbage collector). Prestige—distinction in the eyes of others—is less concrete than wealth and power. It is no less important, however. In fact, if they had the opportunity to choose, many would probably rather have prestige than wealth. As Davis and Moore have mentioned, the prestige and status accorded one's position are determined by its scarcity or importance to society and by the amount of training or talent needed to obtain the position.[3] Logically, we would expect that one holding a position high in prestige would receive greater financial rewards than would one in a position of less prestige. This is usually true, but not always. A carpenter or plumber often makes more money than a schoolteacher, but the teacher, whose skill is scarcer and requires more training, has higher occupational prestige (which may make the teacher *feel* better, but won't pay the bills).

A person in the situation just described—material wealth but low prestige, or vice versa—we say is a victim of *status inconsistency*. He is status-inconsistent because the factors that determine his rank in society are not consistent with each other. If we recall that there are many stratification systems—race, religion, age, sex, as well as socioeconomic factors—it is clear that there are many possibilities for status inconsistency. Examples of status-inconsistent people would include a Negro court justice, a college-educated carpenter, a female doctor, a wealthy businessman with an eighth-grade education, a Catholic President, or a person of recent wealth but no prestige. The problem for the status-inconsistent person, as Broom and Selznick have pointed out, is that he behaves toward others in terms of his high rank (court justice) but others may tend to behave toward him in terms of his low rank (Negro). Some sociologists

[3] Kingsley Davis and Wilbert Moore, "Some Principles of Stratification," *American Sociological Review*, 10 (April 1945), pp. 242–249.

report that status inconsistency may lead to other things: stress, political liberalism, involvement in social movements, withdrawal, or psychosomatic illness.[4]

How Many Social Classes?

A variety of factors, then, produce a layered society. The question of just exactly *how many* layers or social classes exist has long been of interest to sociologists. Karl Marx was an economic determinist in that he felt that a person's position in the economic structure of society "determined" his life style, his values, his beliefs, and his behavior. In his writings in the mid-nineteenth century, Marx described societies as composed of two classes, the *bourgeoisie,* or capitalists, and the *proletariat,* or workers. The bourgeoisie controls the capital, the means of production. The proletariat owns only their own labor. Marx saw a continuing struggle between these two classes leading to the overthrow of the bourgeoisie by the proletariat, a "classless" society, and socialism as a new system of government.

[4] See Leonard Broom and Phillip Selznick's discussion of status consistency and incon sistency, *Sociology*, 5th Ed. (New York: Harper & Row, 1973), pp. 186–187

Studies of social class in the United States have produced varying results. Lloyd Warner studied a New England community and discovered six social classes. August Hollingshead, using a technique similar to Warner's in a Midwestern town, found five social classes. Joseph Kahl also developed a system of five social classes. According to Kahl, the upper two classes (upper and upper-middle) account for about ten percent of the population and include the "big people," the important people. The other three classes (lower-middle, working, and lower) account for about ninety percent of the population and include the "little people," or the "common man." Others have performed similar studies of a number of communities, and the results are often the same —five or six social classes.

Harold Hodges has summarized the characteristics of a typical six-social-class community as follows: The "upper-upper" class has wealth, power, social repute gained through long residence, and a prominent family name. One can only be born, or occasionally marry, into this level. The "lower-upper" class has adequate wealth and power, but their tradition of "upper-classness" is lacking. Their money is too new. Communities with a short history and characterized by mobility (people moving in and out) are less likely to have the "prominent old family names," and therefore they have few people in the upper-upper class. According to Hodges, the two upper classes seldom account for more than two or three percent of a town's citizens. The "upper-middle" class has somewhat less wealth and prestige and is made up of professionals and successful merchants. They may belong to the country club and they have college degrees, but they didn't graduate from Ivy League schools as did the uppers. The "lower-middle" class is average in income and education (high school plus), and is made up of small businessmen, salesmen, clerks, and foremen. The "lower-middle" is probably somewhat more religious and family-centered than other classes. Hodges estimates that about thirty percent of the people in a community are members of the "lower-middle" class and about the same percentage are members of the "upper-lower" class. The "upper-lower" earns less, probably didn't graduate from high school, and is more likely to be an employee than an employer. The bottom fifteen or twenty percent are members of the "lower-lower" class. They are unskilled, dropped out of school early, and are frequently unemployed. According to Hodges, the "lower-lower" is characterized by pessimism, resignation, and apathy. They are "on the outside looking in."

Other students of stratification believe that it distorts the picture to speak in terms of specific social classes, whether it be two, three, five, six, nine, or whatever. It is more accurate, they feel, to speak of a stratification continuum, consisting of many rankings with small gradations between them (much like a thermometer) and with no readily discernible social-class categories. Logically, this approach makes sense and may be the most accurate description of "the way things really are." However, since people seem to believe in social classes,

and since teachers and researchers often find it easier to make distinctions between several broad categories than between numerous slightly differing gradations, we usually view stratification in terms of specific classes. Most often
this involves the Warner or Kahl categories or a similar modification.[5]

Determining Social Class

One's social-class affiliation seems to be related to other factors. A person's
values and beliefs and his behavior in a variety of ways are affected by the
social class to which he belongs. Sociologists, therefore, have developed several
ways of determining social-class rank. These methods include the subjective,
reputational, and objective techniques. In the *subjective* method, the person is
asked what social class he thinks he belongs to. This seems a rather crude
method possibly, but many argue as Marx did that the world is divided along
class lines and that a man's social class identification is very much a part of his
self-image—it is much of what he *is*. This view holds that social class is important to people, that these people therefore have a high degree of "class
consciousness," and that they should be able to place themselves accurately in
the social-class spectrum.

The *reputational* method involves finding out "what others think." People
from the community are selected to act as prestige judges, and these judges in
turn evaluate others in the community. Social class becomes what selected
people say it is. This method is similar to the subjective technique, and again
it hinges on community members' "class consciousness." The *objective* method
differs from other methods in that individuals are evaluated in terms of certain specific factors that sociologists assume are related to social class. For example, Warner examined four factors when he used the objective technique:
the individual's occupation, his source of income, the type of house he lives
in, and the area of the city in which he lives. By knowing these facts about a
person, Warner felt that he could objectively place him in a specific social

---

[5] In this section we have directly or indirectly referred to several classic works in stratification. Lloyd Warner's study of Newburyport, Massachusetts was first described in Lloyd
Warner and Paul S. Lunt, *The Social Life of a Modern Community* (New Haven, Conn.:
Yale University Press, 1941). Robert S. Lynd and Helen M. Lynd described stratification
in a Midwestern city in *Middletown* and *Middletown in Transition,* as did August Hollingshead in *Elmtown's Youth.* (The Lynds' work appeared in the 1920s and 1930s, while
Hollingshead's book appeared in 1949.) Joseph Kahl's theories are found in his book, *The
American Class Structure* (New York: Holt, Rinehart and Winston, 1957). Stratification
along a continuum is discussed by John Cuber and William Kenkel in their book, *Social
Stratification in the United States* (New York: Appleton-Century-Crofts, 1954). The description of six social classes comes from the book by Harold M. Hodges, Jr., *Social Stratification* (Cambridge, Mass.: Schenkman Publishing Co., 1964), Chapter 4.

class. Other objective factors that have been used include years of education, amount of income, type of possessions, even type and quality of home furnishings.

Using any of these methods, especially the objective, may give the impression that social class is a very clear-cut phenomenon and each person can be adequately plugged in. This, of course, is an oversimplification. The categories are not precise and are not always related one to another. For example, in what social class do we put the status-inconsistent fellow whose occupational prestige is low, income is high, who lives in an apartment in a slum, and is a college graduate—and when we ask him, he says he doesn't believe in social class?[6]

Social Class and Behavior

Social-class membership is related to various patterns of behavior. Lower-class people seem oriented more toward taking pleasures in the present than toward planning for future goals. Middle-class people are more prone to defer gratification. There is an apparent link between low status and prejudice. In examining people who are mentally ill, psychiatrists more often diagnose middle-class people as neurotic, and lower-class people as psychotic. From among numerous other examples of class-related behavior patterns, we will briefly discuss three: leisure and recreation patterns, child-training practices, and explanations for delinquent and criminal behavior.

Several sociologists have studied social-class variations in patterns of leisure and recreation. Hodges found in his survey of "Peninsula People" that upper-class people watched television an average of sixteen minutes per week night, while lower-lower-class people watched an average of 180 minutes a night. Thirty-three percent of the uppers said that they never watched television, while only six percent of the lower-lowers said they never watched. Reading books and magazines increases as one goes up the social-class ladder. The higher one's social class, the more he is likely to be involved in sports as a participant; the lower his class, the more likely he is to be involved as a spectator. Al Clarke compared upper- and lower-class people and found that the uppers favored playing bridge, watching movies, and going to museums, while the lowers liked playing poker, watching baseball, and going to the zoo.[7]

[6] Methods of determining social class and critiques of these methods are covered in more detail by Hodges in *Social Stratification,* Chapter 5.

[7] Hodges, *Social Stratification,* p. 161, and Alfred C. Clarke, "The Use of Leisure and Its Relation to Levels of Occupational Prestige," *American Sociological Review,* 21 (June 1956), pp. 301–306.

In terms of the way they raise their children, middle-class mothers are probably more permissive, lower-class mothers more rigid. Melvin Kohn reports that middle-class mothers value self-control, dependability, and consideration, while lower-class mothers value obedience and the ability in a boy to defend himself. The middle-class child is raised in an atmosphere in which achievement and "getting ahead" are encouraged. The lower-class child is raised in an atmosphere that emphasizes the immediate and the concrete, that focuses on "getting by," and that counsels him to shy away from the new or unfamiliar. We should note here that there is much change in social-class-linked child-rearing practices. What is "fashionable" or "correct" at one time may change drastically a few years later.[8]

Many of the current theories attempting to explain delinquent and criminal behavior are based on social class. Walter Miller, for example, argues that lower-class juveniles who become delinquents do so because of the lower-class value system. Lower-class values and beliefs important to lower-class youth include trouble, toughness, smartness, excitement, fate, and autonomy (resistance to being bossed or controlled). Miller believes that the more marked presence of these values in the lower class than in other social classes makes it inevitable that many lower-class children will run afoul of the law. In a way he is saying that we have two different cultures—middle-class and lower-class—but the *laws* in United States society emerge solely from the middle-class culture and therefore one should expect that most *illegal* behavior will come from the lower-class culture. The rather pessimistic inference from this theory is that the only way to make it is to become middle-class.

Several other theories examine the social-class-linked motivations for delinquency in a slightly different way. Albert Cohen and Richard Cloward and Lloyd Ohlin agree that ours is a middle-class-based society, but they do not believe that it is a lower-class value system or culture that leads one to delinquency. Rather, they feel that the basic problem arises out of the lower-class individual's attempt to move into the middle class. It is Cohen's view that most who try to make it will not. Anticipating failure, their reaction is to invert the middle-class system—to do just the opposite of what middle-class people say is correct. The result is malicious, non-utilitarian, frequently criminal behavior. Cloward and Ohlin agree with Cohen up to the point of the "spite," invert-the-middle-class-values reaction. Cloward and Ohlin believe that the lower-class individual still wants to make it, and when he sees he cannot succeed legally he decides to try it illegally. He becomes involved, therefore, in utilitarian property crime which allows him to collect the good things, the symbols of status associated with middle-class culture. Whether or not the theorists agree on particulars,

---

[8] See Hodges' discussion in *Social Stratification,* Chapter 8, especially pp. 178–186. Melvin Kohn's research is discussed by Hodges, pp. 181–182. Also see Melvin Kohn's book, *Class and Conformity* (Homewood, Ill.: Dorsey Press, 1969).

the important factor in all of these theories is that they are based on social class. The social class to which a person belongs apparently provides him with a characteristic view of the world that does much to determine his behavior.

The theories discussed above deal only with lower-class crime and may leave one with the impression that all crime is committed by lower-class people. This is a common error that is made if one looks only at arrest figures, which *are* higher among the lower class. Middle-class people commit different types of crime—fraud, embezzlement, white-collar offenses—that are less easily detected and punished. Also, middle-class people have the financial resources to deal with the law, to avoid arrest to begin with, and to obtain better legal defense should arrest occur. Typically, the middle-class juvenile delinquent is informally apprehended and returned to his parents while the lower-class delinquent is formally arrested and sent to a juvenile hall. The actual extent of "hidden" middle-class crime is hard to assess. It may be that if all offenses could be known, the differences between social classes would be only in types of offenses, not in number of offenses.[9]

Social Mobility

Horizontal social mobility refers to movement from one occupation to another within the same social class. If an architect becomes a minister, or if the mailman becomes a carpenter, we would say that horizontal social mobility has occurred—occupational change but no change in social class. The term "horizontal social mobility" is also used by sociologists to describe geographical mobility, moving one's home from one place to another. *Vertical* social mobility is more relevant to our discussion here, however. Vertical social mobility refers to movement up or down the social-class ladder, movement from one rank to another.

Societies with unlimited possibilities for vertical social mobility are described as "open." Those with no possibilities for mobility are called "closed." In reality, all societies rank somewhere between the extremes of completely open and completely closed. India's system of stratification, for example, is

[9] The original works referred to in this section include: William C. Kvaraceus and Walter B. Miller, *Delinquent Behavior: Culture and the Individual* (Washington, D.C.: National Education Association, 1959), Walter Miller, "Lower-Class Culture as a Generating Milieu of Gang Delinquency," *Journal of Social Issues,* 14 (1958), pp. 5–19, Albert K. Cohen, *Delinquent Boys: The Culture of the Gang* (New York: Free Press, 1955), and Richard Cloward and Lloyd Ohlin, *Delinquency and Opportunity* (New York: Free Press, 1960). These and other class-related theories of delinquency are summarized in Hodges, *Social Stratification,* Chapter 10, and in many textbooks on criminology—for example, Walter C. Reckless, *The Crime Problem,* 5th Ed. (New York: Appleton-Century-Crofts, 1973), Chapter 2.

closer to the closed end of the continuum. Lines between levels or castes are often firmly drawn—moving from the caste into which one is born may be difficult if not impossible. Some have suggested that we have a type of caste system in the United States relative to blacks and whites. That is, there is a firm line between black and white stratification systems and although a black may rise within the black class system, he is either blocked from the white system or is automatically assigned low rank in the white system. In societies with stratification systems that rank more toward the "open" end of the continuum, mobility from one level to another may be both possible and frequent.

Examining mobility in a given country is a complicated procedure. Americans, for example, have traditionally looked at their own system as completely open. Mobility and achievement were available to anyone who worked hard and led a clean life. We *know* that the "rags-to-riches," Horatio Alger story is *true* and *we* can make it too. America is not like other countries where class lines are difficult to cross. In fact and contrary to these beliefs, mobility is very much the same in all modern industrialized countries. The dramatic leap from rags to riches is a rare occurrence indeed. Mobility, when it occurs, is usually in a series of small steps and possibly over several generations. There is more mobility within classes (horizontal mobility) than between classes (vertical mobility). There seems to be more upward vertical mobility than downward, but though many are mobile, few are very mobile.

If one wants to become upwardly mobile, aside from a simple reliance on luck, there are a few general rules to follow. Defer gratification, marry late, and have a small family if you must have a family. If you live in a small town, leave. Vertical mobility is easier in large cities. If you are an immigrant to the United States, be Japanese, Jewish, or Scottish. These groups are more mobile than other immigrant groups, who more often than not come in at the bottom of the social-class ladder and stay there. In modern societies in which skills and knowledge are increasingly important, education is essential for upward mobility. In the United States a college degree is necessary. For some it is not only the degree, but the "right school"—Harvard, Yale, Radcliff, Princeton—that is essential to mobility. Finally, if all else fails in your quest for upward mobility, marry someone who has followed the above rules. . . .

But before you decide for sure to move up, beware of the consequences. Sociologists have been studying the social-psychological effects of upward mobility. One result of uprooting oneself from the past and moving to a new level is that it becomes difficult to form satisfying relationships. One becomes alone, a marginal man between two worlds and a member of neither. Another view agrees that socially mobile people are isolates, but argues that they were isolates to begin with. They were unhappy and isolated and this led to attempts at mobility, so they are really no worse off. A third view of the situation is that socially mobile people have few problems because they are so anxious to get to the next level that they adopt the patterns of behavior of that level long before they ever get there (anticipatory socialization). Consequently, they are accepted and much at home when they finally arrive.[10]

In a society that is oriented upwards, downward mobility is hard to take. Studies cite relationships between downward mobility and both suicide and mental illness (especially schizophrenia). The same factors that are related to upward mobility are related in their converse to downward mobility. Marrying early, having a large family, or failing to get an education may do it. Personal factors may help: business failure, sickness, or rejection of the ethic that says that climbing the social ladder is important.

Race and Ethnicity

In the previous section we found that people differ and are ranked by such socioeconomic factors as wealth, education, occupation, power, and prestige. People also differ and are ranked by their race and ethnicity. A person's race and ethnic affiliation confer on him a status or position in society—sometimes a minority status. The term "minority status" is an important one and is probably more useful than a term such as "race." Minority status refers to a social condition, not necessarily a statistical one. A "minority" may actually represent a majority of a society's population but they have *minority status* in that they are treated as lower in social ranking and are subject to domination by other segments of the population. For example, women in the United States are a numerical majority but have minority status because they are not treated on a level of equality with men. In most instances minority groups do represent a smaller proportion of the population—blacks and Mexican-Americans in the United States, for example—but it is important to recall the *social* nature of minority status.

Race is a vague and ambiguous term. It is generally defined as people bound together by hereditary physical features. The difficulty with the category "race" is that practically no "pure" races exist. Substantial biological mixing has blurred boundaries to the point that it is difficult to outline uniform "hereditary physical features." Scientists attempting to define race have come up with systems for anywhere from three racial categories to more than thirty. Three definitions of race—biological, legal, social—seem to intermingle.[11] A biological definition is based on observable physical features such as skin color, hair texture, and eye color, or on differences in gene frequencies. The legal definition is carried by the

---

[10] See Hodges' discussion of social mobility and its effects in *Social Stratification*, Chapters 12 and 13, especially p. 266.

[11] This distinction is suggested by Brewton Berry in *Race and Ethnic Relations*, 3rd Ed. (Boston: Houghton Mifflin, 1965), Chapter 2.

laws of states or nations. The law in one of our states has defined a black as a person who had "one-eighth or more Negro blood" and in other states a black is a person with "any ascertainable trace of Negro blood." The social definition refers to what members of society feel to be the important distinctions about race. Berry has suggested that in the United States the social definition of a black is anyone who identifies himself as black or who has any *known* trace of black ancestry. It can be seen from this that the term "race" is not a particularly precise term, but it is nevertheless widely used.

A sociology class is shown slides of people who identify themselves as blacks but who, because of an absence of "typical" racial characteristics, don't *look* like blacks. The class (which is predominantly white) is asked to identify the race or nationality of the light-skinned, straight-haired people on the slides and the guesses range across the globe. Finally the class is told, "they are all American Negroes." The reaction is astonishment of course, because "they don't look like blacks." This illustrates several things, among them the difficulty of defining race, the blurring of racial boundaries, and the importance of the social definition— once the class is told that the people on the slides identify as blacks (probably because of some black ancestry), to the class they *are* blacks. No question about it, regardless of how they look.

When race is discussed, the question of racial differences inevitably comes up. That is, do races biologically differ in I.Q., in achievement, in susceptibility to diseases, in perception? The haziness in definitions of race supplies part of the answer: If the boundaries of race are unclear, how can any statements about racial differences be made? Nevertheless, they are, as witness the current controversy over inherent racial I.Q. differences. A conclusion to this discussion that is favored by most social scientists is that there are no significant differences *caused* by race. There are numerous differences between people caused by cultural, social, and geographic factors, however, and these are often incorrectly identified as racial differences. For example, certain gene frequencies and blood characteristics have developed in particular areas of the world. Population groups migrating from those areas—regardless of race—carry these characteristics to other parts of the world. Apparently, a specific blood characteristic that has survival value in high malaria areas has developed in populations in parts of Africa and the Middle East. This same blood characteristic also leads to sickle-cell anemia, a disease that has victimized blacks in the United States. Is sickle-cell anemia race-linked? No, for nonblacks who have migrated to other parts of the world from those same areas of Africa and the Middle East may also have it. Likewise, differences in attitude, achievement, and perception are explained by cultural differences—one culture emphasizes achievement, another tranquility, one is aggressive, another encourages passivity, and so on. In short, social scientists argue from a cultural determinist viewpoint and reject the idea of racially caused differences. Many people remain unconvinced, however, and the argument will undoubtedly continue.

"Ethnicity" or "ethnic group" are more useful terms than "race," at least from the sociological viewpoint. *Ethnicity* refers to people bound together by cultural ties. These cultural ties may have several origins. When nationality groups immigrate to a new area their ties to their previous culture may remain strong. Religious beliefs may also provide the basis for ethnicity, and examples in the United States might include Jews, the Amish, and the Hutterites. The term ethnicity is useful because it appropriately brings the focus on cultural similarities, which to the social scientist are more important and have more explanatory power than racial similarities.

Prejudice and Discrimination

Prejudice has been defined as a favorable or unfavorable attitude toward a person or thing, prior to, or not based on, actual experience. A prejudiced person ignores the individual and his particular qualities or characteristics and groups him with others who happen to have the same skin color (brown or yellow), or speak with the same accent (New England), or have the same type of name (Cohen, Greenberg), or come from the same part of the country (South). Finally, prejudice tends to be generalized. People who are prejudiced against one group will probably be prejudiced against others. In fact, Hartley found that college students who were prejudiced against Negroes also were prejudiced against Jews, Wallonians, and Daniereans. (There are about 14 million Jews in the world, but no Daniereans or Wallonians.)

Discrimination is actual behavior unfavorable to a specific individual or group. When people desire equality of treatment and are denied it, they are being discriminated against. Discrimination occurs when a person is denied a desired position or right because of "irrelevant" factors—for example, when skin color is used to determine eligibility to vote or when religious affiliation is used to determine where one may reside.

Prejudice and discrimination are usually associated, but not always. It is possible to be prejudiced and not discriminate, as in the case of the person who has negative beliefs about a certain group but treats all individuals equally in his business dealings. It is also possible to discriminate but not be prejudiced, as in the case of the Southern businessman who is not prejudiced against Negroes but who follows the mores of the area and discriminates against them in his business activities. Generally, however, prejudice (the attitude) precedes discrimination (the behavior).

The origins of prejudice are explained in varying ways. Some psychologists feel that there is a certain type of personality—called an Authoritarian Personality—that is especially prone to prejudice. The Authoritarian Personality is also ethnocentric, rigidly conformist, and worshipful of authority and strength. According to psychologists, the Authoritarian Personality can most often be traced to faulty emotional development born of harsh discipline and lack of affection and love from parents during one's childhood. Most sociologists believe that prejudice, like other attitudes and behaviors, is learned in interaction with others, mainly in the family, and that personality is not as important as the social or cultural situation in which one interacts. We learn race prejudice in the same way we learn how to eat with a fork, study for a test, or drive a car. Also, certain life situations affect how this learning takes place. For example, people who are downwardly mobile—moving from middle to lower class—show more intense feelings of prejudice toward Negroes and Jews; and in times of rapid social change, prejudice and discrimination may become more intense and more generalized.

Sociologists also associate stereotyping with prejudice. In stereotyping, we apply a common label and set of characteristics to all the people in a certain category, even though none or only some of the people in that category fit the image we are applying. The stereotyped college professor is absent-minded, smokes a pipe, is an extreme liberal, wears horn-rimmed glasses and a tweed jacket with elbow patches, and generally is not much in touch with the real world. This image is applied to everyone in the college professor category even though most do not fit the part. The professor will probably survive his stereotype without serious damage since the characteristics of the stereotype are not particularly "bad" in our society, and since a person *chooses* as an adult to become a college teacher and, therefore, to enter a stereotyped category.

A Negro, on the other hand, who is stereotyped from birth as ignorant, lazy, dirty, happy-go-lucky, morally primitive, emotionally unstable, and fit only for menial work, can be psychologically damaged by the effects of the lifelong stereotype. Likewise, women have been stereotyped as weak, submissive, unintelligent, noncompetitive, and suited only for housework. When others react to us on the basis of such stereotypes, it strongly affects our self-concept—the way we see ourselves.

Several theories have been offered to explain prejudice and discrimination. One such theory explains conflict between unlike groups in terms of scapegoating. If attention can be focused on some out-group, this may strengthen the boundaries and unity of the in-group. It is suggested that the Nazis' attack on the Jews before and during World War II had this motivation. Marxist theory holds that economic competition is the best explanation for prejudice and discrimination. When access to desired goods or valued positions in society is limited, discrimination against certain categories of people helps insure that others can more easily dominate and obtain their goals. By reducing the status of others to second-class citizens, by eliminating certain people from highly valued jobs, education, and access to wealth, we can guarantee that our own path is free of obstacles. Some have said that the conflict that arises when unlike groups meet may be best and most simply explained as resulting from a struggle for status between competing groups.

The common areas of discrimination in the United States include employment, education, housing, and, to a lesser extent, voting. In the following paragraphs we will take a brief look at some patterns of prejudice and discrimination as they affect blacks, Indians, Mexican-Americans, and Jews.

There are 22½ million blacks in the United States, or roughly 11 percent of the population. Blacks are a part of American history from its beginning; from the earliest days of the settlement of this country our economy was based on slavery. We are still trying to survive the effects that the culture of slavery had on blacks and whites in America. Certain dates stand out:

1619   *twenty blacks purchased from a Dutch ship*
1644   *first slaves imported directly from Africa*
1861–1865   *civil war with emancipation as a major issue*
1865   *legal abolishment of slavery by the thirteenth amendment to the Constitution*
1918 on   *black migration from the rural south to jobs in the urban north*
1954   *Brown v. Board of Education decision by the Supreme Court states that "separate facilities are inherently unequal"*
1956   *Montgomery bus boycott led by Martin Luther King, Jr.*
1960–1965   *passive resistance, sit-ins, demonstrations*
1965–1970   *urban riots, beginning of black militancy, and "Black Power"*
1970s   *prison riots, widespread disagreement over busing to achieve school desegregation*

The Kerner (riot commission) Report in 1968 stated that "our nation is moving toward two societies, one black, one white—separate and unequal." Median income for whites in 1972 was $11,549; for nonwhites, it was $6,864. The unemployment rate for nonwhites is double that of whites (10.6 percent to 5.3 percent for the first quarter 1972). Blacks represented a larger proportion of the poverty group in 1970 than they did in 1959 despite the fact that average income has gone up. In other words, the economic position of blacks has improved, but it has improved much faster for whites. Education presents a confusing picture. The Supreme Court outlawed segregated schools in the *Brown* v. *Board of Education* decision in 1954, but integration of schools did not proceed very rapidly—more than two-thirds of the Southern black children were still attending all black schools by 1968. According to the Department of Health, Education, and Welfare, however, a dramatic change did take place between 1968 and 1971–72. In 1972 only 9 percent of Southern black children were still in all black schools, whereas in the North and West 11 percent of black students were in all black schools in 1972. More black students (44 percent) were in majority white schools in 1972 in the South than in the North and West according to HEW. These statistics reveal that despite a tendency to point the finger of accusation toward the South when discussing racism in America, all parts of the nation share the guilt. Housing (especially de facto) segregation has certainly been increasing much more rapidly in the ghettos of Northern cities than it has been in the South.

Finding adequate housing is difficult for blacks. First restrictive covenants and now "gentleman's agreements" keep blacks out of the better districts in most cities and suburbs of the North, West, and South. Also, because middle-class whites are leaving the cities for the suburbs, de facto segregation is turning the inner cities into black ghettos. Blacks isolated in these areas find their housing, their public facilities, and their schools automatically "segregated" and made inadequate by the lowered tax base, the backwardness (and often helplessness) of city government, and the exploitation or apathy of absentee landlords and local businessmen.

Blacks have been denied the vote for years in the South. However, implementation of the Civil Rights Act, which called for federal voting registrars in the South, seemed to change this form of discrimination. Voter registration figures in eleven Southern states in 1960 indicated that 61 percent of the eligible whites were registered while only 29 percent of the eligible blacks were registered. By 1970, however, 69 percent of the whites were registered and 62 percent of the blacks.

There are approximately 800,000 American Indians. Indians have a life expectancy of 44 years (compared to 71 for whites); the average per family income of Indians is $1,500, and Indian unemployment runs to 10 times the national average. The average years of schooling received by Indians is 5.5. Reservation housing is substandard. Incidence of tuberculosis among Indians is eight times the national average, and infant mortality and suicide rates are both double the national average. Suicide rates are even higher for Indians in their late teens and twenties. Rates of alcoholism and homicide are also very high. The birth rate of Indians—2½ times that of whites—makes them the nation's fastest growing minority. We have systematically taken over Indian land. They held 138 million acres in 1887—this had been reduced to 55 million acres by 1970. Dr. Bertram Brown, director of the National Institute of Mental Health, stated that "because of the general neglect of many generations, America's oldest minority suffers greatly the effects of isolation and alienation from society. Racism and bigotry have an adverse effect on mental health and the Indian has been the victim of this abuse longer than any other American."

The Mexican-American is the Southwest's largest culturally distinct minority group. According to a May 1972 report by the U.S. Commission on Civil Rights, however, schools in the Southwest exclude the Chicano's Spanish language, exclude their Mexican heritage, and discourage their participation in school affairs. Nearly 50 percent of the Mexican-American first graders do not speak English as well as the average Anglo first grader. They have to learn a new language in addition to the other material being taught. By the twelfth grade, 63 percent of all Chicano students read at least six months below grade level. Before the end of the twelfth grade, 47 percent of the Chicanos will have left school. Only 7 percent of the secondary schools in the Southwest had a course in Mexican-American history. Four million persons in the Southwest identify Spanish as mother tongue, but the schools (75 percent of the elementary, 90 percent of the secondary) communicate with parents (send notices, conduct meetings) only in English. Many Chicanos in the west are migrant workers performing farm labor in the fields of California and Oregon. Farm labor is seasonal, uncertain, underpaid, and subject to bad working conditions. Farm laborers were overrepresented among the poor in 1970. Recent efforts by Cesar Chavez and the United Farmworkers Union have begun to change conditions, but the fight with the growers promises to be a long and difficult one.

There are approximately 14 million people of the Jewish faith in the world. There are six million Jews in the United States or roughly 3 percent of our population. In the past, Jews have faced prejudice and discrimination in a variety of areas. For a time, many jobs were not open to Jews. Until recently, colleges and universities, especially in the Eastern United States, had quotas covering the percentage of Jews they would accept. As recently as 1958, 33 percent of the real estate agents in a large midwestern city reported they did not want to rent to Jews, and a study of 3,000 resorts across the country in the same year found that 22 percent discriminated against Jews. In the late 1960s and 1970s, such overt discrimination against Jews has probably declined, although anti-Jewish prejudice remains. Of some current concern are the quotas and preferential treatment being received by some groups in education and employment which, it is argued, favors one minority to the exclusion of others.

Patterns of Interaction

When populations that differ by race or ethnicity meet, a number of different types of reactions may occur. Some of these reactions are quite peaceful, others are not.[12] *Annihilation* refers to the elimination of one group by another. This may be done intentionally, such as the Nazis' treatment of the Jews, or U.S. policies toward Indians in the nineteenth century. The practice of deliberately exterminating a whole race or ethnic group is called genocide. Annihilation may occur unintentionally when one group brings disease that decimates the other group. Again, American Indians are examples as they fell victim in great numbers to illnesses brought over by European settlers. *Expulsion* refers to the

---

[12] These paragraphs on patterns of interaction are drawn from Berry, *Race and Ethnic Relations,* Chapters 7–12.

removal of a group from the territory in which it resides. Japanese on the West Coast during World War II were removed from their homes and placed in detention camps, and yes, American Indian tribes were forced from their homes onto reservations. *Segregation* refers to the setting apart of one group. It is not as extreme as expulsion but the separation is nevertheless obvious. The segregation may be physical—a separate area of the city—or it may be social as when people living together are constrained in how and with whom they may interact. Segregation (from the minority's viewpoint) may be involuntary—blacks in the U.S.—or voluntary. Avoidance (voluntary self-segregation) occurs when a culture such as the Amish in America wants to maintain its identity and uniqueness against the onslought of the dominant culture and therefore voluntarily separates itself.

Assimilation and amalgamation represent less violent patterns of interaction between unlike groups. *Assimilation* refers to the mixing and merging of unlike cultures so that two groups come to have a common culture. When two cultures meet, one outcome would be that each culture adopts some of the other's traits so that the result is a true melting pot—the emergence of a new culture different from either of the old cultures. More often, however, assimilation means that the incoming or minority culture adapts to the dominant culture. *Amalgamation* refers to biological (rather than cultural) mixing. Amalgamation seems invariably to accompany the meeting of racial and ethnic groups, despite the best efforts of some societies (the United States, for example) to legislate against it. The *marginal man* is defined as a person who is between two antagonistic cultures, a product of both but a member of neither. Studies indicate that in some cases the consequences of marginality may be severe—personality disturbance, feelings of inferiority. Marginality is often defined as a product of amalgamation, but it may also result from cultural mixing (the Southern rural migrant to the urban North, for example).

Cultural pluralism describes a pattern of interaction in which unlike cultures maintain their own identity and yet interact with each other relatively peacefully. Switzerland is usually cited as the best example of pluralism in that peoples of several nationalities and religions and even three or four different languages are able to get along peacefully. According to Berry, few countries have been able to successfully accomplish a system of pluralism. Some minorities at some times in the United States have voiced a preference for cultural pluralism but the dominant culture seems to look either toward integration or toward discrimination and segregation.

Minority Group Reactions

The patterns of interaction described above are usually dictated by the dominant group. What then of minority group reactions to domination? Allport has outlined some types of reactions in his book, *The Nature of Prejudice.*[13] The simplest response is to *deny membership* in the minority group—members of one race "pass" as members of another, people change their names to get rid of their ethnic identification. Similarly, *acculturation* refers to attempts by members of minority groups to assimilate, to blend in and take on as many characteristics of the dominant culture as possible. Hiding resentment in *withdrawal* and passivity—"a mask of contentment"—is another reaction. *Self-hatred* may develop and the minority group may identify with the dominant group. Studies of Nazi concentration camps showed that after years of suffering, inmates began identifying with the guards: the prisoners wore bits of the guards' clothing, they became anti-Semitic, and in general they adopted the mentality of the oppressor. Likewise, if blacks value light skin more than dark, they may be accepting whites' evaluation of skin pigmentation. Self-hate may lead to aggression against one's own group, as when a "higher class" segment of the minority takes out its frustrations on a lower ranked segment. Minorities sometimes show greater *prejudice* against other minorities, and in other cases the opposite reaction—greater *sympathy.*

A *strengthening of in-group ties* is another reaction of minorities to domination. Nativism—a rejection of the dominant culture and a reaffirming of the characteristics of the minority culture—may result. This has been seen recently in the United States with slogans such as "Black Power" and "Don't buy where you can't work," and by the focus on the development of ethnic identity through emphasizing the minority's cultural and historical roots. Minorities may react to domination by using *aggression.* The aggression may be individual and reflected in crime patterns, or could be collective and culminate in urban disturbances or riots. In milder form, the aggression may appear in the literature and humor of the minority group as it makes fun of or shows its bitterness toward the majority group. In fact, humor is a common way of expressing feelings about other groups. In the following not very representative examples, who is putting down whom?

> *A black woman from Harlem wins the Irish sweepstakes and decides to buy a fur coat. She tries on a coat at Saks Fifth Avenue and it comes down to her ankles. As she looks at herself in the mirror, she turns to the saleslady and says, "Do you think this makes me look too Jewish?"*
>
> *A priest and a rabbi are each driving down a New York street. The rabbi stops at a light and the priest runs into him. An Irish cop comes up to the priest and asks, "Ah Father,*

---

[13] See *The Nature of Prejudice* by Gordon Allport (Garden City, New York: Doubleday, 1958), Chapter 9.

*how fast might the rabbi have been going when he backed
into you?"*

*Dick Gregory: "I sat in at this place for three years and when
they finally waited on me I found out they didn't have what I
wanted."*

*What do you have when you cross a WASP and a chimpan-
zee? A three foot tall, blond, company president. . . .*

Summary

Sociologists examine the social organization of society by studying groups
and non-groups. In the previous chapter we focused on groups. This chapter
covered non-groups with specific attention to social class and race–ethnicity,
categories of social differentiation. Our study of social stratification included
a discussion of the numerous factors that stratify people, differing descriptions of
social classes in America, several ways of determining social class, descriptions
of some class-related behaviors, and social mobility.

Race, ethnicity, and minority status were defined and the question of racial
differences was discussed. Some of the patterns of prejudice and discrimination
that occur in the United States were described. Finally, the patterns of interaction and reaction that occur when unlike groups meet were outlined. Even at
the more detailed level of analysis used in the discussion of social class and
race–ethnicity, the general concepts introduced earlier—socialization, self,
norms, roles, culture, group—continue to be important.

The four readings that follow cover some of the ideas introduced in this
chapter. Norman Podhoretz describes his own first awareness of social class and
his encounter with a teacher who encouraged him to be socially mobile. The
second article, by the editors of the *New York Times,* describes a status symbol
that is currently popular. The third selection, an excerpt from John Howard
Griffin's *Black Like Me,* describes the interaction of people who differ by race.
Finally, Paula Stern analyzes the female role in American society and illustrates
the concepts of status, role, and stereotype.

Making It:
The Brutal Bargain

Norman Podhoretz

There is much variation in how conscious people are of social class. In societies where class lines are strictly drawn, there is probably greater "class consciousness." In such societies the individual is likely to have a well-developed sense of his own class position, of others who are like him, and of those who rank higher or lower. In societies where class is more fluid and lines are easily crossed, there is probably less class consciousness. And in any society, some individuals are more conscious of class than are others.

Norman Podhoretz is an author and editor of *Commentary* magazine. In this selection from his book, *Making It,* Podhoretz describes his growing awareness of social class. Podhoretz was of lower- or working-class background, but he encountered an English teacher who decided he was a "gem in the rough and took it upon herself to polish [him] to as high a sheen as she could manage . . . ." This process illustrates a growing class consciousness and the processes and problems of upward social mobility as well.

One of the longest journeys in the world is the journey from Brooklyn to Manhattan—or at least from certain neighborhoods in Brooklyn to certain parts of Manhattan. I have made that journey, but it is not from the experience of having made it that I know how very great the distance is, for I started on the road many years before I realized what I was doing, and by the time I did realize it I was for all practical purposes already there. At so imperceptible a pace did I travel, and with so little awareness, that I never felt footsore or out of breath or weary at the thought of how far I still had to go. Yet whenever anyone who has remained back there where I started—remained not physically but socially and culturally, for the neighborhood is now a Negro ghetto and the Jews who have "remained" in it mostly reside in the less affluent areas of Long Island —whenever anyone like that happens into the world in which I now live with such perfect ease, I can see that in his eyes I have become a fully acculturated citizen of a country as foreign to him as China and infinitely more frightening.

That country is sometimes called the upper middle class; and indeed I am a member of that class, less by virtue of my income than by virtue of the way my speech is accented, the way I dress, the way I furnish my home, the way I entertain and am entertained, the way I educate my children—the way, quite simply, I look and live. It appalls me to think what an immense transformation I had to work on myself in order to become what I have become: if I had known what I was doing I would surely not have been able to do it, I would surely not have wanted to. No wonder the choice had to be blind; there was a kind of treason in it—treason toward my family, treason toward my friends. In choosing the road I chose, I was pronouncing a judgment upon them, and the fact that they themselves concurred in the judgment makes the whole thing sadder but no less cruel.

When I say that the choice was blind, I mean that I was never aware—obviously not as a small child, certainly not as an adolescent, and not even as a young man already writing for publication and working on the staff of an important intellectual magazine in New York—how inextricably my "noblest" ambitions were tied to the vulgar desire to rise above the class into which I was born; nor did I understand to what an astonishing extent these ambitions were shaped and defined by the standards and values and tastes of the class into which I did not know I wanted to move. It is not that I was or am a social climber as that term is commonly used. High society interests me, if at all, only as a curiosity; I do not wish to be a member of it; and in any case, it is not, as I have learned from a small experience of contact with the very rich and fashionable, my "scene." Yet precisely because social climbing is not one of my vices (unless what might be called celebrity climbing, which very definitely *is* one of my vices, can be considered the contemporary variant of social climbing), I think there may be more than a merely personal significance in the fact that class has played so large a part both in my life and in my career.

But whether or not the significance is there, I feel certain that my long-time blindness to the part class was playing in my life was not altogether idiosyncratic. "Privilege," Robert L. Heilbroner has shrewdly observed in *The Limits of American Capitalism,* "is not an attribute we are accustomed to stress when we consider the construction of *our* social order." For a variety of reasons, says Heilbroner, "privilege under capitalism is much less 'visible,' especially to the favored groups, than privilege under other systems" like feudalism. This "invisibility" extends in America to class as well

No one, of course, is so naïve as to believe that America is a classless society or that the force of egalitarianism—powerful as it has been in some respects—has ever been powerful enough to wipe out class distinctions altogether. There was a moment during the 1950s, to be sure, when social thought hovered on the brink of saying that the country had to all intents and purposes become a wholly middle-class society. But the emergence of the civil-rights movement in the 1960s and the concomitant discovery of the poor—to whom, in helping to discover them, Michael Harrington interestingly enough applied, in *The Other America,* the very word ("invisible") that Heilbroner later used with reference to the rich—has put at least a temporary end to that kind of talk. And yet if class has become visible again, it is only in its grossest outlines—mainly, that is, in terms of income levels—and to the degree that manners and style of life are perceived as relevant at all, it is generally in the crudest of terms. There is something in us, it would seem, which resists the idea of class. Even our novelists, working in a genre for which class has traditionally been a supreme reality, are largely indifferent to it—which is to say, blind to its importance as a factor in the life of the individual.

In my own case, the blindness to class always expressed itself in an outright and very often belligerent refusal to believe that it had anything to do with me at all. I no longer remember when or in what form I first discovered that there was such a thing as class, but whenever it was and whatever form the discovery took, it could only have coincided with the recognition that criteria existed by which I and everyone I knew were stamped as inferior: we were in the *lower* class. This was not a proposition I was willing to accept, and my way of not accepting it was to dismiss the whole idea of class as a prissy triviality.

Given the fact that I had literary ambitions even as a small boy, it was inevitable that the issue of class would sooner or later arise for me with a sharpness it would never acquire for most of my friends. But given the fact also that I was on the whole very happy to be growing up where I was, that I was fiercely patriotic about Brownsville (the spawning ground of so many famous athletes and gangsters), and that I felt genuinely patronizing toward other neighborhoods (especially the "better" ones like Crown Heights and East Flatbush which seemed by comparison colorless and unexciting)—given the fact, in other words, that I was not, for all that I wrote poetry and read books, an "alienated" boy dreaming of escape, my confrontation with the issue of class would probably have come later rather than sooner if not for an English teacher in high school who decided that I was a gem in the rough and took it upon herself to polish me to as high a sheen as she could manage and I would permit.

I resisted—far less effectively, I can see now, than I then thought, though even then I knew that she was wearing me down far more than I would ever give her the satisfaction of admitting. Famous throughout the school for her altogether outspoken snobbery, which stopped short by only a hair (and sometimes did not stop short at all) of an old-fashioned kind of patrician anti-Semitism, Mrs. K. was also famous for being an extremely good teacher; indeed, I am sure that she saw no distinction between the hopeless task of teaching the proper use of English to the young Jewish barbarians whom fate had so unkindly deposited into her charge and the equally hopeless task of teaching them the proper "manners." (There were as many young Negro barbarians in her charge as Jewish ones, but I doubt that she could ever bring herself to pay very much attention to them. As she never hesitated to make clear, it was punishment enough for a woman of her background—her family was old-Brooklyn and, she would have us understand, extremely distinguished —to have fallen among the sons of East European immigrant Jews.)

For three years, from the age of thirteen to the age of sixteen, I was her special pet, though that word is scarcely adequate to suggest the intensity of the relationship which developed between us. It was a relationship right out of *The Corn Is Green,* which may, for all I know, have served as her model; at any rate, her objective was much the same as the Welsh teacher's in that play: she was determined that I should win a scholarship to Harvard. But whereas (an irony much to the point here) the problem the teacher had in *The Corn Is Green* with her coal-miner pupil in the traditional class society of Edwardian England was strictly academic, Mrs. K.'s problem with me in the putatively egalitarian society of New Deal America was strictly social. My grades were very high and would obviously remain so, but what would they avail me if I continued to go about looking and sounding like a "filthy little slum child" (the epithet she would invariably hurl at me whenever we had an argument about "manners")?

Childless herself, she worked on me like a dementedly ambitious mother with a somewhat recalcitrant son; married to a solemn and elderly man (she was then in her early forties or thereabouts), she treated me like a cruelly ungrateful adolescent lover on whom she had humiliatingly bestowed her favors. She flirted with me and flattered me, she scolded me and insulted me. Slum child, filthy little slum child, so beautiful a mind and so vulgar a personality, so exquisite in sensibility and so coarse in manner. What would she do with me, what would become of me if I persisted out of stubbornness and perversity in the disgusting ways they had taught me at home and on the streets?

To her the most offensive of these ways was the style in which I dressed: a T-shirt, tightly pegged pants and a red satin jacket with the legend "Cherokees, S.A.C." (social-athletic club) stitched in large white letters across the back. This was bad enough, but when on certain days I would appear in school wearing, as a particular ceremonial occasion required, a suit and tie, the sight of those immense padded shoulders and my white-on-white shirt would drive her to even greater heights of contempt and even lower depths of loving despair than usual. *Slum child, filthy little slum child.* I was beyond saving; I deserved no better than to wind up with all the other horrible little Jewboys in the gutter (by which she meant Brooklyn College). If only I would listen to her, the whole world could be mine: I could win a scholarship to Harvard, I could get to know the best people, I could grow up into a life of elegance and refinement and taste. Why was I so stupid as not to understand?

II

In those days it was very unusual, and possibly even against the rules, for teachers in public high schools to associate with their students after hours. Nevertheless, Mrs. K. sometimes invited me to her home, a beautiful old brownstone located in what was perhaps the only section in the whole of Brooklyn fashionable enough to be intimidating. I would read her my poems and she would tell me about her family, about the schools she had gone to, about Vassar, about writers she had met, while her husband, of whom I was frightened to death and who to my utter astonishment turned out to be Jewish (but not, as Mrs. K. quite unnecessarily hastened to inform me, *my* kind of Jewish), sat stiffly and silently in an armchair across the room squinting at his newspaper through the first pince-nez I had ever seen outside the movies. He spoke to me but once, and that was after I had read Mrs. K. my tearful editorial for the school newspaper on the death of Roosevelt—an effusion which provoked him into a full five-minute harangue whose blasphemous contents would certainly have shocked me into insensibility if I had not been even more shocked to discover that he actually had a voice.

But Mrs. K. not only had me to her house; she also—what was even more unusual—took me out a few times, to the Frick Gallery and the Metropolitan Museum, and once to the theater, where we saw a dramatization of *The Late George Apley,* a play I imagine she deliberately chose with the not wholly mistaken idea that it would impress upon me the glories of aristocratic Boston.

One of our excursions into Manhattan I remember with particular vividness because she used it to bring the struggle between us to rather a dramatic head. The familiar argument began this time on the subway. Why, knowing that we would be spending the afternoon together "in public," had I come to school that morning improperly dressed? (I was, as usual, wearing my red satin club jacket over a white T-shirt.) She realized, of course, that I owned only one suit (this said not in compassion but in derision) and that my poor parents had, God only knew where, picked up the idea that it was too precious to be worn except at one of those bar mitzvahs I was always going to. Though why, if my parents were so worried about clothes, they had permitted me to buy a suit which made me look like a young hoodlum, she found it very difficult to imagine. Still, much as she would have been embarrassed to be seen in public with a boy whose parents allowed him to wear a zoot suit, she would have been somewhat less embarrassed than she was now by the ridiculous costume I had on. Had I no consideration for her? Had I no consideration for myself? Did I want everyone who laid eyes on me to think that I was nothing but an ill-bred little slum child?

My standard ploy in these arguments was to take the position that such things were of no concern to me: I was a poet and I had more important matters to think about than clothes. Besides, I would feel silly coming to school on an ordinary day dressed in a suit. Did Mrs. K. want me to look like one of those "creeps" from Crown Heights who were all going to become doctors? This was usually an effective counter, since Mrs. K. despised her middle-class Jewish students even more than she did the "slum children," but probably because she was growing desperate at the thought of how I would strike a Harvard interviewer (it was my senior year), she did not respond according to form on that particular occasion.

"At least," she snapped, "they reflect well on their parents."

I was accustomed to her bantering gibes at my parents, and sensing, probably, that they arose out of jealousy, I was rarely troubled by them. But this one bothered me; it went beyond banter and I did not know how to deal with it. I remember flushing, but I cannot remember what if anything I said in protest. It was the beginning of a very bad afternoon for both of us.

We had been heading for the Museum of Modern Art, but as we got off the subway, Mrs. K. announced that she had changed her mind about the museum. She was going to show me something else instead, just down the street on Fifth Avenue. This mysterious "something else" to which we proceeded in silence turned out to be the college department of an expensive clothing store, De Pinna. I do not exaggerate when I say that an actual physical dread seized me as I followed her into the store. I had never been inside such a store; it was not a store, it was enemy territory, every inch of it mined with humiliations. "I am," Mrs. K. declared in the coldest human voice I hope I shall ever hear, "going to buy you a suit that you will be able to wear at your Harvard interview." I had guessed, of course, that this was what she had in mind, and even at fifteen I understood what a fantastic act of aggression she was planning to commit against my parents and asking me to participate in. Oh no, I said in a panic (suddenly realizing that I *wanted* her to buy me that suit), I can't, my mother wouldn't like it. "You can tell her it's a birthday present. Or else I will tell her. If I tell her, I'm sure she won't object." The idea of Mrs. K. meeting my mother was more than I could bear: my mother, who spoke with a Yiddish accent and whom, until that sickening moment, I had never known I was so ready to betray.

To my immense relief and my equally immense disappointment, we left the store, finally, without buying a suit, but it was not to be the end of clothing or "manners" for me that day—not yet. There was still the ordeal of a restaurant to go through. Where I came from, people rarely ate in restaurants, not so much because most of them were too poor to afford such a luxury— although most of them certainly were—as because eating in restaurants was not regarded as a luxury at all; it was, rather, a necessity to which bachelors were pitiably condemned. A home-cooked meal was assumed to be better than anything one could possibly get in a restaurant, and considering the class of restaurants in question (they were really diners or luncheonettes), the assumption was probably correct. In the case of my own family, myself included until my late teens, the business of going to restaurants was complicated by the fact that we observed the Jewish dietary laws, and except in certain neighborhoods, few places could be found which served kosher food; in midtown Manhattan in the 1940s, I believe there were only two and both were relatively expensive. All this is by way of explaining why I had had so little experience of restaurants up to the age of fifteen and why I grew apprehensive once more when Mrs. K. decided after we left De Pinna that we should have something to eat.

The restaurant she chose was not at all an elegant one—I have, like a criminal, revisited it since—but it seemed very elegant indeed to me: enemy territory again, and this time a mine exploded in my face the minute I set foot through the door. The hostess was very sorry, but she could not seat the young gentleman without a coat and tie. If the lady wished, however, something could be arranged. The lady (visibly pleased by this unexpected—or was it expected?—object lesson) did wish, and the so recently defiant but by now utterly docile young gentleman was forthwith divested of his so recently beloved but by now thoroughly loathsome red satin jacket and provided with a much oversized white waiter's coat and a tie—which, there being no collar to a T-shirt, had to be worn around his bare neck. Thus attired, and with his face supplying the touch of red which had moments earlier been supplied by his jacket, he was led into the dining room, there to be taught the importance of proper table manners through the same pedagogic instrumentality that had worked so well in impressing him with the importance of proper dress.

Like any other pedagogic technique, however, humiliation has its limits, and Mrs. K. was to make no further progress with it that day. For I had had enough, and I was not about to risk stepping on another mine. Knowing she would subject me to still more ridicule if I made a point of my revulsion at the prospect of eating non-kosher food, I resolved to let her order for me and then to feign lack of appetite or possibly even illness when the meal was served. She did order—duck for both of us, undoubtedly because it would be a hard dish for me to manage without using my fingers.

The two portions came in deep oval-shaped dishes, swimming in a brown sauce and each with a sprig of parsley sitting on top. I had not the faintest idea of what to do—should the food be eaten directly from the oval dish or not?— nor which of the many implements on the table to do it with. But remembering that Mrs. K. herself had once advised me to watch my hostess in such a situation and then to do exactly as she did, I sat perfectly still and waited for her to make the first move. Unfortunately, Mrs. K. also remembered having taught me that trick, and determined as she was that I should be given a lesson that would force me to mend my ways, she waited too. And so we both waited, chatting amiably, pretending not to notice the food while it sat there getting colder and colder by the minute. Thanks partly to the fact that I would probably have gagged on the duck if I had tried to eat it—dietary taboos are very powerful if one has been conditioned to them—I was prepared to wait forever. And, indeed, it was Mrs. K. who broke first.

"Why aren't you eating?" she suddenly said after something like fifteen minutes had passed. "Aren't you hungry?" Not very, I answered. "Well," she said, "I think we'd better eat. The food is getting cold." Whereupon, as I watched with great fascination, she deftly captured the sprig of parsley between the prongs of her serving fork, set it aside, took up her serving spoon and delicately used those two esoteric implements to transfer a piece of duck from the oval dish to her plate. I imitated the whole operation as best as I could, but not well enough to avoid splattering some partly congealed sauce onto my borrowed coat in the process. Still, things could have been worse, and having more or less successfully negotiated my way around that particular mine, I now had to cope with the problem of how to get out of eating the duck. But I need not have worried. Mrs. K. took one bite, pronounced it inedible (it must have been frozen by then), and called in quiet fury for the check.

Several months later, wearing an altered but respectably conservative suit which had been handed down to me in good condition by a bachelor uncle, I presented myself on two different occasions before interviewers from Harvard and from the Pulitzer Scholarship Committee. Some months after that, Mrs. K. had her triumph: I won the Harvard scholarship on which her heart had been so passionately set. It was not, however, large enough to cover all expenses, and since my parents could not afford to make up the difference, I was unable to accept it. My parents felt wretched but not, I think, quite as wretched as Mrs. K. For a while it looked as though I would wind up in the "gutter" of Brooklyn College after all, but then the news arrived that I had also won a Pulitzer Scholarship which paid full tuition if used at Columbia, and a small stipend besides. Everyone was consoled, even Mrs. K. Columbia was at least in the Ivy League.

The last time I saw her was shortly before my graduation from Columbia and just after a story had appeared in the *Times* announcing that I had been awarded a fellowship which was to send me to Cambridge University. Mrs. K. had passionately wanted to see me in Cambridge, Massachusetts, but Cambridge, England, was even better. We met somewhere near Columbia for a drink, and her happiness over my fellowship, it seemed to me, was if anything exceeded by her delight at discovering that I now knew enough to know that the right thing to order in a cocktail lounge was a very dry martini with lemon peel, please.

III

Looking back now at the story of my relationship with Mrs. K. strictly in the context of the issue of class, what strikes me most sharply is the astonishing rudeness of this woman to whom "manners" were of such overriding concern. (This, as I have since had some occasion to notice, is a fairly common characteristic among members of the class to which she belonged.) Though she would not have admitted it, good manners to Mrs. K. meant only one thing: conformity to a highly stylized set of surface habits and fashions which she took, quite as a matter of course, to be superior to all other styles of social behavior. But in what did their superiority consist? Were her "good" manners derived from or conducive to a greater moral sensitivity than the "bad" manners I had learned at home and on the streets of Brownsville? I rather doubt it. The "crude" behavior of my own parents, for example, was then and is still marked by a tactfulness and a delicacy that Mrs. K. simply could not have approached. It is not that she was incapable of tact and delicacy; in certain moods she was (and manners apart, she was an extraordinarily loving and generous woman). But such qualities were neither built into nor expressed by the system of manners under which she lived. She was fond of quoting Cardinal Newman's definition of a gentleman as a person who could be at ease in any company, yet if anything was clear about the manners she was trying to teach me, it was that they operated—not inadvertently but by deliberate design—to set one at ease *only* with others similarly trained and to cut one off altogether from those who were not.

While I would have been unable to formulate it in those terms at the time, I think I must have understood perfectly well what Mrs. K. was attempting to communicate with all her talk about manners; if I had not understood it so well, I would not have resisted so fiercely. She was saying that because I was a talented boy, a better class of people stood ready to admit me into their ranks. But only on one condition: I had to signify by my general deportment that I acknowledged them as *superior* to the class of people among whom I happened to have been born. That was the bargain—take it or leave it. In resisting Mrs. K. where "manners" were concerned—just as I was later to resist many others—I was expressing my refusal to have any part of so brutal a bargain.

But the joke was on me, for what I did not understand—not in the least then and not for a long time afterward—was that in matters having to do with "art" and "culture" (the "life of the mind," as I learned to call it at Columbia), I was being offered the very same brutal bargain and accepting it with the wildest enthusiasm.

I have said that I did not, for all my bookishness, feel alienated as a boy, and this is certainly true. Far from dreaming of escape from Brownsville, I dreaded the thought of living anywhere else, and whenever my older sister, who hated the neighborhood, began begging my parents to move, it was invariably my howls of protest that kept them from giving in. For by the age of thirteen I had made it into the neighborhood big time, otherwise known as the Cherokees, S.A.C. It had by no means been easy for me, as a mediocre athlete and a notoriously good student, to win acceptance from a gang which prided itself mainly on its masculinity and its contempt for authority, but once this had been accomplished, down the drain went any reason I might earlier have had for thinking that life could be better in any other place. Not for nothing, then, did I wear that red satin jacket to school every day. It was my proudest possession, a badge of manly status, proving that I was not to be classified with the Crown Heights "creeps," even though my grades, like theirs, were high.

And yet, despite the Cherokees, it cannot be that I felt quite so securely at home in Brownsville as I remember thinking. The reason is that something extremely significant in this connection had happened to me by the time I first met Mrs. K.: without any conscious effort on my part, my speech had largely lost the characteristic neighborhood accent and was well on its way to becoming as neutrally American as I gather it now is.

Now whatever else may be involved in a nondeliberate change of accent, one thing is clear: it bespeaks a very high degree of detachment from the ethos of one's immediate surroundings. It is not a good ear alone, and perhaps not even a good ear at all, which enables a child to hear the difference between the way he and everyone else around him sound when they talk, and the way teachers and radio announcers—as it must have been in my case—sound. Most people, and especially most children, are entirely insensitive to such differences, which is why anyone who pays attention to these matters can, on the basis of a man's accent alone, often draw a reasonably accurate picture of his regional, social, and ethnic background. People who feel that they belong in their familiar surroundings—whether it be a place, a class, or a group— will invariably speak in the accent of those surroundings; in all likelihood, indeed, they will never have imagined any other possibility for themselves. Conversely, it is safe to assume that a person whose accent has undergone a radical change from childhood is a person who once had fantasies of escaping to some other world, whether or not they were ever realized.

But accent in America has more than a psychological or spiritual significance. "Her kerbstone English," said Henry Higgins of Eliza Doolittle, "will keep her in the gutter to the end of her days." Most Americans probably respond with a sense of amused democratic superiority to the idea of a society in which so trivial a thing as accent can keep a man down, and it is a good measure of our blindness to the pervasive operations of class that there has been so little consciousness of the fact that America itself is such a society. While the broadly regional accents—New England, Midwestern, Southern—enjoy more or less equal status and will not affect the economic or social chances of those who speak in them, the opposite is still surely true of any accent identifiably influenced by Yiddish, Italian, Polish, Spanish—that is, the languages of the major post-Civil War immigrant groups (among which may be included American-Irish). A man with such an accent will no longer be confined, as once he would almost automatically have been, to the working class, but unless his life, both occupational and social, is lived strictly within the milieu in whose tone of voice he speaks, his accent will at the least operate as an obstacle to be overcome (if, for example, he is a schoolteacher aspiring to be a principal), and at the most as an effective barrier to advancement (if, say, he is an engineer), let alone to entry into the governing elite of the country. (For better or worse, incidentally, these accents are not a temporary phenomenon destined to disappear with the passage of the generations, no more than ethnic consciousness itself is. I have heard third-generation American Jews of East European stock speaking with thicker accents than their parents.)

Clearly, then, while fancying myself altogether at home in the world into which I was born, I was not only more detached from it than I realized; I was also taking action—and of very fundamental kind—which would eventually make it possible for me to move into some other world. Yet I still did not recognize what I was doing—not in any such terms. My ambition was to be a great and famous poet, not to live in a different community, a different class, a different "world." If I had a concrete image of what greatness would mean socially, it was probably based on the famous professional boxer from our block who had moved to a more prosperous neighborhood but still spent his leisure time hanging around the corner candy store and the local poolroom with his old friends (among whom he could, of course, experience his fame far more sharply than he could have done among his newly acquired peers).

But to each career its own sociology. Boxers, unlike poets, do not undergo a cultural change in the process of becoming boxers, and if I was not brave enough or clever enough as a boy to see the distinction, others who knew me then were. "Ten years from now, you won't even want to talk to me, you won't even recognize me if you pass me on the street," was the kind of comment I frequently heard in my teens from women in the neighborhood, friends of my mother who were fond of me and nearly as proud as she was of the high grades I was getting in school and the prizes I was always winning. "That's crazy, you must be kidding," I would answer. They were not crazy and they were not kidding. They were simply better sociologists than I.

As, indeed, my mother herself was, for often in later years—after I had become a writer and an editor and was living only a subway ride away but in a style that was foreign to her and among people by whom she was intimidated—she would gaze wistfully at this strange creature, her son, and murmur, "I should have made him for a dentist," registering thereby her perception that whereas Jewish sons who grow up to be successes in certain occupations usually remain fixed in an accessible cultural ethos, sons who grow up into literary success are transformed almost beyond recognition and distanced almost beyond a mother's reach. My mother wanted nothing so much as for me to be a success, to be respected and admired. But she did not imagine, I think, that she would only purchase the realization of her ambition at the price of my progressive estrangement from her and her ways. Perhaps it was my guilt at the first glimmerings of this knowledge which accounted for my repression of it and for the obstinacy of the struggle I waged over "manners" with Mrs. K.

For what seemed most of all to puzzle Mrs. K., who saw no distinction between taste in poetry and taste in clothes, was that I could see no connection between the two. Mrs. K. knew that a boy from Brownsville with a taste for Keats was not long for Brownsville, and moreover would in all probability end up in the social class to which she herself belonged. How could I have explained to her that I would only be able to leave Brownsville if I could maintain the illusion that my destination was a place in some mystical country of the spirit and not a place in the upper reaches of the American class structure?

Saint Paul, who was a Jew, conceived of salvation as a world in which there would be neither Jew nor Greek, and though he may well have been the first, he was very far from the last Jew to dream such a dream of transcendence—transcendence of the actual alternative categories with which reality so stingily presents us. Not to be Jewish, but not to be Christian either; not to be a worker, but not to be a boss either; not—if I may be forgiven for injecting this banality out of my own soul into so formidable a series of fantasies—to be a slum child but not to be a snob either. How could I have explained to Mrs. K. that wearing a suit from De Pinna would for me have been something like the social equivalent of a conversion to Christianity? And how could she have explained to me that there was no socially neutral ground to be found in the United States of America, and that a distaste for the surroundings in which I was bred, and ultimately (God forgive me) even for many of the people I loved—and so a new taste for other kinds of people—how could she have explained that all this was inexorably entailed in the logic of a taste for the poetry of Keats and the painting of Cézanne and the music of Mozart?

Questions

1. *What is the function of the manners that Mrs. K. sought to teach?*
2. *What was the "brutal bargain"? Mr. Podhoretz rejected the "brutal bargain" but later accepted it—how and why?*
3. *Identify the symbols of class that concerned Mrs. K.*
4. *What were the strains or problems that upward social mobility presented for Mr. Podhoretz?*
5. *From information presented in this article, develop a convincing argument that (a) America has an open class system, and (b) America has a closed class system.*

Vuitton: Status Never
Comes Cheap

New York Times

It is important to let others know how "well-off" we are and status symbols do the job. Certain cars help—Porsche, Mercedes-Benz. The spectacular house at the right address with old master paintings on the wall certainly won't hurt. However, the super status symbols are known to only a few (what's a Facel Vega?) and the following article describes one of 1973's superstars.

NEW YORK

At one count, Barbara Hutton had 55 pieces of Vuitton luggage. Marlene Dietrich flew into New York last month with 23 Vuitton cases that took an entire limousine to transport.

The rich and fashionable who buy their groceries at London's Fortnum & Mason, their wines at Fauchon and their watches at Boucheron in Paris have always flocked to the Vuitton shop on the avenue Marceau in Paris or to Saks Fifth Avenue here when they needed a small trifle like a change purse ($75) or a wardrobe trunk tagged at over $2000.

Vuitton prices, most people agree, are outrageous. But status never comes cheap. The famous brown plastic (originally it was leather), embellished with geometric flowers and the crossed initials LV—for Louis Vuitton—makes one a member of a special coterie that understands quality and is willing to pay for it.

But now this exclusive club is being invaded even by people who can't pronounce the name (Vweetohn). Young mothers are hitching their Vuitton totes to baby carriages, hairdressers are carrying their brushes in them, and a housewife recently plunked down close to $500 for two cases at Saks' Vuitton shop.

As the Pucci dress was the visible status symbol of the 1960s, when secretaries skimped on lunches to buy the $200 Pucci prints and wore them day after day, the Vuitton bag now is the token that bestows instant good taste on its owner. Where once the happy few could spot their cases as they came off the luggage belts at airports, now they have to resort to distinguishing devices to find their possessions in a sea of Vuitton prints.

"I see every girl in town carrying a Vuitton satchel that costs $85," remarks a woman who prides herself on her fashion good sense. "Since it's nothing more than a half yard of plastic, a zipper and a couple of handles, why this ridiculous fad?"

Why indeed: Why did so many dogs receive Vuitton leashes (prices from $22.50 to $30) for Christmas that Saks is sold out of them? Why do people beg to buy the plastic by the yard to upholster their cars or cover their walls? (Vuitton refuses to sell the fabric.) Why did one Saks customer have an expensive case cut up so she could have shoes made?

"My bag is five years old," said a mink-coated young woman shopping on Fifth avenue. "It's getting to be embarrassing, now that you see so many of them."

However, most Vuitton carriers around New York are enthusiastic about theirs.

"It's the greatest," said blond Joyce Shindle, who is in theatrical management. "They're expensive, but you can carry them in the rain and nothing happens."

Just as the signed Pucci dress and designer scarves had their legions of imitators, Vuitton's LVs have boiled up an alphabet soup of initial-patterned bags.

Not all of them are as blatant copies as the plastic bags designed by Adolfo, where As replace LVs, but the colors and geometrics are similar. The Adolfo plastic tends to sag after a season's wear, but it can fool the uninitiated and prices are much lower: $21 for a shape similar to Vuitton's $115 one.

Will the Beautiful People be perturbed enough to boycott Vuitton now that they find their pet possession carried by the folks in tourist class? The next season or so should tell.

1. What is so special about a plastic bag? Why and how are status symbols created?

2. What are the status symbols common among your peers?

Black Like Me

John Howard Griffin

Race relations—relationships between people of differing racial categories—is a major area of sociological study. Often the focus is on the prejudice and discrimination that occur when people who differ by race or ethnicity come in contact with each other. Prejudice ignores the individual and his particular qualities or characteristics and groups him with others who happen to have the same skin color, the same religious beliefs, come from the same part of the country or world, or have some other characteristic in common. Discrimination refers to actual behavior unfavorable to a specific individual or group.

The following is from John Howard Griffin's book *Black Like Me*. Griffin is a white man who temporarily darkened his skin with chemicals and then traveled through the Deep South as a black.

November 14

In the bus station lobby, I looked for signs indicating a colored waiting room, but saw none. I walked up to the ticket counter. When the lady ticket-seller saw me, her otherwise attractive face turned sour, violently so. This look was so unexpected and so unprovoked I was taken aback.

"What do you want?" she snapped.

Taking care to pitch my voice to politeness, I asked about the next bus to Hattiesburg.

She answered rudely and glared at me with such loathing I knew I was receiving what the Negroes call "the hate stare." It was my first experience with it. It is far more than the look of disapproval one occasionally gets. This was so exaggeratedly hateful I would have been amused if I had not been so surprised.

I framed the words in my mind: "Pardon me, but have I done something to offend you?" But I realized I had done nothing—my color offended her.

"I'd like a one-way ticket to Hattiesburg, please," I said and placed a ten-dollar bill on the counter.

"I can't change that big a bill," she said abruptly and turned away, as though the matter were closed. I remained at the window, feeling strangely abandoned but not knowing what else to do. In a while she flew back at me, her face flushed, and fairly shouted: "I *told* you—I can't change that big a bill."

"Surely," I said stiffly, "in the entire Greyhound system there must be some means of changing a ten-dollar bill. Perhaps the manager—"

She jerked the bill furiously from my hand and stepped away from the window. In a moment she reappeared to hurl my change and the ticket on the counter with such force most of it fell on the floor at my feet. I was truly dumfounded by this deep fury that possessed her whenever she looked at me. Her performance was so venomous, I felt sorry for her. It must have shown in my expression, for her face congested to high pink. She undoubtedly considered it a supreme insolence for a Negro to dare to feel sorry for her.

I stooped to pick up my change and ticket from the floor. I wondered how she would feel if she learned that the Negro before whom she had behaved in such an unladylike manner was habitually a white man.

With almost an hour before bus departure, I turned away and looked for a place to sit. The large, handsome room was almost empty. No other Negro was there, and I dared not take a seat unless I saw some other Negro also seated.

Once again a "hate stare" drew my attention like a magnet. It came from a middle-aged, heavy-set, well dressed white man. He sat a few yards away, fixing his eyes on me. Nothing can describe the withering horror of this. You feel lost, sick at heart before such unmasked hatred, not so much because it threatens you as because it shows humans in such an inhuman light. You see a kind of insanity, something so obscene the very obscenity of it (rather than its threat) terrifies you. It was so new I could not take my eyes from the man's face. I felt like saying: "What in God's name are you doing to yourself?"

A Negro porter sidled over to me. I glimpsed his white coat and turned to him. His glance met mine and communicated the sorrow, the understanding.

"Where am I supposed to go?" I asked him.

He touched my arm in that mute and reassuring way of men who share a moment of crisis. "Go outside and around the corner of the building. You'll find the room."

The white man continued to stare, his mouth twisted with loathing as he turned his head to watch me move away.

In the colored waiting room, which was not labeled as such, but rather as COLORED CAFÉ, presumably because of interstate travel regulations, I took the last empty seat. The room was crowded with glum faces, faces dead to all enthusiasm, faces of people waiting.

December 1

I developed a technique of zigzagging back and forth. In my bag I kept a damp sponge, dyes, cleansing cream and Kleenex. It was hazardous, but it was the only way to traverse an area both as Negro and white. As I traveled, I would find an isolated spot, perhaps an alley at night or the brush beside a highway, and quickly apply the dye to face, hands and legs, then rub off and reapply until it was firmly anchored in my pores. I would go through the area as a Negro and then, usually at night, remove the dyes with cleansing cream and tissues and pass through the same area as a white man.

I was the same man, whether white or black. Yet when I was white, I received the brotherly-love smiles and the privileges from whites and the hate stares or obsequiousness from the Negroes. And when I was a Negro, the whites judged me fit for the junk heap, while the Negroes treated me with great warmth.

As the Negro Griffin, I walked up the steep hill to the bus station in Montgomery to get the schedule for buses to Tuskegee. I received the information from a polite clerk and turned away from the counter.

"Boy!" I heard a woman's voice, harsh and loud.

I glanced toward the door to see a large, matriarchical woman, elderly and impatient. Her pinched face grimaced and she waved me to her.

"Boy, come here. Hurry!"

Astonished, I obeyed.

"Get those bags out of the cab," she ordered testily, seeming outraged with my lack of speed.

Without thinking, I allowed my face to spread to a grin as though overjoyed to serve her. I carried her bags to the bus and received three haughty dimes. I thanked her profusely. Her eyebrows knitted with irritation and she finally waved me away.

I took the early afternoon bus for Tuskegee, walked through a Southern town of great beauty and tranquility. The famed Tuskegee Institute was, I learned, out of the city limits. In fact the major portion of Negro residential area is out of the city limits—put there when the city fathers decided it was the simplest way to invalidate the Negro vote in local elections.

The spirit of George Washington Carver hangs strongly over the campus— a quiet, almost hauntingly quiet area of trees and grass. It radiates an atmosphere of respect for the work of one's hands and mind, of human dignity. In interviews here, my previous findings were confirmed: with the exception of those trained in professions where they can set up independent practice, they can find jobs commensurate with their education only outside the South. I found an atmosphere of great courtesy, with students more dignified and more soberly dressed than one finds on most white campuses. Education for them is a serious business. They are so close to the days when their ancestors were kept totally illiterate, when their ancestors learned to read and write at the risk of severe punishment, that learning is an almost sacred privilege now. They see it also as the only possible way out of the morass in which the Negro finds himself.

Later that afternoon, after wandering around the town, I turned back toward the Institute to talk with the dean. A white man stood in front of a Negro recreation parlor near the college entrance gates and waved to me. I hesitated at first, fearing he would be just another bully. But his eyes pleaded with me to trust him.

I crossed slowly over to him.

"Did you want me?" I asked.

"Yes—could you tell me where is Tuskegee Institute?"

"Right there," I said, pointing to the gates a block away.

"Aw, I know it," he grinned. I smelled whisky in the fresh evening air. "I was just looking for an excuse to talk to you," he admitted. "Do you teach here?"

"No, I'm just traveling through," I said.

"I'm a Ph.D.," he said uncomfortably. "I'm from New York—down here as an observer."

"For some government agency?"

"No, strictly on my own," he said. I studied him closely, since other Negroes were beginning to watch us. He appeared to be in his early fifties and was well enough dressed.

"How about you and me having a drink?" he said.

"No, thanks," I said and turned away.

"Wait a minute, dammit. You people are my brothers. It's people like me that are your only hope. How do you expect me to observe if you won't talk to me?"

"Very well," I said. "I'll be glad to talk with you."

"Hell, I've observed all I can stomach," he said. "Let's us go get just roaring blinko drunk and forget all this damned prejudice stuff."

"A white man and a Negro," I laughed. "We'd both hear from the merciful Klan."

"Damned right—a white man and a Negro. Hell, I don't consider myself any better than you—not even as good, maybe. I'm just trying to show some brotherhood."

Though I knew he had been drinking, I wondered that an educated man and an observer could be so obtuse—could create such an embarrassing situation for a Negro.

"I appreciate it," I said stiffly. "But it would never work."

"They needn't know," he whispered, leaning close to me, an almost frantic look in his eyes as though he were begging not to be rejected. "I'm going to get soused anyway. Hell, I've had all this I can stand. It's just between you and me. We could go into the woods somewhere. Come on—for brotherhood's sake."

I felt great pity for him. He was obviously lonely and fearful of rejection by the very people he sought to help. But I wondered if he could know how offensive this over-weaning "brotherhood" demonstration was. Others stood by and watched with frowns of disapproval.

At that moment a Negro drove up in an old car and stopped. Ignoring the white man, he spoke to me. "Would you like to buy some nice fat turkeys?"

"I don't have any family here," I said.

"Wait a minute there," the white man said. "Hell, I'll buy all your turkeys . . . just to help out. I'll show you fellows that not all white men are bastards. How many've you got in there?" We looked into the car and saw several live turkeys in the back seat.

"How much for all of them?" the white man asked, pulling a ten-dollar bill from his wallet.

The vendor looked at me, puzzled, as though he did not wish to unload such a baggage on the generous white man.

"What can you do with them when you get them out of the car?" I asked.

"What're you trying to do," the white man asked belligerently, "kill this man's sale?"

The vendor quickly put in: "No . . . no, mister, he's not trying to do that. I'm glad to sell you all the turkeys you want. But where you want me to unload them? You live around here?"

"No, I'm just an observer. Hell, take the ten dollars. I'll give the damned turkeys away."

When the vendor hesitated, the white man asked: "What's the matter—did you steal them or something?"

"Oh, no sir . . ."

"You afraid I'm a cop or something?"

The unpardonable had been said. The white man, despite his protestations of brotherhood, had made the first dirty suggestion that came to his mind. He was probably unaware of it but it escaped none of us. By the very tone of his question he revealed his contempt for us. His voice had taken on a hard edge, putting us in our place, as they say. He had become just like the whites he decried.

"I didn't steal them," the turkey man said coldly. "You can come out to my farm. I've got more there."

The white man, sensing the change, the resentment, glared at me. "Hell, no wonder nobody has any use for you. You don't give a man a chance to be nice to you. And damn it, I'm going to put that in my report." He turned away grumbling. "There's something 'funny' about all of you." Then he raised his head toward the evening sky and announced furiously: "But before I do anything else, I'm going to get drunk, stinking drunk."

He stamped off down the road toward open country. Negroes around me shook their heads slowly, with regret. We had witnessed a pitiful one-man attempt to make up for some of the abuses the man had seen practiced against the Negro. It had failed miserably. If I had dared, I would have gone after him and tried to bridge the terrible gap that had come between him and us.

Instead, I walked to the street lamp and wrote in my notebook.

"We must return to them their lawful rights, assure equality of justice—and then everybody leave everybody else to hell alone. Paternalistic—we show our prejudice in our paternalism—we downgrade their dignity."

It was too late to visit the dean of Tuskegee, so I went to the bus station and boarded a bus for Atlanta, via Auburn, Alabama.

The trip was without incident until we changed buses at Auburn. As always, we Negroes sat at the rear. Four of us occupied the back bench. A large, middle-aged Negro woman sat in front of us to the left, a young Negro man occupied the seat in front of us to the right.

At one of the stops, two white women boarded and could find no place to sit. No gallant Southern white man (or youth) rose to offer them a place in the "white section."

The bus driver called back and asked the young Negro man and the middle-aged Negro woman to sit together so the white women could have one of the seats. Both ignored the request. We felt the tensions mount as whites craned to stare at us.

A redheaded white man in a sports shirt stood up, faced the rear and called to the Negro. "Didn't you hear the driver? Move out, man."

"They're welcome to sit here," the Negro said quietly, indicating the empty seat beside him and the one beside the woman across the aisle.

The driver looked dumfounded and then dismayed. He walked halfway to the rear and, struggling to keep his voice under control, said: "They don't want to sit with you people, don't you know that? They don't want to—is that plain enough?"

We felt an incident boiling, but none of us wanted the young Negro, who had paid for his ticket, to be forced to vacate his seat. If the women did not want to sit with us, then let one of the white men offer his seat and he could come and sit with us. The young Negro said no more. He gazed out the window.

The redhead bristled. "Do you want me to slap these two jigaboos out of their seats?" he asked the driver in a loud voice.

We winced and turned into mummies, staring vacantly, insulating ourselves against further insults.

"No—for God's sake—please—no rough stuff," the driver pleaded.

One of the white women looked toward us apologetically, as though she were sorry to be the cause of such a scene. "It's all right," she said. "Please . . ." asking the driver and the young man to end their attempts to get her a seat.

The redhead flexed his chest muscles and slowly took his seat, glaring back at us. A young teen-ager, sitting halfway to the front, sniggered: "Man, he was going to slap that nigger, all right." The white bully was his hero, but other whites maintained a disapproving silence.

At the Atlanta station we waited for the whites to get off. One of them, a large middle-aged man, hesitated, turned and stepped back toward us. We hardened ourselves for another insult. He bent over to speak to the young Negro. "I just wanted to tell you that before he slapped you, he'd have had to slap me down first," he said.

None of us smiled. We wondered why he had not spoken up while whites were still on the bus. We nodded our appreciation and the young Negro said gently: "It happens to us all the time."

"Well, I just wanted you to know—I was on your side, boy." He winked, never realizing how he had revealed himself to us by calling our companion by the hated name of "boy." We nodded wearily in response to his parting nod.

I was the last to leave the bus. An elderly white man, bald and square of build, dressed in worn blue work clothes, peered intently at me. Then he crimped his face as though I were odious and snorted, "Phew!" His small blue eyes shone with repugnance, a look of such unreasoning contempt for my skin that it filled me with despair.

It was a little thing, but piled on all the other little things it broke something in me. Suddenly I had had enough. Suddenly I could stomach no more of this degradation—not of myself but of all men who were black like me. Abruptly I turned and walked away. The large bus station was crowded with humanity. In the men's room, I entered one of the cubicles and locked the door. For a time I was safe, isolated; for a time I owned the space around me, though it was scarcely more than that of a coffin. In medieval times, men sought sanctuary in churches. Nowadays, for a nickel, I could find sanctuary in a colored rest room. Then, sanctuary had the smell of incense-permeated walls. Now it had the odor of disinfectant.

The irony of it hit me. I was back in the land of my forefathers, Georgia. The town of Griffin was named for one of them. Too I, a Negro, carried the name hated by all Negroes, for former Governor Griffin (no kin that I would care to discover) devoted himself heroically to the task of keeping Negroes "in their place." Thanks in part to his efforts, this John Griffin celebrated a triumphant return to the land from which his people had sprung by seeking sanctuary in a toilet cubicle at the bus station.

I took out my cleansing cream and rubbed it on my hands and face to remove the stain. I then removed my shirt and undershirt, rubbed my skin almost raw with the undershirt, and looked into my hand mirror. I could pass for white again. I repacked my duffel, put my shirt and coat back on and wondered how I could best leave the colored rest room without attracting attention. I guessed it was near midnight, but the traffic in and out remained heavy.

Oddly, there was little of the easy conversation one generally hears in public rest rooms, none of the laughter and "woofing." I waited, listening to footsteps come and go, to the water-sounds of hand-washing and flushing.

Much later, when I heard no more footsteps, I stepped from my cubicle and walked toward the door that led into the main waiting room. I hurried into the crowd unnoticed.

The shift back to white status was always confusing. I had to guard against the easy, semiobscene language that Negroes use among themselves, for coming from a white man it is insulting. It was midnight. I asked a doorman where to find a room for the night. He indicated a neon sign that stood out against the night sky—YMCA, only a block or so away. I realized that though I was well dressed for a Negro, my appearance looked shabby for a white man. He judged me by that and indicated a place where lodging was inexpensive.

Questions

1. *"A caste system accurately describes America's relations between the races. . . ." Discuss.*
2. *Describe the forms of racism (differential treatment because of race) that took place in the incident with the white "observer" and in the incident on the bus.*
3. *Analyze and explain Griffin's experiences in terms of (a) prejudice and discrimination, and (b) status differences.*

The Womanly Image:
Character Assassination
Through the Ages

Paula Stern

Women in the U.S. represent a numerical majority but have minority status. Traditionally, women, like blacks, have been the last hired and the first fired. Even when a woman does the same work as a man she gets paid less for it. Women make up about 3 percent of the nation's lawyers and 8 percent of our doctors; women constitute 85 percent of the elementary school teachers but only 21 percent of the principals.

Paula Stern analyzes how women historically have been typed and stereotyped into status and role. "It's marriage and motherhood for girls, while it's education and career for boys." She describes how our society (even in the face of women's liberation movements) continually socializes women into subservient positions.

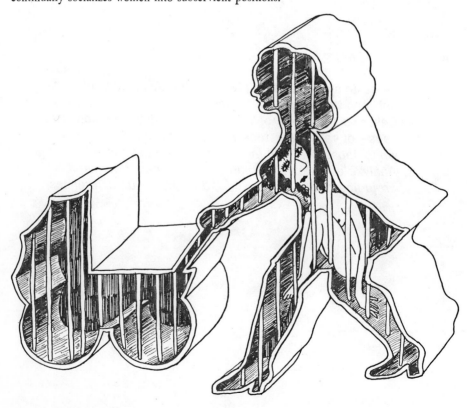

I had a job interview several weeks ago. Friends warned me not to be too aggressive. During the interview, I tried to present myself as a competent candidate, able to "think like a man" and yet not to be a "masculine" female. After fielding several questions relevant to the job, I suddenly heard, "Miss Stern, are you in love?"

Do you think they asked my competition—seven men—the same question? No, for a cultureful of reasons. Jacqueline Kennedy Onassis was quoted once as saying, "There are two kinds of women: those who want power in the world and those who want power in bed." And the majority seem to agree with Jackie that the latter is socially more acceptable. That's how many men think women ought to think.

Children are taught sexual stereotypes early, as well as the appropriate behavior for a sex-determined role in life. Asking a little boy, "What do you want to be when you grow up?" implies to him unlimited possibilities in his future. But most often we ask a little girl, "Where did you get that pretty dress?" suggesting she has only one real option open to her. If we do ask her what she wants to be, she's likely to give the conditioned female response—"A mother." Why? So she can replace her dolls with real babies.

The inspiration for teaching girls to expect less than boys comes from a range of cultural sources, religious, literary, psychiatric, and pop. Even in the Bible, exceptional, independent women like Rebecca, Sarah, Deborah, or Ruth are practically "unknowns" compared with infamous Eve or Delilah.

Eve was made from one of Adam's spare parts, almost as an afterthought, to help him out on earth: "And the Lord God said: 'It is not good that the man should be alone; I will make him a helpmeet for him.'"

There is a contrary legend of the first female, Lilith, who was created equal to man.

> When the Lord created the world and the first man, he saw that man was alone, and quickly created a woman for him, made like him from the earth, and her name was Lilith. Right away, they began to quarrel. He would say "You sleep on the bottom," and she would say "No, you sleep on the bottom, since we are equals and both formed from the earth. . . ." When Lilith saw what the situation was, she pronounced the Ineffable Name and disappeared into thin air.

But Eve, not Lilith, is the prototypal woman—man's little helper, and his temptress.

Today the heirs to the Bible in America—Jews and Christians—have formalized biblical biases in laws and ceremonies and thereby elevated folklore to religious truths. Among the Orthodox Jews, for example, discrimination against women is so blatant that they are forced to sit segregated behind a curtain or in a balcony. The rationale is that women will distract men from their prayers. It is no wonder that men thank God every morning in their ritual prayer "that Thou has not made me a woman."

The majority of Jews have modified most traditional formalities, but independent female expression is still discouraged if outside the confines of the home or not channeled through husband and children.

A Jewish wife is less subservient to her husband than a gentile wife; so say comparative studies on the subject. That's somewhat understandable since Christianity owes much to a prominent classical heritage, that held the second sex in even lower esteem. Utopia for the male chauvinist is Demosthenes' description of Hellenic male-female arrangements: "We have hetairae for the pleasure of the spirit, concubines for sensual pleasure, and wives to bear our sons."

Aristotle's definition of femininity was "a certain lack of qualities; we should regard the female nature as afflicted with a natural defectiveness." And his disciple Saint Thomas Aquinas echoed him religiously: ". . . a female is something deficient and by chance."

Contempt for women helps explain why they can't become Catholic priests, and why theologians, religious education courses, and Catholic marriage manuals highlight the supposedly inferior and passive qualities of women, who "naturally" subordinate themselves to men.

Traditional Protestant marriage services also perpetuate the attitude that the female is a second-class human being. Like a piece of property, the bride is "given" by her father to the groom, whom she promises to "obey." (Although formally removed from the liturgy, this vow still persists in the popular image of the wedding ceremony.) The clergyman reminds her of her proper place when he says, "I pronounce that they are man and wife." Not husband and wife. Not man and woman. The man keeps his status, while she takes on a new one. Her identity vanishes when she sheds her maiden name for his identification. (Blackstone's *Commentaries* on the law strips a married woman of her rights altogether as she legally dies on her wedding day and becomes "incorporated and consolidate with her husband." Accordingly, "A man cannot grant anything to his wife for the grant would be to suppose her separate existence.")

Although reputedly "progressing" beyond the attitudes of antiquity and the Middle Ages, our enlightened European ancestors continued furnishing us some not too enlightened guidelines on a woman's place—or lack of it—in the world.

High school English students learn from Shakespeare that "Frailty, thy name is woman." Rousseau's contribution to the ideas of man's equality and natural goodness makes one exception: "Woman was made to yield to man and put up with his injustice."

Samuel Johnson's word to the wise woman is that "a man is in general better pleased when he has a good dinner upon his table, than when his wife talks Greek." Honoré de Balzac adds, "A woman who is guided by the head and not the heart is a social pestilence: she has all the defects of a passionate and affectionate woman with none of her compensations: she is without pity, without love, without virtue, without sex."

When in 1776 in America, Abigail Adams asked her husband, John Adams, to "be more generous and favorable to them [women] than your ancestors" and to see to it that the new government not "put such unlimited power into the hands of the husbands," John reportedly chuckled. The Continental Congress ignored her. Two hundred years later Spiro Agnew said: "Three things have been difficult to tame—the ocean, fools, and women. We may soon be able to tame the ocean; fools and women will take a little longer."

America's twentieth-century gospel is the work of Freud. Although Freud supposedly has altered the entire course of Western intellectual history, many of his ideas about women are simply male chauvinism. Letters he wrote his fiancée reveal that he, too, wanted his woman kept relatively docile and ignorant so she couldn't compete with him.

His theories have given scientific status to prejudice. The Freudians— psychiatrists, clinical psychologists, psychiatric social workers, marriage counselors, pastoral counselors, educators, writers, literary critics, historians, anthropologists, sociologists, criminologists, and just plain subway psychiatrists in the newspapers, magazines, and on TV—all subscribe to the belief that "anatomy is destiny." In other words, biological differences between the sexes determine personality differences; standards of mental health depend on the sex of the sick.

How? Dr. Judd Marmor, clinical professor of psychiatry at UCLA, has summarized Freud's views on feminine psychology:

The most significant of the biological factors . . . is the lack of penis, which inevitably leads to "penis envy" in the woman. Freud considered penis envy to be a dominant theme in all feminine life, and one that inevitably causes women to feel inferior to men. These deep seated feelings of inadequacy can be compensated for only partially by giving birth to a male child. . . .

Masochism and passivity . . . are natural aspects of normal femininity and whenever a woman behaves in non-passive or aggressive ways or competes with men, she is being neurotically unfeminine. . . .

The most complicated sequence of personality development that women are subject to . . . leads inevitably . . . to less adequate superego formation than in men. This presumably is reflected in women having a poorer sense of justice and weaker social interests than men have.

The myths of marriage counselor G. C. Payetter (from his book *How To Get and Hold a Woman*) have been praised by a number of psychiatrists, and he is consulted in earnest by troubled people. Payetter counsels:

> *Feelings, moods, and attitude . . . rule a woman, not facts, reason, nor logic.*
> *By herself woman is all mixed-up but superb as an auxiliary (Genesis: helper).*
> *Woman is inanimate or on the defensive until you create a feeling such as a praise. Then she goes all out.*
> *Never scold or explain when she is angry, remember she is feeling not thinking. . . .*
> *Stop bossing; just manipulate her in her feelings. . . .*
> *The acquisition of knowledge or responsibilities does not lessen women's need for support, guidance, and control. Quite the contrary.*
> *Why ask women when they only need to be told? Why ask women when they hope to be taken?*

Any resemblance between women and pet dogs or mute concubines is purely coincidental. No doubt, Payetter's model woman is the runner-up to this year's Miss America, who said women shouldn't try to run things "because they are more emotional and men can overcome their emotions with logic."

Even more objectionable are psychiatrist-authors who pronounce final judgment on the mental health of thousands of women reading books like *The Power of Sexual Surrender*. Featured in the book, which has had at least ten paperback printings and been excerpted in *Pageant* magazine, is "The Masculine Woman." (Doctor, how can a woman be a female and be masculine simultaneously?) She's "frigid"—"a driving, competitive woman who was very successful in the business world, having graduated from a leading woman's college." "Clear thinking and logical mind, her emotionless almost masculine forthrightness in expressing herself belied her softly feminine appearance." Surrendering to her "real nature," the doctor's cure, is the only way she can be mentally healthy. Then miraculously

> *. . . those details of life that once seemed so difficult become simple. And because they are feminine tasks, household work, planning and getting dinners, keeping the children busy or in line—whatever life demands—soon lose*

*their irksome and irritating quality and become easy, even
joyful. . . . At this juncture, or closely following on it, a
woman begins to feel her full power, the power that comes
to her for her surrender to her destiny.*

The spuriously Freudian vision of a truly "feminine" female serves the
purposes of admen who woo women to spend millions on clothes and cosmetics
in vain pursuit of their "real nature." To sell a new product, industry need only
simultaneously make the product and manufacture anxiety in gals, pressing
them to consume or be consumed in a female identity crisis. For example, featured in every women's magazine, including those for teen-agers, are the latest
advertising campaigns for vaginal deodorants, a "female necessity." One
called Cupid's Quiver comes in four flavors—Orange Blossom, Raspberry,
Champagne, or Jasmine. Madison Avenue courts the female, even seducing
minors. Teenform, Inc., manufacturers of bras for teen-agers, estimates that
nine-year-olds spend $2 million on bras annually.

Ingenue magazine pushes teen-agers into adult posturing. The format is
peppered with advertisements for engagement rings, pictures of desirable
adolescent boys, and occasionally a plan of attack such as dinners for two.
The ads for cosmetics and clothes are practically identical to those in magazines
designed for their mothers. Typical of women's magazines, *Ingenue* includes
at least one psychologically centered article. Recently, it explained in "The
Hardest Thing About Growing Up" that "inevitably, relationships with boys
affect relationships with girls." It condoned the statement, "I don't trust other
girls in the same way anymore. They become rivals." This is how girls learn
the platitudes: women can't work with other women when men are around,
and never work for a woman.

If a girl manages to survive *Ingenue* without succumbing to marriage,
Glamour picks her up. ("How Five Groovy Men Would Make You Over
Into Their Dream Girls") Where the boys are is where it's at for the reader
who is shunted from high school to college to career to marriage to mother-
hood—"Find Your New Look. College Into Career Make-over. Job Into Mother
Make-over."

The lucky gal who's made the grade by landing a man is promoted to
Modern Bride, which induces her to buy "utterly feminine" wedding gowns,
bride-and-groom matching wedding rings, silver, china, furniture, ad nauseam.
The wedding itself is big business; Wediquette International, Inc., offers total
planning—the place, time, invitations, gown, caterers, florist, photographer . . . .

Ah, then conjugal bliss—and of course, a magazine for mothers. *Redbook*
boasts its biggest year because it knows "Young Mamas Spend More Than Big
Daddies" and so talks "to that 18–34 year old the way she wants to be
talked to," which means in baby talk or kitchen chatter.

McCall's claims 16 million matrons who "buy more than the readers of any other woman's service magazine." Its reader "buys more cosmetics and toiletries, more prepared foods, owns more life insurance, more automobiles . . . ."

Although *Cosmopolitan* says its reader is the career woman who desires success in her own right, it is pitched to the gal who missed the marriage boat the first time around. Female passivity is still the accepted mode of behavior. She can be assertive in the office, but when man-hunting after five, she must be seductively submissive. Who knows? She might hook a divorced man or married man looking for an affair.

Cosmo repeats an old tip from Jackie and Delilah—sex is a woman's hidden arsenal. Under a pseudonym, "a well-known American gynecologist" instructs readers "How to Love Like a Real Woman." "If your man bawls at you and you know you are in the right, what should you do?" "You should take your clothes off. Sex is a woman's strongest weapon. It is her proper weapon."

Taking a cue from *The Power of Sexual Surrender,* the expert explains, "Women must give and give and give again because it is their one and only way to obtain happiness for themselves." Further, "To argue is a male activity. To fight is a male activity. I say to women: 'Don't become a man in skirts. Don't fight. Don't argue. . . .' " Any female who would practice this advice must be masochistic—typical of a "normal" female, according to Freudian thought.

A popular misconception is that in time education will erase all the ill effects of thinking in stereotypes. But the educational system takes over where cultural myths, Freudian folklore, and the media leave off in depressing a girl's aspirations and motivations. All along, she's taught to accept a double standard for success and self-esteem: It's marriage and motherhood for girls, while it's education and career for boys. She's pushed to be popular, date, and marry young (more than half of all American women are married before the age of twenty-one). Success in school only inhibits her social life. Intellectual striving, a necessity for academic success, is considered competitively aggressive; that is unnatural and unladylike behavior, since the essence of femininity, she has learned, is repressing aggressiveness. Telling her she thinks like a man is a backhanded compliment, which is discouraging if she has tried to be a woman using her brains, not sex, in the classroom and office.

While girls outperform boys intellectually in prepuberty, attrition in IQ sets in during adolescence when they learn from new, extracurricular lessons that looks, not brains, are what counts. After high school, achievement in terms of productivity and accomplishment drops off even more. More than 75 percent (some say as high as 95 percent) of all qualified high-schoolers not entering college are girls. Those who go attend more for husband-hunting than for educational self-advancement; one study at a Midwestern university revealed 70 percent of the freshmen women were there for an MRS. Women

BA's are less than half as likely to try for a graduate degree as equally qualified men.

Women should not be given an even break in education and careers, says a clichéd argument, because they will get married and quit anyway. But that's because they are given an arbitrary, unfair option which men aren't forced to accept—either career or marriage. Career opportunities and salary levels for women are so poor that a calculating female would figure marriage is a better bargain. Once married, she can stop fighting the stereotypes and start teaching them to her children.

Questions

1. Describe the typical socialization process that prepares women for the role of motherhood.
2. Our culture broadcasts a desirable female stereotype and an undesirable female stereotype. Describe these.
3. How would Marxist theory explain discrimination against women?
4. Argue the proposition that motherhood for American women is an ascribed rather than an achieved status.
5. Do any of the minority group reactions discussed in the text apply to women? If so, show how.

6

Institutions

The concept *institution* is a major unit of analysis and description for sociologists. Like many words, "institution" has a variety of meanings in general usage. For most of us the word "institution" brings to mind a prison— San Quentin or Sing Sing—or a mental hospital. Or "institution" may refer to a building or to a particularly familiar practice or object. Most sociologists, however, use "institution" in a different and specific way. Horton and Hunt define an institution as "an organized system of social relationships which embodies certain common values and procedures and meets certain basic needs of society." According to Bierstedt, an institution represents an organized way of doing something.[1] All societies have certain important central needs, problems, or functions that must be dealt with, and it is around these

---

[1] Paul Horton and Chester Hunt, *Sociology*, 3rd Ed. (New York: McGraw-Hill Book Co., 1972), p. 177; and Robert Bierstedt, *The Social Order*, 3rd Ed. (New York: McGraw-Hill Book Co., 1970), p. 320.

that institutions—systems of social relationships, ways of doing something—evolve. For example, the following are some of the central needs and concerns that societies face: reproduction of the species, socialization of the young, a way of dealing with the unknown or uncertain, distribution of goods and services, a way of governing people. Different societies handle these concerns in different ways, but eventually an institution emerges that is made up of shared values and practices relating to the core concern. We may relate the societal concerns just mentioned to their evolving institutions. For example, reproduction and maintenance of the species give rise to the institution of the *family*. Socialization and training of the young to take an active part in society describes the central focus of the institution of *education*. The institution of *religion* might arise because of a need to deal with the unknown. Systems for distribution of goods and services relate to *economic* institutions, and *governmental* institutions arise from the necessity for rules and regulations governing man's behavior. In fact, sociologists frequently talk in terms of these five major, basic institutions: familial, educational, religious, economic, and governmental. By describing them as basic we mean that all societies show evidence of these institutions in some form. This does not mean, however, that these are the only institutions. Indeed, one might argue that in modern industrialized societies with emerging and constantly changing needs, other "newer" institutions have surpassed some older ones in significance and importance. For example, we see the institution of *science* (explanation for the unknown again?) and the institution of *leisure* (what does man do with his ever-increasing free time, time away from work?).

Although the same institutions are found in many societies, the content of the institution is not the same in every society. The mountain-dwelling Arapesh of New Guinea and the campus-dwelling college students of America both operate within an institution of the family, for example, which involves elaborate procedures for "courtship," "marriage," and raising of children, and yet, within this institution, the specific practices of the two "societies" are vastly different. Not only will the content be different, but the same institution in different societies may focus on different cultural concerns and serve different functions.

Institutions change, as do all aspects of human behavior. Change in institutions probably occurs more slowly than does change in values and attitudes of people or in other aspects of social organization. Institutional change also varies from one society to another. To make a comparison of extremes, modern industrialized countries for the most part change more rapidly than primitive preliterate societies. Even within one society, one institution will change slowly, another rapidly. We will discuss social change in more detail in a later chapter.

In the previous chapter we approached social organization by discussing groups, categories, and aggregations of people. Here we approach social organization by considering institutions. The concept "institution" is more abstract and possibly more difficult to understand than the previous concepts dealing with concrete entities—numbers of people. These two approaches are not really separate but represent two different levels of analysis. My family constitutes a small group within the institution of the family. I belong to a sociology department (smaller, somewhat primary group) at a college (larger, more secondary and bureaucratic group) within the institution of education. Part of my behavior in each situation is best explained by understanding the dynamics and characteristics of group behavior and of the particular type of group to which I belong. Another part of my behavior is best explained by understanding the attitudes, values, norms, procedures, and symbols that are part of the institutions of the family or education.

"Institution," then, is a concept that sociologists use to describe a certain type of social organization. This concept will be better understood if we see how it is applied to specific areas of human behavior. Following are discussions of two institutions—family and religion.

Family

Sociologists have always looked with great interest on the institution of the family. This is partly because we tend to see the family as the most basic of all institutions, and probably also because there are such tremendous variations in family practices from one culture to another. These variations fascinate us—sociologists and sociology students alike—because we are, most of us, at least a little ethnocentric. We know that our way is the right way and best way and it amazes us how some weird tribes could behave so differently. In discussing the family here, we will first examine these structural variabilities, then functional uniformities or similarities, and conclude with a brief analysis of the family in the United States.

Structural Variabilities

Anthropologists, after studying primitive societies all over the world, report that the structure of the family is almost infinitely variable. Imagine almost anything, and there is probably at least one society someplace that practices it (and they would be aghast if they knew the strange things *we* were doing).

It all starts (usually) by "marriage." This may involve extensive dating leading up to the fateful act. Or you may inherit a wife—often a dead brother's widow. Or the parents may make the choice for you. Or you may buy a wife or two. Or you may capture one. On the east coast of Greenland, the man goes to the girl's tent, grabs her by the hair, and drags her off to his tent. Violent scenes result because single women always act very shy and resistant to marriage. Otherwise they might lose their reputation for modesty and be considered loose women. At any rate, whom you may date, buy, inherit, or capture is determined by whether your society practices *endogamy* (marriage within a certain group) or *exogamy* (marriage outside that certain group). In the United States we practice both. We forbid marriage within the immediate family, and it is necessary to marry an outsider: exogamy. At the same time interracial marriages are often discouraged, and some religious groups encourage their members to marry people of the same faith: endogamy. The number of spouses you may have at one time varies depending on the culture in which you live. Two major types of marriage are called monogamy and polygamy. *Monogamy* means one man for one wife at a time. It is estimated that most people in the world practice monogamy. The United States is technically monogamous, but with our high rate of divorce and family instability it might be more accurate to say that we practice a type of serial, consecutive, or musical-chairs monogamy. *Polygamy* means plural marriage and includes three types: polygyny, polyandry, and group marriage. Polygyny refers to the practice of one man having several wives at a time. G. P. Murdock studied 250 societies and found that polygyny was the preferred form of marriage in seventy-seven percent of them, although, as mentioned above, most people in the world practice monogamy.[2] Even in polygynous societies, most people practice monogamy. Although both sexes favor polygyny in such societies, the wealthy are more able to afford it and are more likely to practice it. Polyandry refers to the very rare practice of one woman having several husbands, and group marriage describes the practice of "mutual marriage" between several men and several women. Polyandry, when it occurs, is usually found in poor societies with a shortage of women. Occasionally such societies kill girl babies to keep the population down. When the woman becomes pregnant, deciding which husband is the father is a problem. This is usually solved by some sort of ceremony—possibly by shooting arrows at a distant target and designating the owner of the nearest arrow to be the father.

Rules of residence prescribe where the newlyweds may live after marriage, and these also vary from one society to another. In *patrilocal* societies the couple lives with the husband's family. In *matrilocal* societies they live with the wife's family, while in *bilocal* societies they alternate between wife's and husband's families. Some tribes are *neolocal*—the couple lives apart from both families (as in the United States). Ancestry is traced in a variety of ways, which gives rise to rules of descent. Some of the popular methods include *patrilineal* (ancestry traced through males), *matrilineal* (ancestry traced through females), and *bilateral* (both sides equally). As to who has the authority in

[2] George P. Murdock, *Social Structure* (New York: Macmillan Co., 1949), p. 28.

the family and makes the decisions, in *patriarchal* societies it is the male and in *matriarchal* societies, the female. It is interesting to note that many of the different practices we have mentioned arise at least partially in reaction to the incest taboo. All societies deny sexual access between certain family members, and these restrictions are called incest taboos. The particular lines of the taboo vary from one society to another. To help regulate the situation, various rules—residence, descent, etc.—were developed. It should be clear by now that almost any imaginable practice exists in some society somewhere. Anything and everything seem to "work."

A number of other terms have emerged that help describe aspects of family structure. The family one is born into is called the family of *orientation*. The family of which one is a parent is called the family of *procreation*. The *nuclear* family, a much-used term today, refers to the married couple and their children. The *conjugal* family is one related by marital ties; the *consanguine* family is one related by blood ties. Finally, *extended* and *compound* families differ from the nuclear family in that the extended family includes more than two generations in close association or under the same roof and the compound family refers to marriages involving multiple spouses—several wives and/or husbands at the same time.

In summary, we could describe the peculiar American family as a nuclear, monogamous, bilateral, neolocal, patriarchal, conjugal, exogamous structure practicing marriage by mutual capture.

Functional Uniformities

The institution of the family exists in all societies in some form. Therefore it must serve a purpose, fill basic needs, and perform essential tasks. Those who have studied family institutions have discovered a number of such functions, some obvious and important and some less obvious. An obvious function of the family is to provide for continuation of the species. Societies, to exist, need people; the institution of the family functions to control reproduction. A second function of the family is control of sex expression. The family institution attempts to deal with powerful sexual needs and desires by defining the who, when, where, why, and how of sexual activity.

A third function of the family is to care for and socialize children. The baby cannot survive without the substantial care which the family provides. Socialization of the young by the family transmits the culture and prepares the child for participation in the adult world. Much of the child's later life is patterned on family models. It is possible that personal pathology and individual unhappiness will follow from inadequate family models or a bad family atmosphere. It may frequently be the case that the child is the defenseless target of the parents' own frustrations, anxieties, neuroses, and maladjustments.

The family may also function to provide close affectional and emotional ties for the individual. In some societies, many groups and associations may perform this function, but in mass, industrialized, secondary societies like the United States, the family may be one of the few remaining places where primary relationships are possible. The family also functions to provide placement or status ascription. The family we are born into provides us with a *place* in society. If a person is a Protestant, middle-class, Midwestern, American Democrat, it is more than likely that he is because he "inherited" certain statuses—religion, social class, region, nationality, political preference—from his family of orientation.

These are some of the functions of the family, and there are probably others. These functions are not necessarily completely separate from each other —reproduction of the species and control of sex expression would seem to be related. And further, other institutions may serve some of the same functions the family institution serves. The institution of education certainly deals with socialization of the young and transmission of culture, as does the institution of religion.

Family in America

The American family of today is smaller than it used to be in several ways. On the average there are fewer children. Birth control techniques and changing values have led to fewer large families. The American family is also small in that it is a nuclear rather than an extended family. Grandparents and other relatives live elsewhere, and in fact the children will leave too at an earlier age. The family today is probably more egalitarian and less patriarchal than it used to be. Some observers argue that in some segments of the U.S. population—the suburban middle class, for example—authority has switched, and now the woman of the family is making many of the important decisions. If these families are not matriarchal, they are at least matricentric—woman-centered. The woman has developed equality in other ways relating to family structure. She is more likely to be working outside the home while married. The possibility of career has given her alternatives to early marriage or even marriage at all. If she does marry, she has a greater choice in the type of role she may play as wife.

The family of today is more urbanized, more geographically mobile, and less rigid or orthodox in religious beliefs. The family used to be the all-powerful institution, but gradually other institutions—religious, educational, governmental—have taken over some of the functions that the family formerly handled. So far this has resulted not in the disappearance of the family but in increased emphasis or importance of the remaining functions that the family fills and a jealous guarding of them: "Sex education in the schools?? Certainly not!!! In the home where it belongs!" As mentioned before, it may be that one of the major functions of the family in mass society is to provide for the affectional and emotional needs of people. The family is nearly the last refuge of the true primary type of relationship, and if it is accurate to call this a basic social need, then this function of the family becomes exceedingly important as other functions decrease in importance.

Finally, the American family shows many elements of instability. Our divorce rate ranks high compared to other countries. Nationwide, there is more than one divorce for every four marriages, while in California currently the ratio is one divorce for every two marriages. Crime and delinquency are on the increase, and to a certain extent the family must bear responsibility. Youth are increasingly challenging the authority and wisdom of their elders. When we note these factors in the family, we are really calling attention to conditions in the society at large. Many aspects of American society are undergoing challenge and change—religious, educational, governmental, and economic institutions as well. But inevitably, much of the attention focuses on what is considered the most basic and revered institution of all—the family.

Since increasing instability seems to be the case, let us speculate for a moment and ask ourselves if maybe some other institution might do better, might take over the functions of the family and replace it. That is a challenging question, and many authors—Huxley, Skinner, Orwell, for example—have turned their attention to it. With advances in the biological sciences, it now appears that reproduction of the species can take place in test tubes, as Aldous Huxley suggested in *Brave New World*. Educational institutions, especially with new inventions in teaching machines and programmed learning, can probably do a much better job of socializing the young and transmitting the culture than the family currently does. Machines are so much more efficient than people anyway, and they don't have the biases, prejudices, and emotional hang-ups that parents have. Control of sex expression? Some would argue that even now more of the control is by law than by the family. The ethic of today is to decide for yourself and exercise individual responsibility in the area of sexual behavior, as in other areas of living. Placement in society is described as a function of the family, but doesn't the individual really make his own place? Status is achieved more than ascribed, and few today follow blindly in the footsteps of their parents as in former generations. All this leaves us with a family system whose only important function is to fill the affectional and emotional needs for the individual. But other agencies might become able to handle this—the church, or the state, or a special hospital, or maybe even the U.S. Marine Corps. These groups are not as primary, to be sure, but societies change, and we are becoming more and more secondary every day in mass society. Without doubt, man can adapt to this change as he did to the car and airplane. In the future, the true primary relationship may seem as outmoded as the pioneer family seems to us. Noting the changes the family is undergoing and the sources of instability, it might be argued that we are currently at a sort of evolutionary way station, holding on to or having some trouble ridding ourselves of vestiges of the past (the "family"), and avoiding or failing to recognize the future although it is nearly upon us.

Religion

Like the family, religion has appeared in all societies although its form varies greatly from society to society. Very rough estimates of worldwide membership in the five largest religions show Christian, 900 million; Moslem, 450 million; Hindu, 350 million; Confucian, 310 million; and Buddhist, 160 million. Of the 900 million Christians, about two-thirds are Roman Catholics. In the United States roughly two-thirds of the population are identified as Protestants, approximately twenty-five percent are Catholic, three percent Jewish, and three percent not identified with any religion.[3] All countries have at least one religion, although not all people are religious. Ethnocentrism relates to our discussion of religion as it does to discussion of the family. The lack of acceptance of others' ways of doing things, the hostility to difference, is probably even more pronounced in regard to religion. Whereas people with peculiar practices (different from ours) in marriage, family, clothing, or eating are seen as "different," primitive, or ignorant, people of different religious beliefs are frequently seen as evil, pagan, or guided by the devil. Great rivalries and conflicts have occurred between religious groups, for religious faith and conviction can be a powerful force. Knowing that "it's God's will" or that "God is on our side" gives a justification and motivation for behavior that is difficult to duplicate by any other means.

Elements and Functions of Religion

We should mention here that sociologists who study religion are not concerned with the possible truth or falsity of beliefs. They are interested in what people believe, and especially in what believing does for people. Although there is great variation among religions, a discussion of some common definitions and descriptions may help our understanding of the institution of religion. Religion may be described as a unified system of beliefs, feelings, and behaviors related to things defined as sacred. Societies define things as sacred—objects (a tree, the moon, a cross, a book), animals, ideas (science, communism, democracy), people (Buddha, Christ, saints). When things become sacred, they are endowed with a special quality or power and are

---

[3] As mentioned, these figures are very rough estimates. The world figures are especially suspect. Data for the United States were collected by the Census Bureau in 1957.

treated with awe, reverence, and respect. Beliefs about the sacred things develop, and often what people choose to believe is of a supernatural quality. A set of appropriate feelings—reverence, happiness, sadness, fear, terror, ecstasy—are established. Finally, behaviors (or rituals) are developed consistent with the beliefs and feelings—confessional, rosary, communion, dietary laws, or the content of a particular worship service.[4]

Religion, like the family, serves a number of functions. Religion provides a way for man to deal with the unknown; it supplies some measure of certainty in an uncertain world. There are a number of things man cannot explain. There are many other things that can be explained and understood but are still difficult to accept—the certainty of death, the loss of loved ones. Religion enables man to adjust to these situations by providing a sacred, supernatural being or object to explain the unknowable; religion provides a belief system to deal with situations difficult to accept—for the certainty of death, a life after death. Anthropologists have noted that sacred rituals and beliefs are usually found in situations that are hardest to control, where there is most uncertainty. Our own appeals for divine guidance and support usually come at intervals when uncertainty is present: when the jet accelerates for takeoff, or just before a particularly difficult test. Karl Marx was critical of religion because of man's tendency to use it in times of uncertainty or stress. Marx described religion as the opiate of the masses because he felt that it took their minds off their real problems in favor of the other-worldly answers of Christianity. The working class's real problem in Marx's view was its manipulation and exploitation by the wealthy industrialists—the bourgeoisie—in capitalist economic systems. Religion was a needless distraction that could only slow the workers' revolt and subsequent freedom from oppression. In Marx's view, therefore, religion serves a negative function.

Religion also functions to provide man with a perspective, a viewpoint, a way of looking at the world. It provides value orientations as to how the world ought to be; it gives meaning to life. Max Weber held that people are motivated by ideologies or beliefs that stem in great part from religious origins, and that these are more basic than the economic values believed by Marx to be so important. In his classic work *The Protestant Ethic and the Spirit of Capitalism* Weber's analysis of history led him to the conclusion that the beliefs surrounding Protestantism were central to the rise of capitalism. For example, Protestant values encourage the view that work is a "calling": to work hard is virtuous, acquisition is supported, sobriety is encouraged. Far from being a needless distraction, religion is the source, according to Weber, of many of a society's most basic values, perspectives, and orientations to the world.

[4] This definition of religion is close to that of Glock and Stark and also borrows some from Cuber. Glock and Stark trace the background of their definition, which includes the works of Durkheim, Yinger, Parsons, Nottingham, and Williams. Much of our discussion in this section is drawn from the book by Charles Glock and Rodney Stark, *Religion and Society in Tension* (Chicago: Rand McNally & Co., 1965). Also see John Cuber, *Sociology*, 6th Ed. (New York: Appleton-Century-Crofts, 1968).

Religion may serve an integrative function in that it promotes solidarity. People with similar beliefs and viewpoints are drawn together, are more unified than those without this common experience. The presence of religion does not guarantee solidarity within a society, however, as other factors are also important. Many societies—the United States, for example—have several religions, and these may be in conflict with each other. In this case there may be a degree of solidarity among those of the same faith but an absence of solidarity in the society—religion may prove to be disintegrative for society while being integrative for the individual.

Religion may function as an agency of social control. We noted earlier that religion provides man with a value orientation, a perspective on life, a view of the world. From shared viewpoints, common agreements arise as to what people should and should not do. Since these norms emerge from a religious base, the church becomes involved in ensuring that they are observed. They may be informally encouraged or enforced, or they may be enacted into law. For example, many religions provide for the education of the young in schools run by the church. Some churches do not recognize marriages that take place outside the church. Ministers perform marriages and engage in marriage counseling. A little more indirectly, through pressure groups and lobbies, religions are involved in ensuring the passage or rejection of laws that they feel are crucial; laws dealing with liquor, pornography, abortion, and birth control are recent examples in the United States. In countries where there is less separation of church and state, religious organizations and their representatives are more directly involved with government in determining right and wrong. In a variety of ways then, organized religious groups assert moral authority and attempt to provide guidance—they act as agents of social control. Problems may arise when values and viewpoints on issues change, as they have, for example, on legalized abortion and birth control in the United States. Formal church doctrines change much slower than the values and attitudes of the people change. The result is that the social control function of the church is compromised when it espouses values its members no longer hold. It is likely that if this occurs on many issues, the authority of the church will be seriously undermined.

These four functions—to explain the unknown or uncertain, to provide a perspective or viewpoint, solidarity, and social control—represent some of the more obvious functions of religion. These are not mutually exclusive, and there are others as well. It is interesting to note here while we are discussing functions that *magic* in primitive societies and *science* in more advanced societies serve many of the same functions as religion. In fact, it is sometimes difficult to distinguish between what is magic, science, or religion.[5]

---

[5] Ely Chinoy has an interesting discussion of the comparisons between science, magic, and religion in his introductory text, *Society* (New York: Random House, 1961), pp. 274–276.

So far we have examined the elements of religion (beliefs, feelings, and be-havior related to sacred objects) and some of the functions religion may serve. Religion may also be studied from the viewpoint of the organizational struc-ture of religious groups. What we know about bureaucracies and large organi-zations may be applied to churches. Terminology has been developed to describe different types of church organization. One distinction that is com-monly made is between church and sect. The *church* is large and highly organ-ized, represents and supports the *status quo,* is respectable, and membership is automatic—one is born into the church. The *sect* on the other hand is smaller and less organized, and membership is voluntary. Members of sects usually show greater depth and fervor in their religious commitment than members of churches. The sect is more closely associated with the lower classes, the church with the middle and upper classes. The sect usually arises because of protest when church members become disaffected. They may feel that the church is too compromising or religiously too conservative, or in some other way is not responding to the wishes or convictions of its membership. The disaffected, deciding they would rather switch than fight, establish a sect based on purity of belief and the individual religious needs of its mem-bership.[6]

Yinger sees "church" and "sect" as two types on a continuum of religious organizations. He adds several other types, including ecclesia, denomination, and cult. *Ecclesia* is defined as the church in a state of rigidification. It is even more conservative and *status quo*-oriented than the church. The *denomi-nation* continues this trend and appeals to an even smaller category of people —a racial, ethnic, or social-class grouping. Yinger defines *cult* as a small, short-lived, often local group, frequently built around a dominant leader. The cult is smaller, less organized, and more transitory than the sect and represents the opposite end of the continuum from the church. Cults and sects arise, it is argued, because people feel deprivation in some form—poverty, ill health, value conflict, anomie. It is this deprivation that leads to the formation of new religious movements. Once formed, the movement may later die out, or it may become larger, more established and conservative, and move to another category of organization—from cult to sect to denomination, for example.

Religion in America

To a sociologist looking at religion in the United States, certain aspects stand out. In America as in other countries there is *differential involvement*

[6] These paragraphs on types of religious organizations make use of material from Glock and Stark, *Religion and Society in Tension,* Chapter 13, and from J. Milton Yinger's book, *Religion, Society and the Individual* (New York: Macmillan Co., 1957), Chapter 6, espe-cially pp. 142–155.

in religious activities. If we take church attendance as a measure of religious involvement, we find that women are more active than men, Catholics more
than Protestants, college-educated more than those with high school education
or less, people over thirty more than those under thirty, and people in the
East most and people in the West least. Middle- and upper-class people
attend and participate in church activities more than those of the lower class,
while lower-class people tend to show greater intensity and emotionality in
religious feeling. Religious groups seem to be stratified according to social
class. Episcopalians, Congregationalists, and Jews tend to be of higher social
class than Presbyterians and Methodists, who in turn tend to rank higher
than Baptists and Catholics. Often this ranking is related to ethnic or national
origin and recency of migration to the United States, but there is also a tendency for Americans to change their religious affiliation as they move up the
social-class ladder.[7]

Great *religious diversity* characterizes this country. The United States has no
official state-supported religion. America, unlike some countries, has attempted
to maintain a separation between church and state. Broadly speaking, three
religious bodies—Protestant, Catholic, and Jewish—dominate. However, there
are numerous Protestant denominations, of which the largest are Baptist,
Methodist, Lutheran, and Presbyterian, as well as a multitude of sects and
cults. Some authorities have noted this diversity in American religious groups
and have argued that, on the contrary, the differences are in name only. They
feel that there is a growing consensus on religious beliefs and that we are approaching a common religion in America that is eroding the traditional differences between Protestantism, Catholicism, and Judaism. Glock and Stark
tested this idea by asking a number of members of Protestant and Catholic
churches about their beliefs. They conclude that great diversity *does* exist,
not only between Protestants and Catholics, but between various Protestant
denominations as well. In fact, Glock and Stark feel that the differences between various Protestant denominations are so great that it is inappropriate to
speak of "Protestants"—there is no such thing as a unified Protestant religion.
Some of the results of Glock and Stark's research are shown in Table 1. It is
apparent from these data that members of different Protestant denominations
have marked differences in belief. These differences are reflected in numerous
areas and seem to indicate that a common American religion, at least in terms

[7] George Gallup conducts a yearly poll on church attendance. See Leonard Broom and
Phillip Selznick, *Sociology*, 5th Ed. (New York: Harper & Row, 1973), pp. 408–409, for
a discussion of social class and denominational differences. More recent data on family income and occupational status as related to denomination are provided by Galen Gockel,
"Income and Religious Affiliation: A Regression Analysis," *American Journal of Sociology*,
24, 6 (May 1969), pp. 632–647. Gockel's data confirm the ranking given here (Jewish,
Episcopalian, Congregationalist, Presbyterian, Methodist, Catholic, and Baptist, from high
income and status to low).

of beliefs, does not now exist.[8] On the other hand, Protestantism, Catholicism, and Judaism in the United States are probably peculiarly American. Often they differ markedly from their antecedents in other countries. The melting pot has modified traditional religions so that they all probably reflect the cultural values of the United States. In this sense, at least, there is a "common American religion," and we will return to this when we discuss the secularization of American religion.

Table 1. Percentage of Members of Various Religious Groups Who Held the Following Beliefs To Be "Completely True."

	Congregationalists	Methodists	Presbyterians	Missouri Lutherans	Southern Baptists	Catholics
Belief in the existence of God	41	60	75	81	99	81
Belief that Jesus was born of a virgin	21	34	57	92	99	81
Belief in life after death	36	49	69	84	97	75
Belief in the existence of the Devil	6	13	31	77	92	66
Belief in original sin	2	7	21	86	43	68

Adapted from Glock and Stark, *Religion and Society in Tension*, Chapter 5.

Religion in America is *losing functions*. Other institutions are taking over the traditional functions that religion has served. Education and socialization of the young is handled for the most part by educational institutions rather than by the church. More dramatic is the rise in the importance of science. Today we tend to put our faith in science rather than religion when dealing with the unknown or uncertainty. Scientific knowledge increasingly forces a redefining of religious beliefs. How do you describe heaven when rockets and spaceships are racing through the universe to the moon and beyond? What is the "soul" when hearts and possibly even brains can be transplanted from one

[8] For a more complete analysis of this topic, see Glock and Stark, *Religion and Society in Tension,* Chapters 4 and 5.

body to another? Today we look to science for the answers, not religion—the scientist is our folk hero, not the minister. We might predict that either religion will change to adapt to a scientific world or that religion will have ever-decreasing influence. Some religious organizations, in a spirit of "if you can't lick 'em, join 'em," are attempting to develop new functions to replace those they have lost. Usually this means becoming more "this-worldly" and less "other-worldly." The new church looks like a social work agency, and religious leaders frequently lead the way in speaking out on social issues. Ministers and priests put their bodies on the line in the 1960s in civil rights demonstrations in the South. Individual representatives of the church have spoken out on the draft and on the war in Vietnam. Churches in some areas have provided food and shelter for hippies and for other youth "doing their own thing." It is frequently noted that the minister in the pulpit sounds more like his college degree were in psychology or sociology than in theology.

These trends may not be widespread or even widely accepted in the very churches in which they are taking place. Some argue that these changes are certain guarantees of the decline of religion. After all, formerly churches were offering something different, a special way of looking at the world unattainable elsewhere. Now the church is no different from other secular activities and loses any unique appeal it might have had. Others feel, however, that in a changing world, religion too must change or run the risk of becoming irrelevant.

Finally, the *secularization of American religion* bears discussion. By secular we mean non-spiritual, non-sacred, this-worldly. Americans seem to be religious and non-religious at the same time. Millions of Bibles are sold yearly, and polls indicate that over ninety percent of Americans say they believe in God, and yet fifty-three percent of the people asked could not name one of the four authors of the first four books of the New Testament. Americans believe in prayer, in heaven and hell, and in life after death, and yet church attendance has dropped from forty-nine percent in a given week in 1958 to forty percent in 1971. In 1957, ninety-seven percent of Americans identified with a religious denomination, and yet at about the same time a panel of outstanding Americans, when asked to rate the most significant events in history, gave first place to Columbus' discovery of America while Christ, his birth or crucifixion, came in fourteenth, tied with the discovery of the X ray and the Wright brothers' first flight.[9] Religion used to be of vital significance; it guided the pioneers' way of life. The Bible was read regularly at family gatherings, it was the law, and its teachings were carefully followed. Today people join churches and say they are religious, but the meaning and the reasons are different. People are religious for social and secular reasons—"it looks right," it makes one respectable. Religion is used to get other desired things. Belonging to the "right" church will

---

[9] Figures on attendance come from the Gallup Poll, 1971. Other facts in this section come from Will Herberg's interesting book, *Protestant—Catholic—Jew* (Garden City, N.Y.: Doubleday & Co., Anchor Books, 1960), Chapter 1. Also Glock and Stark, *Religion and Society in Tension,* Chapter 4.

help the aspiring businessman make the right contacts, meet the right people, have the right friends. Athletic teams pray before games; even the U.S. Marine Corps holds special religious services before shooting the rifle on qualification day. We seem to feel that if we "have religion"—belong or go to church—other good things will happen to us. The result is an increasing secularization of American religion. As Will Herberg puts it, contemporary American religion is *man-centered*. Man, not God, is the beginning and end of the spiritual system of much of present day American religiosity. The result is a religiousness without religion, a way of sociability or "belonging" rather than a way of orienting life to God.[10] The increasing interest in the Pentecostal religious movements shown by today's young people may indicate a temporary countertrend, or it may signify a more general moving back to the spiritual and emotional aspects of religion.

Summary

The major topics of the first two chapters in this section on social organization were groups, categories, and aggregations. These concepts permit the study of a number of different types of collectivities of people. In this chapter we moved to another, somewhat more abstract level, and focused on social institutions. Sociologists define an institution as a system of social relationships, an organized way of doing things that meets certain basic needs of society. All societies have basic needs—reproduction of the species, socialization of the young, for example. Consequently, many of the same institutions—family, religion, education, government, economics—appear in all societies, although the content of a given institution may vary from one society to another. As societies develop and change, other institutions—science, leisure—may emerge.

Sociological research and study is more apt to be concerned with specific institutions than it is with the concept itself. The major part of this chapter has presented an analysis of the family and religion in order to illustrate the application of the concept "institution" to specific areas of human behavior. In the section on the family, cross-cultural variations were examined. The constants or uniformities were discussed, and it was observed that the family everywhere seems to fulfill similar functions. Finally, an analysis of the family in America showed substantial change over time and increasing instability. This led to a discussion of functional alternatives to the family.

In our analysis of religion, we outlined those common elements and functions that religions seem to have. Religious organizations were analyzed using

---

[10] Herberg, *Protestant—Catholic—Jew*, Chapter 11, especially p. 268.

Yinger's "church-sect" typology. A description of religion in America included discussion of differential involvement, religious diversity, loss or change in functions, and the apparent secularization of American religion.

Four readings follow. The first two are short excerpts from books by Margaret Mead and Ruth Benedict, and they illustrate the point that within a given institution, the cultural variability in behavior is vast. The third reading is an excerpt from Snell Putney's book, *The Conquest of Society,* in which he describes the current American family as a "people-wrecker." The final article, by Nathan Gerrard, deals with serpent-handling religions. Gerrard again makes the point that there is great diversity in practices within a given institution. More importantly, we again see the combination of several methods of analysis—social-class and institution—with one helping to explain characteristics of the other.

Courtship among the Dobu

Ruth Benedict

Although the same institutions are common to many societies, the specific content of an institution may vary greatly from one society to another. The institution of the family is no exception. In these short selections from two of their books, anthropologists Ruth Benedict and Margaret Mead describe courtship practices in two societies that they studied.

Marriage is set in motion by a hostile act of the mother-in-law. She blocks with her own person the door of her house within which the youth is sleeping with her daughter, and he is trapped for the public ceremony of betrothal. Before this, since the time of puberty, the boy has slept each night in the houses of unmarried girls. By custom his own house is closed to him. He avoids entanglements for several years by spreading his favours widely and leaving the house well before daylight. When he is trapped at last, it is usually because he has tired of his roaming and has settled upon a more constant companion. He ceases to be so careful about early rising. Nevertheless he is never thought of as being ready to undertake the indignities of marriage, and the event is forced upon him by the old witch in the doorway, his future mother-in-law. When the villagers, the maternal kin of the girl, see the old woman immobile in her doorway, they gather, and under the stare of the public the two descend and sit on a mat upon the ground. The villagers stare at them for half an hour and gradually disperse, nothing more; the couple are formally betrothed.

From this time forward the young man has to reckon with the village of his wife. Its first demand is upon his labour. Immediately his mother-in-law gives him a digging-stick with the command, "Now work." He must make a garden under the surveillance of his parents-in-law. When they cook and eat, he must continue work, since he cannot eat in their presence. He is bound to a double task, for when he has finished work on his father-in-law's yams he has still to cultivate his own garden on his own family land. His father-in-law gets ample satisfaction of his will to power and hugely enjoys his power over his son-in-law. For a year or more the situation continues. The boy is not the only one who is caught in this affair, for his relatives also are loaded with obligations. So heavy are the burdens upon his brothers in providing the necessary garden stuff and the valuables for the marriage gift that nowadays young men at their brother's betrothal escape from the imposition by signing up with the white recruiter for indentured labour.

*Courtship among
the Mundugumor*

Margaret Mead

Girls of this age are also divided by their experience; some are married and living in the houses of their mothers-in-law, some have been successfully kept at home by jealous fathers. While the betrothed girls may be fretting over the indignity of having husbands too young to copulate with them, or too old to be desirable, the unbetrothed girls are fretting because their fathers follow them about everywhere and never permit them any privacy. Temporary alliances are sometimes formed in pursuance of love-affairs, but for the most part each pair of Mundugumor lovers acts in complete secrecy. The implications of a love-affair are so dangerous that it is inadvisable to trust anyone. In the face of all Mundugumor conflicts about arranged marriages there exists a violent preference for individual selection of one's mate. Children who have been accustomed to fight even for their first drops of milk do not docilely accept prescribed marriages arranged for other people's convenience. Almost every girl, betrothed or not, goes about with her skin polished and her grass skirt gay and stylish, with her eye out for a lover, and boys and men are watchful for the slightest sign of favour. The love-affairs of the young unmarried people are sudden and highly charged, characterized by passion rather than by tenderness or romance. A few hastily whispered words, a tryst muttered as they pass on a trail, are often the only interchange between them after they have chosen each other and before that choice is expressed in intercourse. The element of time and discovery is always present, goading them towards the swiftest possible cut-and-run relationship. The words in which a slightly older man advises a boy give the tone of these encounters: "When you meet a girl in the bush and copulate with her, be careful to come back to the village quickly and with explanations to account for your disappearance. If your bow-string is snapped, say that it caught on a passing bush. If your arrows are broken, explain that you tripped and caught them against a branch. If your loin-cloth is torn, or your face scratched, or your hair disarrayed, be ready with an explanation. Say that you fell, that you caught your foot, that you were running after game. Otherwise people will laugh in your face when you return." A girl is similarly advised: "If your ear-rings are torn out of your ears, and the cord of your necklace broken, if your grass skirt is torn and bedraggled, and your face and arms scratched and bleeding, say that you were frightened, that you heard a noise in the bush and ran and fell. Otherwise people will taunt you with having met a lover." Foreplay in these quick encounters takes the form of a violent scratching and biting match, calculated to produce the maximum amount of excitement in the minimum amount of time. To break the arrows or the basket of the beloved is one standard way of demonstrating consuming passion; so also is tearing off ornaments, and smashing them if possible.

Before she marries, a girl may have a number of affairs, each characterized by the same quick violence, but it is dangerous. If the matter is discovered the whole community will know that she is no longer a virgin, and the Mundugumor value virginity in their daughters and brides. Only a virgin may be offered in exchange for a virgin, and a girl whose virginity is known to be lost can be exchanged only for one whose exchange value has been similarly damaged. However, if a man marries a girl and then discovers she is not a virgin, he says nothing about it, for his own reputation is now involved and people would mock him. Sometimes the bush meetings are varied by an accepted lover's slipping into the girl's sleeping basket at night. Fathers may, if they wish, sleep with their adolescent daughters until they marry, and mothers have a similar right to sleep with their sons. Particularly jealous fathers and particularly possessive mothers exercise this privilege. Often, however, two girls are allowed to sleep together in a basket; if one of the pair is away, the other temporarily has the basket to herself. If she receives a lover in her sleeping-basket, she risks not only discovery but actual injury, for an angry father who discovers the intruder may fasten up the opening of the sleeping-bag and roll the couple down the house-ladder, which is almost perpendicular and some six or seven feet in height. The bag may receive a good kicking and even a prodding with a spear or an arrow before it is opened. As a result, this method of courtship, although very occasionally resorted to by desperate lovers in the wet season when the bush is flooded, is not very popular. Young men relate with bated breath the most conspicuous mishaps that have befallen their elders, mishaps so uproariously humiliating and damaging to pride and person that they have become sagas of mirth. While the lover from another hamlet will therefore seldom risk a tryst within the house, new relationships between people temporarily housed together are often set up in this way, where the risk is much smaller.

Questions

1. *The variabilities or differences are obvious, but describe the uniformities or similarities between Dobu, Mundugumor, and U.S. institutions of the family.*

2. To the extent that you can, describe the Dobu and Mundugumor using rules of marriage, residence, descent, authority, and so on.

The Family as a People Wrecker

Snell Putney

In this excerpt from his book, *The Conquest of Society,* Snell Putney examines the family in America today. He is concerned that the present family system is not meeting people's needs but is forced on them by the "autosystem": a social system pursuing its own objectives by its own means which has largely ceased to be under the effective control of men. Snell Putney is a professor of sociology at California State University, San Jose.

It is emotional fulfillment that Americans want from the family. But the existing family system evolved as a means of operating small farms. Small wonder there are problems. The autosystems enforce the present family system, teaching people that it is their own fault that their marriages fail. And people believe it.

Once everyone had to belong to a family. The apprentice became a member of the master craftsman's household because there was no place for him in society as an employee living separately. The Eskimo who had no wife had a mother or sister living with him, or he lived with another man who had a wife.

Today the laundromat, prepackaged foods, sexual liberalism, and employment outside the home have removed the necessity for marriage. Yet marriage remains popular; most Americans marry, and many marry more than once. Those unmarried past the usual age of marriage are a small and persecuted minority. The married do missionary work among them; the bachelor learns not to be surprised to find a young lady present when a married couple asks him to dinner.

Why Marry?

Why did you get married? An Eskimo would have found the question absurd; for him marriage was an aspect of survival. But the American marries by choice, and has usually pondered the reasons for his action. He may give a variety of explanations, but almost always they involve the fulfillment of emotional needs. He may say he married to escape loneliness, or because he found someone warm and rewarding, because he wanted to live with the one he loved, or because he found someone who seemed to lack the faults of his previous spouse. All of these reasons are based on the expectation that marriage will contribute to the fulfillment of emotional needs.

Emotional fulfillment has always occurred in the family; probably more so in the past than is usual today. But it was never before seen as the primary *function* of the family. It was the lucky by-product.

Australia was first colonized by male convicts. On their release, they were encouraged to go into the outback and establish farms. They were forbidden to return to England. Quite a traffic in mail-order brides resulted. Some men wrote to relatives in England asking for a girl who would come to Australia to marry them. Commercial enterprises arose which brought young women to Australia where they met their prospective husbands. Most of these marriages seem to have been successful for the simple reason that the prospective husband

and wife expected things of each other that the other could provide. The man needed the assistance and companionship of a woman in the arduous task of making a farm, and he wanted sons to help him. He expected certain skills in his wife, but all girls raised in rural England were likely to have them. Her expectations were similarly pragmatic. She expected him to know farming, to work hard, and to protect her. Neither thought of the other as a happiness machine. If they found happiness together more often than American couples do, it may have been because they were not looking so hard for it. They fulfilled each other *because* they shared a life; they did not share a life in the hope of being fulfilled.

The modern American lives much of his life within the sockets of the giant autosystems where his needs for intimacy, meaning, and uncomplicated enjoyment are difficult to fulfill. It is not surprising that he turns to the smaller world of the family for fulfillment. He *is* looking for a happiness machine.

Sex and Children

There are a few other functions remaining to the family. Approved sexual relations remain a monopoly of the family (although the strength of disapproval of nonmarital sex seems to be weakening). Similarly, the bearing and socialization of children remain a presumed monopoly of the family (although the diminishing importance of children and the intrusion of other agencies of socialization, such as television and the nursery school, affect this).

There is an interesting tendency to group the sexual and child-rearing functions together under the general and pervasive quest for emotional fulfillment. In the past, a man had children in order to claim the labor of the child and to perpetuate his lineage. These two reasons have largely disappeared. Children now constitute one of the greatest economic liabilities that can be undertaken, and they do not effectively continue lineage when they depart to far corners of the country and pursue lives incomprehensible to their parents.

Today, people have children for different reasons. Of course some people, having grown up expecting to have children, have them without thinking much about it (perhaps to their later regret). Those who *decide* to have children usually do so for about the same reasons they got married: to enhance their opportunity to fulfill emotional needs. The specific reasons may be as healthy as liking to watch children develop or as pathological as wanting to relive their lives vicariously. But all of them are emotional.

In a similar way, sex is incorporated into the idea of emotional fulfillment. Americans see the goal of the family as "togetherness," and sex is viewed as the ultimate form of togetherness. This is a very limited theory of sexuality. It is true that people who are fond of each other within a stable and monogamous relationship can enjoy sex—if they work at reducing the inevitable boredom. But it is also true that people can enjoy sex in very different situations.

An indication of the degree to which sex and children are subsumed under the pervasive goal of emotional fulfillment is the fact that when the family ceases to fulfill emotional needs for the spouses, sexual relations are generally terminated, and it is assumed that the children might be better off if the marriage were dissolved. All of the eggs are in one basket, and when it drops, all of them break. The wife of the outback farmer may not have "loved" her husband, but she did not think much about it, and she certainly did not contemplate taking the children and leaving because she was not emotionally fulfilled. She had too many other things to do.

The Family versus Its Functions

The system of the family as we know it evolved gradually over a long period of time. It was presumably well suited to the functions which the family served on the subsistence farms where most people lived. But it would be amazing if this same system were well adapted to fulfill the different functions expected of it in modern urban society.

Once things are viewed in this light, a number of questions arise. For example, the demand that marriage should entail sexual monogamy may have made sense in an era when contraception was largely impossible and questions of lineage and inheritance were of considerable moment. And in any case, long hours of hard labor used to restrict sexual energies. But it is by no means certain that the demand for monogamy contributes to marital success under present conditions. American society constantly suggests the delights of sexual variety, and forbids the enjoyment of it. It teaches people to experience intense sexual jealousy, and provides innumerable opportunities for sexual infidelity. A vast amount of energy is unhappily consumed in repression, fantasy, scheming, guilt, and quarreling over sexual matters. There is bound to be a better way of arranging things!

The present family system encourages viewing spouses and children as property—marriage confers rights of ownership. Such attitudes may have had some utility in days when brides were purchased, and wives and children were largely regarded as instruments of production, but these attitudes are grossly inappropriate to marriages among individualistic Americans. They have enough problems without a system which encourages them to think of each other as chattels.

The family system insists that children belong in the home of their biological parents. Yet this is hardly easy to achieve as people change partners looking for the greatest emotional fulfillment. Countless people find themselves living stunted lives because it is financially impractical for them to escape each other, or because they have separated and the burdens of separate households and child support ruin them financially. Nor is the picture necessarily brighter from the child's viewpoint. Parents may insist on their inalienable right to produce children and then drive them neurotic, but where is the child's right to a mentally healthy childhood in an uncrowded world? It is interesting that we require barbers to be licensed to protect people from getting poor haircuts, but allow anyone at all to attempt to shape and rear another human being.

The present family system holds up the ideal of a lifetime relationship—which made a great deal of sense in the Australian outback or the English village. But it is not at all clear that such an exception makes sense under present circumstances. Probably one marriage in three ends in divorce, and another one in three becomes a protracted struggle to destroy one another. If the function of the family is to help the individual find fulfillment, it is only logical to encourage him to experiment until he finds a situation to his liking. But even in the one marriage in three which might be termed amiable, it is unclear just why there should necessarily be a lifetime commitment. The man who leaves a successful career in the middle of his life to seek new experiences in another field is applauded, yet it seems shocking to think of someone leaving a happy marriage in order to experience other intimate and rewarding relationships. But why not?

The Hand of the Autosystems

The family system did not evolve to do what we now expect of it, and yet we seem bewildered that it does not work. The family system itself is at such a low level of centralization that it does not become a formidable autosystem. But the highly centralized institutional sectors—especially the state—undertake to enforce the existing family structure. Legislation is directed against experimentation which might uncover family forms—for example, communes—more propitious to yielding what we want from the family. And the church, school, and advertising join the state in teaching people to believe that there is something unalterable about the present system.

The autosystems thus force people to fit an arbitrary family system, rather than let people create a system which will fit them. The family as it exists is a people-wrecking machine of awesome effectiveness. It hardly seems excessive to estimate that two-thirds of the unhappiness which Americans experience derives from the family—if not from marital conflict, then from parent-child conflict. But Americans are massively programmed to assume that the system is all right, and that their unhappiness is the result of their own deficiencies or those of their spouses and children.

I recall talking to a young bride who told me that her entire evaluation of herself as a person would depend on the success of her marriage. She defined success as finding happiness herself, and in making her husband happy. I shuddered and said nothing, but I felt a real sense of tragedy that this young lady was so willing to play the system's game against the odds, and with her ego at stake. A few months later, I heard that she and her husband had separated.

It is long past time to reexamine the whole question of the family from the *human* point of view, and to withdraw the misplaced loyalty we have been taught to render unto the present system.

Since the only real function for the family is to make people happy, why not just encourage them to work out whatever kind of family arrangements suit them best? Why let the autosystems surround us with rules and preconceptions?

Free Form

An alternative to the present family is leaving everyone free to remain single, or to join with other people in whatever way seems most congenial to his desires and needs. Let individuals form families of two, three, four, five, or any number, and in any combination of sexes they choose: three men, two men and four women, one woman and three men, two women—or one man and one woman. Within these families let them play whatever roles they choose without regard to traditional sex roles: let the cooking, wage earning, faucet fixing, and child care (if any) fall where they may according to people's personalities and not according to their sex.

Such a proposal flies in the face of traditional regulating of family behavior, but whereas past societies may have needed to control the family, our society can afford to allow people to do what they want.

Necessary Changes

To establish a free-form family system would require various changes. First, the interference of the autosystems in family relations would have to cease. Legislation regulating family groupings would have to be repealed, and pressures to maintain the present family system eliminated.

Fortunately there seems to be a trend in this direction. We are seeing the gradual repeal of various types of legislation relating to the traditional family. Changes in divorce and abortion laws are a case in point.

A second necessary change would be the institution of some form of guaranteed annual wage so that everyone could live apart from a family if he chose. To a degree the family is still a means of economic distribution: the wife may live by her husband's wage or pension, having none of her own. For economic reasons unrelated to the family, it is probable that at least a minimal guaranteed annual wage will be established.

An alternative child-rearing system would also have to be provided. If people were allowed to choose their family forms freely, it seems inevitable that only some of these forms would provide the continuity necessary to raise children. Of course with adequate contraception and a free-form family system, many people would probably decide not to have children. Certainly many people who have them today do so more in response to the pressures and expectations of society than out of a deep desire for children.

But children must be produced and reared if the race is to continue, and if the family is no longer to take full responsibility, other agencies must be provided. And, in fact, we are seeing a trend toward child-care centers wherein children of working mothers can receive day care; it is only another step to allow (as they do in Russia) the children to spend most of their time in these centers if the child or the parent desires it. Our present state-supervised foster homes are another beginning of a child-care system external to the family.

Professional child rearing outside the home could have advantages from the viewpoint of the child. He could receive care from people who had elected child rearing as a profession because they were interested in children, rather than fallen into it because they forgot to take their pill. Each child could also be given a guaranteed annual income independent of the family. The child could then (as some children of divorced parents can do now) take his child support and move from one situation to another according to his wishes and preference instead of being sentenced to a particular situation by his parents or the state. It is appealing to think of a child having the option of staying in a child center, with his biological parents, with other families, or even going on his own without financial or legal barriers. It is now recognized that a child can determine what he needs to eat; he may also be capable of determining where he should live.

Perhaps the biggest change necessary to implement a free-form family system is in the programming of people. Rather extensive change in attitudes would be essential. People would have to stop claiming the right to regulate other people's personal lives. The insistence on traditional sex roles would have to be abandoned, both in the family and in the economy. The prejudice against homosexuality would have to be eradicated. The concept of sexual monogamy as a precious aspect of human relationship would also have to be relinquished. And it would be necessary to cease regarding other people as personal property; we would have to become secure enough to stop demanding that society coerce our lovers and children to remain with us.

There is evidence that all these changes in attitudes are slowly coming to pass. The interest in the liberation movements—women's lib, gay lib, and others— is evidence of a trend toward greater flexibility. And there is a general liberalization of attitudes. The hand of the autosystem is weakening, and it is about time. Now we need to study the situation very carefully and decide what it is that *we* want to do.

Questions

1. *What are the functions of the U.S. family in the mid-1970s? How do these differ from the U.S. family of a century ago, and the family in other societies?*
2. *In American society in the mid-1970s, why do people marry?*
3. *Putney is nuts—the American family system of today provides all sorts of positive and worthwhile benefits for its members. Discuss.*
4. *What is a "free-form family system?" What are the obstacles to its adoption? Analyze the positive and negative aspects of such a system.*
5. *Should individuals be licensed to become parents? Support your argument.*

The Serpent-Handling Religions of West Virginia

Nathan L. Gerrard

There is great diversity in religious practices, as this article by sociologist Nathan Gerrard makes clear. Gerrard feels that a group's religious practices are at least partly explained by the social class of the members. He also outlines the functions that the serpent-handling religions seem to provide for their members.

. . . And these signs shall follow them that believe; In my name shall they cast out devils; they shall speak with

*new tongues; They shall take up serpents; and if they drink
any deadly thing, it shall not hurt them; they shall lay hands
on the sick, and they shall recover. Mark 16:17–18.*

In Southern Appalachia, two dozen or three dozen fundamentalist congre-
gations take this passage literally and "take up serpents." They use copper-
heads, water moccasins, and rattlesnakes in their religious services.

The serpent-handling ritual was inaugurated between 1900 and 1910,
probably by George Went Hensley. Hensley began evangelizing in rural
Grasshopper Valley, Tenn., then traveled widely throughout the South, particularly in Kentucky, spreading his religion. He died in Florida at 70—of
snakebite. To date, the press has reported about 20 such deaths among the
serpent-handlers. One other death was recorded last year, in Kentucky.

For seven years, my wife and I have been studying a number of West
Virginia serpent-handlers, primarily in order to discover what effect this unusual form of religious practice has on their lives. Although serpent-handling
is outlawed by the state legislatures of Kentucky, Virginia, and Tennessee and
by municipal ordinances in North Carolina, it is still legal in West Virginia. One
center is the Scrabble Creek Church of All Nations in Fayette County, about
37 miles from Charleston. Another center is the Church of Jesus in Jolo,
McDowell County, one of the most poverty-stricken areas of the state. Serpent-
handling is also practiced sporadically elsewhere in West Virginia, where it is
usually led by visitors from Scrabble Creek or Jolo.

The Jolo church attracts people from both Virginia and Kentucky, in addition to those from West Virginia. Members of the Scrabble Creek church speak
with awe of the Jolo services, where people pick up large handfuls of poisonous
snakes, fling them to the ground, pick them up again, and thrust them under
their shirts or blouses, dancing ecstatically. We attended one church service in
Scrabble Creek where visitors from Jolo covered their heads with clusters of
snakes and wore them as crowns.

Serpent-handling was introduced to Scrabble Creek in 1941 by a coal miner
from Harlan, Ky. The practice really began to take hold in 1946, when the
present leader of the Scrabble Creek church, then a member of the Church of
God, first took up serpents. The four or five original serpent-handlers in Fayette County met at one another's homes until given the use of an abandoned
one-room school house in Big Creek. In 1959, when their number had swelled
several times over, they moved to a larger church in Scrabble Creek.

Snakebites, Saints, and Scoffers

During the course of our seven-year study, about a dozen members of the church received snakebites. (My wife and I were present on two of these occasions.) Although there were no deaths, each incident was widely and unfavorably publicized in the area. For their part, the serpent-handlers say the Lord causes a snake to strike in order to refute scoffers' claims that the snakes' fangs have been pulled. They see each recovery from snakebite as a miracle wrought by the Lord—and each death as a sign that the Lord "really had to show the scoffers how dangerous it is to obey His commandments." Since adherents believe that death brings one to the throne of God, some express an eagerness to die when He decides they are ready. Those who have been bitten and who have recovered seem to receive special deference from other members of the church.

The ritual of serpent-handling takes only 15 or 20 minutes in religious sessions that are seldom shorter than four hours. The rest of the service includes singing Christian hymns, ecstatic dancing, testifying, extemporaneous and impassioned sermons, faith-healing, "speaking in tongues," and foot-washing. These latter rituals are a part of the firmly-rooted Holiness movement, which encompasses thousands of churches in the Southern Appalachian region. The Holiness churches started in the 19th century as part of a perfectionist movement.

The social and psychological functions served by the Scrabble Creek church are probably very much the same as those served by the more conventional Holiness churches. Thus, the extreme danger of the Scrabble Creek rituals probably helps to validate the members' claims to holiness. After all, the claim that one is a living saint is pretentious even in a sacred society—and it is particularly difficult to maintain in a secular society. That the serpent-handler regularly risks his life for his religion is seen as evidence of his saintliness. As the serpent-handler stresses over and over, "I'm afraid of snakes like anybody else, but when God anoints me, I handle them with joy." The fact that he is usually not bitten, or if bitten usually recovers, is cited as further evidence of his claim to holiness.

After we had observed the Scrabble Creek serpent-handlers for some time, we decided to give them psychological tests. We enlisted the aid of Auke Tellegen, department of psychology, University of Minnesota, and three of his clinical associates: James Butcher, William Schofield, and Anne Wirt. They interpreted the Minnesota Multiphasic Personality Inventory that we administered to 50 serpent-handlers (46 were completed)—and also to 90 members of a conventional-denomination church 20 miles from Scrabble Creek. What we wanted to find out was how these two groups differed.

What we found were important personality differences not only between the serpent-handlers and the conventional church members, but also between the older and the younger generations within the conventional group. We believe that these differences are due, ultimately, to differences in social class: The serpent-handlers come from the nonmobile working class (average annual income: $3000), whereas members of the conventional church are upwardly mobile working-class people (average annual income: $5000) with their eyes on the future.

But first, let us consider the similarities between the two groups. Most of the people who live in the south central part of West Virginia, serpent-handlers or not, have similar backgrounds. The area is rural, nonfarm, with only about one-tenth of the population living in settlements of more than 2500. Until recently, the dominant industry was coal-mining, but in the last 15 years mining operations have been drastically curtailed. The result has been widespread unemployment. Scrabble Creek is in that part of Appalachia that has been officially declared a "depressed area"—which means that current unemployment rates there often equal those of the depression.

There are few foreign-born in this part of West Virginia. Most of the residents are of Scottish-Irish or Pennsylvania Dutch descent, and their ancestors came to the New World so long ago that there are no memories of an Old World past.

Generally, public schools in the area are below national standards. Few people over 50 have had more than six or seven years of elementary education.

Religion has always been important here. One or two generations ago, the immediate ancestors of both serpent-handlers and conventional-church members lived in the same mining communities and followed roughly the same religious practices. Today there is much "backsliding," and the majority seldom attend church regularly. But there is still a great deal of talk about religion, and there are few professed atheists.

Hypochondria and the Holy Spirit

Though the people of both churches are native-born Protestants with fundamentalist religious beliefs, little education, and precarious employment, the two groups seem to handle their common problems in very different ways. One of the first differences we noticed was in the ways the older members of both churches responded to illness and old age. Because the members of both churches had been impoverished and medically neglected during childhood and young adulthood, and because they had earned their livelihoods in hazardous and health-destroying ways, they were old before their time. They suffered from a wide variety of physical ailments. Yet while the older members of the conventional church seemed to dwell morbidly on their physical disabilities, the aged serpent-handlers seemed able to cheerfully ignore their ailments.

The serpent-handlers, in fact, went to the opposite extreme. Far from being pessimistic hypochondriacs like the conventional-church members, the serpent-handlers were so intent on placing their fate in God's benevolent hands that they usually failed to take even the normal precautions in caring for their health. Three old serpent-handlers we knew in Scrabble Creek were suffering from serious cardiac conditions. But when the Holy Spirit moved them, they danced ecstatically and violently. And they did this without any apparent harm.

No matter how ill the old serpent-handlers are, unless they are actually prostrate in their beds they manage to attend and enjoy church services lasting four to six hours, two or three times a week. Some have to travel long distances over the mountains to get to church. When the long sessions are over, they appear refreshed rather than weary.

One evening an elderly woman was carried into the serpent-handling church in a wheelchair. She had had a severe stroke and was almost completely paralyzed. Wheeled to the front of the church, she watched everything throughout the long services. During one particularly frenzied singing and dancing sessions, the fingers of her right hand tapped lightly against the arm of the chair. This was the only movement she was able to make, but obviously she was enjoying the service. When friends leaned over and offered to take her home, she made it clear she was not ready to go. She stayed until the end, and gave the impression of smiling when she was finally wheeled out. Others in the church apparently felt pleased rather than depressed by her presence.

Both old members of the conventional denomination and old serpent-handlers undoubtedly are frequently visited by the thought of death. Both rely on religion for solace, but the serpent-handlers evidently are more successful. The old serpent-handlers are not frightened by the prospect of death. This is true not only of those members who handle poisonous snakes in religious services, but also of the minority who do *not* handle serpents.

One 80-year-old member of the Scrabble Creek church—who did not handle serpents—testified in our presence: "I am not afraid to meet my Maker in Heaven. I am ready. If somebody was to wave a gun in my face, I would not turn away. I am in God's hands."

Another old church member, a serpent-handler, was dying from silicosis. When we visited him in the hospital he appeared serene, although he must have known that he would not live out the week.

The assertion of some modern theologians that whatever meaning and relevance God once may have had has been lost for modern man does not apply to the old serpent-handlers. To them, God is real. In fact, they often see Him during vivid hallucinations. He watches over the faithful. Misfortune and even death do not shake their faith, for misfortune is interpreted, in accordance with God's inscrutable will, as a hidden good.

Surprisingly, the contrast between the optimistic old serpent-handlers and the pessimistic elders of the conventional church all but disappeared when we shifted to the younger members of the two groups. Both groups of young people, on the psychological tests, came out as remarkably well adjusted. They showed none of the neurotic and depressive tendencies of the older conventional-church members. And this cheerful attitude prevailed despite the fact that many of them, at least among the young serpent-handlers, had much to be depressed about.

The young members of the conventional church are much better off, socially and economically, than the young serpent-handlers. The parents of the young conventional-church members can usually provide the luxuries that most young Americans regard as necessities. Many conventional-church youths are active in extracurricular activities in high school or are attending college. The young serpent-handlers, in contrast, are shunned and stigmatized as "snakes." Most young members of the conventional denomination who are in high school intend to go on to college, and they will undoubtedly attain a higher socioeconomic status than their parents have attained. But most of the young serpent-handlers are not attending school. Many are unemployed. None attend or plan to attend college, and they often appear quite depressed about their economic prospects.

The young serpent-handlers spend a great deal of time wandering aimlessly up and down the roads of the hollows, and undoubtedly are bored when not attending church. Their conversation is sometimes marked by humor, with undertones of cynicism and bitterness. We are convinced that what prevents many of them from becoming delinquent or demoralized is their wholehearted participation in religious practices that provide an acceptable outlet for their excess energy, and strengthen their self-esteem by giving them the opportunity to achieve "holiness."

Now, how does all this relate to the class differences between the serpent-handlers and the conventional-church group? The answer is that what allows the serpent-handlers to cope so well with their problems—what allows the older members to rise above the worries of illness and approaching death, and the younger members to remain relatively well-adjusted despite their grim economic prospects—is a certain approach to life that is typical of them as members of the stationary working class. The key to this approach is hedonism.

Hopelessness and Hedonism

The psychological tests showed that the young serpent-handlers, like their elders, were more impulsive and spontaneous than the members of the conventional church. This may account for the strong appeal of the Holiness churches to those members of the stationary working class who prefer religious hedonism to reckless hedonism, with its high incidence of drunkenness and illegitimacy. Religious hedonism is compatible with a puritan morality—and it compensates for its constraints.

The feeling that one cannot plan for the future, expressed in religious terms as "being in God's hands," fosters the widespread conviction among members of the stationary working class that opportunities for pleasure must be exploited immediately. After all, they may never occur again. This attitude is markedly different from that of the upwardly mobile working class, whose members are willing to postpone immediate pleasures for the sake of long-term goals.

Hedonism in the stationary working class is fostered in childhood by parental practices that, while demanding obedience in the home, permit the child license outside the home. Later, during adulthood, this orientation toward enjoying the present and ignoring the future is reinforced by irregular employment and the other insecurities of stationary working-class life. In terms of middle-class values, hedonism is self-defeating. But from a psychiatric point of view, for those who actually have little control of their position in the social and economic structure of modern society, it may very well aid acceptance of the situation. This is particularly true when it takes a religious form of expression. Certainly, hedonism and the associated trait of spontaneity seen in the old serpent-handlers form a very appropriate attitude toward life among old people who can no longer plan for the future.

In addition to being more hedonistic than members of the conventional church, the serpent-handlers are also more exhibitionistic. This exhibitionism and the related need for self-revelation are, of course, directly related to the religious practices of the serpent-handling church. But frankness, both about others and themselves, is typical of stationary working-class people in general. To a large extent, this explains the appeal of the Holiness churches. Ordinarily, their members have little to lose from frankness, since their status pretensions are less than those of the upwardly mobile working class, who are continually trying to present favorable images of themselves.

Because the young members of the conventional denomination are upwardly mobile, they tend to regard their elders as "old fashioned," "stick-in-the-muds," and "ignorant." Naturally, this lack of respect from their children and grandchildren further depresses the sagging morale of the older conventional-church members. They respond resentfully to the tendency of the young "to think they know more than their elders." The result is a vicious circle of increasing alienation and depression among the older members of the conventional denomination.

Respect for Age

There appears to be much less psychological incompatibility between the old and the young serpent-handlers. This is partly because the old serpent-handlers manage to retain a youthful spontaneity in their approach to life. Then too, the young serpent-handlers do not take a superior attitude toward their elders. They admire their elders for their greater knowledge of the Bible, which both old and young accept as literally true. And they also admire their elders for their handling of serpents. The younger church members, who handle snakes much less often than the older members do, are much more likely to confess an ordinary, everyday fear of snakes—a fear that persists until overcome by strong religious emotion.

Furthermore, the young serpent-handlers do not expect to achieve higher socioeconomic status than their elders. In fact, several young men said they would be satisfied if they could accomplish as much. From the point of view of the stationary working class, many of the older serpent-handlers are quite well-off. They sometimes draw two pensions, one from Social Security and one from the United Mine Workers.

Religious serpent-handling, then—and all the other emotionalism of the Holiness churches that goes with it—serves a definite function in the lives of its adherents. It is a safety valve for many of the frustrations of life in present-day Appalachia. For the old, the serpent-handling religion helps soften the inevitability of poor health, illness, and death. For the young, with their poor educations and poor hopes of finding sound jobs, its promise of holiness is one of the few meaningful goals in a future dominated by the apparent inevitability of life-long poverty and idleness.

Questions

1. *What are the functions that the serpent-handling religions provide? Relate your discussion to the four functions covered in the text.*
2. *How are these functions related to the social class of the members?*
3. *Analyze the serpent-handlers in terms of religious organization—church, denomination, sect, etc.*

7

Population and Ecology

In previous chapters in this section on social organization we have examined concepts dealing with groups, categories, aggregations, and institutions. In this chapter, we will show how social organization may be analyzed through the study of population and human ecology. Population refers to the number of people in a given unit, as in a state, society, world, or universe. Human ecology refers to the adaptation of people to their physical environment, their location in space. Demography is the study of human population, its distribution, composition, and change.

As an introduction to some of the important techniques and variables, suppose we try a demographic analysis of a college sociology class. What does the professor see as he looks out at the mass of eager young faces? The total population of the class selected is 130, of which eighty are females and fifty are males —a very favorable sex ratio (unless you're female). There are four Afro-Americans, eleven Asian-Americans, and 115 Caucasian-Americans. The age distribution of this "society" is overwhelmingly in the nineteen to twenty-three categories, with trace amounts in ages up to forty-five. Both birth and death rates for this "society" are exceedingly low. Apparently this represents a very healthy but non-fertile tribe. The life expectancy for the majority will be one semester, although for some it may be at least double that. Migration variables are peculiar for this tribe. Temporary immigration ("in-migration") occurs on those occasions when the class is going to discuss sex or deviant behavior. Permanent emigration ("out-migration") occurs just before tests are scheduled or papers are due.

Ecologically, this class is also interesting. After several meetings, they arrange themselves in space consistently and predictably. There are occasional shifts as dating alliances change, but generally they sit in the same seats throughout the semester. Part of the patterning may be explained by classical ecological processes. Cooperation—X takes great notes, so she is constantly surrounded by A, B, and C (at least I think that's the reason). Competition—when asked why they sit in front, several have said they pay more attention to what is being said and they feel the instructor is more likely to remember them; consequently, they will get better grades. Films of migrating apes have shown ecological processes at work: older males proceed in front, younger males at the rear, and females protected in the middle. Applying these principles to the classroom, we could predict that around the edge will be the physical education majors and football players, next circle will include the older, more experienced females, and in the middle and well protected will be the young, beautiful virgins. . . .

Population

Population, then, involves the study of the numbers of people classified according to a series of variables. Demographers look at the total number of people in a society. They look at the sex ratio—the number of males per hundred females (a ratio of about sixty-three in the sociology class discussed above). Data are collected on the number of people in racial, ethnic, and religious categories. Age distributions are calculated. Birth rates and death rates are computed, as are indications of life span or life expectancy. Migration affects the population of a society, so rates of migration—how many as well as who—are collected for those entering as well as leaving a country. Migration patterns within the country are examined also. Population growth for an area is determined by net migration (in-migration minus out-migration) plus natural increase (births minus deaths). Using these variables, a demographer might describe the United States as follows.

The Census Bureau reported that the population of the United States in January 1973 was approximately 209,712,000. The world population was over 3.7 billion. The sex ratio in 1970 in the United States was 94.8 (about ninety-five males for every hundred females). Regionally, New England and the Atlantic states have a low sex ratio, Mountain and Western states have a high sex ratio (more males than females). In 1970, New York and Massachusetts were lowest with sex ratios of less than 92; Alaska and Hawaii were highest with ratios of 119 and 108. American cities have more women than men—in central cities the sex ratio in 1970 was 90.7, while in rural areas it was 101.

Population pyramids on the following pages illustrate the distinctive age and sex profiles produced by different types of communities. The first pyramid gives an age/sex profile for the United States in 1970. The second describes Norfolk, Virginia. Norfolk is a city with a large military base and, consequently, a concentration of young people, especially young males. The third pyramid describes Ann Arbor, Michigan, a college town. The fourth gives an age/sex profile of St. Petersburg, Florida, a city that attracts older, retired people.

Blacks make up about 11 percent of the U.S. population, while Mexican-Americans account for about two percent and Orientals less than one percent. In 1957 census data, 66 percent reported that they were Protestant, 26 percent were Catholic, and 3 percent were Jewish. The median age of the U.S. population in 1970 was 28.1 (a drop from 29.5 in 1960). The median age for males was 26.8, for females 29.3. There was variation between states as well with Alaska having the youngest population (median age = 22.9) and Florida the oldest (32.3). There are more older people (sixty-five and older) and more younger people (in their late teens and twenties) than there were thirty years ago.

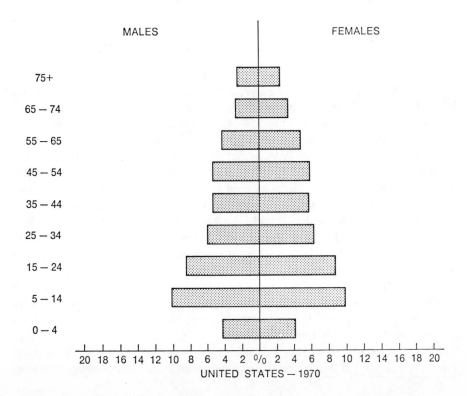

UNITED STATES — 1970

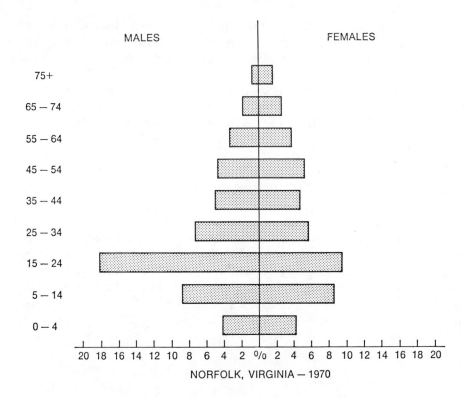

MALES   FEMALES

75+

65 — 74

55 — 64

45 — 54

35 — 44

25 — 34

15 — 24

5 — 14

0 — 4

20 18 16 14 12 10 8 6 4 2 %/o 2 4 6 8 10 12 14 16 18 20

NORFOLK, VIRGINIA — 1970

The U.S. birthrate in 1972 was 15.6 per 1,000 population. The birthrate reached a high of twenty-six in 1947, remained constant at about twenty-five from 1952 to 1957, and has dropped since to its 1972 low. The general fertility rate—births per 1,000 women age 15–44—dropped to 73.4. This was its lowest level in U.S. history (or at least since such records have been kept). The previous low was 75.8 in 1936. Children per family dropped to 2.03 in 1972, another new low (1971 = 2.28, 1936 = 2.12) and below the "replacement level" of 2.1 children per family. "Replacement level" is defined as the average number of births per woman over her lifetime necessary for the population eventually to reach zero growth (which would take about 70 years). Population experts don't know whether this birth decline will continue but they have come up with some reasons for why it is happening now. Women are getting married later and divorced more. Increased freedom of women to work means they are putting off marriage and child rearing. Increased use of contraception and liberalization of abortion laws as well as changing viewpoints about the family have helped drop the birth rate. And finally, unemployment rates and a sluggish economy are also cited as contributing factors.

For purposes of comparison, countries in Europe have about the same birth rates as the United States, while some countries (Mexico, Guatemala, Indonesia,

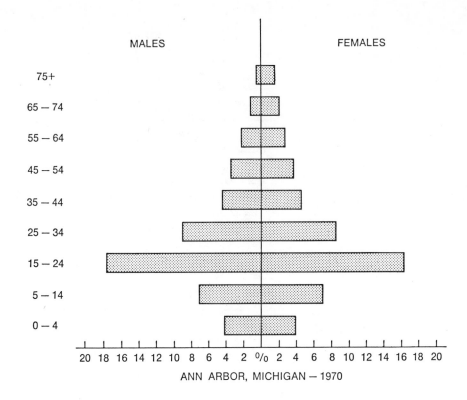

MALES   FEMALES

| 75+ |
| 65 — 74 |
| 55 — 64 |
| 45 — 54 |
| 35 — 44 |
| 25 — 34 |
| 15 — 24 |
| 5 — 14 |
| 0 — 4 |

20 18 16 14 12 10 8 6 4 2 % 2 4 6 8 10 12 14 16 18 20

ANN ARBOR, MICHIGAN — 1970

India, Pakistan) have birth rates more than double ours. The death rate in this country is approximately 9.5 per 1,000. Over a long period of time this rate has been dropping slowly, but it has remained nearly constant since the early 1950s. European countries have about the same rate, but the rates in countries like Guatemala, India, and Pakistan are about double. Life expectancy in America has slowly risen to its present point of around 72 years for whites (75 for females, 68 for males), and 65 years for non-whites (69 for females, 61 for males). In 1971, approximately 370,000 people immigrated to the United States. Because of our quota restrictions, immigrants come predominantly from Western Europe, Great Britain, and from other countries in North America.

Internally, Americans move around a great deal with one family in five changing its home in a given year. Forty-seven percent of Americans did not live in the same house in 1970 that they did in 1965. Migration is from farm to city and from city to suburb. Population is generally concentrated around centers of industrialization and transportation, areas near important natural resources. This remains true, but it is interesting to note that migration arrows in the U.S. now point to "riviera" areas. Part of the explanation for this is that population is increasingly becoming distributed in terms of recreation and leisure patterns. Sun and climate are the important new natural resources. People are

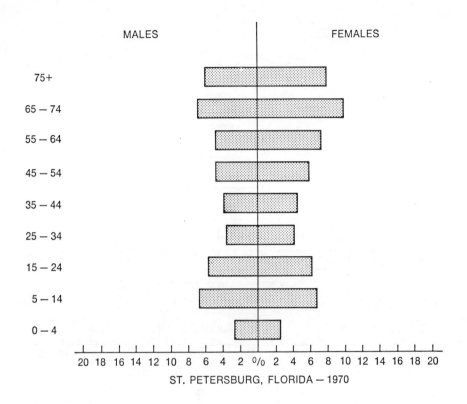

MALES   FEMALES

75+

65 – 74

55 – 64

45 – 54

35 – 44

25 – 34

15 – 24

5 – 14

0 – 4

20 18 16 14 12 10 8 6 4 2 %/o 2 4 6 8 10 12 14 16 18 20

ST. PETERSBURG, FLORIDA – 1970

moving to states like California, Nevada, Arizona, Alaska, Colorado, Florida, Delaware, and Maryland, all of which gained twenty percent or more in population between 1960 and 1970. Some New England and Atlantic states (Maine, Pennsylvania, West Virginia), Southern states (Mississippi, Alabama), Midwestern states (North and South Dakota, Iowa, Kansas, Nebraska), and Western states (Wyoming, Montana) are losing population relative to the rest of the country. The 1970 census reports that, in general, Americans continue to migrate from the interior to the Atlantic, Pacific, and Gulf coasts.[1]

Besides giving us a statistical description of collectivities, population data are useful in social planning. Population profiles in terms of age and sex enable planners to determine the number of schools needed, the number and proportion of apartments and homes to build, the type of recreation facilities required, the

[1] The figures in this section on population come from the Census Bureau and have been published in their *Current Population Reports,* or come from news releases on population projections and estimates. The international data come from the Statistical Office of the United Nations as published in the *Statistical Yearbook* and *Demographic Yearbook.*

necessary facilities for the aged and for child care, and a number of other similar needs. When we hear that a group of city planners is developing a community with no schools (because there are no children), no tennis courts (because tennis is too strenuous), and many recreation centers and shuffleboard courts, it is apparent that the planners have designed a community for elderly retired people.

Human Ecology

Biologists have for some time studied the interrelationships and interdependence of plants and animals—the "balance of nature." Living organisms are dependent on other organisms and pattern themselves in space accordingly. Why don't porcupines live in the desert? It may be because they would get sand in their quills, but it is certainly because their food supply—the bark of certain trees—does not grow in the desert. Likewise, all organisms live in certain places and patterns but not in others. Social scientists noticed that people too locate themselves in space in specific patterns, and this gave rise to the study of human ecology.

Flying over the United States, we see that people are not equally distributed but are grouped in clusters. There are fewer clusters in the West and more in the East. Most of the clusters are on rivers, lakes, or oceans. Highways run through the clusters, and various natural resources are nearby. There are fewer clusters where the climate is severe or the terrain rugged. People pattern themselves in space in predictable ways. They group together in cities, for in cities mutual cooperation and a complex division of labor allow people to accomplish much more than they could as isolated individuals. These cities are located to take maximum advantage of natural factors—waterways for transportation, resources for technological needs.

If we look more closely at the cities, we see that they also have consistent patterns. One city patterning commonly cited by ecologists has five concentric circles or zones. The small inner circle is called the central business district and contains the major stores, banks, offices, and government buildings, the "downtown" area of the city. The next circle is called the zone in transition and contains rundown buildings, slums, a high proportion of minority groups, some industry, and higher rates of unemployment. The third ring is called the workingman's zone and contains small apartment buildings and older single-dwelling units. The middle-class residential district is the fourth zone and contains better private residences and high-class apartments. Finally, the suburban or commuter's zone contains larger estates, golf courses, and makes up the upper-class residential district. Generally speaking, as one moves from Zone I (central business district) outward toward the suburbs, population density decreases, home ownership increases, the proportion of foreign-born decreases, social class rises, crime rate decreases, land cost decreases, and family size decreases. The pattern of the city may be affected by how fast the city develops, by the influence of cars, and by natural obstacles—hills, oceans, rivers. So a given city may not fit this design exactly, but many cities are close to this general pattern.[2]

Other consistent city patternings have been noted. Multiple nuclei describes a city in which a number of specialized centers or "downtowns" develop and each exerts dominance over its particular area. Industry and residential areas grow up around each nucleus. Perhaps Los Angeles, "a bunch of suburbs in search of a city," is an example of multiple-nuclei development. Hoyt feels that cities are more accurately described as sectors with a specific type of land use than as concentric zones.

How are these patterns explained? People arrange themselves in space according to social and cultural values that they believe to be important. It is apparent from previous paragraphs that economic competition has much to do with spatial arrangement in cities. Land is in greatest demand and, therefore, is most expensive in the center of the city. Banks, large stores, businesses, office buildings, and government buildings can afford the cost of locating here because of their importance, business volume, and/or financial base. Structures whose economic effect is less dramatic—homes, apartment buildings, schools, country clubs—are usually located away from the center of the city where land is cheaper. Other social values are also reflected. Many cities have set aside large green areas in those parts of the city where land is most expensive. Parks near the centers of London and Paris, the Boston Commons, and Central Park in New York are but a few of numerous examples illustrating that economic competition is not the sole determining factor in spatial arrangement. Racial and religious minority groups generally reside in separate areas of the city. This separation or segregation sometimes occurs by choice of the minority group, but more often it represents the wishes and values of the majority group. Social-class groupings also separate themselves into different parts of the city, and inevitably areas develop "reputations" which attract certain types of people and discourage others. As the Duncans have pointed out, "spatial distances between occupation groups are closely related to their social distance."[3] In a variety of ways, then, we see that spatial arrangement reflects social and cultural values.

It is both important and interesting to note that spatial arrangement *affects* social interaction. People interact with those who live next door or across the street, unless it's a wide and busy street. People living toward the middle of the

[2] More detailed explanations of the theories discussed in this section may be found in any text on urban sociology. See, for example, Noel Gist and Sylvia Fava, *Urban Society*, 5th Ed. (New York: Thomas Y. Crowell Co., 1964), Chapter 6; or Ralph Thomlinson, *Urban Structure* (New York: Random House, 1969), Chapter 8.

[3] The article by Otis Dudley Duncan and Beverly Duncan, "Residential Distribution and Occupational Stratification," is quoted here from Thomlinson's book, *Urban Structure*, pp. 12–13.

block have more social contacts than those living on corners. Friendships develop more on the side of the house where the driveway is located, especially if there are adjacent driveways—driveways are natural areas for gathering and talking. A family that doesn't mix or "fit" or is unfriendly often acts as a boundary—neighbors have difficulty interacting past this boundary as they would across a busy street. Such habits become so ingrained that when a new family moves into the house, it may inherit the previous family's reputation as a social boundary.[4]

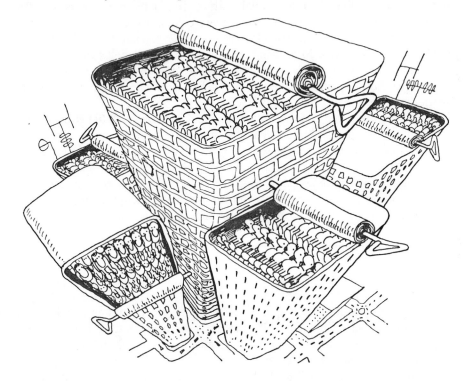

William Michelson in his book *Man and His Urban Environment* outlines a number of factors that correlate with spatial arrangements in addition to those we have already mentioned. He finds, for example, that physical and social pathologies—social and physical illness, and crime—are related to certain spatial factors. The health of women and their children living in self-contained houses was compared with the health of those living in three- and four-story apartments. The sickness rate of the apartment dwellers was 57 percent greater than the sickness rate of those living in houses as measured by first-consultation rates for any ailment. The differences were attributed to the cramped space and

[4] For a detailed description of these interaction patterns, see William H. Whyte, Jr. *The Organization Man* (New York: Simon and Schuster, 1956), Chapter 25.

greater isolation of women in apartments removed from the ground. This conclusion is underlined by the fact that the women in apartments who did not have young children and were therefore able to come and go from their homes more freely had excellent health. High noise levels are related to the incidence of diseases that involve tension. Studies of overcrowding (many persons per room) and high density (many persons per acre) have found generally that *density* is more related to pathology than is overcrowding. For example, in one study (after controlling for other social characteristics) the researchers found in several instances that domestic internal overcrowding (that is, at home) was not related to students' achievement in school while the number of families on the block (density) was. Michelson reminds us that although spatial arrangement may be important, its effects are modified by cultural values. Compare, for example, how Japanese make use of internal and external space with how Americans make use of the same space.

Different types of people have different spatial preferences. Michelson reports that people who highly value convenience are likely to prefer more mixed land uses and small lot sizes; people who highly value individualism prefer larger lot sizes. People with "cosmopolitan" life-styles desire more physical separation from neighbors and place less emphasis on being near facilities and services than do people whose interests are local. Concerning high-rise apartment living, research indicates that children up to about the age of seven in such buildings cling much more closely to their parents than do children in single-family homes who become independent at an earlier age. But past that age the patterns reverse —when they become more mobile, children in high-rise apartment buildings spend much more time away from home than do children living in single-family houses. Finally, one study reports that while apartment dwellers do suffer more from noise disturbance than people living in homes, their main complaint is the restriction they feel on making noise themselves—this affects their leisure patterns and leads them to such sedentary practices as watching television.[5]

Ecologists use the terms "centralization," "decentralization," "segregation," "invasion," and "succession" to describe specific types of spatial arrangements. *Centralization* describes the tendency of people to gather around some central or pivotal point in a city. Centralization allows citizens to better fulfill social and economic needs and functions and is represented in most American cities by the central business district. *Decentralization,* on the other hand, refers to the tendency to move away from the central focus. Decentralization probably occurs at least partly because of dissatisfaction with certain of the consequences of centralization—traffic, crowds, noise, concrete, and so on—and is seen in the U.S.

---

[5] See *Man and His Urban Environment* by William Michelson (Reading, Mass.: Addison-Wesley, 1970). The comments in these two paragraphs are drawn especially from pp. 98–99, 158, 161, and 193–195.

in the rush to the suburbs. *Segregation* refers to the clustering together of similar people. These similarities may be along the lines of occupation, race, religion, nationality, ethnicity, or education. *Invasion* refers to the penetration of one group or function into an area dominated by another group or function. *Succession* refers to the complete displacement or removal of the established group and represents the end product of invasion. The invasion-succession process often produces tension, hostility, and possibly overt conflict.[6]

A brief look at the ongoing drama of the local faculty dining room illustrates some of these ecological concepts. The room was originally segregated: faculty ate there, students ate elsewhere. Segregation also existed within the room: faculty generally sat on the south side of the room, and non-teaching staff—secretaries and administrators—sat on the north side of the room. As the college population grew, students were crowded out of other eating areas and began moving into the faculty room. Invasion had begun. Students found that the room made a convenient study area, and they brought stacks of books and papers which further crowded out the faculty. Finally, the faculty gave up and moved elsewhere as the students took over the room. Alas, succession had occurred. . . .

Ecological arrangement in the United States has undergone change. This used to be a predominantly rural country; now most Americans live in cities or very near them. Recent Census data indicate that between 1960 and 1970 farm population declined by one-third, from fifteen million to ten million. In 1971 farm population was down to nine million or 4.6 percent of the total U.S. population. As nations undergo technological and industrial development, probably it is inevitable that they become more and more urbanized. The transformation from rural to urban and the increased problems of the urbanized society have led to comparisons between the two ways of life. Urban life is seen as secondary, tense, complicated, and anonymous, and rural life is seen as primary, simple, peaceful, and benign. This tendency to idealize rural life may partially explain the current rush to the suburbs. Nostalgia for the rural existence may be based on fact or on wishful thinking, but some rural-urban behavioral differences do exist. There seems to be greater religious and political tolerance in cities and greater religious observance (church attendance) in rural areas. There is more change in cities, more stability in rural areas. There is a higher level of education and a lower birth rate in cities. There is more suicide, divorce, and a lower proportion of married people in the cities. Rates of mental illness, illegitimacy, and crime may be slightly higher in cities, but because cities keep statistics better than rural areas, we cannot be sure.[7] Technological change and

---

[6] This is summarized from Thomlinson, *Urban Structure*, pp. 152–153.

[7] Rural-urban differences are discussed and summarized in Bernard Berelson and Gary Steiner's book, *Human Behavior* (New York: Harcourt Brace Jovanovich, 1964), pp. 606–607.

the spreading influence of the mass media have in a sense given all—rural and urban dwellers alike—contact with a similar culture and set of values. The result is that many former differences between rural and urban people are rapidly disappearing.

A related ecological phenomenon is the exodus from the city to the suburbs, especially by whites. The area near the center of the city ("zone in transition," "workingman's zone") often offers the least expensive housing in the city. As a result, lower-class and minority group members migrate into these areas, and as they move in others who can afford it leave for the suburbs. This has been occurring for several decades and with ever-increasing frequency in the 1960s. The Bureau of the Census estimated in 1969 that for the two preceding years, 500,000 people migrated from city to suburb per year. This was nearly three times the yearly rate in the years between 1960 and 1966. The Bureau of the Census reported in 1970 that for the first time, suburbanites outnumbered city dwellers. Of the twenty-five largest cities in 1970, thirteen had less population than they had in 1960.

It was also estimated in 1969 that for every black who moved into central cities, three whites left for the suburbs. Between 1960 and 1970, the percentage of whites living in central cities declined while whites living outside central cities increased by nearly 30 percent. In 1970, 72 percent of all whites and 81 percent of all blacks lived in urban areas. Several of our largest cities already have black majorities. The obvious result is that America is becoming more and more racially segregated. More and more schools are becoming all white or all black, and the gaps in understanding and tolerance between races seem to be widening rather than narrowing. This is an urgent problem that American cities in particular and society in general must solve. We should note that all is not well even in white middle-class suburbia: crime rates are going up in suburbs as fast as or faster than in center cities.

Another ecological trend occurring in the United States in the latter half of the twentieth century is the development of strip cities or megalopolises. One city and its suburbs merge and grow into an adjacent city and its suburbs. The eventual result is an unbroken series of cities for tens, possibly hundreds, of miles. Travelers at night over the East Coast report a constant chain of lights from north of Boston to south of Richmond, a 600-mile "city." Strip cities may be anticipated along the West Coast from San Francisco to San Diego, in the Midwest around the Great Lakes, in the Pacific Northwest, along both Florida coasts, and in many other places throughout the country.

Problem Aspects

As well as providing important information about the characteristics of societies, the study of population and human ecology calls attention to several important problems. Study of population trends has caused demographers to alert us to what many feel will become our most serious social problem: the population explosion. "Demographic transition" refers to the movement of a population through three stages: (1) high birth rates and high death rates, (2) high birth rates and low death rates, and (3) low birth rates and low death rates. Western industrialized nations are in the third stage, but nations in the underdeveloped regions of the world are generally in the second stage, which means rapid population growth. With increasing control of disease and death, population is exploding in many countries of the world. We mentioned earlier, for example, that the birth rate in Mexico is more than double that of the United States; Mexico's death rate, however, has dropped to the point where it is roughly the same as ours. The result of this lowered death rate but constant high birth rate is tremendous population growth. World population is growing at a rate of well over one million people per week. At current growth rates it is reported that in 600 years or so we will have about one square foot of land per person. (*Then* maybe further reproduction will be impossible.) Thomas Malthus said in 1789 that population would increase faster than would our ability to produce food and that eventually we would run out of food. He may have been right, for in certain countries today, population pressure is linked to serious problems: poverty, disease, starvation, war.

Many population experts are quite worried about this situation, and organizations all the way from the United Nations to your local Planned Parenthood Association are attempting to inform and enlighten people on the problem and on how to deal with overpopulation. Malthus thought later marriage would solve the problem. Today, birth control—the pill, abortion, sterilization—is seen as the answer. As we noted earlier in this chapter, birth rates in the U.S. have currently been reduced to the lowest levels in history. Whether this will continue is unknown. The rates will have to stay below the replacement level for some 70 years before population will indeed level off. Many American demographers continue to be cautious, believing that there is a population bomb latent, but not armed, in present society. A Zero Population Growth spokesman states that "The birth rate is notably fluid and capricious, strongly affected by such psychological factors as the economy or changing attitudes about the role of women." Some countries with high birth rates have encountered difficulty in introducing new population-control measures, especially when they run counter to local customs. Distrust of doctors, ignorance about biological facts or the consequences of overpopulation, desire for many sons to help farm the land, and numerous other cultural values have frustrated the efforts of people interested in population control. If the problem is ignored, or if we give up on it, it may be taken out of our hands—involuntary death control through starvation, war, or selective annihilation may be the last answer. Governmental intervention and national planning already occurring in some countries will have to become worldwide if this problem is to be effectively dealt with. On the encouraging side, recent evidence in some developing nations indicates that their high birth rates are beginning to decline. Ben Wattenberg has summarized research that reports some significant birth-rate drops between 1960 and 1970: South Korea from 41 to 31, Taiwan from 40 to 28, Costa Rica from 48 to 33. Many of the declines were modest, but of the 85 nations with complete birth-registration data, 78 reported declining rates.[8]

Some people optimistically suggest that population redistribution will help solve the problem, and they cite as evidence high population densities in some countries (over 800 people per square mile in Belgium and Holland, over 700 per square mile in Japan) and low population densities in other countries (five people per square mile in Canada and Australia, 28 per square mile in Russia, 57 in the U.S.). It is obvious, they suggest, that some countries are underpopulated and population redistribution would help. Paul Ehrlich disputes this and argues that overpopulation is a *world* problem, not a problem of individual countries, and redistribution of population will aggravate rather than solve the problem. More densely populated countries (like Holland) are seldom self-sufficient and depend on the "underpopulated" countries for resources and food. Measurements around the globe indicate that atmospheric dustiness is increasing by perhaps thirty percent per decade, and this poses a serious threat to the climatological balance. Fuels are being burned at rates that will exhaust estimated world reserves in well under a century. Pesticide residues are found everywhere—even in the fat of Antarctic penguins and in the Greenland ice cap. These facts indicate that the *world* has a population problem. Population distribution does present problems, especially in overcrowded urban areas, but the first priority in Ehrlich's opinion is not population redistribution but stopping population growth.[9]

Ecologists and urban sociologists call attention to other serious problems that are as difficult to solve as the population explosion. Specifically, they are worried about the ways we are using and destroying the environment. The automobile has taken over the American city. Most of the land area in our cities must be devoted to car-related functions—streets, highways, parking lots. With the advent of drive-in movies, drive-in restaurants, drive-in banks, drive-in stores, and now even drive-in church services, drive-in marriage ceremonies, and drive-in funeral parlors, it will soon be possible for man to go from birth to death almost without ever leaving his car. Industries and the car are

[8] See Wattenberg's article, "The Decline of the American Baby," *World,* August 29, 1972, pp. 20–23.

[9] Paul Ehrlich has written a number of articles and several books on population and ecological problems. The ideas that I have summarized here come from Paul Ehrlich and John Holdren, "Why Do People Move?" which appeared in *Saturday Review* (September 5, 1970), p. 51.

polluting our environment. Two rivers in Ohio were recently declared fire hazards. Chemicals developed to control insects have turned out to be more effective than was anticipated and are now destroying other forms of wildlife. Cities are becoming uglier, and urban sprawl is gutting the landscape. Cities are having increasing difficulty disposing of the huge amounts of garbage and refuse that people are producing (on the average, Americans produce more than four pounds of pure garbage per person per day). City centers are being abandoned, and we are creating slums at fantastic rates. More and more people feel that the city is an unfit place to live—only those live there who are forced to.[10]

Perhaps we came too quickly into an urban world. It is a fact that living in cities, especially large cities, is a relatively new experience. In 1800 only about three percent of the world's population lived in cities of 5,000 or more. By 1900, the proportion living in cities had grown to fourteen percent, and by 1950, to thirty percent.[11] The U.S. has changed from a sparsely settled rural country to an extremely urbanized nation. Possibly our problems are to be expected due to man's lack of experience with the phenomenon of urbanization.

In his book *The Human Zoo,* zoologist Desmond Morris suggests that man is basically a tribal or small-group animal. Man is used to interacting on a localized, interpersonal basis. Relatively recently in man's history he has, because of population growth and economic advantage, been forced into a super-tribal or urban existence. Morris describes this new existence as "a human zoo." Man has adapted well to some aspects of the super-tribe—the urban environment has stimulated "man's insatiable curiosity, his inventiveness, his intellectual athleticism." Man has adapted less well to other aspects, however, and we see suicide, war, crime, mental illness, and destruction of the environment. The simple tribesman became a citizen, but according to Morris man has not had time to evolve into a new, genetically civilized species. Man has adapted somewhat to his new environment through learning and conditioning, but biologically he is still a simple tribal animal. Morris concludes, "If he is given the chance he may yet contrive to turn his human zoo into a magnificent human game-park. If he is not, it may proliferate into a gigantic lunatic asylum, like one of the hideously cramped menageries of the last century."[12]

[10] A detailed account of the problems facing cities is provided by Mitchell Gordon in his book *Sick Cities* (Baltimore: Penguin Books, 1965).

[11] This is summarized from Thomlinson, *Urban Structure,* pp. 46–48.

[12] Desmond Morris, *The Human Zoo* (New York: McGraw-Hill, 1969), especially Chapter 1. The quote is from page 248.

Summary

In the previous chapters in this section on social organization we dealt with groups, categories, aggregations, and institutions. These are abstract concepts, but they are valuable for their capacity to describe and analyze the social organization of society. In this chapter, we continue to study social organization but in a somewhat different manner. The focus changes to population and human ecology, and we move from the abstract to the concrete.

Population and human ecology involve the study of numbers of people and their location in space. Population variables that are examined include birth and death rates, life expectancy figures, numbers of people in sex, age, race, ethnic, and religious categories, and migration rates. Ecological variables that are examined include study of city patterns (slums, suburbs, strip cities), ecological processes, reasons for spatial patterning, and consequences of spatial patterning. The study of population and human ecology supplies descriptive data about a society. These data, usually of a statistical nature, develop a picture of a society that often provides an interesting contrast to the picture supplied by the more abstract studies of groups and institutions. Finally, the study of population and ecology has today called attention to several serious problems facing mankind—overpopulation, urbanization, the destruction of the environment—and has encouraged development of the social planning needed to solve these problems.

Numerous books and articles have called attention to the almost insurmountable problems that the city faces. In the first of two readings which follow, Gus Tyler summarizes some of these problems and suggests possible solutions. At the moment, overcrowded countries like India seem to have much more of a population problem than the United States. Wayne Davis in his article "Overpopulated America" suggests that, in fact, just the reverse is true. Given our numbers, our affluence, and our standard of living, we are in much more serious difficulty than India.

Can Anyone Run a City?

Gus Tyler

In the summer of 1970, Tokyo had a five-day smog crisis that sent more than 8,000 people to hospitals. New York City had, simultaneously, a heat wave, a smog alert, and a power shortage. And in Sydney, Australia, citizens were having trouble swimming on beaches where 200 million gallons of sewage were being dumped daily.

Gus Tyler describes the many and severe problems faced by that ecological phenomenon, the city. He discusses migration, population pressure and density, race, city government, and economic policies to illustrate that the situation is serious. It is not insurmountable, however, if we immediately get at the task of careful urban planning.

Can anyone run a city? For scores of candidates who have run for municipal office across the nation this week, the reply obviously is a rhetorical yes. But if we are to judge by the experiences of many mayors whose terms have brought nothing but failure and despair, the answer must be no. "Our association has had a tremendous casualty list in the past year," noted Terry D. Schrunk, mayor of Portland, Oregon, and president of the U.S. Conference of Mayors. "When we went home from Chicago in 1968, we had designated thirty-nine mayors to sit in places of leadership. . . . Today, nearly half of them are either out of office or going out . . . most of them by their own decision not to run again." Since that statement, two of the best mayors in the country—Jerome P. Cavanagh of Detroit and Richard C. Lee of New Haven—have chosen not to run again.

Why do mayors want out? Because, says Mayor Joseph M. Barr of Pittsburgh, "the problems are almost insurmountable. Any mayor who's not frustrated is not thinking." Thomas G. Currigan, former mayor of Denver, having chucked

it all in mid-term, says he hopes "to heaven the cities are not ungovernable, [but] there are some frightening aspects that would lead one to at least think along these lines." The scholarly Mayor Arthur Naftalin of Minneapolis adds his testimony: "Increasingly, the central city is unable to meet its problems. The fragmentation of authority is such that there isn't much a city can decide anymore: it can't deal effectively with education or housing."

Above all, the city cannot handle race. Cavanagh, Naftalin, and Lee—dedicated liberal doers all—were riot victims. Mayor A. W. Sorensen of Omaha had to confess that after he'd "gone through three-and-a-half years in this racial business," he'd had it.

Although frictions over race relations often ignite urban explosives, the cities of America—and the world—are proving ungovernable even where they are ethnically homogeneous. Tokyo is in hara-kiri, though racially pure. U Thant, in a statement to the U.N.'s Economic and Social Council, presented the urban problem as world-wide: "In many countries the housing situation . . . verges on disaster. . . . Throughout the developing world, the city is failing badly."

What is the universal malady of cities? The disease is density. Where cities foresaw density and planned accordingly, the situation is bad but tolerable. Where exploding populations hit unready urban areas, they are in disaster. Where ethnic and political conflict add further disorder, the disease appears terminal.

Some naturalists, in the age of urban crisis, have begun to study density as a disease. Crowded rats grow bigger adrenals, pouring out their juices in fear and fury. Crammed cats go through a "Fascist" transformation, with a "despot" at the top, "pariahs" at the bottom, and a general malaise in the community, where the cats, according to P. Leyhausen, "seldom relax, they never look at ease, and there is continuous hissing, growling, and even fighting."

How dense are the cities? The seven out of every ten Americans who live in cities occupy only 1 per cent of the total land area of the country. In the central city the situation is tighter, and in the inner core it is tightest. If we all lived as crushed as the blacks in Harlem, the total population of America could be squeezed into three of the five boroughs of New York City.

This density is, in part, a product of total population explosion. At some point the whole Earth will be as crowded as Harlem—or worse—unless we control births. But, right now, our deformity is due less to overall population than to the lopsided way in which we grow. In the 1950s, half of all the counties in the U.S. actually lost population; in the 1960s, four states lost population. Where did these people go? Into cities and metropolitan states. By the year 2000, we will have an additional 100 million Americans, almost all of whom will end up in the metropolitan areas.

The flow of the population from soil to city has been underway for more than a century, turning what was once a rural nation into an urban one by the early 1900s. Likewise, the flow from city to suburb has been underway for almost half a century. "We shall solve the city problem by leaving the city," advised Henry Ford in a high-minded blurb for his flivver. But, in the past decade, the flow has become a flood. Modern know-how dispossessed millions of farmers, setting in motion a mass migration of ten million Americans from rural, often backward, heavily black and Southern counties to the cities. They carried with them all the upset of the uprooted, with its inherent ethnic and economic conflict. American cities, like Roman civilization, were hit by tidal waves of modern Vandals. Under the impact of this new rural-push/urban-pull, distressed city dwellers started to move—then to run—out. Hence, the newest demographic dynamic: urban-push and suburban-pull. In the 1940s, half the metropolitan increase was in the suburbs; in the 1950s, it was two-thirds; in the 1960s, the central cities stopped growing while the suburbs boomed.

Not only people left the central city; but jobs, too, thereby creating a whole new set of economic and logistic problems. Industrial plants (the traditional economic ladder for new ethnic populations) began to flee the city in search of space for factories with modern horizontal layouts. Between 1945 and 1965, 63 per cent of all new industrial building took place outside the core. At present 75 to 80 per cent of new jobs in trade and industry are situated on the metropolitan fringe. In the New York metropolitan area from 1951 to 1965, 127,753 new jobs were located in the city while more than three times that number (387,873) were located in the suburbs. In the Philadelphia metropolis, the city *lost* 49,461 jobs, while the suburbs gained 215,296. For the blue-collar worker who could afford to move to the suburbs or who could commute (usually by car) there were jobs. For those who were stuck in the city, the alternatives were work in small competitive plants hungry for cheap labor and no work at all.

Ironically, the worthwhile jobs that did locate in the cities were precisely those most unsuited for people of the inner core, namely, white-collar clerical, administrative, and executive positions. These jobs locate in high-rise office buildings with their vertical complexes of cubicles, drawing to them the more affluent employees who live in the outskirts and suburbs.

This disallocation of employment, calling for daily commuter migrations, has helped turn the automobile from a solution into a problem, as central cities have become stricken with auto-immobility; in midtown New York, the vehicular pace has been reduced from 11.5 mph in 1907 to 6 mph in 1963. To break the traffic jam, cities have built highways, garages, and parking lots that eat up valuable (once taxable) space in their busy downtowns: 55 per cent of the land in central Los Angeles, 50 per cent in Atlanta, 40 per cent in Boston, 30 per cent in Denver. All these "improvements," however, encourage more cars to come and go, leaving the central city poorer, not better.

Autos produce auto-intoxication: poisoning of the air. While the car is not the only offender (industry causes about 18 per cent of pollution; electric generators, 12 per cent; space heaters, 6 per cent; refuse disposal, 2.5 per cent), it is the main menace spewing forth 60 per cent of all the atmospheric filth. In 1966, a temperature inversion in New York City—fatefully coinciding with a national conference on air pollution—brought on eighty deaths. In 1952, in London, 4,000 people died during a similar atmospheric phenomenon.

The auto also helped to kill mass transit, the rational solution to the commuter problem. The auto drained railroads of passengers; to make up the loss, the railroads boosted fares; as fares went up, more passengers turned to autos; faced with bankruptcy, lines fell behind in upkeep, driving passengers to anger and more autos. Between 1950 and 1963, a dozen lines quit the passenger business; of the 500 intercity trains still in operation, fifty have applied to the ICC for discontinuance. Meanwhile, many treat their passengers as if they were freight.

Regional planners saw this coming two generations ago and proposed networks of mass transportation. But the auto put together its own lobby to decide otherwise: auto manufacturers, oil companies, road builders, and politicians who depend heavily on the construction industry for campaign contributions.

The auto is even failing in its traditional weekend role as a means to get away. On a hot August weekend this year, Jones Beach had to close down for a full hour, because 60,000 cars tried to get into parking lots with a capacity of 24,000. The cars moved on to the Robert Moses State Park and so jammed the 6,000-car lot there as to force a two-hour shutdown.

Overcrowding of the recreation spots is due not only to more people with more cars but to the pollution of waters by the dumping of garbage—another by-product of metropolitan density.

Viewed in the overall, our larger metropolises with their urban and suburban areas are repeating the gloomy evolution of our larger cities. When Greater New York was composed of Manhattan (then New York) and the four surrounding boroughs, the idea was to establish a balanced city: a crowded center surrounded by villages and farms. In the end, all New York became citified. Likewise, the entire metropolitan area is becoming urbanized with the suburbanite increasingly caught up in the city tangle.

The flow from city to suburb does not, surprisingly, relieve crowding within the central city, even in those cases where the city population is no longer growing. The same number of people—especially in the poor areas—have fewer places to live. In recent years, some 12,000 buildings that once housed about 60,000 families in New York City have been abandoned, with tenants being dispossessed by derelicts and rats; 3,000 more buildings are expected to be abandoned this year. The story of these buildings, in a city such as New York, reads like a Kafkaesque comedy. For the city to tear down even one of these menaces involves two to four years of red tape; to get possession of the land takes another two to four years. Meanwhile, the wrecks are inhabited by human wrecks preparing their meals over Sterno cans that regularly set fire to the buildings. By law, the fire department is then charged with the responsibility of risking men's lives to put out the fire, which they usually can do. However, when the flames get out of hand, other worthy buildings are gutted, leaving whole blocks of charred skeletons—victims of the quiet riot.

Other dwellings are being torn down by private builders to make way for high-rise luxury apartments and commercial structures. *Public* action has destroyed more housing than has been built in all federally aided programs. As a result, the crowded are more crowded than ever. Rehabilitation instead of renewal doesn't work. New York City tried it only to discover that rehabilitation costs $38 a square foot—a little *more* than new luxury housing.

The result of all this housing decay and destruction (plus FHA money to encourage more affluent whites to move to the suburbs) has been, says the National Commission on Urban Problems, "to intensify racial and economic stratification of America's urban areas."

While ghetto cores turn into ghost towns, the ghetto fringes flare out. The crime that oozes through the sores of the diseased slum chases away old neighbors, a few of whom can make it to the suburbs; the rest seek refuge in the "urban villages" of the low-income whites. Cities become denser and tenser than they were. In the process, these populous centers of civilization become—like Europe during the Dark Ages—the bloody soil on which armed towns wage their inevitable wars over a street, a building, a hole in the wall. Amid this troubled terrain, the free-lance criminal adds to the anarchy.

All these problems (plus welfare, schooling, and militant unions of municipal employees) hit the mayors at a time when, according to the National Commission on Urban Problems, "there is a crisis of urban government finance . . . rooted in conditions that will not disappear but threaten to grow and spread rapidly." The "roots" of the "crisis"? The mayor starts with a historic heavy debt burden. His power to tax and borrow is often tethered by a rural-minded state legislature. He has lost many of the city's wealthy payers to the suburbs. His levies on property (small homes) and sales are prodding Mr. Middle to a tax revolt. The bigger (richer) the city is, the worse off it is. As population increases, per capita cost of running a city goes up—not down: density makes for frictions that demand expensive social lubricants. Municipalities of 100,000 to 299,000 spend $14.60 per person on police; those of 300,000 to 490,000 spend $18.33; and those of 500,000 to one million spend $21.88. New York City spends $39.83. On hospitalization, the first two categories spend $5 to $8 per person; those over 500,000 spend $12.54; New York spends $55.19.

Expanding the economy of a city does not solve the problem; it makes it worse. Several scholarly studies have come up with this piece of empiric pessimism: if the gross income of a city goes up 100 per cent, revenue rises only 90 per cent, and expenditures rise 110 per cent. Consequently, when a city's economy grows, the city's budget is in a worse fix than before. This diseconomy of bigness and richness applies even when cities merely limit themselves to prior levels of services. But cities, unable to cling to this inadequate past, have had to step up services to meet the rising expectations of city dwellers.

The easy out for a mayor is to demand that the federal coffers take over cost or hand over money. But is that the real answer? The federal income tax as presently levied falls most heavily on an already embittered middle class—our alienated majority. Unable to push this group any harder and unwilling to "soak the rich," an administration, such as President Nixon's, comes up with revenue-sharing toothpicks with which to shore up mountains. Nixon has proposed half a billion for next year and $5-billion by 1975, while urban experts see a need for $20- to $50-billion each year for the next decade. A Senate committee headed by Senator Abe Ribicoff calls for a cool trillion.

But even if a trillion were forthcoming, it might be unable to do the job. To build, a city must rebuild: bulldoze buildings, redirect highways, clear for mass transportation, remake streets—a tough task. But even tougher, a city must bulldoze people who are rigidified in resistant economic and political enclaves. The total undertaking could be more difficult than resurrecting a Phoenix that was already nothing but a heap of ashes.

What powers does a mayor bring to these complex problems? Very few. Many cities have a weak mayor setup, making him little more than a figurehead. If he has power, he lacks money. If he has power and money, he must find real—not symbolic—solutions to problems in the context of a density that turns "successes" into failures. If a mayor can, miraculously, come up with comprehensive plans, they will have to include a region far greater than the central city where he reigns.

A mayor must try to do all this in an era of political retribalism, when communities are demanding more, not less, say over the governance of their little neighborhoods. In this hour, when regional government is needed to cope with the many problems of the metropolitan area as a unity, the popular mood is to break up and return power to those warring factions—racial, economic, religious, geographic—that have in numerous cases turned a city into a no man's land.

Is there then no hope? There is—if we putter less within present cities and start planning a national push-pull to decongest urban America. Our answer is not in new mayors but in new cities; not in urban renewal but in urban "newal," to use planner Charles Abrams's felicitous word.

We cannot juggle the 70 per cent of the American people around on 1 per cent of the land area to solve the urban mess. We are compelled to think in terms of new towns and new cities planned for placement and structure by public action with public funds. "All of the urbanologists agree," reported *Time* amidst the 1967 riot months, "that one of the most important ways of saving cities is simply to have more cities." The National Committee on Urban Growth Policy proposed this summer that the federal government embark on a program to create 110 new cities (100 having a population of 100,000, and ten even larger) over the next three decades. At an earlier time, the Advisory Commission on Intergovernmental Relations proposed a national policy on urban growth, to use our vast untouched stock of land to "increase, rather than diminish, Americans' choices of places and environments," to counteract our present "diseconomics of scale involved in continuing urban concentration, the locational mismatch of jobs and people, the connection between urban and rural poverty problems, and urban sprawl."

New towns would set up a new dynamic. In the central cities, decongestion could lead to real urban renewal, starting with the clearing of the ghost blocks where nobody lives and ending with open spaces or even some of those dreamy "cities with a city." The new settlements could be proving grounds for all those exciting ideas of city planners whose proposals have been frustrated by present structures—physical and political. "Obsolete practices such as standard zoning, parking on the street, school bussing, on-street loading, and highway clutter could all be planned out of a new city," notes William E. Finley in the Urban Growth report. These new towns (cities) could bring jobs, medicine, education, and culture to the ghost towns in rural America, located in the counties that have lost population—and income—in the past decades. Finally, a half-century project for new urban areas would pick up the slack in employment when America, hopefully, runs out of wars to fight.

The cost would be great, but no greater than haphazard private development that will pop up Topsy-like to accommodate the added 100 million people who will crowd America by the year 2000. Right now we grow expensively by horizontal or vertical accretion. We sprawl onto costly ground, bought up by speculators and builders looking for a fast buck. Under a national plan, the federal government could buy up a store of ground in removed places at low cost or use present government lands. Where private developers reach out for vertical space, they erect towers whose building costs go up geometrically with every additional story. On the other hand, as city planners have been pointing out for a couple of decades, "it has been proved over and over again, by such builders as Levitt, Burns, and Bohannon" that efficient mass production of low-risers "can and do produce better and cheaper houses." Cliff dwellings cost more than split-levels.

The idea of new towns is not untested. "There is little precedent in this country, but ample precedent abroad," notes the Committee on Urban Growth. "Great Britain, France, the Netherlands, the Scandinavian countries—all have taken a direct hand in land and population development in the face of urbanization, and all can point to examples of orderly growth that contrast sharply with the American metropolitan ooze." To the extent that the U.S. has created new communities it has done so as by-products: Norris, Tennessee, was built for TVA to house men working on a dam; Los Alamos, Oak Ridge, and Hanford were built for the Atomic Energy Commission "to isolate its highly secret operations."

What then is the obstacle to this new-cities idea? It runs contrary to the traditional wisdom that a) where cities are located, they should be located, and b) that the future ought to be left to private enterprise. Both thoughts are a hangover from a hang-up with laissez faire, a Panglossian notion that what is, is best.

The fact is, however, that past reasons for locating cities no longer hold—at least, not to the same extent. Once cities grew up at rural crossroads; later at the meeting of waters; still later at railroad junctions; then near sources of raw material. But today, as city planner Edgardo Contini testified before a Congressional committee, these reasons are obsolete. "Recent technological and transportation trends—synthesis rather than extraction of materials, atomic rather than hydroelectric or thermoelectric power, air rather than rail transportation—all tend to expand the opportunities for location of urban settlements." Despite this, the old cities, by sheer weight of existence, become a magnetic force drawing deadly densities.

Furthermore, concluded Mr. Contini and a host of others, "the scale of the new cities program is too overwhelming for private initiative alone to sustain, and its purposes and implications are too relevant to the country's future to be relinquished to the profit motive alone." The report of the Urban Growth Committee stresses the limited impact of new towns put up by private developers such as Columbia, Maryland and Reston, Virginia. "They are, and will be, in the first place, few in number, serving only a tiny fraction of total population growth. A new town is a 'patient' investment, requiring large outlays long before returns begin; it is thus a non-competitive investment in a tight money market. Land in town-size amounts is hard to find and assemble without public powers of eminent domain. Privately developed new towns, moreover, by definition must serve the market, which tends to fill them with housing for middle- to upper-income families rather than the poor."

The choice before America is really not between new cities and old. Population pressure will force outward expansion. But by present drift, this will be unplanned accretion—plotted for quick profit rather than public need. What is needed is national concern for the commonweal in the location and design of new cities: a kind of inner space program.

Questions

1. Forces influencing human ecology have changed. Cities no longer have to be located at rail junctions, on rivers, or near natural resources. Explain why.

2. *Discuss what Tyler feels to be the major problem or "universal malady" of the cities.*
3. *Analyze in detail the problems for the city that are caused by the automobile.*
4. *The solution is urban "newal," not urban renewal—building new cities rather than changing old ones. Explain why.*

Overpopulated America

Wayne H. Davis

Population pressure may be assessed by means of many different variables: number of people, population density, ability of the land to produce food, trends in birth rates and death rates. Wayne Davis introduces the variables of affluence and standard of living and suggests that they may be at least as important as number of people. He compares America's population problem to India's by using the concept "Indian equivalents." Professor Davis teaches in the school of biological sciences at the University of Kentucky.

I define as most seriously overpopulated that nation whose people by virtue of their numbers and activities are most rapidly decreasing the ability of the land to support human life. With our large population, our affluence and our technological monstrosities the United States wins first place by a substantial margin.

Let's compare the US to India, for example. We have 203 million people, whereas she has 540 million on much less land. But look at the impact of people on the land.

The average Indian eats his daily few cups of rice (or perhaps wheat, whose production on American farms contributed to our one percent per year drain in quality of our active farmland), draws his bucket of water from the communal well and sleeps in a mud hut. In his daily rounds to gather cow dung to burn to cook his rice and warm his feet, his footsteps, along with those of millions of his countrymen, help bring about a slow deterioration of the ability of the land to support people. His contribution to the destruction of the land is minimal.

An American, on the other hand, can be expected to destroy a piece of land on which he builds a home, garage and driveway. He will contribute his share to the 142 million tons of smoke and fumes, seven million junked cars, 20 million tons of paper, 48 billion cans, and 26 billion bottles the overburdened environment must absorb each year. To run his air conditioner we will strip-mine a Kentucky hillside, push the dirt and slate down into the stream, and burn coal in a power generator, whose smokestack contributes to a plume of smoke massive enough to cause cloud seeding and premature precipitation from Gulf winds which should be irrigating the wheat farms of Minnesota.

In his lifetime he will personally pollute three million gallons of water, and industry and agriculture will use ten times this much water in his behalf. To provide these needs the US Army Corps of Engineers will build dams and flood farmland. He will also use 21,000 gallons of leaded gasoline containing boron, drink 28,000 pounds of milk and eat 10,000 pounds of meat. The latter is produced and squandered in a life pattern unknown to Asians. A steer on a Western range eats plants contining minerals necessary for plant life. Some of these are incorporated into the body of the steer which is later shipped for slaughter. After being eaten by man these nutrients are flushed down the toilet into the ocean or buried in the cemetery, the surface of which is cluttered with boulders called tombstones and has been removed from productivity. The result is a continual drain on the productivity of range land. Add to this the erosion of overgrazed lands, and the effects of the falling water table as we mine Pleistocene deposits of groundwater to irrigate to produce food for more people, and we can see why our land is dying far more rapidly than did the great civilizations of the Middle East, which experienced the same cycle. The average Indian citizen, whose fecal material goes back to the land, has but a minute fraction of the destructive effect on the land that the affluent American does.

Thus I want to introduce a new term, which I suggest be used in future discussions of human population and ecology. We should speak of our numbers in "Indian equivalents." An Indian equivalent I define as the average number of Indian citizens required to have the same detrimental effect on the land's ability to support human life as would the average American. This value is difficult to determine, but let's take an extremely conservative working figure of 25. To see how conservative this is, imagine the addition of 1000 citizens to your town and 25,000 to an Indian village. Not only would the Americans destroy much more land for homes, highways and a shopping center, but they would contribute far more to environmental deterioration in hundreds of other ways as well. For example, their demand for steel for new autos might increase the daily pollution equivalent of 130,000 junk autos which *Life* tells us that US Steel Corp. dumps into Lake Michigan. Their demand for textiles would help the cotton industry destroy the life in the Black Warrior River in Alabama with endrin. And they would contribute to the massive industrial pollution of our oceans (we provide one third to one half the world's share) which has caused the precipitous downward trend in our commercial fisheries landings during the past seven years.

The per capita gross national product of the United States is 38 times that of India. Most of our goods and services contribute to the decline in the ability of the environment to support life. Thus it is clear that a figure of 25 for an Indian equivalent is conservative. It has been suggested to me that a more realistic figure would be 500.

In Indian equivalents, therefore, the population of the United States is at least four billion. And the rate of growth is even more alarming. We are growing at one percent per year, a rate which would double our numbers in 70 years. India is growing at 2.5 percent. Using the Indian equivalent of 25, our population growth becomes 10 times as serious as that of India. According to the Rienows in their recent book *Moment in the Sun,* just one year's crop of American babies can be expected to use up 25 billion pounds of beef, 200 million pounds of steel and 9.1 billion gallons of gasoline during their collective lifetime. And the demands on water and land for our growing population are expected to be far greater than the supply available in the year 2000. We are destroying our land at a rate of over a million acres a year. We now have only 2.6 agricultural acres per person. By 1975 this will be cut to 2.2, the critical point for the maintenance of what we consider a decent diet, and by the year 2000 we might expect to have 1.2.

You might object that I am playing with statistics in using the Indian equivalent on the rate of growth. I am making the assumption that today's child will live 35 years (the average Indian life span) at today's level of affluence. If he lives an American 70 years, our rate of population growth would be 20 times as serious as India's.

But the assumption of continued affluence at today's level is unfounded. If our numbers continue to rise, our standard of living will fall so sharply that by the year 2000 any surviving Americans might consider today's average Asian to be well off. Our children's destructive effects on their environment will decline as they sink ever lower into poverty.

The United States is in serious economic trouble now. Nothing could be more misleading than today's affluence, which rests precariously on a crumbling foundation. Our productivity, which had been increasing steadily at about 3.2 percent a year since World War II, has been falling during 1969. Our export over import balance has been shrinking steadily from $7.1 billion in 1964 to $0.15 billion in the first half of 1969. Our balance of payments deficit for the second quarter was $3.7 billion, the largest in history. We are now importing iron ore, steel, oil, beef, textiles, cameras, radios and hundreds of other things.

Our economy is based upon the Keynesian concept of a continued growth in population and productivity. It worked in an underpopulated nation with excess resources. It could continue to work only if the earth and its resources were expanding at an annual rate of 4 to 5 percent. Yet neither the number of cars, the economy, the human population, nor anything else can expand indefinitely at an exponential rate in a finite world. We must face this fact *now*. The crisis is here. When Walter Heller says that our economy will expand by 4 percent annually through the latter 1970s he is dreaming. He is in a theoretical world totally unaware of the realities of human ecology. If the economists do not wake up and devise a new system for us now somebody else will have to do it for them.

A civilization is comparable to a living organism. Its longevity is a function of its metabolism. The higher the metabolism (affluence), the shorter the life. Keynesian economics has allowed us an affluent but shortened life span. We have now run our course.

The tragedy facing the United States is even greater and more imminent than that descending upon the hungry nations. The Paddock brothers in their book, *Famine 1975!*, say that India "cannot be saved" no matter how much food we ship her. But India will be here after the United States is gone. Many millions will die in the most colossal famines India has ever known, but the land will survive and she will come back as she always has before. The United States, on the other hand, will be a desolate tangle of concrete and ticky-tacky, of strip-mined moonscape and silt-choked reservoirs. The land and water will be so contaminated with pesticides, herbicides, mercury fungicides, lead, boron, nickel, arsenic and hundreds of other toxic substances, which have been approaching critical levels of concentration in our environment as a result of our numbers and affluence, that it may be unable to sustain human life.

Thus as the curtain gets ready to fall on man's civilization let it come as no surprise that it shall first fall on the United States. And let no one make the mistake of thinking we can save ourselves by "cleaning up the environment." Banning DDT is the equivalent of the physician's treating syphilis by putting a bandaid over the first chancre to appear. In either case you can be sure that more serious and widespread trouble will soon appear unless the disease itself is treated. We cannot survive by planning to treat the symptoms such as air pollution, water pollution, soil erosion, etc.

What can we do to slow the rate of destruction of the United States as a land capable of supporting human life? There are two approaches. First, we must reverse the population growth. We have far more people now than we can continue to support at anything near today's level of affluence. American women average slightly over three children each. According to the *Population Bulletin* if we reduced this number to 2.5 there would still be 330 million people in the nation at the end of the century. And even if we reduced this to 1.5 we would have 57 million more people in the year 2000 than we have now. With our present longevity patterns it would take more than 30 years for the population to peak even when reproducing at this rate, which would eventually give us a net decrease in numbers.

Do not make the mistake of thinking that technology will solve our population problem by producing a better contraceptive. Our problem now is that people want too many children. Surveys show the average number of children wanted by the American family is 3.3. There is little difference between the poor and the wealthy, black and white, Catholic and Protestant. Production of children at this rate during the next 30 years would be so catastrophic in effect on our resources and the viability of the nation as to be beyond my ability to contemplate. To prevent this trend we must not only make contraceptives and abortion readily available to everyone, but we must establish a system to put severe economic pressure on those who produce children and reward those who do not. This can be done within our system of taxes and welfare.

The other thing we must do is to pare down our Indian equivalents. Individuals in American society vary tremendously in Indian equivalents. If we plot Indian equivalents versus their reciprocal, the percentage of land surviving a generation, we obtain a linear regression. We can then place individuals and occupation types on this graph. At one end would be the starving blacks of Mississippi; they would approach unity in Indian equivalents, and would have the least destructive effect on the land. At the other end of the graph would be the politicians slicing pork for the barrel, the highway contractors, strip-mine operators, real estate developers, and public enemy number one—the US Army Corps of Engineers.

We must halt land destruction. We must abandon the view of land and minerals as private property to be exploited in any way economically feasible for private financial gain. Land and minerals are resources upon which the very survival of the nation depends, and their use must be planned in the best interests of the people.

Rising expectations for the poor is a cruel joke foisted upon them by the Establishment. As our new economy of use-it-once-and-throw-it-away produces more and more products for the affluent, the share of our resources available for the poor declines. Blessed be the starving blacks of Mississippi with their outdoor privies, for they are ecologically sound, and they shall inherit a nation. Although I hope that we will help these unfortunate people attain a decent standard of living by diverting war efforts to fertility control and job training, our most urgent task to assure this nation's survival during the next decade is to stop the affluent destroyers.

1. *What point is Davis attempting to make by introducing the concept "Indian equivalents"?*
2. *Davis suggests that there are two approaches to America's problem of overpopulation. What are the difficulties likely to be encountered in following these two approaches?*

THREE

Social Change and Social Deviation

In Part 2 we dealt with the individual as a member of society and the social organization of society. We saw that social organization could be studied using the following concepts: group, category and aggregation, institution, population, and human ecology. In Part 3 we will focus on change and deviation in society. The concepts discussed in this section will suggest that all is not as predictable and organized as previous sections may have implied. Uncertainty and instability exist in all societies and are the result of a variety of factors. *Social change* occurs and affects the way individuals and groups relate to each other. If social change is rapid and extreme, the organization of society may break down and *social disorganization* may result. In some situations, behavior occurs that is spontaneous and unstructured but not necessarily disorganized. This type of behavior is called *collective behavior*. We learned in Part 1 that norms and roles describe what people are expected to do in certain situations and positions. But inevitably, many individuals do *not* behave in the ways they are expected to. Societies, in turn, devise ways to encourage or even force conformity. This leads us to the final topics of *deviation* and *social control*.

8

Social Change and Social Disorganization

All societies are dynamic and constantly changing. Some societies change more rapidly than others, and within a society some parts will change more rapidly than others. Frequently, change may lead to problems because, although some individuals and institutions will adjust rapidly, others will have difficulty adapting to change. We can anticipate that social change will occasionally lead to periods of social disorganization as old ways erode and collapse and new ways of behaving are developed.

Strictly speaking, *social* change refers only to change in the structure and functioning of the social relationships of a society. *Cultural* change refers to changes in aspects of the culture (the learned and shared customs, beliefs, habits, and traditions) of that society.[1] However, these two types of change

[1] See the chapter on social change by Alvin Boskoff in Howard Becker and Alvin Boskoff, *Modern Sociological Theory* (New York: Dryden Press, 1957). Also see the discussion by Paul Horton and Chester Hunt in their introductory book, *Sociology*, 3rd Ed. (New York: McGraw-Hill Book Co., 1972), Chapter 20.

are similar. One usually affects the other, and it is often difficult to view them separately. In this chapter, the term "social change" is being used in the broad sense to include both social and cultural change.

Factors Related to Social Change

Various attempts have been made to relate social change to other factors in the physical and social environment.[2] Some of these hypothesized relationships seem farfetched; others seem more reasonable. For example, social change has been related to the biological characteristics of a nation. Adherents of "master race" theories believe that societies fortunate enough to be graced by the presence of a superior race will have greater progress (and more rapid social change) than will less fortunate nations. Bierstedt points out that such theories—present at all times in all societies—are only a primitive form of ethnocentrism. A more realistic approach might hold that certain mixtures of racial or ethnic categories in a given society could lead to greater or lesser conflict and correspondingly, greater or lesser social change. Geographical factors may be related to change. Some countries are more favored by climate and natural resources and this may affect their rates of technological advancement and social change. As we discussed in the previous chapter, demographic factors may lead to change. When a country faces population growth to the point of overcrowding, social relationships change, both within that society and with surrounding societies which may be less crowded.

Social change may be related to the appearance of certain "great men." Recall how societies, and perhaps even the world, were affected and changed by Hitler, Napoleon, Einstein, Lincoln, Karl Marx, and Julius Caesar. The course of events in the United States in the mid-twentieth century has been altered by men like Franklin D. Roosevelt and Martin Luther King, Jr. It is sometimes argued that "great men" alone initiate significant social changes, while others maintain that such men are merely products of their society, and that if they had not appeared, someone else of the same caliber would have. The truth probably lies somewhere between these views. The cultural and societal conditions might be seen as a stage where men perform, a few in unique ways having lasting effects, many others in more commonplace and predictable ways. And, certainly, the historical aspect cannot be overlooked as a factor in change. Many "great men" were made by historical conditions—"accidents" of history. Had they appeared at another time, they would probably have passed unnoticed.

----

[2] This discussion is drawn in part from Robert Bierstedt, *The Social Order*, 3rd Ed. (New York: McGraw-Hill Book Co., 1970), Chapter 20.

Ideological and technological factors are related to social change. The appearance of and commitment to ideas of socialism, democracy, Christianity, science, or progress have led to major social changes. The industrial revolution of the eighteenth and nineteenth centuries was a major force for change in the United States and elsewhere; its dramatic consequences are still with us today. Technological innovations and inventions that have produced tremendous social change include the wheel, the car, the birth control pill, the atom bomb, the gun, the telephone, the airplane, and the computer. It is easy to point to the dramatic inventions that affect societies, probably because their emergence seems sudden, rather than slow and evolutionary as are many changes. Sometimes the effects of inventions are less obvious. William Ogburn recorded numerous examples of the widespread effects of technological innovations.[3] The self-starter on cars aided in the emancipation of women: it allowed women to use cars on an equal basis with men. The invention of the elevator made possible the construction of tall apartment buildings. Living in these buildings, in turn, changed the family: rearing of large families was more difficult, and consequently the urban birth rate declined. The invention of the cotton gin was a major factor leading to the Civil War. Invention of the six-shooter, barbed wire, and the windmill made possible the settling of the Great Plains. To imply that inventions have such far-reaching effects no doubt seems as much of an oversimplification as did the "great men" theory. The lesson probably is that we cannot single out any one element or invention in a culture and attribute change to it alone.

[3] These examples come from a number of different works by Ogburn, and are quoted here from Bierstedt, *The Social Order*, pp. 522–524.

Social change is introduced in a culture through two processes: invention and diffusion. *Invention* refers to the creation of a new object or idea. Usually, although the end product of the invention (car, airplane, telescope) is new, the parts that make it up are not. The elements have been around and are now arranged or put together in a new way. *Diffusion* refers to the spread of objects or ideas from one society to another (Egypt to England) or from one group to another within the same society (upper class to lower class or black to white). Although innovation or invention attracts the most attention, most change is introduced through the process of diffusion.

To sum up the many factors related to social change, we could generalize and say that social change represents the coming together of a number of events: the conditions in a particular culture at a given time in history and the change agent or catalyst—a great man or the invention or diffusion of a new technique, object, or idea.

Rates of Change

It is frequently the case that different segments of a given society change at different rates. William Ogburn called this condition *cultural lag.* A new element may be introduced which requires change in other areas of society, and when these other areas are slow to change, problems result. Faster cars were built in advance of highways that could handle them. Jumbo jets arrived before airports were constructed that could accommodate the increased passenger load. But these are examples of an analogous technological lag. An example of cultural lag is that despite the easy access of a variety of birth control measures, most people still place a high social premium on premarital chastity.

A society's receptivity to change is an important factor in the rate of social change. If a society has a strictly defined system of stratification or rigid institutional structure, change will be slower. If a society is isolated from others, change will be slower. Change will be more rapid in a society that emphasizes values like individualism and self-determination than in a society that emphasizes conformity and reverence for the past and custom. Arnold Green believes that there is a basic resistance to change in all societies in that men are basically conservative and seek stability or "strain for consistency." Resistance to change is balanced to a certain extent by man's curiosity. People continue to seek new knowledge and better ways of doing things, so change must occur.[4]

[4] Arnold Green, *Sociology,* 4th Ed. (New York: McGraw-Hill Book Co., 1964), Chapter 25.

Planned Social Change and Social Movements

It may be that social change is an evolutionary process beyond man's control—man is at the mercy of forces that he can do nothing about. Many people believe, however, that man can do something more than just describe and accept his social environment. Rather, the environment can actually be manipulated for man's benefit. One view of the process of change, as expressed by William Graham Sumner, is that social change must be slow, and change in people's attitudes must precede change in legislation. Sumner believed that laws should not move ahead of the customs of the people, or in his words, "stateways cannot change folkways." An opposite view is that new laws can lead the way—they can change people's attitudes and behavior in necessary and beneficial ways. From 1954 on, court decisions and legislative acts have attempted to change the pattern of interaction between the races in the United States. Civil rights groups in the 1960s, feeling that change had been too slow, tried sit-ins, non-violent demonstrations, and passive resistance to speed up the process. Both sides—those who feel change is beyond control and those who feel that change can be planned and controlled—have fuel for their arguments. The latter group can state that the conditions of minorities in America have improved. The former group, however, can call attention to unanticipated changes that have also occurred: increasing violence between the races in the 1960s, and probably a hardening of racial attitudes on the part of many people. At any rate, social scientists today feel that change within limits can be a planned phenomenon. As a result, we see the development of commissions and agencies focusing on a number of areas where it is felt that planned social change is needed.

Social change may occur through a form of collective behavior called a social movement. According to Turner and Killian, a *social movement* is a group of people acting with some continuity to promote or to resist a change in their society or group. Social movements are lasting rather than temporary, they have a distinctive perspective or viewpoint, they are oriented toward a specific goal or goals, and members have a sense of solidarity or *esprit de corps*.[5] Social movements seem to be especially popular in modern mass society. In mass society there is mass confusion; that is, there are a variety of viewpoints on every issue. The United States, like other mass societies, has a multiplicity of groups from numerous backgrounds, and each group has its own values, its own way of looking at things. Individual discontent, anxiety, and frustration about the condition of the world and about one's own chances are all conducive to social movements.[6] Mass communication exposes us to all the con-

---

[5] Ralph Turner and Lewis Killian, *Collective Behavior*, 2nd Ed. (Englewood Cliffs, N.J.: Prentice-Hall, 1972), p. 246.

[6] See C. Wendell King's book, *Social Movements in the United States* (New York: Random House, 1956), Chapter 1, for a discussion of social movements in mass society.

fusing aspects of the mass society and puts us immediately in touch with others who may also be frustrated and anxious and looking for a way to change things. The combination of these elements—complex societies with a variety of peoples and viewpoints, numbers of people who feel discontented or shortchanged, and a system of mass communication to tie them together—provides fertile soil for social movements.

Examples of social movements in the United States might include the following: the civil-rights movement (which includes organizations like SNCC, NAACP, CORE, Black Muslims, and Black Panthers), the student New Left (SDS), women's rights movements, peace movements, anti-communist movements (John Birch Society, Minutemen), religious movements (Billy Graham, Campus Crusade), and numerous others. Some of these movements are *revolutionary*, in that they demand a complete change in the social order. Others are *reform*, in that they seek modification in certain aspects of society.[7] Social movements of either type, however, provide an important impetus for social change.

Often one social movement will develop to counter the effects of another. A current example centers upon legalization of abortion. As recently as 1966, abortion was illegal throughout the United States although a few states would allow it if the mother's life were in danger. A social movement developed among people who, for a variety of reasons—rights of women, population control, objection to laws that discriminated against the poor—felt that abortion should be legalized. Pamphlets to citizens, letters to senators, articles in newspapers and magazines made people aware of the issue. In 1967, Colorado passed a liberalized abortion law, and soon California, New York, Hawaii, and other states followed. By early 1972, 16 states and the District of Columbia had changed their laws. Then, in January 1973, the U.S. Supreme Court overruled all state laws that prohibited or restricted women from obtaining abortions during the first three months of pregnancy. Seldom is social change, especially legal social change, so rapid, and seldom are the effects of a social movement so dramatic. There was an immediate outcry from those who objected to the Supreme Court's action. Groups of people began getting together—"Right to Life" is the name of one—and a social movement desiring restrictive abortion legislation started to develop. Whether this movement will have the success of the earlier pro-abortion movement appears doubtful, but if the amount of reaction and intensity of feeling are any indication, the movement is not likely to be short-lived.

Collective behavior experts feel that social movements have a life history. One description of the life span of movements sees them going through four stages.[8] The *preliminary* stage involves individual excitement, unrest, and

---

[7] Turner and Killian give a brief discussion of reform and revolutionary movements in *Collective Behavior*, pp. 257–258.

[8] This description of the life history of a social movement is from Rex Hopper, "The Revolutionary Process: A Frame of Reference for the Study of Revolutionary Movements," *Social Forces*, Vol. 28 (March 1950), pp. 270–279.

some milling. Mechanisms of suggestion, imitation, and propaganda are important, and an "agitator" type of leader appears. The *popular* stage involves crowd or collective excitement or unrest. The unrest is now open and widespread, and *esprit de corps* and an ideology or viewpoint become important mechanisms. The leader at this stage is a "prophet" (who puts forth a general ideology) or a "reformer" (who focuses on specific evils and develops a clearly defined program). Eric Hoffer believes that the early stages of social movements are dominated by "true believers." These are people of fanatical faith for whom mass movements have an almost irresistible appeal. The true believer is ready to sacrifice his life for a cause, any cause.[9] The third or *formal* stage of the social movement involves the formulation of issues and formation of publics. The movement becomes "respectable" in order to gain wider appeal. Issues are discussed and debated. The leaders are ' statesmen." The *institutional* stage involves the legalization of the movement; the movement becomes part of the society. The leaders are of the "administrator-executive" type.

Remember that this is a generalized description, and not all social movements follow this pattern. The time involved in any one stage is variable. The unsuccessful social movement disappears before it can progress through all stages. The successful social movement which attains its objectives must adapt and broaden its goals, or it too will die out.

CHARISMATIC MOVEMENT CONTINUING — EVEN IN LEADERS ABSENCE.

Finally, the *charismatic* leader figures prominently in both sociological and popular literature. Charisma refers to a certain quality an individual may have which sets him apart from other men. He is treated as though he were

[9] See *The True Believer* by Eric Hoffer (New York: New American Library, 1951).

super-human and capable of exceptional acts. The charismatic movement follows the charismatic leader—such a leader is a symbol for the movement and he is above criticism.[10] Some movements are so closely identified with the leader that they have no goal beyond that of following him. Other movements, although they follow such a leader, have well-defined goals which allow the movement to continue even if the charismatic leader is lost. Examples of charismatic leaders might include Gandhi, Martin Luther King, Jr., Hitler, Fidel Castro, and Charles de Gaulle.

Patterns of Social Change

Is there any pattern to social change? Is its course predictable? Some scholars think so.[11] Some who have studied change in a number of societies conclude that all change is good and in the direction of progress; others argue very nearly the opposite. Oswald Spengler believed that societies, like people, go through a cycle of birth, youth, maturity, decline, and disintegration. Arnold Toynbee sees societies developing through continuing cycles of *challenge* and *response*. Challenges are at first of a geographical nature, later of a social nature. Toynbee, in contrast to Spengler, is optimistic and sees change going in an upward spiral with ever-higher achievements. Pitirim Sorokin believes that societies fluctuate back and forth in pendulum fashion between two types of orientations: the sensate and the ideational. The *sensate* culture emphasizes the senses; it is objective, scientific, materialistic, profane, and instrumental. Sorokin's sensate culture is probably similar to Tonnies' *Gesellschaft*. The *ideational* culture emphasizes feelings and emotions; it is more subjective, expressive, and religious. Ideational culture is more like Tonnies' *Gemeinschaft*. Karl Marx's interpretation of social change was based on economic factors. He held that class conflict was the vehicle for social change. In his analysis of history, Marx saw societies progressing through a series of states ending inevitably in a form of Communism and a classless society.

These speculations are interesting to examine, but they are only speculations. Perhaps the history of man is too short for scholars to accurately record permanent historical trends. And possibly we will find when we get to the proper place in history that social change follows no predictable pattern but occurs randomly and inevitably, in spite of man's best efforts to modify its speed or direction.

---

[10] See Turner and Killian, *Collective Behavior*, pp. 388–392, for a more detailed discussion of the charismatic movement.

[11] Bierstedt provides a summary of social change theories in *The Social Order*, Chapter 20. The brief comments in this paragraph are drawn in part from his summary.

Social Disorganization

Social disorganization refers to the breakdown of norms and roles with the result that customary ways of behaving no longer operate. Suppose the star halfback in the weekend football game is given the ball to run through the opposing team's line, but instead he turns and runs fifty yards the wrong way over his own goal line! The spectators are aghast. Several plays later, a player is running with the ball (in the right direction) only to be tackled by the referee. Again, consternation, because "that's not the way the game is played." The norms are so well-known that when they are flagrantly violated and seem to be breaking down, effects on participants are marked. So unusual are these events that sometimes the "norm violators" become famous. A football player had broken loose on a touchdown run in a college game not long ago. No one had a chance to get him, when suddenly an opposing player who was out of the game and sitting on the bench raced onto the field and tackled the ball carrier. The incident made the sports pages throughout the country next day, and the two players (ball carrier and tackler from the bench) appeared on a nationwide television program a few days later to describe the great event. Again, the reason it was so remarkable was because the game just isn't played that way.

But let's get back to the spectators at our peculiar game in which on every play something strange happens: a player runs the wrong way, the wrong person is tackled, eight players come into the game as substitutes but only three leave, and the quarterback runs up into the stands to lead cheers. How long would the spectators tolerate this behavior? It is my guess that very soon they would start leaving the stands. "This is ridiculous—the rules seem to change on every play—you don't know what to expect. . . ." In like manner, extensive breakdown in a society's norms and roles may produce a condition of social disorganization. Extreme social disorganization may lead to personal disorganization in which the individual becomes upset, disaffected, demoralized, and apathetic—he may want to "leave the game."

The term social disorganization is often used to describe the living conditions in the inner cities of large urban areas. The disorganized nature of life arises from the effects of poverty, anonymity, overcrowding, absence of "roots" or ties to the community. Consequences of these conditions are higher rates of crime, mental illness, infant mortality, disease, and family instability. This is not meant to imply that social disorganization "causes" these to occur, but rather that social disorganization describes a general set of conditions under which these social problems flourish.

The word "anomie" has also been used to describe a generalized condition of normlessness. French sociologist Emile Durkheim used the concept of anomie to describe a condition in societies in which norms and rules governing men's aspirations and moral conduct had eroded.[12] There is loss of solidarity in that old group ties tend to break down, and a loss of consensus in that felt agreement on values and norms tends to disappear. It is difficult for the individual to know what is expected of him or for him to feel a sense of close identity with the group. Anomie describes a demoralized society without norms or goals. Durkheim felt that a particular type of suicide occurs in such societies: anomic suicide, in which the individual feels lost and disaffected due to an absence of clear-cut rules and standards for behavior. Durkheim felt that abrupt economic changes—sudden inflation or depression, poverty, or wealth—might lead to anomie. This concept has received much attention recently, especially from sociologists in the areas of criminology and delinquency. Although we will return to it later, the term "anomie" is being introduced here to describe a particular type of social and personal disorganization that results when norms regulating men's aspirations and expectations begin to collapse.

Social disorganization may result from rapid social change. As social change takes place, new norms replace older ones, role behavior is modified, conflict in values occurs, and institutions assume different forms and functions. Individuals, groups, institutions, and societies must adapt to change, and for some of these it may be difficult, especially if change is rapid or if change is defined as unacceptable and is therefore resisted. In such situations we might anticipate social disorganization.

Some sociologists feel that the concept of social disorganization is not very useful. They maintain that the organization of society is constantly in flux, is always changing, and that the result is not disorganization but *reorganization*. They believe that we are really talking about another stage in the social change process rather than about social disorganization. Further, argue the critics of the concept, there is a tendency to apply the label of social disorganization to those things we dislike, to things that may contradict our own particular values or what we are used to. For example, suppose that in the United States we have high divorce and illegitimacy rates, birth control pills are freely available, and teenagers commit more crime than any other age group. Does this mean that the institution of the family in America is a victim of social disorganization, or that it is changing to a different form of organization? Is the current situation regarding relations between blacks and whites in America symptomatic of a disorganized society or of a society undergoing change and reorganization? Youth are challenging institutions of higher education throughout the country, and in other parts of the world as well. Does this mean we have social disorganization in the institution of education, or change and reorganization?

Our view is that the concept of social disorganization may be helpful in

---

[12] Emile Durkheim, *Suicide,* translated by John A. Spaulding and George Simpson (Free Press, New York, 1951). Also see Leonard Broom and Phillip Selznick's summary of Durkheim's ideas on suicide in their introductory book, *Sociology,* 5th Ed. (New York: Harper & Row, 1973), pp. 44–46.

identifying a particular stage which may occur in groups or institutions as they undergo change and reorganization. To produce social disorganization, rapid social change would probably be necessary. In our view, social disorganization involves confusion, disaffection, demoralization, disorientation for individuals—in short, personal disorganization as well. At the same time, it is important to keep from using the concept of social disorganization only to describe those conditions with which we disagree.

Summary

In the previous section of this book, we focused on social organization, the *social fabric* of society. There is a tendency in studying social organization to emphasize the constant, recurring, normal, stable nature of society. In fact, however, all is not as organized, predictable, and fixed as previous sections may have implied. Change and deviation are present in all societies, and this section addresses itself to those topics.

This chapter dealt with the concepts of social change and social disorganization. Social change occurs at varying rates in all societies—on this at least there is general agreement. On some other issues there is more debate: Which, if any, factors are related to change? Can overall patterns of social change be identified? Is change automatic and inexorable or subject to man's intervention and control? Assuming that planned social change is possible, we have examined one vehicle through which such change occurs—the social movement. Finally, social disorganization is the condition that sometimes results when norms have broken down and behavior becomes unpredictable. Although there is some disagreement over the usefulness of the concept of social disorganization, it probably is helpful in describing what may happen in periods of rapid and traumatic social change.

In the first of the readings which follow, Robert Dryfoos describes social change among Eskimos and Indians in Canada. There are numerous factors that tend to encourage change. The article by Dryfoos illustrates the point that some cultures are more effective than others at resisting change. Most often, probably, change occurs slowly without creating much disturbance in the society in which it takes place. Occasionally, however, change may be sudden and far-reaching, with dramatic effects. Lauriston Sharp describes the consequences of the introduction of steel axes into a society of Australian aboriginals. Individuals or groups frequently come to the conclusion that change is occurring too slowly, and that they must do something to speed its progress. A social movement—a group of people acting with some continuity to promote or resist a change—may result. The United States has been fertile ground for social movements, and the last article in this section is an excerpt from Eric Lincoln's book about the Black Muslims, the Negro movement which preaches black supremacy and black union against the white man.

Two Tactics for Ethnic
Survival—Eskimo and Indian

Robert J. Dryfoos, Jr.

Social change takes place at varying rates, even within a given geographical area. Some cultures or subcultures are more successful than others at maintaining their identity in the face of a dominant culture that tends to absorb them. Both of these situations are described in anthropologist Robert Dryfoos's article on Eskimos and Indians in Canada.

On the isolated eastern shore of Hudson Bay, about 700 miles northwest of Montreal, lies the community of Great Whale River, Quebec. It cannot be reached by road. When the ice breaks up, in mid-May, the Hudson Bay Company boat makes its way bringing stock for the store. There is an aircraft landing strip, enabling weekly service from Montreal and twice weekly service from Moosonee, Ontario. But outside visitors are usually restricted to the federal or provincial authorities, police, doctors and dentists who serve the community.

At Great Whale River, subarctic temperatures of minus 50 degrees Fahrenheit are not uncommon during the short (six-hour) days of winter. Summer brings 18-hour days, balmy temperatures (up to 85), and swarms of flies and mosquitoes. The surrounding terrain is flat and sandy rising to low, rocky hills to the east and northeast. As the village lies only 100 miles south of the timber line, the trees are small and sparse. Berries grow in season, which is short. Life is hard. The community consists of about 450 Eskimos, 225 Indians and 100 Euro-Canadians. The latter include teachers, medical personnel, Hudson Bay Company employees, representatives of both the federal Canadian government and the Quebec government, and missionaries of the Anglican and Catholic churches. The Indians are trappers and hunters, trapping beaver and mink in the winter, hunting bear and smaller game year around. Although they now use rifles and shot guns, the Indians still hunt in the bush country to the east as they did in earlier times. The Eskimos are more frequently employed by the government and the Hudson Bay Company. They still hunt seal, and they too have adopted the rifle and shot gun to wound the animals initially before they are harpooned and landed. They have also continued to hunt whale and they trap in the summer, though none of this could be considered their major endeavor. The authorities recognize the difficulties of life in Great Whale River, and most of the people are eligible for and receive welfare payments and child allotments.

While both the Eskimo and the Indians have become settled residents of the village and have largely adopted the material culture of the white man, each group has maintained its own individuality and continues to speak its own language. And although very few rituals, practices or beliefs persist among members of the two native groups, considerable knowledge of the old ways still survives.

Remembrance of things past is the focus of this study; particularly the curious contrast between the remembrances of the Eskimos and the Indians of Great Whale River. The Eskimo has very largely left the past behind with his entry into the modern world; he looks back, if at all, to see a life of hardship and insecurity which he has little wish to perpetuate. Not so the Indian. His past is tenacious, and the days before the coming of the white man are meaningful, valued and well remembered. It is as if the bush still calls to him, and the old life holds something of the fascination of a "lost horizons" for the town-dwelling Indian.

The fact that sharp differences in recall do exist between the two native groups emerged in the course of a seven-month field study I conducted during the summers of 1964 and 1965. Why these differing perceptions should exist simultaneously is an intriguing question, especially as the history of contact with modern culture has been almost identical for each group in regard to both duration and intensity. Explanations involve the complex interplay between past and present, and among the three ethnic groups living side by side.

During my two summers in Great Whale River I interviewed approximately half the members of each native group, in most cases more than once. To try to insure that "no response" to questions about the past resulted from lack of traditional knowledge and not from unwillingness to answer, I attempted to establish a cordial relationship with each person I interviewed, and came to know some quite well. I also established good rapport with my interpreters, some of whom I used throughout the two summers, and relied heavily on their judgement in determining the truthfulness of the replies.

Among the Eskimos, only 12 percent were able to give information about former customs and beliefs, compared to 75 percent of the Indians. Not a single Eskimo under 35 could demonstrate any recall of the traditional ways; the average age for Eskimo informants was over 65. The average age for Indian informants was 42, and several Indian teen-agers as well as one child of 11 were able to give information about their past.

The amount and depth of knowledge retained shows a similar pattern. Members of both groups were asked for information about religion, rites of passage, rites of intensification, marriage and residence patterns, myths and legends, kinship. political organization and economic activities. The Indians were able to recall a total of about 85 such items, and almost invariably discussed them in considerable detail. The Eskimos recalled only 25 items, and could usually give only a skeletal version of the material they remembered.

In the traditional legends of both the Eskimos and the Indians there appears a great sea spirit which takes the form of a mermaid. Present-day experience with this mermaid is the closest to a survival of a traditional belief that I was able to discover. About 20 Indians reported that they, or someone they knew, had had some contact with the mermaid, whom they call Mentoxo—either seeing, hearing, or being affected in some way by this sea creature, in whose present existence they expressed belief. Only two Eskimos reported knowing of anyone who had encountered the Eskimo version of the mermaid, whom they call Tariup Inunga. (In most ethnographic literature this Eskimo spirit is known as Sedna, but none of the Eskimos at Great Whale River had ever heard this name, or were even able to pronounce it.) Several of the Indians who said they confronted Mentoxo dated these events within very recent years, whereas the two Eskimo reports of Tariup Inunga occurred perhaps 40 or 50 years ago.

The vitality of the past among the Indians is easily explained on one level: most Indian fathers say it is desirable for their children to learn of traditional Indian customs, and take pains to tell them about the "way things were done, and what we believed before the white man came." Practically every Eskimo, on the other hand, has dispensed with such teaching, explaining that the "old days have little value for today's children." This is true not just in the area of custom and belief, but for practical skills as well. Most Indian parents say it is valuable for the young men to be able to engage in "real" Indian activities, and teach their sons the proper techniques for hunting in the bush. Only a few Eskimo parents want their children to learn how to hunt sea mammals; most adults dismiss the idea, saying it is "too difficult for people today," or "hunting does not pay enough."

The harsh physical environment and the problems of sheer survival in traditional times may provide one clue to both what and how much of the past is recalled today. Although life was difficult for both peoples, the Eskimos faced an environment that was more continuously threatening than did the Indians. Certainly this is how it is viewed in retrospect: many more Eskimos than Indians comment that the old days were "bad," or that "there was great hunger and starvation many years ago." The Eskimos, then, may well have been more apt to recognize the advantages of Euro-Canadian culture and to welcome a way of life offering security and comfort. The Indians, with their less oppressive past, may have adopted the material culture of the white man less wholeheartedly, and this may have carried over to ideological areas as well. For example, although both groups are Christians today, the Eskimos appear to have internalized the Christian faith to a greater extent than the Indians.

Traditionally, both Indian and Eskimo culture was loosely structured, but some of the available ethnographies indicate that Indian culture was the more highly structured of the two and I would hold that this is one reason for its greater persistence. Today, Indians continue to view themselves as comprising a "tribe" or society; knowledge of the past functions as an integrating mechanism and helps to provide a sense of identity as members of an enduring, albeit fragmenting, society. The Eskimos have never considered themselves members of a cohesive group, so identification with the past would have little meaning from this point of view.

The favored position enjoyed by the Eskimos today in the eyes of the dominant white community, and the comparatively inferior status of the Indians, may well be significant in explaining their different regard for the past. I interviewed about three-fourths of the Euro-Canadian population during my study, and learned that they greatly favor the Eskimos. In general, Eskimos are regarded as more industrious and honest, practical and pragmatic, while Indians are often characterized as "dreamers." Both the Eskimos and the Indians are well aware of these attitudes; the Indians also believe they have less chance of being hired for wage labor than the Eskimos, and that they do not have equal access to government funds. Quite naturally, the Indians feel some resentment and hostility toward the white community as a result.

It is my belief that perpetuation of traditional knowledge serves the Indians as a relatively safe outlet for aggression against the whites. The passing on of stories, myths and beliefs of bygone days may also be seen as a nativistic movement, similar to the present-day mask-carving among the Onendaga, as suggested by Jean Hendry. The perpetuation of traditional knowledge may well serve to strengthen the Indians' image of themselves in the face of hostile white attitudes, especially vis-à-vis the Eskimos. Given their preferred status in relation to the Indians, the Eskimos would have no such reason to perpetuate the past, and might only alienate the dominant whites by doing so.

Shifting ecocultural patterns of the two groups may also suggest reasons for their differential recall of the past. Traditionally the Eskimos were oriented toward the sea, spending much of their time hunting seal and walrus on Hudson Bay. Today however, when an Eskimo leaves the village in the morning to hunt seal, he usually returns the same evening to a rather bustling village life. Hunting has become more and more a sideline activity, and at the urging of the white man during the last 20 to 25 years, the Eskimos have turned increasingly to various craft pursuits, especially soapstone-carving. (Soapstone-carving, formerly done only as a pleasant pastime during the long winter nights to ornament children's toys, was not a traditional economic activity of the Eskimos.) In other words, the Eskimo ecological orientation has shifted from the coast to the entirely novel one of the village; in this process, the traditional ties with the whole fabric of the past have been attenuated.

The ecocultural patterns of the Indian have not changed nearly so drastically, and he is still to some degree bush-oriented. The hunters and trappers of today must leave the village for extended periods to reach adequate game supplies— they cannot limit these activities to "off-business hours" as the Eskimos can. Indians are constantly reminded of their past by their present hunting and trapping patterns. Craft production is much less developed, though current efforts are being made to increase it. For the present, however, the Indians continue to think and talk largely in terms of their traditional bush orientation. The bush, and the old way of life that went with it, still linger as a powerfully nostalgic image to the Indians, even to those who never venture from the village now.

In summary, recollection of the past is meaningful to the Indians; it functions as a mechanism to make them "more Indian," to provide a sense of current identity. But the Eskimos have little interest in being "more Eskimo," and their past is being forgotten at an ever increasing rate.

Questions

1. *Dryfoos suggests that the two groups—Indians and Eskimos—have changed at different rates. What types of evidence does he have for this conclusion?*
2. *What explanations are there for these different rates of change? Which of the factors related to change discussed in the text seem to fit best?*
3. *Which group—Eskimos or Indians—is held in higher regard by the dominant white community? Why? In your opinion, is this a typical or unusual occurrence when unlike races or ethnic groups come in contact?*

Steel Axes for
Stone Age Australians

Lauriston Sharp

Social change occurs in all societies. Often change takes place without much disruption in the lives of people. Sometimes, however, change is extremely disturbing. This may be because the change is rapid and extensive, or because, regardless of the speed with which it takes place, people are unable to adapt to it. Social change which disrupts the order of a society may lead to social disorganization, possibly even the disintegration of the society. Anthropologist Lauriston Sharp describes what happened when missionaries gave steel axes to the Yir Yoront.

Like other Australian aboriginals, the Yir Yoront group at the mouth of the Coleman River on the west coast of tropical Cape York Peninsula originally had no knowledge of metals. Technologically their culture was of the old stone age or paleolithic type; they supported themselves by hunting and fishing, obtaining vegetable foods and needed materials from the bush by simple gathering techniques. Their only domesticated animal was the dog, and they had no domesticated plants of any kind. Unlike some other aboriginal groups, however, the Yir Yoront did have polished stone axes hafted in short handles, and these implements were most important in their economy.

The production of a stone axe required a number of simple skills. With the idea of the axe in its various details well in mind, the adult men—and only the adult men—could set about producing it, a task not considered appropriate for women or children. First of all, a man had to know the location and properties of several natural resources found in his immediate environment: pliable wood, which could be doubled or bent over the axe head and bound tightly to form a handle; bark, which could be rolled into cord for the binding; and gum, with which the stone head could be firmly fixed in the haft. These materials had to be correctly gathered, stored, prepared, cut to size, and applied or manipulated. They were plentifully supplied by nature, and could be taken by a man from anyone's property without special permission. Postponing consideration of the stone head of the axe, we see that a simple knowledge of nature and of the technological skills involved, together with the possession of fire (for heating the gum) and a few simple cutting tools, which might be nothing more than the sharp shells of plentiful bivalves, all of which were available to everyone, were sufficient to enable any normal man to make a stone axe.

The use of the stone axe as a piece of capital equipment for the production of other goods indicates its very great importance in the subsistence economy of the aboriginal. Anyone—man, woman, or child—could use the axe; indeed, it was used more by women, for theirs was the onerous daily task of obtaining sufficient wood to keep the campfire of each family burning all day for cooking or other purposes and all night against mosquitoes and cold (in July, winter temperature might drop below forty degrees). In a normal lifetime any woman would use the axe to cut or knock down literally tons of firewood. Men and women, and sometimes children, needed the axe to make other tools, or weapons, or a variety of material equipment required by the aboriginal in his daily life. The stone axe was essential in making the wet-season domed huts, which keep out some rain and some insects; or platforms, which provide dry storage; or shelters, which give shade when days are bright and

Excerpted from "Steel Axes for Stone Age Australians" by Lauriston Sharp in *Human Problems in Technological Change* edited by Edward H. Spicer, © 1952 by the Russell Sage Foundation, Publishers, New York.

hot. In hunting and fishing and in gathering vegetable or animal food the axe was also a necessary tool; and in this tropical culture without preservatives or other means of storage, the native spends more time obtaining food than in any other occupation except sleeping.

In only two instances was the use of the stone axe strictly limited to adult men: Wild honey, the most prized food known to the Yir Yoront, was gathered only by men who usually used the axe to get it; and only men could make the secret paraphernalia for ceremonies, an activity often requiring use of the axe. From this brief listing of some of the activities in which the axe was used, it is easy to understand why there was at least one stone axe in every camp, in every hunting or fighting party, in every group out on a "walk-about" in the bush.

While the stone axe helped relate men and women and often children to nature in technological behavior, in the transformation of natural into cultural equipment, it also was prominent in that aspect of behavior which may be called conduct, primarily directed toward persons. Yir Yoront men were dependent upon interpersonal relations for their stone axe heads, since the flat, geologically recent alluvial country over which they range provides no stone from which axe heads can be made. The stone they used comes from known quarries four hundred miles to the south. It reached the Yir Yoront through long lines of male trading partners, some of these chains terminating with the Yir Yoront men, while others extended on farther north to other groups, having utilized Yir Yoront men as links. Almost every older adult man had one or more regular trading partners, some to the north and some to the south. His partner or partners in the south he provided with surplus spears, and particularly fighting spears tipped with the barbed spines of sting ray, which snap into vicious fragments when they penetrate human flesh. For a dozen spears, some of which he may have obtained from a partner to the north, he would receive from a southern partner one stone axe head.

Not only was it adult men alone who obtained axe heads and produced finished axes, but it was adult males who retained the axes, keeping them with other parts of their equipment in camp, or carrying them at the back slipped through a human hair belt when traveling. Thus, every woman or child who wanted to use an axe—and this might be frequently during the day—must get one from some man, use it promptly, and return it to the man in good condition. While a man might speak of "my axe," a woman or child could not; for them it was always "your axe," addressing a male, or "his axe."

This necessary and constant borrowing of axes from older men by women and children was done according to regular patterns of kinship behavior. A woman on good terms with her husband would expect to use his axe unless he were using it; a husband on good terms with his wives would let any one of them use his axe without question. If a woman was unmarried or her husband was absent, she would go first to her older brother or to her father for an axe. Only in extraordinary circumstances would she seek a stone axe from a mother's brother or certain other male kin with whom she had to be most circumspect. A girl, a boy, or a young man would look to a father or an older brother to provide an axe for her or his use, but would never approach a mother's brother, who would be at the same time a potential father-in-law, with such a request. Older men, too, would follow similar rules if they had to borrow an axe.

It will be noted that these social relationships in which the stone axe had a place are all pair relationships and that the use of the axe helped define and maintain the character of the relationships and the roles of the two individual participants. Every active relationship among the Yir Yoront involved a definite and accepted status of superordination or subordination. A person could have no dealings with any other on exactly equal terms. Women and children were dependent on, or subordinate to, older males in every action in which the axe entered.

The stone axe was an important symbol of masculinity among the Yir Yoront (just as pants or pipes are among ourselves). By a complicated set of ideas which we would label "ownership" the axe was defined as "belonging" to males. Everyone in the society (except untrained infants) accepted these ideas. Similarly spears, spear throwers, and fire-making sticks were associated with males, were owned only by them, and were symbols of masculinity. But the masculine values represented by the stone axe were constantly being impressed on all members of society by the fact that non-males had to use the axe and had to go to males for it, whereas they never borrowed other masculine artifacts. Thus, the axe stood for an important theme that ran all through Yir Yoront culture: the superiority and rightful dominance of the male, and the greater value of his concerns and of all things associated with him. We should call this androcentrism rather than patriarchy; the man ("andros") takes precedence over feminine values, an idea backed by very strong sentiments among the Yir Yoront. Since the axe had to be borrowed also by the younger from the older, it also represented the prestige of age, another important theme running all through Yir Yoront behavior.

The introduction of the steel axe indiscriminately and in large numbers into the Yir Yoront technology was only one of many changes occurring at the same time. It is therefore impossible to factor out all the results of this single innovation alone. Nevertheless, a number of specific effects of the change from stone axes to steel axes may be noted; and the steel axe may be used as an epitome of the European goods and implements received by the aboriginals in increasing quantity and of their general influence on the native culture. The use of the steel axe to illustrate such influences would seem to be justified, for it was one of the first European artifacts to be adopted for regular use by the Yir Yoront; and the axe, whether of stone or steel, was clearly one of the most important items of cultural equipment they possessed.

The shift from stone to steel axes provided no major technological difficulties. While the aboriginals themselves could not manufacture steel axe heads, a steady supply from outside continued; and broken wooden axe handles could easily be replaced from bush timbers with aboriginal tools. Among the Yir Yoront the new axe never acquired all the use it had on mission or cattle stations (carpentry work, pounding tent pegs, use as a hammer, and so on); and, indeed, it was used for little more than the stone axe had been, so that it had no practical effect in improving the native standard of living. It did some jobs better, and could be used longer without breakage; and these factors were sufficient to make it of value to the native. But the assumption of the white man (based in part on a realization that a shift from steel to stone axe in his case would be a definite regression) that his axe was much more efficient, that its use would save time, and that it therefore represented technical "progress" toward goals which he had set for the native was hardly borne out in aboriginal practice. Any leisure time the Yir Yoront might gain by using steel axes or other western tools was invested, not in "improving the conditions of life," and certainly not in developing aesthetic activities, but in sleep, an art they had thoroughly mastered.

Having acquired an axe head through regular trading partners of whom he knew what to expect, a man wanting a stone axe was then dependent solely upon a known and an adequate nature and upon his own skills or easily acquired techniques. A man wanting a steel axe, however, was in no such self-reliant position. While he might acquire one through trade, he now had the new alternative of dispensing with technological behavior in relation with a predictable nature and conduct in relation with a predictable trading partner and of turning instead to conduct alone in relation with a highly erratic missionary. If he attended one of the mission festivals when steel axes were handed out as gifts, he might receive one simply by chance or if he had happened somehow to impress upon the mission that he was one of the "better" bush aboriginals (their definition of "better" being quite different from that of his bush fellows). Or he might—but again almost by pure chance—be given some brief job in connection with the mission which would enable him to earn a steel axe. In either case, for older men a preference for the steel axe helped create a situation of dependence in place of a situation of self-reliance and a behavior shift from situations in technology or conduct which were well structured or defined to situations in conduct alone which were ill defined. It was particularly the older ones among the men, whose earlier experience or knowledge of the white.man's harshness in any event made them suspicious, who would avoid having any relations with the mission at all, and who thus excluded themselves from acquiring steel axes directly from that source.

The steel axe was the root of psychological stress among the Yir Yoront even more significantly in other aspects of social relations. This was the result of new factors which the missionary considered all to the good: the simple numerical increase in axes per capita as a result of mission distribution; and distribution from the mission directly to younger men, women, and even children. By winning the favor of the mission staff, a woman might be given a steel axe. This was clearly intended to be hers. The situation was quite different from that involved in borrowing an axe from a male relative, with the result that a woman called such an axe "my" steel axe, a possessive form she never used for a stone axe. Furthermore, young men or even boys might also obtain steel axes directly from the mission. A result was that older men no longer had a complete monopoly of all the axes in the bush community. Indeed, an old man might have only a stone axe, while his wives and sons had steel axes which they considered their own and which he might even desire to borrow. All this led to a revolutionary confusion of sex, age, and kinship roles, with a major gain in independence and loss of subordination on the part of those able now to acquire steel axes when they had been unable to possess stone axes before.

The trading partner relationship was also affected by the new situation. A Yir Yoront might have a trading partner in a tribe to the south whom he defined as a younger brother, and on whom as an older brother he would therefore have an edge. But if the partner were in contact with the mission or had other easier access to steel axes, his subordination to his bush colleague was obviously decreased. Indeed, under the new dispensation he might prefer to give his axe to a bush "sweetheart" in return for favors or otherwise dispose of it outside regular trade channels, since many steel axes were so distributed between natives in new ways. Among other things, this took some of the excitement away from the fiesta-like tribal gatherings centering around initiations during the dry season. These had traditionally been the climactic annual occasions for exchanges between trading partners, when a man might seek to acquire a whole year's supply of stone axe heads. Now he might find himself prostituting his wife to almost total strangers in return for steel axes or other white men's goods. With trading partnerships weakened, there was less reason to attend the fiestas, and less fun for those who did. A decline in one of the important social activities which had symbolized these great gatherings created a lessening of interest in the other social aspects of these events.

The most disturbing effects of the steel axe, operating in conjunction with other elements also being introduced from the white man's several subcultures, developed in the realm of traditional ideas, sentiments, and values. These were undermined at a rapidly mounting rate, without new conceptions being defined to replace them. The result was a mental and moral void which foreshadowed the collapse and destruction of all Yir Yoront culture, if not, indeed, the extinction of the biological group itself.

From what has been said it should be clear how changes in overt behavior, in technology and conduct, weakened the values inherent in a reliance on nature, in androcentrism or the prestige of masculinity, in age prestige, and in the various kinship relations. A scene was set in which a wife or young son, his initiation perhaps not even yet completed, need no longer bow to the husband or father, who was left confused and insecure as he asked to borrow a steel axe from them. For the woman and boy the steel axe helped establish a new degree of freedom which was accepted readily as an escape from the unconscious stress of the old patterns, but which left them also confused and insecure. Ownership became less well defined, so that stealing and trespass were introduced into technology and conduct. Some of the excitement surrounding the great ceremonies evaporated, so that the only fiestas the people had became less festive, less interesting. Indeed, life itself became less interesting, although this did not lead the Yir Yoront to invent suicide, a concept foreign to them.

The bush Yir Yoront, still trying to maintain their aboriginal definition of the situation, accepted European artifacts and behavior patterns, but fit them into their totemic system, assigning them as totems to various clans on a par with original totems. There is an attempt to have the myth-making process keep up with these cultural changes so that the idea system can continue to support the rest of the culture. But analysis of overt behavior, of dreams, and of some of the new myths indicates that this arrangement is not entirely satisfactory; that the native clings to his totemic system with intellectual loyalty, lacking any substitute ideology; but that associated sentiments and values are weakened. His attitudes toward his own and toward European culture are found to be highly ambivalent.

The steel axe, like most European goods, has no distinctive origin myth, nor are mythical ancestors associated with it. Can anyone, sitting of an afternoon in the shade of a ti tree, create a myth to resolve this confusion? No one has, and the horrid suspicion arises that perhaps the origin myths are wrong, which took into account so little of this vast new universe of the white man. The steel axe, shifting hopelessly between one clan and the other, is not only replacing the stone axe physically, but is hacking at the supports of the entire cultural system.

During a wet season stay at the mission, the anthropologist discovered that his supply of tooth paste was being depleted at an alarming rate. Investigation showed that it was being taken by old men for use in a new tooth paste cult. Old materials of magic having failed, new materials were being tried out in a malevolent magic directed toward the mission staff and some of the younger aboriginal men. Old males, largely ignored by the missionaries, were seeking to regain some of their lost power and prestige. This mild aggression proved hardly effective, but perhaps only because confidence in any kind of magic on the mission was by this time at a low ebb.

For the Yir Yoront still in the bush a time could be predicted when personal deprivation and frustration in a confused culture would produce an overload of anxiety. The mythical past of the totemic ancestors would disappear as a guarantee of a present of which the future was supposed to be a stable continuation. Without the past, the present would be meaningless and the future unstructured and uncertain. Insecurities would be inevitable. Reaction to this stress might be some form of symbolic aggression, or withdrawal and apathy, or some more realistic approach.

Questions

1. *What changes in the Yir Yoront culture followed the introduction of the steel axe?*
2. *Use the terms "social disorganization," "anomie," and "reorganization" to analyze and describe the condition of the Yir Yoront.*
3. *Why did the Yir Yoront have such difficulty adapting to the introduction of the steel axe?*
4. *What elements introduced into American culture have led to dramatic social change? As you list several, discuss why they didn't have the disastrous effect that introduction of the steel axe had for the Yir Yoront.*

The Black Muslims
in America

C. Eric Lincoln

The following is an excerpt from Eric Lincoln's book about the Black Muslims. A number of characteristics of a social movement are illustrated, including the goals, techniques, and methods of recruitment used by this movement. Some movements are centered upon a particularly effective person, and this excerpt describes the leader of the Black Muslims, Elijah Muhammad.

Racial Separation

The Black Muslims demand absolute separation of the black and the white races. They are willing to approach this goal by stages—the economic and political links, for example, need not be severed immediately—but all personal relationships between the races must be broken *now*. Economic severance, the next major step, is already under way, and political severance will follow in good time. But only with complete racial separation will the perfect harmony of the universe be restored.

Those so-called Negroes who seek integration with the American white man are, say the Muslims, unrealistic and stupid. The white man is not suddenly going to share with his erstwhile slaves the advantages and privileges because of their subordinate position. America became the richest and most powerful nation in the world because she harnessed, for more than three hundred years, the free labor of millions of human beings. But she hasn't the slightest intention to share her wealth and privileges with "those who worked so long for nothing, and even now receive but a pittance." The so-called Negroes are still "free slaves.". . .

Reaching for the Masses

Under Fard, the Muslims never had more than eight thousand members, although the conditions for rapid growth were almost ideal. Muhammad claims "a few hundred thousand," and while no objective source is in position to verify that allegation, the evidence does seem to suggest that over the long span of Muhammad's leadership the number of Blacks who have been attracted to the movement has been substantial. The difference may well lie in the fact that Fard was the leader of a cult. Muhammad made that cult a movement.

Muhammad's strategy has been to put the cult on parade—on the streets, in the press, in the temples, *wherever there are people*. And he has done this with impressive success. For local action, he has had an able corps of ministers in the field; but there were not many at first, and their fight was uphill. The press gave him his first major assist, for it made him "controversial": as a columnist in one of the most important black papers in the country, he became a conversation piece for hundreds of thousands of Blacks across America. Thousands of letters were sent to Muhammad and to the *Pittsburgh Courier,* denouncing and defending both the Messenger and the newspaper which provided space for his message.

People went to the temples to see the man whose columns they read. For the most part they were simply curious, but Muhammad and his ministers are masters at capturing the curious. In the temples Muhammad preached a somewhat different message—not completely different, but different in emphasis. His writings in the newspapers were generally filled with vague and cryptic biblical interpretations. But in the privacy of the temples, the white man was unmasked; his mistreatment of the so-called Negro was rehearsed in bizarre detail and with militant outrage.

Moreover, Muhammad appealed to the newcomers not as individuals but as a crowd. All persons entering a temple were (and still are) searched for weapons as a precaution against the assassination of a minister. This requirement intrigued the curious and excited their sense of personal importance. Even to be thought capable of assassinating an important leader was gratifying to some who, in the structure of things, had no real identity whatsoever. At the same time, they were awed and flattered at being admitted, while all white men were rigidly excluded. The initiative had passed to the Muslims: it was now the newcomers who were tentatively accepted, but on trial.

Inside the temples, they were fascinated by the black-suited young males with the red ties and the military bearing. They were impressed by Muhammad's bold denunciation of the white man, and they were enlightened by hearing for the first time the "truth" about themselves, the Black Nation of Islam. For the most receptive among them, the potential true believers, a new vision dawned. They joined—a few at first and then more and more—and the character of the association began to change. The cult had quietly died. The Movement had begun.

The black press helped to supply the initial impetus that brought Muhammad and the Muslims to the attention of his potential followers. The white press has made him famous, and notoriety sharply enhanced his attraction for the masses. In the summer of 1959, Mike Wallace presented a television documentary featuring the Muslim leader, and articles soon followed in *Time, U.S. News and World Report, Reader's Digest,* and other elements of the national press. Muhammad's total following was then less than thirty thousand. A month after he had been "discovered" by the mass media, his following had doubled, and it continued to climb for most of a decade. Ironically, many of these magazines and newspapers sought to "expose" Muhammad as "a purveyor of cold black hatred," or otherwise as a social anomaly with no real future. They underestimated his appeal to an important segment of the dissatisfied black masses who, being born with a cause, needed only a leader. . . .

Muhammad's first and most crucial task is to keep the Movement a *movement* rather than permit it to become an institution. This does not mean that the Muslims must forsake structure and direction; on the contrary, they have one of the most effective organizational structures to be seen outside the military. But to lure the masses, they must seem to be going somewhere, not settling down. They must reflect and mobilize the masses' own dissatisfaction and urgency, building these into the corporate identity. A successful mass movement is always arriving, but never quite arrives.

Muhammad is not unaware of the frustrations and the free-floating hostilities which are the corollaries of America's caste system, and he will continue to use these as capital in his program to bring every "lost black brother" under the Star and Crescent of Islam. This is, to be sure, an ambitious undertaking; but it is well to remember that only Billy Graham has attracted and converted more people in recent years than has Elijah Muhammad, Messenger of Allah, and Dr. Graham enjoys the advantages of social approval, a magnificent TV presence, and a product most Americans are committed to buying anyway. Elijah has none of these, but, unlike Billy Graham's converts, the Blacks who make "decisions for Allah" do not return to the anonymity from which they so briefly emerged. They take on a new identity that is *really* different, and they find a new and satisfying visibility in the corporate image of the Muslim brotherhood.

Lures for the True Believer

To clinch the conversion of those true believers who approach the Movement in simple curiosity, Muhammad offers the lure of personal rebirth. The true believer who becomes a Muslim casts off at last his old self and takes on a new identity. He changes his name, his religion, his homeland, his "natural" language, his moral and cultural values, his very purpose in living. He is no longer a Negro, so long despised by the white man that he has come almost to despise himself. Now he is a black man—divine, ruler of the universe, different only in degree from Allah Himself. He is no longer discontent and baffled, harried by social obloquy and a gnawing sense of personal inadequacy. Now he is a Muslim, bearing in himself the power of the Black Nation and its glorious destiny. His new life is not an easy one: it demands unquestioning faith, unrelenting self-mastery, unremitting loyalty, and a singularity of purpose. He may have to sacrifice his family and friends, his trade or profession, if they do not serve his new-found cause. But he is not alone, and he now knows *why* his life matters. He has seen the truth, and the truth has set him free.

When he has seen the light and has decided to join the Movement, the potential convert is put through certain rites of passage before he is admitted. First he is given a copy of the following letter, which he himself must copy by hand:

Address
City and State
Date

Mr. W. F. Muhammad
4847 So. Woodlawn Avenue
Chicago, Illinois 60015

Dear Savior Allah, Our Deliverer:

I have been attending the teachings of Islam by one of your Ministers, two or three times. I believe in It, and I bear witness that there is no God but Thee, and that Muhammad is Thy Servant and Apostle. I desire to reclaim my Own. Please give me my Original Name. My slave name is as follows:

Name
Address
City and State

The applicant's letter is sent to Chicago, where it is scrutinized. If it contains any errors, it is returned and must be recopied correctly. If the letter is perfect, the applicant receives a questionnaire concerning his marital status and dependents. When this and other forms have been completed and approved, the convert enters his new life as a member of the Black Nation of Islam.

To commemorate his rebirth, the convert drops his last name and is known simply by his first name and the letter X. To facilitate identification among Muslims having the same first name and belonging to the same temple, numbers are prefixed to the X. Thus the first man named John to join the temple is named John X; the second becomes John 2X; and so on. Some temples have gone as high as X to the "17th power"! At a later date, Muhammad may grant the convert a new—that is, an "original"—surname, such as Majied, or Hassan

The symbol X has a double meaning: implying "ex," it signifies that the Muslim is no longer what he was; and as "X," it signifies an unknown quality or quantity. It at once repudiates the white man's name and announces the rebirth of Black Man, endowed with a set of qualities the white man does not have and does not know. "In short," Malcolm X explained, " 'X' is for mystery. The mystery confronting the Negro as to who he was before the white man made him a slave and put a European label on him. That mystery is now resolved. But 'X' is also for the mystery confronting the white man as to what the Negro has become." That mystery will be resolved only when the teachings of Elijah Muhammad have been received by enough of the "Lost Nation" to counter "three hundred years of systematic brainwashing by the white man." When the Lost Nation of Islam in the West has learned its true identity, has gained a realistic appreciation of its past accomplishments, and has seen the "truth about the white man," then the white man will see the black man in a new light— "and he will have no reason to rejoice."

Most Muslims also retain their "slave" surnames for use in such pragmatic affairs as signing checks. On these occasions, however, the surname is always preceded by an X to indicate that the Muslim repudiates it. On other occasions, Muslims may use the tribal name "Shabazz." For example, when Malcolm X toured Egypt and several other Moslem countries in Africa and Asia for the first time, he traveled as Malik Shabazz "so that my brothers in the East would recognize me as one of them." If he had used his "European" name (Malcolm Little), he explained, he would have been rejected as an imposter or ridiculed for retaining that symbol of the white man's ownership.

This change of name is, of course, only the most outward token of rebirth. Perhaps the deepest change promised—and delivered—is the release of energies that had been damned or buried in the old personality. This release may account in part for the regeneration of criminals, alcoholics, and narcotic addicts which is a hallmark of the Movement. At the other extreme, it is often apparent in a change from gentle bewilderment to dogmatic and barely leashed hostility. "When I was in the Pacific," said a Muslim veteran of World War II, "I prayed to God every day that He would not let me die in the jungle, fighting some Japanese who had never done anything to me. I was a Christian then. Now I pray to Allah to let me live to help my people find out who their real enemies are, right here in America."

Recruitment

In pursuit of his goal to make Black Muslims out of black Christians, Muhammad has an ambitious program of recruitment. His ministers go into jails and penitentiaries, pool halls and bars, barbershops and drugstores to talk about Islam. They invade the college campuses, the settlement houses, and the YMCAs. Young Muslim brothers hawk their newspapers along with insistent invitations to attend lectures at the Muslim temples. They speak from street corners and in parks, and they distribute literature wherever large crowds of Blacks may be gathered. Invariably, the proselytizers are young, personable, urbane, and well-dressed men of confidence and conviction.

It is a Muslim boast that the black intellectual will be hardest to reach ("he has been brainwashed more thoroughly than any of the rest of us"), but he will ultimately have no choice other than to accept Islam. He can never be more than marginally acceptable to the white man, so "he will have nobody to lead and no one to honor him when the common people have all become Muslims." Muhammad himself has a sort of calculated patience with black intelligentsia. He regards them as doubly damned: "They have stayed in the white man's schools too long, learning nothing of themselves," and they are fervid in their "hopes that the white man is going to change and treat them like men instead of boys.". . .

In their proselytizing, the Muslims carefully select their approach and their language—and often their speaker—to match the particular audience in mind. For example, Muhammad's long center-fold column in *Muhammad Speaks,* the official Muslim newspaper, is very deftly aimed at the *lumpen proletariat,* the common man. In one of the best edited newspapers published by Blacks, Muhammad's column is filled with biblical eschatology, numerology, and "mystery," all to the embarrassment and shame of the educated classes. However, the pitch here is being made not to the educated classes but to the masses, who are successfully attracted by such techniques. Inside the brotherhood these exotic elements are deemphasized, and more practical concerns are introduced.

When the Muslim is called upon to confront a highly critical audience, the whole panoply of the occult is usually discarded, except when it is needed to protect the speaker or the Movement against too close examination. In the privacy of his home, Mr. Muhammad is not only "rational," but gracious and friendly as well. He does not greet his guests with "*As-salaam-alaikum*" unless they happen to be Muslims. There are no guards anywhere about the house, and none of the physical trappings of the Movement is in evidence. Conversation is at a level consistent with his appraisal of the visitor. To be sure, Muhammad has a professional hostility against the white man, but this hostility does not dominate his private conversation. The Messenger's concern is more likely to center around the Black Man's economic plight. On the other hand, he may become totally incomprehensible about any matter he does not wish to discuss, usually calling upon "Allah" in answer to any questions which might put him at a disadvantage or give away any statistics or other secrets about his movement. . . .

Dramatic productions, songs, and other such entertainment are effective recruiting devices. "People who can put on a play like that—and who wrote it themselves are not just 'everyday' folks," is a common consensus in the black ghetto. But Muhammad does not make entertainment ability the chief attraction of his Movement. Indeed, he is careful to emphasize "that the so-called Negro has already done too much singing and dancing," when he should have been giving his attention to more serious matters like factories and supermarkets. Apart from the public meetings and publications, a good deal of recruiting is done in jails and prisons, among men and women whose resentment against society increases with each day of imprisonment. Here their smoldering hatred against the white man builds up to the point of explosion. But Muhammad's ministers are trained to prevent any such release; they are adept at channeling aggression and hostility into a kind of leakproof reservoir for future use. No act of violence or retaliation against the white man is permitted. Instead, Muslims who join the sect while in prison invariably improve in behavior and outlook. Every Muslim *must* respect constituted authority—no matter what the authority may be. This is one of the cardinal rules of membership in the sect.

The black prisoner is reminded that he is in an institution administered by whites, guarded by whites, built by whites. Even the chaplains are white, "to continue to force upon you the poisonous doctrine that you are blessed by being persecuted." The judge who tried him, the jury who heard his case, the officers who arrested him—all were white. Can he, then, be justly imprisoned? . . .

Muhammad's reclamation program promises a kind of moral and social perfectionism, which is available to all who adopt Islam. In his public addresses, he chides the black community for its juvenile delinquency, which is "caused by parental immorality" and "rips apart the seams of the Christian society." In Islam, echoed Malcolm X, "we don't have any delinquency, either juvenile or adult, and if Mr. Muhammad is given a chance he will clean up the slums and the ghettos—something all the leaders and the social workers and the policemen put together have not been able to do."

The Muslims visualize the reclamation of thousands of Blacks who, through ignorance, despair, and defeat, have found themselves in the gutter or in jail. They have had some impressive successes in rehabilitating certain categories of social outcasts, including narcotic addicts and alcoholics. Muhammad operates on the premise that "knowledge of self" and of the "truth about the white man" —when tied in with a constructive program, such as building the Black Nation— is sufficient to reclaim the most incorrigible. "By nature," the Muslims are taught, "you are divine." Their social tragedies are caused by the white devil's "tricknology," but truth and hard work will soon make them free.

Questions

1. *What is the appeal of the Black Muslim movement? What measures were used to make the movement grow?*
2. *At what stage in the development of social movements are the Black Muslims as described by Lincoln? Why might Muhammad wish to avoid making the Black Muslims an* institution *rather than a* movement?
3. *Of what significance is the granting of a new name to a convert?*

9

Collective Behavior

Collective behavior is group behavior that is spontaneous, unstructured, and unstable. It may be either sporadic and short-term or more continuous and long-lasting.[1] Collective behavior is often hard to predict because it is not rooted in the usual cultural or social norms. Spontaneous and unstructured behavior is hard to observe or record objectively and is, therefore, difficult to study. Although there have been some artificial or laboratory-created studies of rumor and panic, most studies of collective behavior by social scientists are

[1]Treatment of concepts in this chapter in general follows the description given by Ralph Turner and Lewis Killian in their book, *Collective Behavior*, 2nd Ed. (Englewood Cliffs, N.J.: Prentice-Hall, 1972). Also see the chapters on collective behavior in the introductory sociology texts by Paul Horton and Chester Hunt, *Sociology*, 3rd Ed. (New York: McGraw-Hill Book Co., 1972), and by Leonard Broom and Phillip Selznick, *Sociology*, 5th Ed. (New York: Harper & Row, 1973).

after-the-fact analyses and discussions with people who happened to be involved. However, these studies have revealed that collective behavior, although spontaneous, is not as disorganized as it appears and, in fact, follows reasonably consistent patterns. Some of these patterns are examined in this chapter as we look at analyses of crowds (audiences, mobs), rumor, fads and fashions, mass hysteria, disaster behavior, publics, and public opinion.

Crowd

An outline of the major collective behavior concepts would start with the crowd. A *crowd* is a temporary collection of people in close physical contact reacting together to a common stimulus. For example, the passengers on the flight from New York to San Francisco whose pilot suddenly decides he would like to go to the North Pole might be transformed from an aggregation into a crowd (or even a mob). Crowds have certain characteristics in common. *Milling* usually occurs as a crowd is being formed. In one sense milling refers to the excited, restless, physical movement of the individuals involved. In a more important sense milling refers to a process of communication that leads to a definition of the situation and possible collective action. Not long ago, a Berkeley classroom suddenly started shaking with the first tremors of an earthquake. Almost at once the people began turning, shifting, looking at each other, at the ceiling, and at the instructor. They were seeking some explanation for the highly unusual experience and, whether spoken aloud or not, the questions on their faces were clear: "What is it?" "Did you feel it?" "What should we do?" Buzzing became louder talking, and someone shouted, "Earthquake!!!" The students began to get up and move toward the doors. Many continued to watch the ceiling. . . . Milling may involve the long buildup of a lynch mob, or the sudden reaction in a dark and crowded theater when someone shouts, "Fire!!!" Milling helps ensure the development of a common mood for crowd members.

A person when he is part of a crowd tends to be *suggestible*. He is less critical, and he will readily do things that he would not ordinarily do alone. This is in part because, as a member of a crowd, he is *anonymous*. There is a prevailing feeling that it is the crowd that is responsible, not the individual. Once one becomes a member of an acting crowd, it is extremely difficult to step back, get perspective, and objectively evaluate what one is doing. Crowd members have a narrowed focus, a kind of tunnel vision. The physical presence of a crowd is a powerful force—a person almost has to separate himself from the crowd physically before he can critically examine his own behavior. There is also a *sense of urgency* about crowds. Crowds are oriented toward a specific focus or task: "We've got to do *this,* and we've got to do it *now!*" Some form of leadership usually appears in the crowd but, as the mood of the crowd changes, the leadership may shift quickly from one individual or group to another.

There are many different types of crowds. Some are passive—those watching a building burn or those at the scene of an accident. Some are active—a race riot or a lynch mob. Some crowds have a number of loosely defined goals. Other crowds are focused on a specific goal. Turner and Killian distinguish between crowds that direct their action toward some external object—harassing a speaker until he leaves the platform or lynching a criminal—and expressive crowds, that direct their focus on the crowd itself—cheering at a football game or speaking in tongues at a church service.

Controlling the behavior of a crowd is difficult because of the mass of people involved and the spontaneous nature of their behavior. Some methods of dealing with a potentially riotous crowd have been suggested, however: Remove or isolate the individuals involved in the precipitating incident. Reduce the feelings of anonymity and invincibility of the individual—force him to focus on himself and the consequences of his action. Interrupt patterns of communication during the milling process by breaking the crowd into small units. Remove the crowd leaders if it can be done without use of force. Finally, attempt to distract the attention of the crowd by creating a diversion or a new point of interest, especially if this can be accomplished by someone who is considered to be "with" the crowd.[2]

Audience, Mob, Riot

Audiences and mobs are specific types of crowds. An *audience* at a concert, football game, lecture, religious service, or burning building may usually be likened to a passive crowd. Emotional contagion is possible in such situations, and individuals are responsive in a group in ways that they would not be as individuals. Audiences at performances of rock and roll stars and in Pentecostal church services may become very expressive in a variety of possibly unpredictable ways. Comedians expect audiences to laugh at their jokes. But most comedians have "bits" that they do when audiences are unpredictable and don't laugh (Johnny Carson gets audience sympathy by jokingly mentioning his "war injuries"). Much of audience behavior is predictable, or at least predictably unpredictable. The football fan knows he is going to cheer at the game, the comedian's "rejection bits" are well prepared, and rock concerts are adequately staffed with police to protect the musicians and nurses to minister to the fans that pass out. At the same time, audiences demonstrate collective behavior characteristics in that their behavior is frequently spontaneous, and members are suggestible and anonymous.

A *mob* is a focused, acting crowd. It is emotionally aroused, intent on taking aggressive action. A lynch mob would be an example of such a crowd. A water-fight between several fraternities in Berkeley on a warm spring day in 1956

---

[2] For dimensions, types, and control of crowds, see Turner and Killian, *Collective Behavior*, Chapters 5–9.

spontaneously turned into a panty raid. Thousands of eager young males marched with determination through the campus community methodically stealing panties from numerous sorority houses. Afterwards, many of the participants expressed amazement that they had been involved in such behavior.

A *riot* describes the situation in which mob behavior has become increasingly widespread and destructive. Riots may involve a number of mobs acting independently. Throughout our history, the United States has had riots over the issue of race: New York, 1863; Chicago, 1919; Detroit, 1943. In the 1960s, urban riots occurred with increasing frequency. The issues were social class and poverty as well as race. The Watts riot in Los Angeles in the summer of 1965 lasted six days. Nearly 4,000 people were arrested, and property damage was estimated at over $40 million. Thirty-four people were killed and over 1,000 people injured. Most of the killed and injured were Negroes. More than forty people died, and property damage was estimated at $50 million in the Detroit riot in the summer of 1967. The relatively minor incident which set off the week-long confrontation was the police closing of a "blind pig," an after-hours tavern. A crowd collected as the police carted off the tavern's patrons, a stone was thrown, a shoe store was set on fire, and the riot was on. Campus disturbances occurred in the late 1960s at San Francisco State, Berkeley, Harvard, Columbia, Cornell, and at a number of other schools. It is likely, however, that to call these occasions riots, as the press often did, is an exaggeration of what actually happened. Riots have taken place at prisons and sporting events. A highly unusual situation occurred in 1969 when a disagreement at a soccer match led to a riot which in turn led to a short war between the two countries Honduras and El Salvador.

Panic and Mass Hysteria

Panic represents a particular type of reaction in a crowd situation. Sociologically, panic is defined as non-adaptive or non-rational flight resulting from extreme fear and loss of self-control. Usually there is a severe threat, a limited number of "ways out," a feeling of being trapped. Flight in itself does not necessarily mean panic. Some flight is rational and sensible, as when people leave in an orderly manner an area that is threatened by hurricane or flood. Panic refers specifically to flight that is non-adaptive—people stampeding through a burning building and attempting to fight their way out a door that is already hopelessly blocked. Panic differs somewhat from other forms of collective behavior in that, although it is frequently a result of the crowd situation (spontaneous and contagious), it is essentially an individualistic and competitive reaction. In panic, each person is desperately trying to obtain an objective on his own, and since many others are doing the same thing there is a good chance that some will not make it.[3]

The Iroquois Theater fire in Chicago provides an extreme example of panic and its possible consequences. During a performance on a December afternoon in 1903, draperies on the stage caught fire. Somebody yelled "Fire!!!," and most of the audience panicked. Actors and musicians attempted to calm the crowd, but to no avail. There were many exit doors, but some were poorly marked and some hard to open. People were crushed against doors and on stairways, others jumped to their death from fire escapes. The fire was not very serious, and the fire department arrived quickly—the panic lasted only eight minutes. The death toll, however, was 602.

Mass hysteria is in some ways similar to panic and describes the situation in which a particular behavior, fear, or belief sweeps through a large number of people—a crowd, a city, or a nation. Examples of mass hysteria might include fainting at a rock concert, the fear that flying saucers are after us or that the Martians are invading, or the belief that certain women are practicing witchcraft.

Rumor

Rumor is a type of collective behavior that may or may not be crowd-oriented. Much rumor is merely a form of person-to-person communication. Rumor is defined as unconfirmed, although not necessarily false, communication. Rumor is often related to some issue of public concern. Rumors change constantly as they spread. They tend to grow shorter, more concise, and more easily told. Certain "attractive" details of the rumor become magnified. New details are manufactured to "complete" the story or to make it internally consistent. People pass or tell rumors for a variety of reasons. The rumor may fit with what we want to believe, with what "we know to be true": "Negroes are lazy," or "teachers are absentminded," or "sex education is Communist-inspired." We may pass rumors on because it increases our status in the eyes of others. Possibly we were the first to get the news, and we want to let others know that. Or it's such a tremendous story that others are bound to think more of us when we tell it to them. Rumor may have a variety of functions. It may act as gossip and serve to enliven the Thursday Afternoon Bridge Club, or it may provide a core

[3] This discussion of panic is drawn from Duane Schultz, *Panic Behavior* (New York: Random House, 1964), and from Turner and Killian, *Collective Behavior*, Chapters 5 and 6.

of communication during a crowd's milling period. In this latter situation, it may provide the stimulus for crowd action.[4]

Fads, Crazes, and Fashions

Fads, crazes, and fashions are forms of collective behavior that are usually more widespread and long lasting than crowd behavior. *Fads* and *crazes* refer to the relatively short-term "obsessions" that members of society or members of specific groups have toward certain mannerisms, objects, clothes, or ways of speaking. Relatively recent fads include wearing faded levis, riding ten-speed bikes, eating health foods, and using expressions like "far out," "rip off," "right on," and "up tight." Past examples include the super ball, swallowing goldfish, the hula hoop, and stuffing phone booths. Fads and crazes may interest many and burn brightly for a while, but usually they die out quickly. *Fashions* are similar but are more widespread and last longer than fads and crazes. Examples of fashions might include the miniskirt, two-piece bathing suits, long hair on men, wide neckties, Mustang-style in cars, ranch-style in homes, and rock and folk rock in popular music.

Turner and Killian report an interesting peculiarity of fads and fashions: fashions follow the social-class structure, while fads do not necessarily follow the social-class structure. That is, fashions usually start at upper-class levels and seep downward. Fads, on the other hand, may appear anywhere in the class structure and may be adopted more quickly by members of lower social classes than by members of the upper classes. Since following fads and fashions brings prestige to people, fashion supports the *status quo* (the current prestige system), while fads may upset the *status quo* by granting prestige to people who otherwise have low status.[5]

Disaster

Studies of disasters provide us with data about collective behavior. A disaster situation is defined as one in which there is a basic disruption of the social context within which individuals and groups function, a radical departure from the pattern of normal expectations. Such a situation almost by definition results in collective behavior.[6]

---

[4] See Warren A. Peterson and Noel P. Gist's article, "Rumor and Public Opinion," *Amer. Journal of Sociology*, Vol. 57 (September 1951), pp. 159–167, for a summary and analysis of some theories on rumor.

[5] Turner and Killian, *Collective Behavior*, pp. 152–153.

[6] This section on disaster is taken from Charles Fritz's chapter on disaster, which appears in Robert Merton and Robert Nisbet's book, *Contemporary Social Problems* (New York: Harcourt Brace Jovanovich, 1961), Chapter 14.

Disaster research has focused on three time periods: immediately before the disaster, during the disaster, and after the disaster. Predisaster studies have noted that making people aware of impending disaster is extremely difficult unless the group concerned has already experienced a disaster—a flood, a bombing, or an earthquake. Otherwise, people do not take the warning seriously. They look around, note that others don't seem bothered, and define the situation as normal or at least not serious. During Hurricane Camille in Mississippi in August 1969, twenty-some people were killed in an apartment house where they had decided to ride out the storm and have a "hurricane party." People tend to interpret disaster cues as normal or familiar events.

Studies of behavior *during* the disaster indicate that, contrary to popular belief, panic and loss of control are rare. Flight is a frequent response, but it usually represents an adaptive rational reaction to the situation rather than panic. Studies of behavior *after* the disaster indicate that people tend to underestimate the scope and destructiveness of the disaster. Again, people define events in terms of the familiar and normal. Often those who had clearly-defined tasks in case of disaster—civil defense workers, nurses—experience severe role conflict. The conflict is between helping people in general as they are trained to do or finding and helping family and loved ones. Frequently the latter choice is made. Various types of convergence behavior occur after a disaster. People flock *to* the disaster area. Within twenty-four hours after the atom bomb was dropped on Hiroshima, thousands of refugees streamed *into* the city. Airliners in trouble over major airports attract crowds of people to the scene. One such incident at New York's Kennedy Airport brought so much automobile traffic that emergency vehicles had difficulty reaching the scene. Communication lines become clogged with calls coming *into* disaster areas. Material convergence occurs as all sorts and varieties of material are shipped into the disaster area in an effort to help the victims. Within forty-eight hours after a tornado in Arkansas, truckloads full of material began arriving. Among the mass of material that people sent were button shoes, derby hats, a tuxedo, and a carton of falsies. It took 500 workers two weeks to sort the material. After Hurricane Camille in 1969, a great variety of material poured into Mississippi. Authorities had to make television appeals to stop the shipments. Finally, the studies report that in many cases disaster as an immediate threat produces solidarity among those experiencing it. People tend to grow closer together as a result of their attempts to fight and survive the situation.

Publics and Public Opinion

Publics and public opinion represent another aspect of collective behavior. A *public* is a number of people who have an interest in, and difference of opinion about, a common issue. The public engages in communication and discussion (more often indirect than face-to-face) and, contrary to the crowd, the public is dispersed or scattered rather than in close physical contact. *Public opinion* refers to opinions held by a public on a given issue. *Propaganda* refers to attempts to influence and change the public's viewpoint on an issue.[7]

In a complicated mass society, a great number of issues appear, and each issue has its concerned interest group or public. Membership in these publics is transitory and constantly changing. Some members of a public are vitally interested, others only marginally. Members of a public may communicate by special magazines, newspapers, and by television and letter writing. Professional football and baseball have a public, the National Rifle Association is a public, the American Medical Association is a public; the issues of socialized medicine, legalization of prostitution, and elimination of the death penalty all have publics. Some publics are widespread—if the issue is the type of job the President is doing, the whole nation may become the public. Other publics may be much smaller.

Public opinion is registered in a variety of ways. It is registered when an individual running for office is defeated. It is recorded in the "letters to the editor" column of a newspaper or magazine that prints a story with which the public agrees or disagrees. More recently, public opinion polls have become a popular way of determining what the public is thinking. Polls are avidly followed by politicians as well as by the man on the street. Polls have even been criticized because it is feared that some people look at the polls before deciding how to vote or what to think on a given issue.

There are many pitfalls in public opinion polling, and occasionally even the best pollsters go wrong. Probably the most famous miss was the *Literary Digest* poll of 1936 which predicted that Landon (Republican) would defeat Roosevelt (Democrat) for President. The *Literary Digest* obtained a biased sample by mailing ballots to people whose names, for the most part, were selected from telephone directories or from lists of automobile owners. Only 40 percent of all homes had phones in 1936 and 55 percent of all families had cars, so the magazine was sampling people who were economically well-off. Another error was introduced by *mailing* ballots—people of higher income and education are more likely to return mailed questionnaires than are people with low income and education. Ballots were mailed early (September) so that last-minute changes were missed. The upshot was that *Literary Digest* asked a group of reasonably well-to-do people (who generally tend to vote Republican) who they were going to vote for. Their prediction was so grossly wrong that it is given as the reason why the magazine went out of business.[8] A number of polls picked Dewey to

---

[7] For a comprehensive treatment of these concepts, see Turner and Killian, *Collective Behavior*, Chapters 10–12.

[8] This is summarized from Julian Simon's very complete discussion in his book *Basic Research Methods in Social Science* (New York: Random House, 1969), Chapter 8.

beat Truman in 1948; and there was a tremendous uproar in England in June 1970, when the Tories decisively won an election that all the polls predicted would be won by Labour.

Since it is usually impossible in a public opinion poll to talk to all members of the public, a sample is taken. Frequently the success of the poll hinges on the accuracy of the sampling technique. The time at which the poll is taken is also important. Opinions change rapidly and if the latest political poll is three or four weeks before the election, pollsters can expect to have missed many last-minute changes. A more basic fault in polling is that some people are very interested and know much about the issue, and others are only slightly interested and know little or nothing about the issue. Yet in most polls the responses of these two types are given the same weight. Other difficulties in sampling public opinion occur when people give pollsters answers they think the pollsters want, and when a person is a member of several conflicting publics at once, as most of us are. What if a member of the Catholic Church and mother of eleven kids is asked her opinion of government-supported artificial birth control? She may find herself a member of conflicting publics. Finally, as far as action is concerned, it is often much more important to know how a few powerful people or opinion leaders feel about an issue than it is to know what many relatively powerless people think.

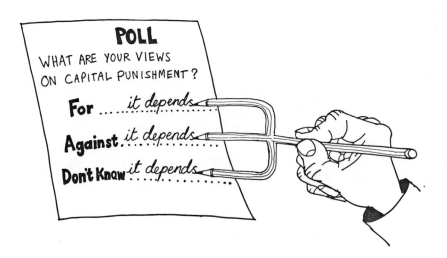

In conclusion, let's examine how the public, public opinion, and propaganda might relate to a given issue, capital punishment. Members of the public interested in this issue would include policemen, prison officials, sociologists, psychologists, social workers, and future criminals. To obtain a measure of public opinion, Gallup might randomly select 1,000 people and ask them what they think about keeping the death penalty. The sample includes interested members of the public and disinterested bystanders, and all opinions are counted equally. (What if, for example, we find thàt most of those who know most about capital punishment are opposed to it, and most of those who know least about it are in favor of it? What do we do?) Suppose we find (as Gallup did in 1972) that fifty-seven percent of those polled want to keep the death penalty. The public in its various forms has spoken. Since the margin is not decisive, however, the other side decides to hire a public relations firm to persuade the public a little. Propaganda begins to appear. A public interest story in a popular magazine tells about how the family of an executed man is getting along. A newspaper story appears describing a famous case in which a condemned man was cleared of the crime he was supposed to have committed—but just too late. . . . An ex-warden of San Quentin is interviewed on a nationwide television news broadcast, and he relates in detail his opposition to the death penalty. A reporter, witness to an execution in the electric chair, describes it in vivid detail in a Sunday Supplement. The effectiveness of the propaganda will depend on its ability to reach the audience, on the sophistication of the audience, and on the receptiveness of the audience to the new viewpoint. Let's assume that the propaganda has been cleverly conceived, and a new sampling indicates that public opinion has changed—now only forty percent want to keep the death penalty. Still, nothing happens until power is applied. A lobbyist in Washington, D.C., working for the Anti-Death Penalty League, puts pressure on legislators. Thirty thousand anti-capital-punishment letters (all remarkably similar) flood in. Finally a new law is passed, more because of the League, lobby, and letters than because of "public opinion." We can see from this imaginary and oversimplified example that boundaries of what constitutes a public are obscure, polls may be misleading, public opinion may change rapidly, propaganda is frequently very useful at building or changing public opinion, and finally, public opinion must be backed by political power if meaningful action is to result.

In June 1972 the U.S. Supreme Court in a 5–4 decision ruled that the death penalty was unconstitutional. Since polls indicate that the public still favors capital punishment we can perhaps follow the reverse of the procedures outlined above as attempts are made to reinstitute the death penalty—which was accomplished in California in September 1973.

Summary

In the previous chapter in this section on change and deviation in society we dealt with social change and social disorganization. In this chapter we examined another form of activity that is outside the organized and ordinary—collective behavior. Collective behavior refers to spontaneous and somewhat unstructured actions by groups of people. A number of concepts and terms central to the study of collective behavior were discussed. We examined types of collectivities: crowds, audiences, and mobs. We described types of behaviors: rumor, panic, mass hysteria, fads, crazes, and fashions. Special situations involving collective behavior were noted: riots and disasters. Our discussion of collective behavior concluded with an analysis of publics, public opinion, and propaganda.

A riot is a situation in which mob behavior has become widespread and destructive. The first reading that follows is an excerpt from the U.S. Riot Commission's Report. It illustrates crowd, mob, and riot behavior in three American cities. Rumor is defined as unconfirmed, although not necessarily false, communication. The essay from *Time* describes a popular rumor of 1969 and illustrates many of the typical characteristics of this form of collective behavior. A mob is a focused, acting crowd. A mob is hard to deal with once set in motion, but the next reading relates how one of the characters in Harper Lee's novel *To Kill a Mockingbird* found a way to distract a lynch mob. A disaster situation is defined as one in which there is a radical departure from the pattern of normal expectations. In the last reading in this section, John Spiegel describes what happened when a small English community was hit by disaster.

U.S. Riot Commission Report

Tampa

The following excerpts from the U.S. Riot Commission's report (the "Kerner Report") describe disturbances that took place in several cities in the summer of 1967. The riot in Tampa was mild in comparison with those in Newark and Detroit. In Newark, twenty-three died—a white detective, a white fireman, and twenty-one Negroes. Damage was estimated at $10 million. In Detroit, forty-three persons were killed—thirty-three blacks and ten whites. Seventeen of the dead were looters. Damage was estimated at between $30 and $50 million. Taken together these examples provide a composite of the life history of a riot They also provide graphic illustrations of crowds and mobs.

On Sunday, June 11, 1967, Tampa, Florida, sweltered in the 94-degree heat. A humid wind ruffled the bay, where thousands of persons watched the hydroplane races. Since early morning the Police Department's Selective Enforcement Unit, designed as a riot control squad, had been employed to keep order at the races.

At 5:30 P.M., a block from the waterfront, a photo supply warehouse was broken into. Forty-five minutes later two police officers spotted three Negro

From the *Report of the National Advisory Commission on Civil Disorders*, Chapter 1.

youths as they walked near the State Building. When the youths caught sight of the officers, they ducked into an alley. The officers gave chase. As they ran, the suspects left a trail of photographic equipment scattered from yellow paper bags they were carrying.

The officers transmitted a general broadcast over the police radio. As other officers arrived on the scene, a chase began through and around the streets, houses, and alleys of the neighborhood. When Negro residents of the area adjacent to the Central Park Village Housing Project became aware of the chase, they began to participate. Some attempted to help the officers in locating the suspects.

R. C. Oates, one of 17 Negroes on the 55-man Tampa police force, spotted 19-year-old Martin Chambers, bare to the waist, wriggling away beneath one of the houses. Oates called for Chambers to surrender. Ignoring him, Chambers emerged running from beneath the house. A white officer, J. L. Calvert, took up the pursuit.

Pursuing Calvert, in turn, were three young Negroes, all spectators. Behind one of the houses a high cyclone fence created a two-foot wide alley twenty-five feet in length.

As Chambers darted along the fence, Officer Calvert rounded the corner of the house. Calvert yelled to him to halt. Chambers ignored him. Calvert pointed his .38 revolver and fired. The slug entered the back of Chambers and passed completely through his body. Raising his hands over his head, he clutched at the cyclone fence.

When the three youths running behind Officer Calvert came upon the scene, they assumed Chambers had been shot standing in the position in which they saw him. Rumor quickly spread through the neighborhood that a white police officer had shot a Negro youth who had had his hands over his head and was trying to surrender.

The ambulance that had been summoned became lost on the way. The gathering crowd viewing the bloody, critically injured youth grew increasingly belligerent.

Finally, Officer Oates loaded Chambers into his car and drove him to the hospital. The youth died shortly thereafter.

As officers were leaving the scene, a thunderstorm broke. Beneath the pelting rain, the spectators scattered. When an officer went back to check the area he found no one on the streets.

A few minutes after 7:00 P.M., the Selective Enforcement Unit, tired and sun-parched, reported in from the races. A half hour later a report was received that 500 persons were gathering. A police car was sent into the area to check the report. The officers could find no one. The men of the Selective Enforcement Unit were told to go home.

The men in the scout car had not, however, penetrated into the Central Park Village Housing complex where, as the rain ended, hundreds of persons poured from the apartments. At least half were teenagers and young adults.

As they began to mill about and discuss the shooting, old grievances, both real
and imagined, were resurrected: discriminatory practices of local stores, advantages taken by white men of Negro girls, the kicking in the face of a Negro
boy by a white man as the Negro lay handcuffed on the ground, blackballing
of two Negro high schools by the athletic conference.

When Officer Oates returned to the area he attempted to convince the
crowd to disperse by announcing that a complete investigation would be made
into the shooting. He seemed to be making headway when a young woman
came running down the street screaming that the police had killed her brother.
Her hysteria galvanized the crowd. Rock throwing began. Police cars driving
into the area were stoned. The police, relying on a previous experience when,
after withdrawal of their units, the crowd had dispersed, decided to send no
more patrol cars into the vicinity.

This time the maneuver did not work. From nearby bars and tawdry night
spots patrons joined the throng. A window was smashed. Haphazard looting
began. As fluid bands of rioters moved down the Central Avenue business
district, stores whose proprietors were particularly disliked were singled out. A
grocery store, a liquor store, a restaurant were hit. The first fire was set.

Because of the dismissal of the Selective Enforcement Unit and the lack of
accurate intelligence information, the police department was slow to react.
Although Sheriff Malcolm Beard of Hillsborough County was in contact with the
Department throughout the evening, it was not until after 11:00 P.M. that a
request for deputies was made to him.

At 11:30 P.M. a recall order, issued earlier by the police department, began
to bring officers back into the area. By this time, the streets in the vicinity of
the housing project were lighted by the flames of burning buildings.

Falling power lines whipped sparks about the skirmish line of officers as they
moved down the street. The popping noise of what sounded to the officers
like gunshots came from the direction of the housing project.

The officers did not return the fire. Police announced from a sound car that
anyone caught armed would be shot. The firing ceased. Then, and throughout
the succeeding two days, law enforcement officers refrained from the use of
firearms. No officer or civilian suffered a gunshot wound during the riot.

Newark

Early on the evening of July 12, a cab driver named John Smith began, according to police reports, tailgating a Newark police car. Smith was an unlikely
candidate to set a riot in motion. Forty years old, a Georgian by birth, he had
attended college for a year before entering the Army in 1950. In 1953 he
had been honorably discharged with the rank of corporal. A chess-playing

trumpet player, he had worked as a musician and a factory hand before, in 1963, becoming a cab driver.

As a cab driver, he appeared to be a hazard. Within a relatively short period of time he had eight or nine accidents. His license was revoked. When, with a woman passenger in his cab, he was stopped by the police, he was in violation of that revocation.

From the high-rise towers of the Reverend William P. Hayes Housing Project, the residents can look down on the orange-red brick facade of the Fourth Precinct Police Station and observe every movement. Shortly after 9:30 P.M., people saw Smith, who either refused or was unable to walk, being dragged out of a police car into the front door of the station.

Within a few minutes at least two civil rights leaders received calls from a hysterical woman declaring a cab driver was being beaten by police. When one of the persons at the station notified the cab company of Smith's arrest, cab drivers all over the city began learning of it over their cab radios.

A crowd formed on the grounds of the housing project across the narrow street from the station. As more and more people arrived, the description of the beating purportedly administered to Smith became more and more exaggerated. The descriptions were supported by other complaints of police malpractice that, over the years, had been submitted for investigation—but had never been heard of again.

Several Negro community leaders, telephoned by a civil rights worker and informed of the deteriorating situation, rushed to the scene. By 10:15 P.M. the atmosphere had become so potentially explosive that Kenneth Melchior, the senior police inspector on the night watch, was called. He arrived at approximately 10:30 P.M.

Met by a delegation of civil rights leaders and militants who requested the right to see and interview Smith, Inspector Melchior acceded to their request.

When the delegation was taken to Smith, Melchior agreed with their observations that, as a result of injuries Smith had suffered, he needed to be examined by a doctor. Arrangements were made to have a police car transport him to the hospital.

Both within and outside of the police station the atmosphere was electric with hostility. Carloads of police officers arriving for the 10:45 P.M. change of shifts were subject to a gauntlet of catcalls, taunts and curses.

Joined by Oliver Lofton, administrative director of the Newark Legal Services Project, the Negro community leaders inside the station requested an interview with Inspector Melchior. As they were talking to the inspector about initiating an investigation to determine how Smith had been injured, the crowd outside became more and more unruly. Two of the Negro spokesmen went outside to attempt to pacify the people. There was little reaction to the spokesmen's appeal that the people go home. The second of the two had just finished speaking from atop a car when several Molotov cocktails smashed against the wall of the police station.

With the call of "Fire!" most of those inside the station, police officers and civilians alike, rushed out of the front door. The Molotov cocktails had splattered to the ground; the fire was quickly extinguished.

Inspector Melchior had a squad of men form a line across the front of the station. The police officers and the Negroes on the other side of the street exchanged volleys of profanity.

Three of the Negro leaders, Timothy Still of the United Community Corporation, Robert Curvin of CORE, and Lofton requested they be given another opportunity to disperse the crowd. Inspector Melchior agreed to let them try, and provided a bullhorn. It was apparent that the several hundred persons who had gathered in the street and on the grounds of the housing project were not going to disperse. Therefore, it was decided to attempt to channel the energies of the people into a nonviolent protest. While Lofton promised the crowd that a full investigation would be made of the Smith incident, the other Negro leaders urged those on the scene to form a line of march toward the city hall.

Some persons joined the line of march. Others milled about in the narrow street. From the dark grounds of the housing project came a barrage of rocks. Some of them fell among the crowd. Others hit persons in the line of march. Many smashed the windows of the police station. The rock throwing, it was believed, was the work of youngsters; approximately 2,500 children lived in the housing project.

Almost at the same time, an old car was set afire in a parking lot. The line of march began to disintegrate. The police, their heads protected by World War I-type helmets, sallied forth to disperse the crowd. A fire engine, arriving on the scene, was pelted with rocks. As police drove people away from the station, they scattered in all directions.

A few minutes later a nearby liquor store was broken into. Some persons, seeing a caravan of cabs appear at city hall to protest Smith's arrest, interpreted this as evidence that the disturbance had been organized, and generated rumors to that effect.

However, only a few stores were looted. Within a short period of time the disorder ran its course.

(The next day) Reports and rumors, including one that Smith had died, circulated through the Negro community. Tension continued to rise. Nowhere was the tension greater than at the Spirit House, the gathering place for Black Nationalists, Black Power advocates, and militants of every hue. Black Muslims, Orthodox Muslims, and members of the United Afro-American Association, a new and growing organization that follows, in general, the teachings of the late Malcolm X, came regularly to mingle and exchange views. Anti-white playwright LeRoi Jones held workshops. The two police-Negro clashes, coming one on top of the other, coupled with the unresolved political issues, had created a state of crisis.

On Thursday, inflammatory leaflets were circulated in the neighborhoods of the Fourth Precinct. A "Police Brutality Protest Rally" was announced for early evening in front of the Fourth Precinct Station. Several television stations and newspapers sent news teams to interview people. Cameras were set up. A crowd gathered.

A picket line was formed to march in front of the police station. Between 7:00 and 7:30 P.M. James Threatt, Executive Director of the Newark Human Rights Commission, arrived to announce to the people the decision of the mayor to form a citizens group to investigate the Smith incident, and to elevate a Negro to the rank of captain.

The response from the loosely milling mass of people was derisive. One youngster shouted "Black Power!" Rocks were thrown at Threatt, a Negro. The barrage of missiles that followed placed the police station under siege.

After the barrage had continued for some minutes, police came out to disperse the crowd. According to witnesses, there was little restraint of language or action by either side. A number of police officers and Negroes were injured.

As on the night before, once the people had been dispersed, reports of looting began to come in. Soon the glow of the first fire was seen.

Without enough men to establish control, the police set up a perimeter around a two-mile stretch of Springfield Avenue, one of the principal business districts, where bands of youths roamed up and down smashing windows. Grocery and liquor stores, clothing and furniture stores, drug stores and cleaners, appliance stores and pawnshops were the principal targets. Periodically police officers would appear and fire their weapons over the heads of looters and rioters. Laden with stolen goods people began returning to the housing projects.

Near midnight, activity appeared to taper off. The Mayor told reporters the city had turned the corner.

As news of the disturbance had spread, however, people had flocked into the streets. As they saw stores being broken into with impunity, many bowed to temptation and joined the looting.

Without the necessary personnel to make mass arrests, police were shooting into the air to clear stores. A Negro boy was wounded by a .22 caliber bullet said to have been fired by a white man riding in a car. Guns were reported stolen from a Sears Roebuck store. Looting, fires, and gunshots were reported from a widening area. Between 2:00 and 2:30 A.M. on Friday, July 14, the mayor decided to request Governor Richard J. Hughes to dispatch the state police, and National Guard troops. The first elements of the state police arrived with a sizable contingent before dawn.

During the morning the governor and the mayor, together with police and National Guard officers, made a reconnaissance of the area. The police escort guarding the officials arrested looters as they went. By early afternoon the National Guard had set up 137 roadblocks, and state police and riot teams were beginning to achieve control. Command of anti-riot operations was taken over by the governor, who decreed a "hard line" in putting down the riot.

Detroit

On Saturday evening, July 22, the Detroit Police Department raided five "blind pigs." The blind pigs had had their origin in prohibition days, and survived as private social clubs. Often, they were after-hours drinking and gambling spots.

The fifth blind pig on the raid list, the United Community and Civic League at the corner of 12th Street and Clairmount, had been raided twice before. Once 10 persons had been picked up; another time 28. A Detroit Vice Squad officer had tried but failed to get in shortly after 10 o'clock Saturday night. He succeeded, on his second attempt, at 3:45 Sunday morning.

The Tactical Mobile Unit, the Police Department's Crowd Control Squad, had been dismissed at 3:00 A.M. Since Sunday morning traditionally is the least troublesome time for police in Detroit—and all over the country—only 193 officers were patrolling the streets. Of these, 44 were in the 10th Precinct where the blind pig was located.

Police expected to find two dozen patrons in the blind pig. That night, however, it was the scene of a party for several servicemen, two of whom were back from Vietnam. Instead of two dozen patrons, police found 82. Some voiced resentment at the police intrusion.

An hour went by before all 82 could be transported from the scene. The weather was humid and warm—the temperature that day was to rise to 86—and despite the late hour, many people were still on the street. In short order, a crowd of about 200 gathered.

A few minutes after 5:00 A.M., just after the last of those arrested had been hauled away, an empty bottle smashed into the rear window of a police car. A litter basket was thrown through the window of a store. Rumors circulated of excess force used by the police during the raid. A youth, whom police nicknamed "Mr. Greensleeves" because of the color of his shirt, was shouting: "We're going to have a riot!" and exhorting the crowd to vandalism.

By 7:50 A.M., when a 17-man police commando unit attempted to make the first sweep, an estimated 3,000 persons were on 12th Street. They offered no resistance. As the sweep moved down the street, they gave way to one side, and then flowed back behind it.

According to witnesses, police at some roadblocks made little effort to stop people from going in and out of the area. Bantering took place between police officers and the populace, some still in pajamas. To some observers, there seemed at this point to be an atmosphere of apathy. On the one hand, the police failed to interfere with the looting. On the other, a number of older, more stable residents, who had seen the street deteriorate from a prosperous commercial thoroughfare to one ridden by vice, remained aloof.

In an effort to avoid attracting people to the scene, some broadcasters cooperated by not reporting the riot, and an effort was made to downplay the extent of the disorder. The facade of "business as usual" necessitated the detailing of numerous police officers to protect the 50,000 spectators that were expected at that afternoon's New York Yankees–Detroit Tigers baseball game.

Numerous eyewitnesses interviewed by Commission investigators tell of the carefree mood with which people ran in and out of stores, looting and laughing, and joking with the police officers. Stores with "Soul Brothers" signs appeared no more immune than others. Looters paid no attention to residents who shouted at them and called their actions senseless. An epidemic of excitement had swept over the persons on the street.

. . . a rumor was threading through the crowd that a man had been bayoneted by the police. Influenced by such stories, the crowd became belligerent. At approximately 1:00 P.M. stonings accelerated. Numerous officers reported injuries from rocks, bottles, and other objects thrown at them. Smoke billowed upward from four fires, the first since the one at the shoe store early in the morning. When firemen answered the alarms, they became the targets for rocks and bottles.

At 2:00 P.M. Mayor Cavanagh met with community and political leaders at police headquarters. Until then there had been hope that, as people blew off steam, the riot would dissipate. Now the opinion was nearly unanimous that additional forces would be needed.

A request was made for state police aid. By 3:00 P.M. 360 officers were assembling at the armory. At that moment looting was spreading from the 12th Street area to other main thoroughfares.

Some evidence that criminal elements were organizing spontaneously to take advantage of the riot began to manifest itself. A number of cars were noted to be returning again and again, their occupants methodically looting stores. Months later, goods stolen during the riot were still being peddled.

A spirit of carefree nihilism was taking hold. To riot and to destroy appeared more and more to become ends in themselves. Late Sunday afternoon it appeared to one observer that the young people were "dancing amidst the flames."

Questions

1. *Apply text definitions of crowd, mob, and riot to the cities described. Point out where "crowd" is the best description, where "mob" is the best description, and where "riot" is the best description.*

2. *List the common factors—the situations or occurrences that were present in each of the three city disturbances described.*

3. *"Urban riots may be seen as a type of social movement . . ." Discuss (see Chapter 8).*

Of Rumor, Myth and a Beatle

A rumor that Beatle Paul McCartney had been killed in an automobile accident swept the country in the fall of 1969. Fans of the rock music group frantically sought further proof of Paul's demise by playing Beatle records backwards and by finding clues on album covers and in photographs of the group. *Time* offers a brief discussion of this collective behavior phenomenon.

> *LONDON AP—Paul McCartney vigorously denied today the rumor that he is alive and well. At a resurrection ceremony held at London's Highgate Cemetery, the 24-year-old Beatle, who would have been 27 had he lived, emerged from his tomb to insist that he was decapitated in a car accident three years ago.*
>
> *"This is the sort of thing one doesn't get over," he told a crowd estimated by Scotland Yard at 3,500. "If I were really alive, wouldn't I be the first to admit it?" Amid a chorus of anguished protest from the audience, McCartney re-entered his crypt and was seen to bolt it from inside.*
>
> *Despite this brief reincarnation, the rumor persists that McCartney lives, strengthened by the report that a new Beatles movie, in which he appears, will be issued next year.*

Silly as his imaginary news dispatch may seem, it is not much sillier than the rumor, currently sweeping U.S. college campuses, that Paul McCartney is dead. As with most rumors, no one really knows its source. It has been variously traced to a thesis by an Ohio Wesleyan University student, a satirical but deadpan story in the Oct. 14 issue of the University of Michigan *Daily,* and a Detroit disk jockey who spread much the same nonsense over radio station WKNR. Since the rumor spread, Beatle fans have diligently parsed the albums of their heroes for clues corroborating what they already wanted to believe; of course, they found them, usually in forced interpretations of Beatle lyrics. That is another characteristic of rumor. It does not require—indeed, it commonly rejects—the discipline of reason.

As McCartney proved by appearing at a Glasgow airport last week, he is indisputably alive. But so is the baseless report that he is not. What is more, the rumor is not likely to die before he does; after the event, which could occur 50 or so years from now, the last surviving mongers of this particular rumor will triumphantly crow: "I told you so." For reasons that go back to the origins of man, the human intellect craves to discover more meaning than facts can supply. What it does not know it will guess at. Airborne by ignorance and insecurity, that supposition will almost always defy the attempts of reason to shoot it down.

Two conditions are essential to the survival of a rumor. One is ambiguity, which can stem from many different sources: a shortage of dependable information, events beyond ordinary understanding. The other condition is man's dislike of ambiguity in situations that vitally affect him.

The Welcome Channel

These two conditions are handsomely fulfilled by an age in which not only events but their meaning strain human understanding. Merely to live with the omnipotence of science and technology is enough to send man back to the safe harbor of primitive myth. Just as myth was the predecessor of science and religion, so may rumor have been the precursor of myth. Long before man registered his thoughts on the pages of history, he committed his anxieties and his faith to rumor—that welcome channel of information and misinformation that made sense of senselessness.

In satisfying the human need for reassurance, rumor plays a role that truth not always can. It goes through three distinct stages. In the first, the fact content is reduced, partly because of the porosity of human memory, partly because of man's inclination to simplify. The Great Blackout of 1965 was a cause of countless rumors; some people immediately assumed that it was the result of a Communist sabotage plot; others believed that it was an unannounced air-raid test by the U.S. Government. In the next stage, the rumor-monger accents certain parts of the story that appeal to him. Last year in Washington, D.C., a rumor swept the black ghetto that Soul Singer James Brown had been killed shortly after finishing a concert in the city. As it happened, Brown had simply flown off for another appearance: because of the ugly connotations of the story, Brown was traced to Los Angeles and persuaded to record a statement declaring that he was still alive. In this case, the rumor suited the sentiment of a bitter, riot-prone community better than the truth.

In the third and final stage of a rumor's life, the information is tailored to suit the vendor's interests and emotional needs. Those who believe that Mc-Cartney is dead, for instance, are in part sublimating their fear of the grave. For whenever death visits another person, it must delay its appointment in Samarra with *you*. Frequently, the death of a public figure breeds a host of rumors about the supposed deaths of other public figures. Within hours after Franklin Roosevelt died in 1945, rumors falsely consigned General George Marshall, Bing Crosby and New York Mayor Fiorello La Guardia to the same end. John Kennedy's assassination touched off false stories that Lyndon Johnson had immediately succumbed to a heart attack. Conversely, ambiguous evidence of a public figure's death will almost certainly provoke rumors that he is alive. Some people believe that Hitler is still at large in Argentina or Paraguay; others contend that J.F.K. carries on a vegetable-like existence in a well-guarded private hospital. Long after his death, many of his fans believed that he was alive, but hopelessly disfigured, in a hospital somewhere.

It is almost impossible for people in the public eye to escape from rumors. That paragon of puritanical virtue, Queen Victoria, was thought by some of her contemporaries to be the secret wife of Disraeli or the secret mistress of her Scottish gillie, John Brown. Since rumor sometimes represents vicarious wish fulfillment, certain movie stars have been popularly credited with sexual exploits that defy physical ability.

Politics and government are simply inconceivable without the ubiquitous presence of rumor; it is a fixture of every state polity. In the form of trial balloons, rumors are deliberately lofted to survey popular sentiment. Before Gutenberg, word of mouth constituted man's principal means for exchanging knowledge, and it would be difficult to prove that modern instruments of communication have improved things much. If legend and myth are solidified rumor, so may be the printed picture and word—secondhand hearsay that is susceptible to the same kind of distortion that rumor undergoes in its journey from one willing ear to the next.

Not even Paul McCartney would claim that the rumor of his death has injured him in any way. Quite the opposite, in fact. It has filled the headlines with his name and generated a bull market for the new Beatle album, *Abbey Road.* Nor is it surprising, really, that such a morbid thought could take root and grow in the public consciousness. The Beatles are a modern and enviable public myth: four young nobodies from Liverpool who, through accident as much as art, caught the public fancy at a moment when there was a need for the society-challenging antihero.

Among other things, the McCartney death story shows that it is impossible for a man to get through life without hearing a lot of rumors, believing some of them and starting or at least embroidering a few himself. It is all so easy. Take, for example, the story that Jackie Onassis has secretly fallen in love with a New York *Daily News* photographer . . . .

Questions

1. *"Attractive" details of rumors tend to become magnified. Illustrate, using the Beatles' rumor.*
2. *List and describe the functions served by starting and/or passing rumors—especially this rumor.*

Maycomb Jail

Harper Lee

A mob is a focused, acting crowd. It is emotionally aroused and intent on taking action. A mob is a powerful force, and it is difficult to change its direction. When the direction is changed (as it is in this fictional account), the change can be understood in collective behavior terms. Here, Scout and Jem Finch help their father, Atticus, protect a black man from a lynch mob in Harper Lee's novel *To Kill a Mockingbird*.

The Maycomb Jail was the most venerable and hideous of the county's buildings. Atticus said it was like something Cousin Joshua St. Clair might have designed. It was certainly someone's dream. Starkly out of place in a town of square-faced stores and steep-roofed houses, wide and two cells high, complete with tiny battlements and flying buttresses. Its fantasy was heightened by its red brick facade and the thick steel bars at its ecclesiastical windows. It stood on no lonely hill, but was wedged between Tyndal's Hardware Store and The Maycomb Tribune office. The jail was Maycomb's only conversation piece: its detractors said it looked like a Victorian privy; its supporters said it gave the town a good solid respectable look, and no stranger would ever suspect that it was full of niggers.

As we walked up the sidewalk, we saw a solitary light burning in the distance. "That's funny," said Jem, "jail doesn't have an outside light."

"Looks like it's over the door," said Dill.

A long extension cord ran between the bars of a second-floor window and down the side of the building. In the light from its bare bulb, Atticus was sitting propped against the front door. He was sitting in one of his office chairs, and he was reading, oblivious of the nightbugs dancing over his head.

I made to run, but Jem caught me. "Don't go to him," he said, "he might not like it. He's all right, let's go home. I just wanted to see where he was."

We were taking a short cut across the square when four dusty cars came in from the Meridian highway, moving slowly in a line. They went around the square, passed the bank building, and stopped in front of the jail.

Nobody got out. We saw Atticus look up from his newspaper. He closed it, folded it deliberately, dropped it in his lap, and pushed his hat to the back of his head. He seemed to be expecting them.

"Come on," whispered Jem. We streaked across the square, across the street, until we were in the shelter of the Jitney Jungle door. Jem peeked up the sidewalk. "We can get closer," he said. We ran to Tyndal's Hardware door—near enough, at the same time discreet.

In ones and twos, men got out of the cars. Shadows became substance as lights revealed solid shapes moving toward the jail door. Atticus remained where he was. The men hid him from view.

"He in there, Mr. Finch?" a man said.

"He is," we heard Atticus answer, "and he's asleep. Don't wake him up."

In obedience to my father, there followed what I later realized was a sickeningly comic aspect of an unfunny situation: the men talked in near-whispers.

"You know what we want," another man said. "Get aside from the door, Mr. Finch."

"You can turn around and go home again, Walter." Atticus said pleasantly. "Heck Tate's around somewhere."

"The hell he is," said another man. "Heck's bunch's so deep in the woods they won't get out till mornin'."

"Indeed? Why so?"

"Called 'em off on a snipe hunt," was the succinct answer. "Didn't you think a' that, Mr. Finch?"

"Thought about it, but didn't believe it. Well then," my father's voice was still the same, "that changes things, doesn't it?"

"It do," another deep voice said. Its owner was a shadow.

"Do you really think so?"

This was the second time I heard Atticus ask that question in two days, and it meant somebody's man would get jumped. This was too good to miss. I broke away from Jem and ran as fast as I could to Atticus.

Jem shrieked and tried to catch me, but I had a lead on him and Dill. I pushed my way through dark smelly bodies and burst into the circle of light.

"H-ey, Atticus!"

I thought he would have a fine surprise, but his face killed my joy. A flash of plain fear was going out of his eyes, but returned when Dill and Jem wriggled into the light.

There was a smell of stale whiskey and pigpen about, and when I glanced around I discovered that these men were strangers. They were not the people I saw last night. Hot embarrassment shot through me: I had leaped triumphantly into a ring of people I had never seen before.

Atticus got up from his chair, but he was moving slowly, like an old man. He put the newspaper down very carefully, adjusting its creases with lingering fingers. They were trembling a little.

"Go home, Jem," he said. "Take Scout and Dill home."

We were accustomed to prompt, if not always cheerful acquiescence to Atticus's instructions, but from the way he stood Jem was not thinking of budging.

"Go home, I said."

Jem shook his head. As Atticus's fists went to his hips, so did Jem's and as they faced each other I could see little resemblance between them: Jem's soft brown hair and eyes, his oval face and snug-fitting ears were our mother's, contrasting oddly with Atticus's graying black hair and square-cut features, but they were somehow alike. Mutual defiance made them alike.

"Son, I said go home."

Jem shook his head.

"I'll send him home," a burly man said, and grabbed Jem roughly by the collar. He yanked Jem nearly off his feet.

"Don't you touch him!" I kicked the man swiftly. Barefooted, I was surprised to see him fall back in real pain. I intended to kick his shin, but aimed too high.

"That'll do, Scout," Atticus put his hand on my shoulder. "Don't kick folks. No—" he said, as I was pleading justification.

"Ain't nobody gonna do Jem that way," I said.

"All right, Mr. Finch, get 'em outa here," someone growled. "You got fifteen seconds to get 'em outa here."

In the midst of this strange assembly, Atticus stood trying to make Jem mind him. "I ain't going," was his steady answer to Atticus's threats, requests, and finally, "Please Jem, take them home."

I was getting a bit tired of that, but felt Jem had his own reasons for doing as he did, in view of his prospects once Atticus did get him home. I looked around the crowd. It was a summer's night, but the men were dressed most of them, in overalls and denim shirts buttoned up to the collars. I thought they must be cold-natured, as their sleeves were unrolled and buttoned at the cuffs. Some wore hats pulled firmly down over their ears. They were sullen-looking, sleepy-eyed men who seemed unused to late hours. I sought once more for a familiar face, and at the center of the semi-circle I found one.

"Hey, Mr. Cunningham."

The man did not hear me, it seemed.

"Hey, Mr. Cunningham. How's your entailment gettin' along?"

Mr. Walter Cunningham's legal affairs were well known to me; Atticus had once described them at length. The big man blinked and hooked his thumbs in his overall straps. He seemed uncomfortable; he cleared his throat and looked away. My friendly overture had fallen flat.

Mr. Cunningham wore no hat, and the top half of his forehead was white in contrast to his sunscorched face, which led me to believe that he wore one most days. He shifted his feet, clad in heavy work shoes.

"Don't you remember me, Mr. Cunningham? I'm Jean Louise Finch. You brought us some hickory nuts one time, remember?" I began to sense the futility one feels when unacknowledged by a chance acquaintance.

"I go to school with Walter," I began again. "He's your boy, ain't he? Ain't he, sir?"

Mr. Cunningham was moved to a faint nod. He did know me, after all.

"He's in my grade," I said, "and he does right well. He's a good boy," I added, "a real nice boy. We brought him home for dinner one time. Maybe he told you about me, I beat him up one time but he was real nice about it. Tell him hey for me, won't you?"

Atticus had said it was the polite thing to talk to people about what they were interested in, not about what you were interested in. Mr. Cunningham displayed no interest in his son, so I tackled his entailment once more in a last-ditch effort to make him feel at home.

"Entailments are bad," I was advising him, when I slowly awoke to the fact that I was addressing the entire aggregation. The men were all looking at me, some had their mouths half-open. Atticus had stopped poking at Jem: they were standing together beside Dill. Their attention amounted to fascination. Atticus's mouth, even, was half-open, an attitude he had once described as uncouth. Our eyes met and he shut it.

"Well, Atticus, I was just sayin' to Mr. Cunningham that entailments are bad an' all that, but you said not to worry, it takes a long time sometimes . . . that you all'd ride it out together . . . ." I was slowly drying up, wondering what idiocy I had committed. Entailments seemed all right enough for living-room talk.

I began to feel sweat gathering at the edges of my hair; I could stand any-thing but a bunch of people looking at me. They were quite still.

"What's the matter?" I asked.

Atticus said nothing. I looked around and up at Mr. Cunningham, whose face was equally impassive. Then he did a peculiar thing. He squatted down and took me by both shoulders.

"I'll tell him you said hey, little lady," he said.

Then he straightened up and waved a big paw. "Let's clear out," he called. "Let's get going, boys."

As they had come, in ones and twos the men shuffled back to their ramshackle cars. Doors slammed, engines coughed, and they were gone.

I turned to Atticus, but Atticus had gone to the jail and was leaning against it with his face to the wall. I went to him and pulled his sleeve. "Can we go home now?" He nodded, produced his handkerchief, gave his face a going-over and blew his nose violently.

"Mr. Finch?"

A soft husky voice came from the darkness above: "They gone?"

Atticus stepped back and looked up. "They've gone," he said. "Get some sleep, Tom. They won't bother you any more."

From a different direction, another voice cut crisply through the night: "You're damn tootin' they won't. Had you covered all the time, Atticus."

Mr. Underwood and a double-barreled shotgun were leaning out his window above The Maycomb Tribune office.

It was long past my bedtime and I was growing quite tired; it seemed that Atticus and Mr. Underwood would talk for the rest of the night, Mr. Underwood out the window and Atticus up at him. Finally Atticus returned, switched off the light above the jail door, and picked up his chair.

"Can I carry it for you, Mr. Finch?" asked Dill. He had not said a word the whole time.

"Why, thank you, son."

Walking toward the office, Dill and I fell into step behind Atticus and Jem. Dill was encumbered by the chair, and his pace was slower. Atticus and Jem were well ahead of us, and I assumed that Atticus was giving him hell for not going home, but I was wrong. As they passed under a streetlight, Atticus reached out and massaged Jem's hair, his one gesture of affection.

Questions

1. *Outline how mob and crowd characteristics are illustrated in this selection.*
2. *Describe in collective behavior terminology why and/or how the lynch mob was broken up.*

The English Flood of 1953

John P. Spiegel

A disaster situation is defined as one in which there is a basic disruption of the social context within which individuals and groups function, a radical departure from the pattern of normal expectations. Studies of disasters provide us with data about a particular type of collective behavior. In this paper, John Spiegel describes what happened when the English community of "Kimbark" (the actual name of the community is not revealed) was overcome by a flood.

Dr. Spiegel is director of the Lemberg Center for the Study of Violence at Brandeis University.

The National Research Council's Committee on Disaster Studies sent us to England about two weeks after the North Sea flood of February 1, 1953, to set up a rather extensive comparative study of the flood's effects in several communities. Unfortunately, the larger study did not materialize and we were compelled to learn what we could by ourselves in about two weeks. The following report, therefore, must be regarded as very tentative. It deals with Kimbark, one of the two flooded communities we were able to study.

Kimbark before the Flood

Kimbark was a relatively new settlement located on an island less than 10 square miles in area in the Thames Estuary about 35 miles from London. Here the estuary is so broad that it resembles the North Sea itself. The island is cut off from the mainland opposite the estuary side by a narrow creek. A single bridge is the only connection to the mainland. Everything that comes in or goes out of the community—all transport and all communication—must pass over this bridge. The land is virtually at sea level and was first settled for farming about two hundred years ago, mainly by Dutch people. Indeed it resembles some of the Dutch communities today in its physical characteristics. Kimbark is protected against the sea by dykes constructed by Dutch engineers, and the streets have Dutch names.

For years Kimbark was settled only by farmers. After World War I it began to be settled more and more by working-class migrants from the east end of London. These people commonly visited Kimbark for brief week-end holidays at first. They found it a pleasant and inexpensive place to bathe inasmuch as it

From *Human Organization,* Summer 1957, 3–5. Reprinted by permission of the author and The Society for Applied Anthropology.

was not one of England's fashionable sea-side resorts or watering places. Then the people who first came for the weekends began to spend longer summer holidays on Kimbark. Finally, many of these Londoners decided it would be a good place to reside the year around when they no longer had to work in London.

The migrants built cottages and shacks in quite unique and ramshackle fashion. Families built their own houses over periods of several years, adding little bits annually until their houses became fairly habitable. There was no order or town plan in this construction between the two world wars when much of the building occurred. Each family or settlers simply staked out what property they desired and built what they wanted and could afford. These working-class people developed a great pride of ownership, for at long last they had land of their own and a house of their own detached from others.

After World War II the settlement of Kimbark continued at a tremendously increased rate. By 1953 there were about 12,000 people living on the island. The town was governed by an urban-district and, as we shall see, the characteristics of the council members turned out to be very important factors in the course of events following the flood.

The Flood

The flood came to Kimbark very rapidly in the early morning of February 1, 1953. Its shattering effects were prominent and dramatic. The flood was the product of a rare combination of wind and tide unlike anything known in the past 250 years. Meteorologists explained that a small cyclone in the Northeast Atlantic in the last week of January, fed by a warm and calm air mass, grew into a big storm center which then pushed eastward across Scotland to the North Sea. By coincidence the storm arrived over the North Sea at its climax with wind clocked officially at 115 to 125 miles an hour, and at the very time when high spring tides were in full flood. The northwesterly gale drove the waters with mounting pressure against the North Sea's southern bottle-neck just as the tides were pushing with maximum force against the low-lying land. Something had to give under the strain, and the weakest spots in the land's defenses—river estuaries and man-made walls—were what gave way in England, Holland and Belgium.

The particular disaster at Kimbark occurred not as a result of the water topping the dykes—the dykes were very high—but because the dykes broke. The pressure of the water scouring against the bottom of the dykes combined with swirling and dribbling over the top, weakened the structures at certain places in the wall. The results were especially catastrophic at Kimbark, because as the town had grown, a new dyke had been constructed without removing the older one. Thus, there was an inner and an outer dyke with numerous houses between them. When the outer wall gave way between 1:00 and 1:30 A.M. on February 1st the area between the inner and outer dykes filled up rapidly. Water rushed in, hit the inside dyke, bounced back and swirled around inside like water flowing rapidly into a bathtub. The force of the water going in and the eddies and currents set up were enormous.

Initial Reactions

The rapidity of the event gave people practically no opportunity to stop and think. Aroused from their sleep, they were faced with a very sudden emergency situation. They were awakened by the sound of water; dribbling, trickling, rushing and gurgling, and often by the sound of their furniture being rustled around in the house. The water came pouring in through cracks in the doors and windows. In some cases a man would reach for his shoes or his pipe, intending to get up and see where the water was coming from—perchance a tap had been left running!—only to find that his hands were in water. In other cases water came over the bed while one was sleeping.

In one way or another, the people had very little time to orient themselves to the stimuli which suddenly confronted them. For this reason many initially made a series of incorrect assumptions as to what was going on. The usual process was an attempt to relate the emergency stimuli to normal events. A wife would say to her husband, "You left the faucet running," or "The pipes have broken." It was very difficult for people to comprehend and accept the reality of the emergency that faced them. When one finally realized that the water was rising very rapidly outside, and could be seen rising within the house as well, a rapid decision had to be made. What to do? Should one try to get out the front door, or try to get up higher in the house? But these were bungalows without second stories, so where was one to go?

Those who made the correct decision saved their lives. The correct decision was to get up through the ceiling onto the roof or up onto the porch if there was a high porch railing. Fortunately, most people did make the correct assessment. Those who did not and who tried to open the door and get out either let in a mountain of water which trapped them in the house, or they were swept away. In those parts of the flooded area which were worst affected, the currents were too violent for one to swim to safety. More than 50 persons lost their lives and for days several hundred others were missing. All of the 12,000 residents had to be evacuated, and Kimbark was reported to have suffered the greatest damage of any British community.

The flood presented a series of immediate threats. First, there was the threat to the very life of the individual. Second, there was the threat to the intactness of one's family. The threat to the family was present throughout the course of the disaster and its aftermath. During the rescue and evacuation period families would get separated, and there was much anxiety and distress as to the whereabouts of mother, father, child, or grandparent. The third threat was to the family's property or possessions. Finally, there was a fourth threat to the existence of the community. Since Kimbark had to be evacuated, the community was disrupted and could only reestablish itself as houses again became habitable.

Processes of Adjustment

Now, permit me to describe some of the mechanisms or processes that took place here, and their effect on the Kimbark community. The first defense against such disasters as floods is an adequate warning system, of course. Warning of disaster makes for preparedness and effective action. Kimbark had no warning of its disaster, even though the flood had struck the north of England and Scotland on the afternoon of January 31st, and did not reach Kimbark until 1:00 A.M. on February 1st. Word of the disaster to the north simply did *not* get down to the south of England. The reason was that the warning system for floods, and anything else having to do with water, is under the control of a number of organizations called "River Boards"—a traditional institution with a long history. Each River Board pays attention only to its own river and its outlet, plus the land immediately adjacent thereof. No board, it seemed, felt responsible for the neighboring rivers, other than to report possible water levels to the other river boards. A few communities received reports from Scotland Yard with a message to expect flood tides, but there was no indication as to just how disastrous the flood might be. Furthermore, there was no mechanism for disseminating the message, once it was received, by the few civil authorities to whom it was sent. Nor was there an apparatus by which the message could be relayed at night, an especially critical omission.

Another element in the country's governmental structure which affected the organizational readiness of the Kimbark community was the Civil Defense apparatus. As a result of World War II and Britain's critical position with respect to any future war in Europe, civil defense is much more highly organized in that country than here. The civil defense plan calls for the principal authority in each local community to be invested in the chief local official, usually the town clerk. The immediate rescue operations incident to any disaster, or enemy action, are to be in the hands of the police. This is what the plan calls for. In the case of a natural disaster such as flood, the actual situation, with regard to instituting of Civil Defense services was at that time highly ambiguous and the officers of the town were under no responsibility to call out Civil Defense measures. However, because of the magnitude of the disaster, the complete disruption of community organization, and the emergency nature of the evacuation and its consequences, most people were thinking in the images of Civil Defense services and the wartime emergency.

There were other reasons for the plan not operating in Kimbark during the emergency. One was that the town clerk failed to arrive on the scene of action, although he had been notified of the emergency. The chief police authority in the town was a constable, and by plan he should have taken charge of the warning system, determined the seriousness of the emergency which confronted the town, and decided what should be done. But this constable, like other constables, was a man trained to take orders, to proceed with caution and not to "stick his neck out." So Kimbark's constable went from one dyke to the other trying to decide the degree of danger and whether he should alert the community. By the time he had decided the flood was going to be disastrous he was isolated by the water himself and was unable to warn anyone.

In consequence of the officially designated leadership being thus incapacitated, the situation demanded spontaneous leadership. Fortunately for Kimbark this occurred. One man saw what was happening and acted promptly. He was a surveyor and engineer of the town who had been a troop commander in World War II. When he first learned of the possibility of flooding, he went directly to his office where he called the telephone exchange and asked them to transfer any messages reporting signs of water to his office. The first call came soon enough. He thereupon mobilized a crew of men and directed them to warn the public by word of mouth. He also put in a phone call immediately to the mainland and requested ambulances, police reserves, boats, and other emergency equipment. Had this man not sent out the emergency message entirely on his own, acting on intuition and minimum information and before he knew the actual extent of the disaster, Kimbark would have been in a far worse position. Immediately after he telephoned his urgent appeal for emergency assistance all communications with the mainland were cut.

From this time on, the whole operation of rescue and evacuation was in the hands of spontaneous, unofficial leaders not designated in the civil defense plan. They came forth from within Kimbark and from the surrounding countryside, the "shock-absorbing" area, so to speak. From an organizational point of view, these spontaneous processes were initiated partly on the basis of individuals' previous war experience. That is, people knew something of the roles they should play. The spontaneous leadership and action also occurred because certain kinds of people took authority for themselves. They cut "red tape," hired entire bus lines, and got the railroads operating with no prior authority. They were willing to await official authorization after the fact. Because of this spontaneous leadership and prompt action hundreds of lives were saved, and the community was spared far greater destruction.

Thousands of people were exposed to cold and wind and water over many, many hours while awaiting rescue. Families were separated and property destroyed. Nevertheless, during the extreme emergency period, while the flood waters filled the town, morale was extremely high in spite of the great threat to life and terrific feats of endurance.

The tensions which developed at Kimbark came *after* the period of extreme emergency and urgent defense was over. It was during the repair period, during the time of longer-run adjustment to the emergency, that tense conditions appeared. This was when the people returned to their homes to clean and restore their houses and possessions, to resume normal life, to reunite their scattered families. All of this had to be done with little or no money, for Kimbark was a poor community to begin with and most of the residents had now lost many of their possessions and much of the little money they had before. At this point the situation of high morale was suddenly reversed. Previously, there had been very little physical or emotional illness despite the exposure and tension incident to the flood which came on top of an influenza epidemic which was raging when the flood came. Now, in the adjustment period, however, people began to get sick; they began to get disturbed and the community began to grumble. Indeed, there was almost a riot against the town officers one time because of their unwillingness to give adequate support to the families.

The viewpoint and values by which the officials acted in this period became an important issue during the reconstruction period. The town officials held, "The important thing is the initiative and responsibility of the individual. We're not just going to give handouts of dole and relief and the Lord Mayor's funds [which was available to them] simply because the people ask for it. They must prove that they need it." This view was widely resented by the citizenry. The officials attempted to allocate money and other forms of aid on an individual basis. However, inasmuch as nearly everyone was in the same socio-economic category, this policy made little sense. Instead, they might better have given everybody as much support as they possibly could.

At the same time, it should be noted that the citizens themselves were ambivalent on the question of welfare and community support versus individuality and initiative. Whereas they had desired to build their own houses with no town planning or interference in the first place, now that they were hard-pressed and under great tension, they desired maximum community support and application of a social welfare concept. When this did not occur, the discord within the community, and between the community and the central government, became very intense. In addition to the near riots, many persons declared they wanted to move away from Kimbark and never come back.

Questions

1. *How do the events of the Kimbark disaster fit with the general characteristics of disaster discussed in the text? How do they differ?*
2. *Relate panic to the Kimbark disaster. Did it occur or not? Why or why not?*
3. *List the collective behavior concepts involved in the study of disaster. Give examples of each from the Kimbark episode.*

10

Deviation and Social Control

Experts tell us that no two people have the same fingerprints. People differ from each other in their appearance and behavior as well. Variation in behavior occurs even though we have norms and roles that specify what *should* happen and what people *should* do in almost any given situation. Social differentiation is not only tolerated but expected in social interaction. We expect people to be different from ourselves in behavior and appearance, and we would be very surprised if they were not. At a particular point, however, when differences from a group norm become great enough, social differentiation becomes social deviation.

Defining Deviation

There are a number of ways of defining deviation. Sometimes deviation and normality are defined statistically. Those around the average are considered normal, while those at the extremes are seen as deviant. If average

height for American males is five feet, ten inches, then males from 5′ 7″ to
6′ 2″ are probably viewed as normal, and a fellow 6′ 8″ or 5′ 2″ is considered deviant. Since most people have an I.Q. of between ninety-five and
115, that I.Q. level is "normal," and a genius with an I.Q. of 145 or a moron
with an I.Q. of fifty-five are both deviants. Because most Americans are heterosexual and fewer are homosexual, heterosexuality is normal and homosexuality
is deviant, if viewed statistically.

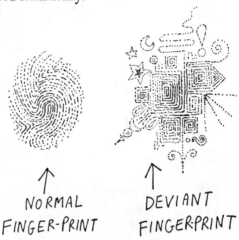

NORMAL   DEVIANT
FINGER-PRINT   FINGERPRINT

Sociologists, however, generally do *not* look at deviation as a statistical
phenomenon, but as a product of group definitions. Becoming a deviant involves
a labeling process—one is a deviant because a particular group so defines him.[1]
Laws in nearly all of our states say that homosexual behavior is not only deviant
but illegal as well. This labeling of homosexuality as deviant and criminal is *not*
because there are numerically more heterosexuals than homosexuals but because
those who make rules saw fit to define one behavior as deviant and the other as
normal. Of course, there is a relationship between numbers and labeling, but
the view of sociologists is that the labeling procedure is the important factor.
For example, in 1919 rule makers succeeded in passing the Eighteenth Amendment to the U.S. Constitution, which made sale or manufacture of intoxicating
beverages a crime. In 1933, the Twenty-first Amendment repealed the Eighteenth
and decreed that drinkers were no longer criminal. Which was the majority view?
Probably the latter, but the important point is that both Amendments resulted
from the action of rule makers who defined an act as deviant and criminal. In
sum, our view is that labeling groups determine who and what is deviant;
deviation is socially defined.

---

[1] This discussion of the labeling aspect of deviance is drawn from Howard S. Becker,
Outsiders (New York: Free Press, 1963), Chapter 1. Also see Chapter 8 for a discussion of
rule creators and rule enforcers.

Why are some acts labeled as deviant and others not? Sometimes the rule makers are motivated by moral or religious beliefs. Or the rule makers may be motivated by profit, or they may be interested in supporting the *status quo* and protecting vested interests. The reasons for it vary, but the labeling process does occur and the result is that some acts and individuals are defined as deviant, others as normal.

A recent example of the labeling process in action has been provided by Stanford psychologist David Rosenhan. Rosenhan and seven colleagues view themselves as quite sane but for the purposes of an experiment each went to the admissions office of a mental hospital and told the same story: They were hearing unclear voices that seemed to be saying words like "empty," "hollow," and "thud." That was enough for the admitting psychiatrists at twelve of the hospitals—Rosenhan and his friends were diagnosed as schizophrenic and admitted. The label was applied and it stuck. The diagnoses were not questioned by other staff members and the pseudo-patients were incarcerated for between 7 and 52 days before being released. Although they behaved calmly and normally in the hospital they were continually given pills (a total of nearly 2100) to "help" them. None were released as cured—"in remission" was the final diagnosis. When a label is successfully applied, the individual's behavior is defined in ways that are consistent with the label. While in the hospitals, the pseudo-patients took careful notes about what was happening—hospital staff either ignored this or saw it as evidence of insane compulsiveness. The pseudo-patient's normal behavior was either overlooked entirely or profoundly misinterpreted. Often they would approach hospital staff with reasonable questions. In response, nurses and attendants would move hurriedly away, eyes averted. Psychiatrists also ignored the questioners. This sort of depersonalization is a predominant characteristic in labeling situations. Rosenhan is discouraged about the inability to correctly diagnose mental illness; but more to the point of our study of labeling is his comment that once a label is applied to people it sticks, a mark of inadequacy forever.[2]

Since deviation is socially defined it should not surprise us to find that sometimes the normal zone of behavior is rather wide and other times it is quite narrow. Moreover, what is defined as deviant by one group may be defined as normal by another. The definition of deviance depends on the variable being defined and the group doing the defining. What is deviant in hair length would vary depending on which of the following groups was doing the defining: the U.S. Marine Corps, college students, hippies, barbers, or an association of baldheaded men. For most males, height of over 6′ 6″ is deviant, while for basketball players, height of below 6′ 1″ is deviant and 6′ 3″ to 7′ is normal.

---

[2] For the complete report, see "On Being Sane in Insane Places," by D. L. Rosenhan, in *Science,* Vol. 179 (January 19, 1973), pp. 250–258. *Saturday Review* also has a good summary of the research in the February 24, 1973 issue, pp. 55–56.

From a sociological viewpoint, deviant behavior is learned behavior, developed through the socialization process. With an occasional exception, deviant behavior is seen not as inborn, but as behavior that is developed and learned through interaction with others. The behavior of a member of an urban delinquent gang could be described as conforming rather than deviant behavior. He is conforming to gang norms when he defends his turf, builds a zip gun, and saves face by fighting rather than backing down to a threat. His "deviant" behavior is learned and is as conforming in its own way as is the behavior of the middle-class college student who conforms to the styles, behavior, and attitudes of those around him.

Categories of Deviation

It is often hard for people to reach agreement on what is deviant and what is normative. There are great differences of opinion in evaluating such things as hair length, sexual behavior, fashion, types of dissent, patriotism, and so on. At the same time, there are some behaviors and characteristics about which there is more general agreement. In the following paragraphs we will briefly examine some of these categories of deviation.

Individuals who lack intelligence to the extent that they are unable to perform normal tasks expected of people their age are victims of *mental deficiency*. Current practice defines five levels of mental deficiency or retardation: *borderline* (I.Q. range of 83–68), *mild* (67–52), *moderate* (51–36), *severe* (35–20), and *profound* (below 20). The extent of mental retardation in the U.S. is estimated at approximately 3 percent of the population. More than half of the retarded receive special educational services, and a great majority of those in the 50-to-80 I.Q. levels make a satisfactory adjustment in the community at the adult level. Those with I.Q. levels between 25 and 50 are viewed as trainable in that they can learn certain skills necessary for living in the home, neighborhood, or sheltered workshop. They will, however, need some care and supervision throughout life. About 5 percent of all retarded fall in the profoundly retarded category, and require complete care and supervision throughout life. Mental deficiency, especially severe retardation, may be related to genetic factors, birth trauma, or diseases of the mother prior to birth. Many instances of retardation particularly at the higher I.Q. levels (50–80) seem to be related to factors in the social environment.[3]

Mental illnesses are commonly classified in two categories: neuroses and psychoses. Neuroses are the mildest and most common, psychoses are more severe and less common. The neurotic is anxious, nervous, compulsive, but generally able to function adequately in society. The psychotic loses touch

[3] This is summarized from *Psychology 73/74 Encyclopedia* (Guilford, Conn.: Dushkin Publishing Group, Inc., 1973), pp. 166–169.

with reality. The psychotic may have hallucinations, incoherent speech and thought, or delusions of persecution, or he may withdraw into a dream world. Psychoses fall into two categories: organic and functional. Organic disorders are those caused by brain injury, hereditary factors, or physiological deterioration (as a result of aging or the effects of alcoholism or syphilis). Functional disorders are those without organic cause; they are based on environmental factors. Functional disorders represent a reaction to such things as stress or rejection, or they may possibly be a chosen alternative to an unlivable and intolerable world. Examples of functional disorders include schizophrenia, manic-depressive psychoses, and paranoia. Social scientists generally are more interested in the functional psychoses because of their relationship to social factors. It is important to note that these categories (organic and functional) are not clear-cut or mutually exclusive. Some research has indicated, for example, that hereditary factors affect schizophrenia and that psychoses resulting from aging may be as much related to social isolation (functional) as to physiological deterioration (organic).[4]

It is difficult to estimate the exact number of neurotics in the United States. Some say we are all a little neurotic; others say anywhere from forty percent to twenty-five percent to five percent of the population are neurotic. It has been estimated that there are over two million psychotics in the U.S. One-half of all hospital beds in the country are used in the care of mental patients, and at current rates one person in ten will be hospitalized for mental illness sometime during his or her life. It is easy to see why mental illness has been called America's *major* health problem.

Drinking alcoholic beverages is relatively common in the United States, but excessive drinking, or *alcoholism*, is viewed as deviant behavior. A 1964 study reported that sixty-eight percent of Americans drink. The proportion of drinkers increases with education and wealth but decreases with age (more young people drink than older people).[5] There are several types of drinkers. The *social drinker* drinks when the occasion suggests or demands it and is relatively indifferent to alcohol—he can take it or leave it. Some social drinkers drink regularly, others infrequently. The *heavy drinker* drinks more frequently and consumes greater quantities when he drinks. He occasionally becomes intoxicated. The *acute alcoholic* has much trouble controlling his use of alcohol. He may go on weekend binges or drunks. He has sober periods, but he relies more and more on alcohol. The *chronic alcoholic* drinks constantly—he "lives to drink, drinks to live." It is difficult if not impossible for him to hold a job, and his health will inevitably be affected. It is estimated that there are five million problem drinkers in the United States, and most of these would be

    [4] A more detailed discussion of mental illness, as well as of alcoholism, narcotics, and suicide, appears in Marshall Clinard's book, *Sociology of Deviant Behavior*, 4th Ed. (New York: Holt, Rinehart, and Winston, 1974).

    [5] Clinard, *Sociology of Deviant Behavior*, 4th Ed., Chapter 12.

termed chronic alcoholics. Of an estimated 8.7 million arrests in 1972, nearly 3.2 million were for offenses directly related to alcohol (drunkenness, drunk driving, and disorderly conduct). Sociologists believe that alcoholism is a learned behavior, since drinking patterns tend to be associated with occupational groups, social classes, religious categories, and nationalities.

Use of *narcotics* is a central issue in American society. Drug use is viewed as deviant in a Protestant ethic society dominated by the values of hard work, self-control, and self-discipline. But use of drugs is increasing. Youth are using marijuana, amphetamines, LSD, and other hallucinogens. Their elders are using tranquilizers, pep pills, and sleeping pills. In the 1960s, drugs, like rock music, became a part of youth culture. As young people became more interested in drugs, adults became more concerned about drugs, at least about those young people were using. The result is a classic example of conflicting views about what is deviant behavior and what is not. Concern about drug usage resulted in passage of new drug control laws and stricter enforcement of older laws. One consequence is that there were more than 400,000 narcotics arrests in 1972. This was an increase of seven percent over 1971. Over half of these arrests were of people under the age of twenty-one. Between 1960 and 1972, narcotics arrests increased by 827 percent—the largest increase in any category.[6] In contrast to the number of arrests for drug usage is the relatively small number of narcotics addicts in the United States, estimated at around 100,000. Our society has been extremely concerned about use of drugs by young people, and the result is seen in arrest statistics.

Suicide is viewed as deviant behavior in the United States, as it is in most societies dominated by Christian and/or Jewish religions. Reactions vary, however. Some countries have called suicide a crime and have buried suicides in special cemeteries. In some Oriental societies suicide is looked upon with less disfavor. Ceremonial self-destruction, known as *hara-kiri,* has long been a custom in Japan. In three states in the U.S. (New Jersey, North and South Dakota) attempted suicide is a crime, but it is unlikely that this has any deterrent effect, except possibly to ensure the success of the attempt. The U.S. suicide rate was approximately eleven per 100,000 people in 1970. Hungary, Austria, Finland, Czechoslovakia, and West Germany all had suicide rates of twenty or more per 100,000, while Italy, Spain, Greece, India, Peru, and Jordan had rates of six or fewer per 100,000. In 1970, it is estimated that 22,630 Americans committed suicide, and probably at least five times as many attempt suicide as actually commit it.[7] However, suicide statistics may be somewhat inaccurate. Countries vary in how they report suicides, and in most places it is probably underreported. In the United States, the coroner usually determines

[6] Information on reported crimes and arrests comes from the *Uniform Crime Reports —1972,* which is put out annually by the FBI.

[7] These figures on suicides come from *Demographic Yearbook* (a U.N. publication), and *Vital Statistics of the United States* (from the Department of Health, Education, and Welfare).

whether a death is reported as suicide; if he is uncertain, he is more likely to
label the death as due to natural causes. In addition, relatives, motivated by
personal or religious beliefs, may press for a "death by natural causes" decision
from the coroner.

Suicides in America are more likely to be male, white, over forty-five,
single, divorced, or widowed, and Protestant. Although men commit suicide
more than women do, more women than men attempt suicide. This has led
some to the conclusion that at least for women, suicide may often be an
attention-getting device. Men more often use guns to commit suicide; women
tend to use poison. Some occupational groups are high in suicide—military officers, policemen, psychiatrists. And, interestinglv. suicide is a leading cause of
death for young people of college age.

In the late nineteenth century Emile Durkheim studied suicide in Europe and
described in detail three types of suicide: egoistic, altruistic, and anomic.[8]
Egoistic suicide occurs in societies in which interpersonal relationships are secondary, distant, and not group-oriented. In such societies, the individual lacks
group attachments, and when personal problems appear, the individual in the
absence of emotional support resorts to suicide. The high suicide rate of single
people might be an example of egoistic suicide. *Altruistic* suicide on the other
hand is the result of strong group attachments. The individual commits suicide
to benefit the group and to follow group norms. Suicides of Japanese soldiers
and airmen during World War II and the self-immolation of Buddhist monks
in Vietnam are described as altruistic suicides. *Anomic* suicide occurs in societies
in which norms are confused or are breaking down. Economic depressions or
rapid social changes that lead to disequilibrium in society and a state of normlessness may result in anomic suicides.

Deviant Behavior and Criminal Behavior

A distinction should be made between deviant behavior and criminal behavior. As we have mentioned, deviant behavior, like beauty, is in the eye
of the beholder. Behaviors are not naturally deviant; they are defined as
deviant by groups. Similarly, reactions to deviation vary greatly. Some deviant
behavior is ignored, some deviant behavior is tolerated, and some deviant
behavior brings severely critical reactions by others. As behaviors fall further outside the range of what is defined as normal, societies feel that they must
formally proscribe the behaviors. Rule makers decide that certain acts are a
threat to the organization and structure of society and must therefore be
prohibited. Laws are passed, and these forms of deviation become illegal or
criminal if performed. More serious acts are called felonies (punished by a

---

[8] Emile Durkheim, *Suicide,* translated by John A. Spaulding and George Simpson
(New York: Free Press, 1951).

year or more in a state prison or by death). Less serious crimes are called misdemeanors. The FBI has developed a list of seven major crimes: homicide, rape, aggravated assault, robbery, burglary, larceny, and auto theft. Trends in crime are studied by noting the number of crimes reported to police throughout the country. For example, in 1972 there were nearly 6,000,000 major crimes reported in the United States. Burglary was the most numerous followed by larceny with these two making up 71 percent of the total. Homicide and rape, together making up about 1 percent of the total, were the least numerous. Aside from the seven major crimes, a number of other acts are illegal—prostitution, gambling, fraud, embezzlement, arson, vandalism, traffic offenses, and so on. Some of the forms of deviant behavior previously discussed in this chapter may fall into criminal categories. If alcoholism becomes drunkenness or drunk driving, it becomes a crime. The sale, possession, and/or use of certain drugs becomes a crime. Attempted suicide is a crime in some states.

One might assume that if an act is defined as criminal, there must be general agreement about it. Such a serious move by a society must mean that people are in accord with each other and group differences and vested interests have been set aside. This, of course, is not necessarily so. One category of behaviors is called crime because it threatens the public order. There is general agreement that acts such as homicide, arson, robbery, and larceny threaten the public order. About other categories of crime, however, there may be less agreement. For example, one such category grew out of the concern, religious beliefs, and moral outrage of our Puritan ancestors, who felt that in certain areas of behavior, the individual must be protected from himself. It is not so much that his behavior may be a threat to society as that his behavior may be a threat to himself. Consequently, a number of acts, some of which we today call "vices," were defined as crimes. These include gambling, prostitution, narcotics use, abortion, and a variety of sexual activities, including homosexuality. Opinions as to the "rightness" or "wrongness" of these acts vary from individual to individual and from group to group. In fact, however, there is a substantial demand to engage in many of these acts.

Gambling is legal in some states and is widely sought and available throughout the country even where not legal. Prostitution is legal in some areas (in all Nevada counties but two, for example) and available in many others. Many young people as well as some of their elders wonder at the current laws punishing marijuana use. Studies show that marijuana is widely used and is relatively easy to obtain. Laws in nearly all our states outlaw sodomy, the "infamous crimes against nature," and yet Kinsey reported that many of these "crimes," which involve various types of sexual behavior, have been relatively common practices. Homosexuals wonder why homosexual acts between consenting adults in private are not legal if heterosexual acts under the same conditions are legal.

Edwin Schur has commented that since all parties involved in these actions (gambling, prostitution, abortion, etc.) are seeking them or at least consenting to them, these are "crimes without victims."[9] If there is no victim, Schur wonders whether anyone should be punished. He points out that when these activities are called crimes, they are forced underground to a certain extent and become more expensive to obtain. This leads to secondary crime—theft, for example, to obtain funds to support the primary crime, such as narcotics or abortion. So, although certain acts are defined as criminal by society, this does not mean that there is universal agreement as to their "wrongness."

"Juvenile delinquency" refers to young people (under twenty-one in some states, under eighteen in others) who commit criminal acts or who are wayward, disobedient, uncontrollable, truant, or runaways. Delinquency is a confusing concept. Young people *are* heavily involved in certain types of crimes. In 1972, seventy-one percent of the arrests for vandalism and at least fifty percent of the arrests for burglary, larceny, auto theft, and arson were of people under the age of eighteen. At the same time, many young people are defined as juvenile delinquents for acts that are ignored if committed by adults (disobedience, running away). American law is such that we are very strict with juveniles. "Get ahold of the bad kid quick and change him so he won't grow up to worse activities. . . ." In fact, however, if the juvenile is thrown into a reform school with other more hardened delinquents, we almost guarantee the result we were trying to avoid. Most countries are more lenient than the U.S. in their treatment of juveniles.

Our purpose throughout this chapter has been to demonstrate that deviation is basically a labeling process which involves group definitions and which may result in many different viewpoints concerning what is deviant and what is not. This same condition extends, unfortunately, to the realm of criminal and delinquent behavior as well.

Explanations for Deviant Behavior

If deviant behavior is the result of a labeling process by selected groups of people, explanations for individual acts of deviant behavior are of only passing interest—the emphasis is on the labeling or defining process rather than on the "deviant behavior." Our time would be well spent attempting to understand how the labeling takes place, who does the labeling, and why. Nevertheless, social scientists have traditionally focused on the deviant individual in an attempt to explain his behavior. The theories that have been developed are quite varied, as we may see by looking at some of the "explanations" for criminal behavior.[10]

[9] In his book, *Crimes Without Victims,* Schur discusses abortion, narcotics use, and homosexuality as victimless crimes (Englewood Cliffs, N.J.: Prentice-Hall, 1965).

[10] Most criminology texts go into causal explanations in great detail. See, for example, Walter Reckless, *The Crime Problem*, 5th Ed. (New York: Appleton-Century-Crofts, 1973).

In 1875, Lombroso stated that deviant behavior was inherited and criminals were throwbacks (closer in the evolutionary chain) to apes. Lombroso came to this conclusion by taking a series of body measurements of institutionalized criminals and non-criminals and comparing these with measurements of primitive man. Subsequent investigators showed the inadequacy of his research and failed to find any support for his theories. Lombroso's claim to fame remains that he was one of the first to try to scientifically discover the causes of crime. Other studies of biological and inheritance factors in crime causation have focused on comparisons of the behavior of identical and fraternal twins, on physique and body type as causal factors, and more recently, on aberrant chromosome patterns among institutionalized violent offenders.

Generally, however, social scientists tend to dismiss the purely biological explanations for behavior. The psychologist looks within the individual at his personality and perceptions and emphasizes the importance of childhood experiences to explain later deviant behavior. The sociologist studies conditions in the social structure and the effects of group affiliations and orientations. Edwin Sutherland's theory of "differential association" is typical of many sociological theories in that it emphasizes that behavior, both normal and deviant, is learned in interaction with others. Other theories attempt to describe the conditions in which this learning takes place. In this regard, several current theories have focused on the lower-class urban delinquent gang. The deviant or anti-social nature of gang behavior is often explained in terms of social-class orientations or conflicts. In the section on social stratification in Chapter 5, we outlined some of these social-class-oriented theories of delinquency when we discussed the ideas of Miller, Cohen, and Cloward and Ohlin. In addition to social class, sociologists have focused on the family, on companionship factors, on culture conflict, or on the individual's self-concept, to explain deviant behavior. The important point, however, is that most sociological theories tend to look at deviant behavior in the same way that they look at non-deviant behavior. Both are forms of social behavior that are developed through the socialization process. These forms of behavior are understood by studying norms, roles, culture, groups, and other aspects of social organization. Deviant behavior is not seen as the strange and peculiar actions of sick people but merely another form of social behavior that can be understood by applying the basic concepts of sociology.

Deviant Behavior in Perspective

Deviant behavior is often seen as a malignant element in society to be eradicated at all costs. To say that something is deviant is to imply that something is wrong and needs to be fixed. This is an incorrect view for several reasons. First, it is important to remember that deviant behavior is basically the product of men's definitions rather than something natural or inherent in an act. This allows us to shift our focus from the person's "deviant behavior" to the question, "Why is his behavior being called deviant?" Second, Durkheim, Erikson, and others have pointed out that deviant behavior is not necessarily harmful to group life. In fact, it often plays an important part in keeping the social order intact. Deviant behavior enables groups to define boundaries—it preserves stability within the group by pointing out the contrast between what is inside the group and what is outside. Erikson suggests that without the battle between "normal" and "deviant," the community would lack a sense of identity and cohesion, a sense of what makes it a special place in the larger world.[11]

Finally, deviant behavior appears to be one of the processes involved in social change. Often, what is deviant today is accepted tomorrow and expected the next day. Maybe the people who seem to be listening to a different drummer just heard the beat before the rest of us. *Some* forms of deviant behavior represent an early adaptation to changing conditions. There are many examples of this: Deviant clothing styles of the past are the fashion of today. Yesterday's pornography is accepted literature today. Compare the reaction to Sherri Finkbine's ideas on abortion ten years ago to the same sort of situation today. Of course, not all of what we call deviant at present is destined to be the norm of tomorrow. Many types of behavior—for example, homicide, theft, incest— are more firmly fixed in deviant definitions. The point, however, is that deviant behavior does not necessarily represent the evil its title implies; often it serves necessary and important functions in society, including those of defining the group's boundaries and as a forerunner of social change.

Social Control

Social control refers to the processes, planned or unplanned, by which people are made to conform to collective norms. A certain amount of conformity seems to be essential in all societies. Predictability and order are necessary to the social organization of group behavior. If man could act in complete isolation, possibly he could ignore the existence of any norms. However, it is almost impossible to imagine such a situation because man is a group animal, and other group members constantly place expectations on one's behavior. Individuality and non-conformity are highly valued; most of us want to be "individualists." We should realize, however, that these words only have meaning when most people, most of the time, conform.

Social control may be provided in a variety of ways. We could, for example, hope that people will naturally conform; that conformity is in the nature of

---

[11] Kai Erikson deals with these ideas in detail in his *Wayward Puritans* (New York: John Wiley, 1966), Chapter 1, and in "Notes on the Sociology of Deviance," in *The Other Side* edited by Howard S. Becker (New York: Free Press, 1964), especially pp. 9–15

man, and it is inherent to conform. Unfortunately, social control doesn't seem to work that way now, although it may in the "brave new world" of the future when we are programmed and conditioned even before birth. Basic social control is taught through the socialization process. Shortly after the child is born, the family begins telling him what he should do and what he should not do, what is right and what is wrong. Sanctions or punishments are applied if he misbehaves. If he fails to conform, the child is told mother won't love him or father will belt him, depending on the family's view of proper child-rearing practices. Later, influences outside the family continue the process. Peers, teachers in the school system, the church, the mass media—all these have a profound effect on inculcating group and societal norms and encouraging conformity to group expectations. Finally, if all else fails, the society can pass laws to ensure conformity. Laws force people to conform and are a response to breakdown in other forms of social control. Again, sanctions are applied for failure. These sanctions may range from a fine to imprisonment to death.

Social control mechanisms vary depending on the type of group or society. In a primary group or small primitive society, rules are not written and social control is informal. Violators may be subjected to gossip or ridicule or possibly even ostracism; although these techniques do not have the dramatic effect of the FBI swooping down, they are surprisingly effective. In secondary groups and larger, urbanized societies, social control becomes more formal, and we have written laws, police, courts, prisons—an exceedingly complicated legal system to guarantee an acceptable degree of conformity.

Social control mechanisms also vary depending on the type of norm being violated. If the violated norm is a folkway regarded as of minor consequence to the group, informal and minor sanctions are called forth: whispering, giggling, or a little mild ridicule. If one of the mores of the group is being abused, however, more formal sanctions may be used.

Individual social control probably emerges from both internal and external sources. Internal constraints would be those aspects of the normative system that one internalizes through the socialization process. Internalized norms become the individual's "conscience." External social control refers to the external mechanisms—rules and laws—applied by society. It would be fortunate if the two were in balance, but as we saw in the previous section on deviant behavior this is frequently not the case. Take, for example, the boy whose little peers happen to be little hoods—his most important primary group is a delinquent gang. He internalizes a set of values and norms from them. He obeys the norms of the gang or he is ridiculed and ostracized. Yet in following gang social control he runs afoul of external societal social control, which in many cases makes opposing demands. To complete the dilemma, it is obvious that the social control system of the primary group, the gang, is much more important for one's behavior than is any external social control system. This type of gap occurs when the values of one segment of society are vastly different from the values of the rule makers of society.

Another type of gap or difference between internal and external social control occurs when people's attitudes, values, and norms change more rapidly than laws change. A cultural lag results. For example, polls indicate that attitudes on prostitution and gambling have moderated to the point that many, if not most people believe that these acts, subject to certain regulation, should not be called crimes. And yet laws will probably be slow to change. We might predict a pattern through which change in laws occurs: (1) attitudes change; (2) laws relating to the changed attitudes are not enforced; and (3) laws change. It is likely, however, that there is a large lapse of time between step 2 and step 3. Consequently, when attitudes change, laws tend to be kept on the books but just not enforced as vigorously as they might be. Law enforcement agencies and other citizens as well often find themselves in a difficult position because of this situation.

White-collar crime and organized crime provide examples of another type of conflict between society's laws and people's attitudes. The public favors and encourages prosecution of offenses such as burglary, assault, larceny, homicide, and sex offenses. On the other hand, white-collar crime is seldom punished. White-collar crime refers to the illegal acts committed by middle- and upper-class people during the course of their regular business activities, and includes such activities as the bank vice-president who embezzles funds, the physician who splits fees or performs unnecessary operations, the businessman who cheats on his income tax, and the disk jockey who accepts payola. Criminologist Edwin Sutherland has maintained that more money is lost yearly through white-collar crime than through all other forms of crime combined, and that the damage to social relationships that results (no one can be trusted, everyone is on the take) is even more serious. And yet, the larceny or theft of the white-collar criminal is seldom punished, and even when it is the penalties are slight compared with the sanctions given for other crimes. Why? Well, the activity may have involved substantial skill and ingenuity and wasn't violent, the victim (often a large organization, or the public in general) is invisible or not easy to identify with, and above all the white-collar criminal is a "good" person (middle-class and respectable). So, the public looks the other way. Likewise, the activities of organized crime go largely unpunished, but the reasons for breakdown in social control in this case are more basic and easier to understand. The public *wants* what organized crime supplies: gambling, narcotics, tax-free cigarettes and alcohol, prostitution, and loan rackets. The point is that the attitudes and values of society are reflected even more in punishment practices than they are in the written laws of society.

Summary

The previous chapters in this section have dealt with social change, social disorganization, and collective behavior. In this chapter we return to the topic of norms, which was first discussed in Chapter 3. A norm is defined as the accepted or required behavior in a specific situation. Most behavior is predictable because it is in accordance with mutually understood norms. However, some behavior is contrary to generally accepted norms, and this is called deviant behavior. Societies attempt to restrict the amount of deviant behavior through social control measures. This chapter addresses itself to these concepts—deviation and social control.

Individual variation and individual differences are a basic part of the human condition. When differences from group norms reach a certain point, however, social differentiation becomes social deviation. Many sociologists feel that deviation is best understood as a *labeling* process. Behaviors and/or characteristics of individuals are deviant when they are defined that way by members of society. Deviation is neither a natural nor statistical phenomenon but is a product of group viewpoints and definitions.

Criminal and delinquent behavior are also seen as products of a defining or labeling process. If society is especially concerned about certain types of behavior, it may define these behaviors as not only deviant but criminal as well. Frequently there are differences of opinion about the "rightness" or "wrongness" of particular acts. Such differences are more likely to occur in large, complex societies in which a variety of viewpoints exist about what is deviant and what is normal. These variations in definitions make it possible that within a society, a given act may be viewed as criminal and deviant, as criminal but not deviant, as deviant but not criminal, or as "normal."

We briefly examined several categories of deviation—mental illness, mental deficiency, alcoholism, drug usage, and suicide—as well as some descriptions of and explanations for criminal and delinquent behavior. Finally, we discussed social control, which refers to the processes by which people are made to conform to collective norms. Social control mechanisms are practiced by all societies and include norms internalized through the socialization process as well as laws enforced by the police and courts of a society.

The first of four readings which follow describes two people who, for quite different reasons, are labeled deviants. The article, written by one of them, relates how they react to their condition, and how society reacts to them. Society is often placed in the peculiar and hypocritical position of condemning a behavior and actively seeking and patronizing it at the same time. Gambling, prostitution, and abortion in some places are among numerous examples of this situation. Businesses and professions develop to satisfy "deviant" needs, and the second reading deals with one such profession, the professional party girl. Most forms of deviant behavior are learned behavior. Barbara Anderson in her article on wine drinking and alcoholism in France illustrates the importance of the socialization process and experiences in the cultural environment in producing a given type of behavior. Society defines certain groups as deviants and outsiders. The reasons for these definitions are sometimes difficult to fathom, but once the process begins, social distance increases, interaction between groups is restricted, inaccuracies abound, and the deviant definitions are reinforced. In the last article in this section, Hunter Thompson writes about the interaction between society and a deviant group, the Hell's Angels.

Two Delicate Conditions

Robin Zehring

People are labeled deviants for a variety of reasons. As this article demonstrates, you don't have to be a criminal to be deviant—being "different" physically is perhaps an even faster way of obtaining the deviant label. Robin Zehring is a free-lance writer living in San Francisco.

One thing about a five-foot-eight-inch-and-obtusely-pregnant woman walking down the street with a considerably-shorter, cerebral-palsied male escort on crutches: They'll get noticed, all right.

Noticed like The Pox.

I, being the pregnant person and Bernard being the shorter, rarely advance more than five City yards before we are not only noticed: we are avoided with a physiological energy so overwhelming that The Natural Order Of Life And Things falls shambled to the sidewalk. On account of our delicate physical conditions, I mean, one public pregnancy partnered by a crippled man and the world goes bananas.

Take, for instance, dogs. Dogs walk backwards, retreating at the mere sight of Bernard and me, misshapen beasts that we are. We've seen dogs forget they are moving and fall off the curb from just looking at us. Seen people fall off too. And trip over fire hydrants, parking meters, invisible trash or their imaginations. We've caused buses to bypass their stops, taxis to pause for red lights, cars to screech in unexpected halts at pedestrian crosswalks ("Lordy, can you imagine

From *California Living Magazine, San Francisco Sunday Examiner & Chronicle,* March 11, 1973. Reprinted by permission of the author.

hitting one of *those"*). Children are hustled away from us ("Hey Mom whatsa-matter with . . ."), adolescents cluster in giggling groups ("I wonder if they're like *married* or somethin'?"). No adult will meet our eyes ("For Godssake, Martha, don't *stare!"*). But their sidelong glances at my swollen torso and Bernard's bent legs indicate Dr. Rubin has plenty more What You Always Wanted To Knows . . . to write about.

Granted, we do walk slowly. Bernard drags his feet to reach each stretch of his stronger crutch and my feet are fluid-retentive and heavy from prenatal pressure of The Occupant (my Unborne Babe, as I call It) and likewise, they drag too. So perhaps the odds of boggled phenomena are directly related to our slow rate of speed: If you walk slowly enough, you're bound to see a dog fall off the curb eventually, or a cow jump over the moon, maybe? But Bernard, who has twenty-six years of public experience being sidetracked as a subhuman, explains to me kindly that those things are just part of it all; in fact, the slower you go, the more willing are people and buses and dogs to accept your physical handicap. Because people like you are *supposed* to go slowly.

"A handicapped person is one thing," cracks Bernard, "But a handicapped person *in a hurry* . . ."

I see what he means. Trudging (slowly) up and down the hills of Powell Street one day, Bernard and I decide to 'run' for the next cable car. Traffic at Bush Street intersection backs up three blocks, not only because we delay it a bit by crossing, but also because astonished drivers in the first few rows can't believe their eyes as down the incline I gallop, full-tilt and waving. The Occupant does cartwheels. Bernard races close behind me, his steel leg braces half-sliding on the concrete. The cable car is already sailing when the gripman sees us, rolls his eyes heavenward, and grabs the brake handle like it's the Titantic anchor, pulling back for all he's worth. The brake snags on the downhill angle. Passengers climb all over themselves (not) to see if we make it, their eyes riveted to my jouncing tummy and Bernard's steel scuttle. Both breathless, we reach the car, Bernard tossing his crutches aboard and hiking himself up. I take a deep breath, conquer the steps and we're off. Gradually, Bush Street traffic resumes. Passengers, now timid with us at close range, study the floor. The gripman is perspiring. The Occupant somersaults. I giggle. Bernard guffaws. "Told you so!" he chortles. "Haw, Haw, Haw!"

I first met Bernard Maxon at The Noble Frankfurter on Powell Street when I was five months pregnant and feeling nauseous. He was at the next table, wolfing down two kosher hot dogs smothered in sauerkraut and mustard and onions, with a side order of potato salad and a hunk of Maria's Bavarian cheesecake waiting for dessert. It all looked enormously tasty and I couldn't help overhearing Bernard's vociferous manner of chewing which made it sound even tastier. I wanted to order six of everything. However, one occupational dilemma of a delicate condition such as mine is relishing the idea of copious food intake and then having The Occupant play soccer with it in my stomach. One learns to nibble Saltines and sip tea instead.

Bernard caught me watching him and listening to his chew. Sure, I had noticed the crutches propped against the chair next to his but I hadn't dwelled on them. I was more intrigued with his food. And yet, when Bernard noticed me noticing, I figured he figured it was for the crutches. But he didn't. He was more interested in figuring me.

"Can't hack the hot dogs these days?" he asked, eyes twinkling behind hornrims.

I shook my head.

"Here, try one of these. I carry a spare." He rolled a pack of TUMS across my table. I blinked at them, dumbfounded. I'd never met anyone under fifty who carried spare TUMS around.

"Ulcer?" I wondered.

He began to answer with a gesture which accidently followed through to the chair with the crutches. A clatter of aluminum banged to the floor. I started to rise.

"Hold it!" he ordered, "No bending over in your condition. It'll make you throw up." It was nice to meet a man who knew about being pregnant.

I sat as Bernard eased himself down to the floor, swept up both crutches and held them together like a canoe paddle, stiffening his body and pushing himself upwards to a standing position, much as a skier remounts with his poles. Then he sat down again and rearranged himself. The entire procedure was complete in about fifteen seconds. I was impressed.

"Pretty tricky," I said.

"That's nothing," said Bernard, "You should see me put on my socks."

I thought carefully for a moment. We had a lot in common.

"The same goes for my pantyhose."

We laughed hard together, knowing we each began the day by dressing on the floor.

In the months following, Bernard and I meet frequently for lunch. I learn to enjoy tea very much and forsake my Saltines for TUMS. We share our life stories and our hope and dream stories and our delicate condition stories which are remarkably similar and occasionally the same. Except that I, as a slightly handicapped person with a temporary condition, don't know the half of it compared to Bernard's life-time experience of prejudice, pain and abuse. Bernard Maxon's got the stiffest upper lip I've ever seen. Why he hasn't drunk himself into oblivion, jumped off the Bridge, or at least clobbered someone with his crutch is beyond me until he reminds:

"Considering that from the moment I was born three months premature and motionless, what have I got to lose?"

I instinctively fold my hands across The Occupant's seven-month Mound and ponder.

What Bernard has got to lose is plenty.

Incidental losses like his balance (when Bernard sneezes hard, he falls down), his public rights to restaurant seating ("They always put me in the back so I won't upset the 'dining decorum' "), hotel reservations, rental privileges (Managers claim they're not insured), some shopping prerogatives (Antique dealers and car salesmen are rarely overjoyed when he comes clomping in; they discourage him from handling the Dresden or testing the gearshift). Also, lost privacy. A lot of people ask Bernard a lot of very personal questions. Also, lost sexual title ("Just once I'd like to be accused of rape."). And the loss of acceptance by his fellow humans as a healthy able-bodied person worthy of friendship, wisdom and strength. People constantly suggest to Bernard that he sit down—at a distance!

Some of the above also goes for being pregnant.

Major losses? Jobs. Bernard has a difficult time finding a good one, despite his six-and-a-half years of college credits, his high I.Q. ratings and physical maneuverability. He was once denied a volunteer job to help recently disabled veterans at Letterman Hospital on grounds that his presence might depress the patients.

"OK, so I'd be lousy at brain surgery or fashion modeling," chides Bernard. "But jobs in management, accounting and teaching are all available to people of my qualifications. Clerical jobs: I can type forty words a minute, with my left hand. But the minute I arrive for an interview, they tell me, 'We're not hiring.' One look at me and they suggest I try elsewhere, like on the street corner selling pencils."

Working the street is not Bernard's bag. He often ends up soliciting books or real estate or vacuum cleaners by phone, dialing the numbers with his typing hand. Telephone sales jobs endure about six weeks before something happens to the Company (bankruptcy, fraud, a quick self-export by the Boss) and the phone is disconnected. So is Bernard from his income, until the next State Disability check comes through. Which doesn't go very far in paying for food and rent and medical bills and custom-altered clothing and new shoes every month and a pair of socks a day and a college education.

So there's money to lose. Ignoring the doom of a butterless future, Bernard admits a weakness for lending whatever cash he does possess. He'll even go to such lengths as borrowing from someone else and re-lending it. And seldom see it again.

"It's true, I'm flattered if people tap me for loans," he says, "It's a rebellion on my part, all related to that crippled pauper image and peddling pencils. I don't think of myself as crippled, I don't wake up in the morning and feel it. I want to live and earn my money through normal channels, not through opportunities specifically for The handicapped, not by dealing in money like that."

Sometimes, money like that deals him. It belongs to people who cannot dissimulate a physical handicap from the downtrodden of the world. No matter that Bernard is dressed from Bullock and Jones—"Only place I can get to alter my pants to a twenty-eight inch waist and a 23 inch inseam without laughing"— and his facial expression maintained with purpose and intent. He finds it necessary to avoid busy City streets around Christmas and Eastertime and on Sunday mornings when pedestrians feel particularly righteous. They press money in his hand or stuff it in his pocket before he can explain that he really doesn't want it. One time a man gave him a personal check.

Another time a lady handed him a huge tin of Almond Roca as he waited for a WALK light. "I had to put it inside my shirt to carry it. Three more blocks, it was chocolate almond soup!"

Once he unknowingly put his crutches down on the sidewalk, leaning forward to tie his shoelace. Got a five dollar bill doing that.

I told Bernard that so far, no one has assessed my delicate condition as pathetic or needy and handed me cash for it. Or Almond Roca either. Bernard advised me to try limping a little.

Most major of losses Bernard has got to lose is affection. Lost affection can be sad for anyone, but it's sadder when a person is excluded beforehand because of a physical handicap. Generally, people suppose that The Handicapped are probably as nice and charming and at least as deserving as anyone else—and all that—but most people don't want to get involved. And don't want their son or daughter marrying one. We are brought up to be kind on the subject. But closed.

The following advertisement that appeared in a local classified section points up reality's grim divide:

> WOMAN, slightly disabled, happy, gentle, sensitive, alive, would appreciate your friendship. Also used paperback books to read. Call or write . . .

As Bernard says, "If you don't advertise for it, you don't get it. In the meantime, you can always read about it."

Beginning with his premature birth Bernard has endured a holocaust of rejections by doctors, therapists, psychiatrists, faith healers, quacks, schoolmates, teachers, employers, relatives, strangers and the public at-large. He doesn't talk about these times very often, apart from periodic shrugs and allusions.

But one day at lunch, Bernard cast his eyes downward at The Occupant's Full-Term Mountain and chuckled.

"Listen," he said, hand on my hand and suddenly serious. "Most people don't let me near their kids, afraid I might rub off on them or something. Do you think maybe I could hold yours once in a while?"

I told him, come time, The Occupant and I would be delighted.

1. *Illustrate the terms "deviance" and "labeling" with examples from this reading.*
2. *Describe the reactions of people to deviants. If, instead of a cripple or pregnant woman, the object of attention were a criminal, movie star, or well-known politician, how would the reactions differ? Why or why not? Explain.*
3. *How did being defined as deviant affect the behavior of Robin and Bernard?*
4. *The reaction to deviants is the same regardless of the particular type of deviation being observed. Discuss.*
5. *Recall the definition of minority group and apply this concept to the people discussed in this article.*

The Corporation Prostitute

There are a number of different types of prostitutes: the streetwalker, the house girl, the high-class call girl. This article describes another type—the girl who works as party girl, hostess, or date for the big business or corporation. She is recruited by the corporation, and her services are sought after and appreciated by the corporation's clients; and society defines her behavior as deviant and criminal although she is never punished. The author of this essay states, "This is an explanation of another field of prostitution that existed twenty some years ago, and even in this more sophisticated era, still does in all probability." This essay was written by a sociology student with a rather varied and unusual past.

"Public Relations Consultant" is to a corporation prostitute what "modeling" is to a call girl, but by whatever name, a whore is a whore. The demands are the same and whether he is chairman of the board or straight off the street, a John is a John.

Assuming that the basic equipment is in order, there are certain refinements that determine your place in the flesh market caste system. Whether or not it is harder work to be a streetwalker is a matter of personal definition, but if a girl has a taste for a classy couch, she should apply at _____. The fringe benefits are good (they had a mandatory health plan), and sometimes you could stumble into a unique retirement plan. It may be temporary, depending upon the vagaries of the market and the Baby's own fickleness—but diamonds are ALWAYS a girl's best friend. There are drawbacks as in everything else—no tenure, you can't collect unemployment, and nobody would believe your references. However, you can tell yourself you were a highclass hooker.

More care was taken in the selection of the women than was given to that of a new vice president. There were stringent requirements and the screening was intensive. Much depended upon the sponsor, which equated to letters of reference in a more legitimate endeavor. This sponsor observed the prospective employee and assessed her qualities sometimes for a period of weeks before the initial contact was made but once the recommendation was in, the girl had her security clearance.

The major prerequisite was that the girl must be a professional prostitute, either from a good house or working her own book. Call girls (even the expensive ones) and hustlers were considered too risky, for their operation involved too many people. They were also over-exposed. It didn't seem to matter if you had started in the streets, but to have improved your situation indicated a fastidiousness and the ambition to do your own thing, which, in turn, denoted a degree of intelligence. The requirements were heavier than have-douche-bag-will-travel. The Company wanted its personal, elite stable, financed by the unsuspecting stockholders at large, covered discreetly by the Auditing Department, administered and controlled in the best tradition of American Corporate efficiency. For this they were willing to pay good money.

Under no circumstances was a freebee considered. Anyone who played for fun and games and no profit was dangerous. They had no ethical standards and the disquieting possibility of emotionalism or involvement was present. Competent detachment is an occupational hazard, or blessing, for the professional. Too often a non-professional falls back on outraged virtue when the demands get rough. No matter how discreetly structured or fiscally disguised, the commodity was still sex and to the businessman with a sentimental conscience, something free smacks of adultery. Besides, he could probably make it with his wife's best friend, or give his secretary a whirl, so what's the big deal.

The girl should have had legitimate experience working with the public—receptionist, hostess, entertainer—that gave her a social poise which if not real was efficiently faked. She had to be aware of the world around her and not just the world of sex, to have read a book or two that wasn't pornographic, to carry on a reasonable conversation and pretend to listen intelligently.

Appearance was important, of course. The girl had to be more than just attractive. Size, shape, personality and disposition all differed, but there was one absolute—she could not look like a prostitute. Hair styles and dress could be modified or brought into line if all the other requirements were in order, but her whole bearing must be in keeping with the carefully constructed sexual fraud—courtesans, classy broads, Princess Grace selling her ass.

Age didn't seem to be a significant factor as long as the girl was over the age of consent. You could tell the older ones, they saved their money. Years of experience was not as important as the quality of experience for some women can turn tricks most of their working lives and end up hustling still for twelve-and-two. There were, however, common characteristics and foremost among them was a taste for the good life, a tough sense of independence, and a determination to be treated as a "lady" even peripherally.

Naturally, there was one other area—sexual expertise. As a professional the talent should have been taken for granted—how many pianists audition for their concerts? If this area was checked out, it was done secretly and never mentioned, but it would have made a great work incentive plan for the recruiter. In a house it was probably a "very important client" and from a book, a favor for your favorite mark.

All these qualities were essential when dealing with men who, because of their positions or their pretensions, will not tolerate a chippy. After genuflecting before the GNP, only the choicest harlots were offered by the high priests. Corporations pimp for the industrial complex and such a select clientele must be catered to, their egos stroked, their reputations protected and their fetishes fanned. Bidding for a factory site? Fly the city fathers on a party to Acapulco. Wooing a merger? Prod it with charm, grace and prowess. Pushing a political issue? Knifing a competitor? Collecting proxies? Oil leases, anyone?

The preliminaries over, the recommendation in and the surveillance completed, the subject was contacted by her sponsor, and if she was interested, an interview was arranged.

It took a really well-trained eye to find potential in me. I was still half-gamin, defiantly determined to escape the streets and refusing to recognize any handicaps I might have. I owe it all to a fighter instinct and my Uncle Harry, a Vaudeville violinist ("The Fiddlin' Coon") and when he died he left his violin up for grabs.

In my family, nothing should be a total waste. Since we were stuck with the instrument, mother managed lessons for me and I promptly fell in love with music. Another cherished family tradition is that if you have a talent you sell it, which made earning a living much easier for the girls than the boys. When I was 10 it was discovered that I could sing—so, why aren't you working? I started paying my way as a band vocalist which drew attention away from my talent as a violinist and its dubious commercial value. At 14 I was on my own, winging to support myself and the violin. Wilhelm Van Hoogstratton was conducting the Portland Symphony and accepted me as a member which gave me a glimpse of a totally new world. It was a schizophrenic existence . . . I could play Hindemith but was incapable of a grammatical conversation. A competent vocalist with poise on the stand, I didn't know there were different folks, and thought everybody slept in their slips. . . . I wore the brightest colors I could find and felt naked without a watch, bracelet, beads, earrings, AND an ankle-chain. Luckily, the Symphony wore uniforms. Having learned submission at a very early age, I also learned about this time to augment my income between music jobs.

By the time I was 20, I was in San Francisco with a child to support and a little black book I used when I needed something. I was running scared but hanging in there, reading books, learning to talk and all the nice, social graces were there, if pretentious. One night it seemed to have all paid off and without even knowing it, I was considered for the big time.

My sponsor was a prominent San Francisco Madam who never offered to hire me herself. I was singing in a Pine Street Club and she came in down the street from her house every once in a while to relax and to see if any of her girls were free-lancing. We became friendly and talked. I think what impressed her most was the way I handled a big-time pimp who wanted to take over my thing for me. Whatever her reasons she decided to be my sponsor.

I wore white gloves to my interview in an office with a view of the bay. He sat behind a mahogany desk and lit my cigarettes with a heavy, silver lighter. When the telephone rang he apologized graciously for the interruption, treating me more like an executive secretary than an executive's whore. I was to be paid every two weeks by mail and he took my social security number for the personnel department. I would be given a wardrobe allowance and there was a prepared list of the types of clothing that should be on hand. I was to move to a "good" address (I lived on Baker Street, just over from Fillmore). Inquiry was made very solicitously as to child care arrangements for I would be traveling a great deal.

My personal life was my own as long as it did not interfere with or threaten the Company; I was made to realize immediately that the company had a battery of lawyers and any attempts at extortion would be handled quickly and efficiently, and I was guaranteed to lose, particularly since the fact of the professionalism made me a loser to start with; he gave me the name of the doctor where I was to have a monthly examination; I would not be "on call" but would be given my assignments in a purely business-like manner and well in advance although there would be emergency calls occasionally as well as luncheon appointments. I was expected to be entertaining, listen attentively even to drunken trivia and to converse as intelligently as I could depending upon the client; however, at no time could I interject my personal affairs.

Under entertainment, the customer was always right with one exception— nothing bizarre and no S&M—if that was the kick, report it to the program director. The company would also not tolerate orgies—just lots of bread and no circuses. He told me my new company name, shook my hand, wished me good luck, courteously escorted me to the door and I never saw him again.

There was a brief training period which consisted of a dinner and some drinks with a half-hearted attempt at erudite conversation. This was to see if I could handle myself and by this time I was pretty confident of the silverware. The staff-members conducting this research were lower echelon and not at all impressed by the Courtesan Corps. They were bored and so was I. The men probably wanted to do more than go to dinner. The woman, I remember, got juiced and had to be sent home in a cab.

The first assignment was a chartered flight to Texas to entertain some board members who were conducting some high-level skullduggery. This was not a sexual scene, but it was probably felt that some women hanging around would disarm somebody. I was also thrilled over the first cruise, until I learned you weren't supposed to watch the water. The clients were politicians, military men, executives and even the young ones ran to pot-bellies. I was hostess several times for conferences and there were a lot of just dinner-dates, but other than these little bonuses it was mostly business as usual except the rhetoric was nicer. It was an organizational meat market although attractively displayed. I got a kick-back from the stores which implemented the clothing allowance, and all the head-waiters split with us but the more money I made the faster I spent it and what I didn't spend, I gave away. I became more and more resentful of the system that hired me because I was intelligent and they treated me with amused contempt because I was. Lay down or go down—it didn't matter that I knew Mozart.

There was something for everyone and our duties were many and varied ranging from the bizarre to the mundane. Sometimes, it took on all the aspects of a Grade-B movie. At informal conferences and board meetings, a few selected women would mix drinks, mingle during breaks, provide a light touch and be generally charming and genial as befits any hostess. Not all the men attending these meetings were to be granted our favors and when the meeting adjourned, those of us who were to be paired off would either be among the last to leave and then go with the client, or we would have discreetly withdrawn and be waiting for them in their hotel room—never ours. As for selection, we were either told beforehand or, as would often happen, some of the men would prefer the same woman and she was held in reserve for one. Sometimes this would provide an ironic domestic touch and occasionally led to bigger and better things for the woman when he decided he didn't want her passed around any longer. The men who were not granted privileges contented themselves with flirting, squeezing, pinching and propositioning. Under no circumstances could we accept the latter. Only the men designated were to be taken to bed and you couldn't make arrangements for later with another one. I don't know how the company would know, but they did know if you started branching off for yourself.

When the company was wooing business or providing favors on a large-scale, it was a different situation. Then we partied. It would be a week-end, lavishly planned—a flight, or a cruise. We would be flown to Las Vegas for instance to meet a group from the East. The women were not assigned, but were up for grabs. We spent a lot of time at Carmel and at Tahoe and once in Mexico City. The scene sometimes reminded me of a Shriner's convention on a small scale. Even this set-up could be surprising, though. Once in Carmel we spent most of the night playing bridge.

For the individual date, you went alone either meeting him at a restaurant or picking him up at his hotel. It was dinner, a show or a round of the clubs and it could be up to that point a very pleasant situation. However, afterwards it often became sticky. On a single you uncovered some strange appetites and it took a lot of handling to let him know how far he was allowed to go. If this didn't work, we reported him and he was "black-listed." However, we also knew that the customer was always right and most of his fetishes were to be catered to.

It was always strange to me that on the parties, sex was almost a secondary thing. The emphasis seemed to be on just plain swinging—drinking, dancing, and a lot of boasting. But the act itself was brief and "normal." As a matter of fact, it seemed as if they never slept and we had to go as long as they did— it was rough on us non-drinkers, believe me.

Occasionally, we acted as tour guides. Using a company car, we would drive the client (and sometimes his wife) or a group of clients around San Francisco and the environs ending up with either a lunch or a dinner at one of the more famous (to the tourist) restaurants. I got awfully sick of the Top of the Mark and Fisherman's Wharf. Once I even acted as a baby sitter for a very important executive's children and took them to the Zoo and Funland at the Beach. Quite often we would be assigned to meet a man at the airport to save him the inconvenience of the limousine and the long, boring drive to the city.

One thing I haven't mentioned was the relationship between the women. Naturally, we all knew each other for we were together quite a bit. However, no friendships ever seemed to develop. We exchanged no personal information nor, to my knowledge, did we ever contact each other away from business. Also, during working hours we did not even discuss the Johns in the powder room. We mixed together beautifully while we were working but it was a me-chanical thing and all our attention was to the men and why we were there—conversations were always general and remote.

We were utilized to some extent for the relaxation of the company executives or board members. If his stay was for a number of days, you were his ex-clusive property during that time. If he decided he wanted a change, you were notified by the office. And his relaxation meant mostly sex. I was hired once for a week to take care of an alcoholic executive whose family was too important to allow the company to fire him.

One night on a dinner date while we were still in the lounge a nightclub hustler tried to solicit my client. I watched her with what I hoped was the proper amount of amusement and doing my best lady bit I told her to make it. She looked at me in my Original and the furs and she laughed. "Bitch," she said, "You're 'hoe-in' just like me." What's more, I knew she was right, and at that moment it seemed I had to make up my mind what I was to be and more importantly, what I wanted to be. I was talented, for my music attested to that, but I had never really failed because I had never really tried. If I put a price on my body, for whatever reason, I couldn't really complain if somebody bought the merchandise. I wasn't even too good at that for I was using the John, he wasn't using me. That particular night was just a preliminary. If I was going to be a whore, then be an honest one. If I didn't want to be a whore, the answer was simple. Don't be one. Walk away from it and keep stepping.

I never went back. I don't know how they wrote me off in Payroll, but no one came after me either. I found an agent and my son and I went on the road with a group. I discovered I was not the best vocalist in the world and the knowledge didn't shatter me for I also discovered I wasn't the worst either and better than most. In 20 years I've made a million mistakes and an equal number of wrong turns, including a very bad marriage that stretched interminably for all the same reasons. I was still whoring, but it was respectable and legitimate. However, I accept the full responsibility. It begins to look as if I might be on my way to being a really classy broad.

Questions

1. *Prostitution is a crime without a victim; if there is no victim, there should be no crime and, therefore, no punishment. Discuss.*
2. *"Prostitution is criminal but not deviant. . . ." Do you agree or disagree? Why? Discuss.*
3. *Where does society focus its attempts at social control —the girl, the "John," the corporation? Why? Where should it? Discuss.*

How French Children
Learn to Drink

Barbara Gallatin Anderson

The French consume more wine than any other people in the world. According to French government figures, thirty percent of France's men consume alcohol in amounts dangerous to their health, and fifteen percent of these are alcoholics. Government campaigns against wine drinking have met with little success, however, because children are taught to drink wine at an early age and their behavior is reinforced later by a number of cultural beliefs. This article by anthropologist Barbara Anderson illustrates how deviant behavior, like normal behavior, is learned through the socialization process and how conflicting definitions of behavior (deviant versus normal) may exist side by side.

Visitors to France—even those with some knowledge of life in Mediterranean cultures—are often startled by the great amount of wine-drinking they find. Frenchmen everywhere drink with unflagging dedication and a quiet passion. For two years, my husband and I lived in the Seine-et-Oise village of Wissous, an area 10 miles from Paris. As anthropologists, we were struck by the tenacity with which villagers clung to their old drinking habits, specifically wine-drinking, despite considerable pressure from the government to abandon or at least cut down on their alcohol consumption. In particular, we were interested in finding out just how these drinking practices were transmitted to the village children.

Our two daughters, Andrea and Robin, then seven and two, were with us, and our son, Scott, was born there. We participated in the village life and, where possible, penetrated behind the scenes, gathering information about village customs. Of course, the questions we asked about children's drinking habits presented problems. The questions had to be very specific, yet apparently off the cuff. Eventually we incorporated them into a rather elaborate questionnaire on child care in general.

On the questionnaire, we asked people what every member of the household had eaten or drunk in the past 24 hours—at home or away from home. When feasible, we called at the villagers' homes during meal hours. Our interest was in what they had drunk, but we tried to give our questions no particular emphasis. We were as scrupulous in our attention to the kinds and quantities of foods they ate as we were in cataloging the beverages they drank. We administered these questionnaires and conducted follow-up interviews beginning in late February and ending in late April—a period of increasing warmth, which lowered the amount of drinking slightly. (To the villagers, cold weather is often a rationale for wine-drinking.)

Now, our interest lay specifically in the village's socially accepted drinking practices. For the French, this amounts to a study of wine-drinking. Our findings: Adult male villagers consumed approximately 1.58 quarts of wine per day. Women drank more than half a quart. The averages for children, however, could not be estimated—for reasons that will become clear later.

Our village was representative of France, where the total consumption of *pure* alcohol for the year 1955 (our study was done in 1957–59) averaged 23.78 quarts per person, or 32.1 for adults over 20. This average for adults was 16.9 quarts more than was consumed that same year by the world's second-largest wine-consuming country—Italy. The Danes drink only 3.17 quarts of pure alcohol per year. Americans drink 9.29 quarts.

According to the French government's figures, 15 percent of France's men are alcoholics, and 30 percent consume alcohol in amounts dangerous to their health. The government's National Institute of Hygiene has said that very active manual workers should not drink over one liter (1.057 quarts) of wine per day. Yet many sedentary workers, who are advised not to drink more than half a liter per day, drink a whole liter—as much as the most active workers. Alcoholism, to the average Frenchman, is identified only with reeling drunkenness.

Children Encouraged to Drink

Now, how does this receptivity to wine-drinking take shape in the children of the village? In other words, how is wine-drinking enculturated?

First of all, in Wissous, a positive value is attached to wine. People view wine-drinking as an act of virility. Men and families cannot socialize without wine. For a host not to offer wine is at best impolite.

In addition, wine is thought to have nutritive value. One reason: Throughout the schools, the very active wine lobby distributes blotters that carry highly dubious statements. One such blotter states that a liter of wine (12 percent alcohol) has nutritive value equivalent to 850 grams of milk, 370 grams of bread, 585 grams of meat, or 5 eggs. The blotter has a drawing of a scale with a wine-bottle balancing these foods.

Wine is also believed to be necessary for working. While at work, a manual or farm worker must have wine at fairly regular intervals. The body can best endure prolonged muscular exertion, it is alleged, with the sustained, revitalizing support of wine. Strong men have a propensity for drink. It is nature's way— *"C'est comme ça."*

Finally, wine may not be purer than any other drink, but Frenchmen think it is. In fact, the alcohol in wine is widely believed to compensate for the unsanitary conditions under which it, and many other food products, are prepared.

These beliefs about wine are strongest among the peasants. The few upper-middle-class families of Wissous also link wine-drinking to vigor. But they are more likely to stress moderation, and they drink less wine than the peasants. The moderation of the upper-middle-class, however, does not appear to extend to *apéritifs* and *digestifs*. They drink considerably more of these than the other villagers do, at home and in cafés.

In contrast with the positive value placed on wine, the French place a negative value on Western Europe's two major *non*alcoholic drinks: water and milk. The Wissous village spring water, which flows from two central fountains, is potable, but little is drunk (except in coffee), especially by the men. The local attitude is that, although a certain amount of water-drinking is inevitable, water takes second place to almost any other beverage. As one of the subway signs posted by France's powerful lobby puts it, "Water is for frogs."

In its campaign against the wine lobby, the French government has recently turned to building the image of fruit juice. Government ads show popular sportsmen drinking fruit juice with apparent gusto. But the wine lobby is still far more successful than any other lobby in France at carrying its message to the people.

As for milk, a precept firmly adhered to by all classes is summed up in a popular 1947 book on child care: "Milk should never constitute the mealtime drink." This book also states that "the quantity of milk drunk in a day should not exceed half a liter, under risk of digestive troubles such as diarrhea." In this regard, the villagers run no risks. When children stop taking the bottle, and stop eating the *bouillies* (thin milk mushes) of babyhood, they rarely drink milk at all, except in *café au lait*, chocolate, or the milk-thinned vegetables called *purées*.

Of course, the fact that milk is unrefrigerated, especially in the villages, does nothing to increase its appeal. And though it is pasteurized, it is *not* homogenized. When poured, it goes clunk-clunk in uneven globs. And in warm weather, it has a strong, almost curdled flavor.

During the time we lived in Wissous, milk was delivered to the village in huge tin urns, and poured into bottles by the grocer. Unknown to him, I once followed him to the back of his shop and saw him slosh a dirty bottle around in a tub of cold water before filling it with milk.

A book on practical child-raising, known in the village since the early twenties, differs little in its warnings about milk, but acknowledges that children cannot be "bad off" if they drink milk almost exclusively for the first two years. I quote: "One can also give at mealtime a half-glass of water lightly reddened with wine, or some beer or cider very diluted with water." In general, the recent literature is more cautious. It suggests, as a more suitable time for introducing children to alcoholic beverages, four years of age rather than two.

Wine Introduced as "Reddened Water"

Here, then, is our major point: Wine-drinking begins while the child is still in near-infancy. And government efforts to show that wine hurts children run into a semantic trap. A child does not drink *wine:* he drinks "reddened water."

To the French, the consumption of wine in quantities of less than a fourth of a quart is equivalent to abstinence. The mother of a boy of 12 will tell you, though the boy may be sitting across from you with a glass of the diluted wine in in his hand, that her son does not drink at all. By this, she means that his "reddened water" contains only a couple of soup-spoons of wine.

One day I bought refreshments for my daughter and her 11-year-old playmate at a cafe. The playmate ordered and drank a bottle of beer. It surprised me a little, because her mother had told me that the girl did not drink. But I am sure that, to the mother, her child's minimal and irregular intake did not constitute drinking.

If parents are drinking wine, beer, or cider, they give some—diluted with water—to their children. The younger ones sip beer or cider from a parent's glass. As they get older and more demanding, they are given small glasses of their own.

Children of lower-class homes drink more wine than children of middle-class homes, and they start drinking when they are younger. One mother even reported putting a drop or two of wine in a baby's bottle to "fortify" the milk. Generally, though, wine is first offered when the child is two or more, can hold his own glass quite safely in his hand, and can join the family at table.

In short, wine-drinking is already a habit before French children are old enough to reflect about it. If they do begin to assess their drinking practices, it is against a cultural backdrop where all the answers are value-loaded. Under the circumstances, it is hardly surprising that the campaigns in France against wine-drinking—led by teachers, social workers, and specialists in child welfare—have met with little success, and that in the past quarter-century the drinking patterns of French villagers, despite much social change and many social pressures, have hardly changed at all.

Questions

1. *Make a case for each of these propositions:* (a) *drinking wine in France is deviant;* (b) *not drinking wine in France is deviant.*
2. *What social control techniques is the French government using to discourage wine drinking? Why aren't they working?*
3. *What kind of social control techniques would be most effective in this situation? Design a program that you think would work.*

Losers and Outsiders

Hunter S. Thompson

Behavior is deviant not because of something inherent in the act but because of the definitions and viewpoints that others apply to the act. Likewise, some groups become defined as deviant: hippies, motorcycle gangs, extremist political or religious groups. Often, social distance and lack of contact or interaction lead to the development of a mythology about the deviant group. Their deeds and "evils" become exaggerated. In his article on the Hell's Angels, Hunter Thompson describes what they are really like, which in some aspects is contrary to the picture presented by the mass media and by law enforcement agencies. Hunter Thompson has written articles and books, including one on the Hell's Angels, and recently ran for sheriff in Aspen, Colorado.

From *The Nation,* May 17, 1965, 522–526. Reprinted by permission of the publisher.

Last Labor Day weekend newspapers all over California gave front-page reports of a heinous gang rape in the moonlit sand dunes near the town of Seaside
on the Monterey Peninsula. Two girls, aged 14 and 15, were allegedly taken
from their dates by a gang of filthy, frenzied, boozed-up motorcycle hoodlums
called "Hell's Angels," and dragged off to be "repeatedly assaulted."

A deputy sheriff, summoned by one of the erstwhile dates, said he "arrived
at the beach and saw a huge bonfire surrounded by cyclists of both sexes. Then
the two sobbing, near-hysterical girls staggered out of the darkness, begging for
help. One was completely nude and the other had on only a torn sweater."

Some 300 Hell's Angels were gathered in the Seaside-Monterey area at the
time, having convened, they said, for the purpose of raising funds among themselves to send the body of a former member, killed in an accident, back to his
mother in North Carolina. One of the Angels, hip enough to falsely identify himself as "Frenchy of San Bernardino," told a local reporter who came out to meet
the cyclists: "We chose Monterey because we get treated good here; most other
places we get thrown out of town."

But Frenchy spoke too soon. The Angels weren't on the peninsula twenty-four
hours before four of them were in jail for rape, and the rest of the troop was
being escorted to the county line by a large police contingent. Several were
quoted, somewhat derisively, as saying: "That rape charge against our guys is
phony and it won't stick."

It turned out to be true, but that was another story and certainly no head-
liner. The difference between the Hell's Angels in the papers and the Hell's
Angels for real is enough to make a man wonder what newsprint is for. It also
raises a question as to who are the real hell's angels.

Ever since World War II, California has been strangely plagued by wild men
and motorcycles. They usually travel in groups of ten to thirty, booming along
the highways and stopping here and there to get drunk and raise hell. In 1947,
hundreds of them ran amok in the town of Hollister, an hour's fast drive south
of San Francisco, and got enough press notices to inspire a film called the *Wild
One,* starring Marlon Brando. The film had a massive effect on thousands of
young California motorcycle buffs; in many ways, it was their version of *The
Sun Also Rises.*

The California climate is perfect for motorcycles, as well as surfboards,
swimming pools and convertibles. Most of the cyclists are harmless weekend
types, members of the American Motorcycle Association, and no more dangerous than skiers or skin divers. But a few belong to what the others call "outlaw
clubs," and these are the ones who—especially on weekends and holidays—
are likely to turn up almost anywhere in the state, looking for action. Despite
everything the psychiatrists and Freudian casuists have to say about them, they
are tough, mean and potentially as dangerous as packs of wild boar. When push
comes to shove, any leather fetishes or inadequacy feelings that may be involved

are entirely beside the point, as anyone who has ever tangled with these boys will sadly testify. When you get in an argument with a group of outlaw motorcyclists, you can generally count your chances of emerging unmaimed by the number of heavy-handed allies you can muster in the time it takes to smash a beer bottle. In this league, sportsmanship is for old liberals and young fools. "I smashed his face," one of them said to me of a man he'd never seen until the swinging started. "He got wise. He called me a punk. He must have been stupid."

The most notorious of these outlaw groups is the Hell's Angels, supposedly headquartered in San Bernardino, just east of Los Angeles, and with branches all over the state. As a result of the infamous "Labor Day gang rape," the Attorney General of California has recently issued an official report on the Hell's Angels. According to the report, they are easily identified:

> *The emblem of the Hell's Angels, termed "colors," consists of an embroidered patch of a winged skull wearing a motorcycle helmet. Just below the wing of the emblem are the letters "MC." Over this is a band bearing the words "Hell's Angels." Below the emblem is another patch bearing the local chapter name, which is usually an abbreviation for the city or locality. These patches are sewn on the back of a usually sleeveless denim jacket. In addition, members have been observed wearing various types of Luftwaffe insignia and reproductions of German iron crosses.* Many affect beards and their hair is usually long and unkempt. Some wear a single earring in a pierced ear lobe. Frequently they have been observed to wear metal belts made of a length of polished motorcycle drive chain which can be unhooked and used as a flexible bludgeon. . . . Probably the most universal common denominator in identification of Hell's Angels is their generally filthy condition. Investigating officers consistently report these people, both club members and their female associates, seem badly in need of a bath. Fingerprints are a very effective means of identification because a high percentage of Hell's Angels have criminal records.*
>
> *In addition to the patches on the back of Hell's Angels jackets, the "One Percenters" wear a patch reading "1%-er." Another badge worn by some members bears the*

---

* Purely for decorative and shock effect. The Hell's Angels are apolitical and no more racist than other ignorant young thugs.

*number "13." It is reported to represent the 13th letter of
the alphabet, "M," which in turn stands for marijuana and
indicates the wearer thereof is a user of the drug.*

The Attorney General's report was colorful, interesting, heavily biased and consistently alarming—just the sort of thing, in fact, to make a clanging good article for a national news magazine. Which it did; both barrels. *Newsweek* led with a left hook titled "The Wild Ones," *Time* crossed with a right, inevitably titled "The Wilder Ones." The Hell's Angels, cursing the implications of this new attack, retreated to the bar of the DePau Hotel near the San Francisco waterfront and planned a weekend beach party. I showed them the articles. Hell's Angels do not normally read the news magazines. "I'd go nuts if I read that stuff all the time," said one. . . .

Newsweek was relatively circumspect. It offered local color, flashy quotes and "evidence" carefully attributed to the official report but unaccountably said the report accused the Hell's Angels of homosexuality, whereas the report said just the opposite. *Time* leaped into the fray with a flurry of blood, booze and semen-flecked wordage that amounted, in the end, to a classic of supercharged hokum: "Drug-induced stupors . . . no act is too degrading . . . swap girls, drugs and motorcycles with equal abandon . . . stealing forays . . . then ride off again to seek some new nadir in sordid behavior. . . ."

Where does all this leave the Hell's Angels and the thousands of shuddering Californians (according to *Time*) who are worried sick about them? Are these outlaws really going to be busted, routed and cooled, as the news magazines implied? Are California highways any safer as a result of this published uproar? Can honest merchants once again walk the streets in peace? The answer is that nothing has changed except that a few people calling themselves Hell's Angels have a new sense of identity and importance.

After two weeks of intensive dealing with the Hell's Angels phenomenon, both in print and in person, I'm convinced the net result of the general howl and publicity has been to obscure and avoid the real issues by invoking a savage conspiracy of bogymen and conning the public into thinking all will be "business as usual" once this fearsome snake is scotched, as it surely will be by hard and ready minions of the Establishment.

Meanwhile, according to Attorney General Thomas C. Lynch's own figures, California's true crime picture makes the Hell's Angels look like a gang of petty jack rollers. The police count 463 Hell's Angels: 205 around Los Angeles and 233 in the San Francisco-Oakland area. I don't know about L.A. but the real figures for the Bay Area are thirty or so in Oakland and exactly eleven with one facing expulsion—in San Francisco. This disparity makes it hard to accept other police statistics. The dubious package also shows convictions on 1,023 misdemeanor counts and 151 felonies—primarily vehicle theft, burglary and assault. This is for all years and all alleged members.

California's overall figures for 1963 list 1,116 homicides, 12,448 aggravated assaults, 6,257 sex offenses, and 24,532 burglaries. In 1962, the state listed 4,121 traffic deaths, up from 3,839 in 1961. Drug arrest figures for 1964 showed a 101 per cent increase in juvenile marijuana arrests over 1963, and a recent back-page story in the *San Francisco Examiner* said, "The venereal disease rate among [the city's] teen-agers from 15–19 has more than doubled in the past four years." Even allowing for the annual population jump, juvenile arrests in all categories are rising by 10 per cent or more each year.

Against this background, would it make any difference to the safety and peace of mind of the average Californian if every motorcycle outlaw in the state (all 901 according to the police) were garroted within twenty-four hours? This is not to say that a group like the Hell's Angels has no meaning. The generally bizarre flavor of their offenses and their insistence on identifying themselves make good copy, but usually overwhelm—in print, at least—the unnerving truth that they represent, in colorful microcosm, what is quietly and anonymously growing all around us every day of the week.

"We're bastards to the world and they're bastards to us," one of the Oakland Angels told a *Newsweek* reporter. "When you walk into a place where people can see you, you want to look as repulsive and repugnant as possible. We are complete social outcasts—outsiders against society."

A lot of this is a pose, but anyone who believes that's all it is has been on thin ice since the death of Jay Gatsby. The vast majority of motorcycle outlaws are uneducated, unskilled men between 20 and 30, and most have no credentials except a police record. So at the root of their sad stance is a lot more than a wistful yearning for acceptance in a world they never made; their real motivation is an instinctive certainty as to what the score really is. They are out of the ball game and they know it—and that is their meaning; for unlike most losers in today's society, the Hell's Angels not only know but spitefully proclaim exactly where they stand.

I went to one of their meetings recently, and half-way through the night I thought of Joe Hill on his way to face a Utah firing squad and saying his final words: "Don't mourn, organize." It is safe to say that no Hell's Angel has ever heard of Joe Hill or would know a Wobbly from a Bushmaster, but nevertheless they are somehow related. The I.W.W. had serious plans for running the world, while the Hell's Angels mean only to defy the world's machinery. But instead of losing quietly, one by one, they have banded together with a mindless kind of loyalty and moved outside the framework, for good or ill. There is nothing particularly romantic or admirable about it; that's just the way it is, strength in unity. They don't mind telling you that running fast and loud on their customized Harley 74s gives them a power and a purpose that nothing else seems to offer.

Beyond that, their position as self-proclaimed outlaws elicits a certain popular appeal, however reluctant. That is especially true in the West and even in California where the outlaw tradition is still honored. The unarticulated link between the Hell's Angels and the millions of losers and outsiders who don't wear any colors is the key to their notoriety and the ambivalent reactions they inspire. There are several other keys, having to do with politicians, policemen and journalists, but for this we have to go back to Monterey and the Labor Day "gang rape."

Politicians, like editors and cops, are very keen on outrage stories, and state Senator Fred S. Farr of Monterey County is no exception. He is a leading light of the Carmel-Pebble Beach set and no friend of hoodlums anywhere, especially gang rapists who invade his constituency. Senator Farr demanded an immediate investigation of the Hell's Angels and others of their ilk—Commancheros, Stray Satans, Iron Horsemen, Rattlers (a Negro club), and Booze Fighters—whose lack of status caused them all to be lumped together as "other disreputables." In the cut-off world of big bikes, long runs and classy rumbles, this new, state-sanctioned stratification made the Hell's Angels very big. They were, after all, Number One. Like John Dillinger.

Attorney General Lynch, then new in his job, moved quickly to mount an investigation of sorts. He sent questionnaires to more than 100 sheriffs, district attorneys and police chiefs, asking for information on the Hell's Angels and those "other disreputables." He also asked for suggestions as to how the law might deal with them.

Six months went by before all the replies were condensed into the fifteen-page report that made new outrage headlines when it was released to the press. (The Hell's Angels also got a copy; one of them stole mine.) As a historical document, it read like a plot synopsis of Mickey Spillane's worst dreams. But in the matter of solutions it was vague, reminiscent in some ways of Madame Nhu's proposals for dealing with the Vietcong. The state was going to centralize information on these thugs, urge more vigorous prosecution, put them all under surveillance whenever possible, etc.

A careful reader got the impression that even if the Hell's Angels had acted out this script—eighteen crimes were specified and dozens of others implied—very little would or could be done about it, and that indeed Mr. Lynch was well aware he'd been put, for political reasons, on a pretty weak scent. There was plenty of mad action, senseless destruction, orgies, brawls, perversions and a strange parade of "innocent victims" that, even on paper and in careful police language, was enough to tax the credulity of the dullest police reporter. Any bundle of information off police blotters is bound to reflect a special viewpoint, and parts of the Attorney General's report are actually humorous, if only for the language. Here is an excerpt:

On November 4, 1961, a San Francisco resident driving through Rodeo, possibly under the influence of alcohol, struck a motorcycle belonging to a Hell's Angel parked outside a bar. A group of Angels pursued the vehicle, pulled the driver from the car and attempted to demolish the rather expensive vehicle. The bartender claimed he had seen nothing, but a cocktail waitress in the bar furnished identification to the officers concerning some of those responsible for the assault. The next day it was reported to officers that a member of the Hell's Angels gang had threatened the life of this waitress as well as another woman waitress. A male witness who definitely identified five participants in the assault including the president of the Vallejo Hell's Angels and the Vallejo "Road Rats" advised officers that because of his fear of retaliation by club members he would refuse to testify to the facts he had previously furnished.

That is a representative item in the section of the report titled "Hoodlum Activities." First, it occurred in a small town—Rodeo is on San Pablo Bay just north of Oakland—where the Angels had stopped at a bar without causing any trouble until some offense was committed against them. In this case, a driver whom even the police admit was "possibly" drunk hit one of their motorcycles. The same kind of accident happens every day all over the nation, but when it involves outlaw motorcyclists it is something else again. Instead of settling the thing with an exchange of insurance information or, at the very worst, an argument with a few blows, the Hell's Angels beat the driver and "attempted to demolish the vehicle." I asked one of them if the police exaggerated this aspect, and he said no, they had done the natural thing: smashed headlights, kicked in doors, broken windows and torn various components off the engine.

Of all their habits and predilections that society finds alarming, this departure from the time-honored concept of "an eye for an eye" is the one that most frightens people. The Hell's Angels try not to do anything halfway, and anyone who deals in extremes is bound to cause trouble, whether he means to or not. This, along with a belief in total retaliation for any offense or insult, is what makes the Hell's Angels unmanageable for the police and morbidly fascinating to the general public. Their claim that they "don't start trouble" is probably true more often than not, but their idea of "provocation" is dangerously broad, and their biggest problem is that nobody else seems to understand it. Even dealing with them personally, on the friendliest terms, you can sense their hair-trigger readiness to retaliate.

This is a public thing, and not at all true among themselves. In a meeting, their conversation is totally frank and open. They speak to and about one another with an honesty that more civilized people couldn't bear. At the meeting I attended (and before they realized I was a journalist) one Angel was being publicly evaluated; some members wanted him out of the club and others wanted to keep him in. It sounded like a group-therapy clinic in progress—not exactly what I expected to find when just before midnight I walked into the bar of the De Pau in one of the bleakest neighborhoods in San Francisco, near Hunters Point. By the time I parted company with them—at 6:30 the next morning after an all-night drinking bout in my apartment—I had been impressed by a lot of things, but no one thing about them was as consistently obvious as their group loyalty. This is an admirable quality, but it is also one of the things that gets them in trouble: a fellow Angel is *always right* when dealing with outsiders. And this sort of reasoning makes a group of "offended" Hell's Angels nearly impossible to deal with.

Here is another incident from the Attorney General's report:

> On September 19, 1964, a large group of Hell's Angels and "Satan's Slaves" converged on a bar in South Gate (Los Angeles County), parking their motorcycles and cars in the street in such a fashion as to block one-half of the roadway. They told officers that three members of the club had recently been asked to stay out of the bar and that they had come to tear it down. Upon their approach the bar owner locked the doors and turned off the lights and no entrance was made, but the group did demolish a cement block fence. On arrival of the police, members of the club were lying on the sidewalk and in the street. They were asked to leave the city, which they did reluctantly. As they left, several were heard to say that they would be back and tear down the bar.

Here again is the ethic of total retaliation. If you're "asked to stay out" of a bar, you don't just punch the owner—you come back with your army and destroy the whole edifice. Similar incidents—along with a number of vague rape complaints—make up the bulk of the report. Eighteen incidents in four years, and none except the rape charges are more serious than cases of assault on citizens who, for their own reasons, had become involved with the Hell's Angels prior to the violence. I could find no cases of unwarranted attacks on wholly innocent victims. There are a few borderline cases, wherein victims of physical attacks seemed innocent, according to police and press reports, but later refused to testify for fear of "retaliation." The report asserts very strongly that Hell's Angels are difficult to prosecute and convict because they make a habit of threatening and intimidating witnesses. That is probably true to a certain extent, but in many cases victims have refused to testify because they were engaged in some legally dubious activity at the time of the attack.

In two of the most widely publicized incidents the prosecution would have fared better if their witnesses and victims *had* been intimidated into silence. One of these was the Monterey "gang rape," and the other a "rape" in Clovis, near Fresno in the Central Valley. In the latter, a 36-year-old widow and mother of five children claimed she'd been yanked out of a bar where she was having a quiet beer with another woman, then carried to an abandoned shack behind the bar and raped repeatedly for two and a half hours by fifteen or twenty Hell's Angels and finally robbed of $150. That's how the story appeared in the San Francisco newspapers the next day, and it was kept alive for a few more days by the woman's claims that she was getting phone calls threatening her life if she testified against her assailants.

Then, four days after the crime, the victim was arrested on charges of "sexual perversion." The true story emerged, said the Clovis chief of police, when the woman was "confronted by witnesses. Our investigation shows she was not raped," said the chief. "She participated in lewd acts in the tavern with at least three Hell's Angels before the owners ordered them out. She encouraged their advances in the tavern, then led them to an abandoned house in the rear. . . . She was not robbed but, according to a woman who accompanied her, had left her house early in the evening with $5 to go bar-hopping." That incident did not appear in the Attorney General's report.

But it was impossible not to mention the Monterey "gang rape," because it was the reason for the whole subject to become official. Page one of the report which *Time's* editors apparently skipped—says that the Monterey case was dropped because ". . . further investigation raised questions as to whether forcible rape had been committed or if the identifications made by victims were valid." Charges were dismissed on September 25, with the concurrence of a grand jury. The deputy District Attorney said "a doctor examined the girls and found no evidence" to support the charges. "Besides that, one girl refused to testify," he explained, "and the other was given a lie-detector test and found to be wholly unreliable."

This, in effect, was what the Hell's Angels had been saying all along. Here is their version of what happened, as told by several who were there:

One girl was white and pregnant, the other was colored, and they were with five colored studs. They hung around our bar—Nick's Place on Del Monte Avenue—for about three hours Saturday night, drinking and talking with our riders, then they came out to the beach with us—them and

*their five boy friends. Everybody was standing around the
fire, drinking wine, and some of the guys were talking to
them—hustling 'em, naturally—and soon somebody asked
the two chicks if they wanted to be turned on—you know,
did they want to smoke some pot? They said yeah, and then
they walked off with some of the guys to the dunes. The
spade went with a few guys and then she wanted to quit, but
the pregnant one was really hot to trot; the first four or five
guys she was really dragging into her arms, but after that
she cooled off, too. By this time, though, one of their boy
friends had got scared and gone for the cops—and that's
all it was.*

But not quite all. After that there were Senator Farr and Tom Lynch and a
hundred cops and dozens of newspaper stories and articles in the national news
magazines—and even this article, which is a direct result of the Monterey "gang
rape."

When the much-quoted report was released, the local press—primarily the
San Francisco Chronicle, which had earlier done a long and fairly objective
series on the Hell's Angels—made a point of saying the Monterey charges
against the Hell's Angels had been dropped for lack of evidence. *Newsweek* was
careful not to mention Monterey at all, but *The New York Times* referred to it
as "the alleged gang rape" which, however, left no doubt in a reader's mind
that something savage had occurred.

It remained for *Time,* though, to flatly ignore the fact that the Monterey rape
charges had been dismissed. Its article leaned heavily on the hairiest and least
factual sections of the report, and ignored the rest. It said, for instance, that the
Hell's Angels initiation rite "demands that any new member bring a woman or
girl [called a 'sheep'] who is willing to submit to sexual intercourse with each
member of the club." That is untrue, although, as one Angel explained, "Now
and then you get a woman who likes to cover the crowd, and hell, I'm no prude.
People don't like to think women go for that stuff, but a lot of them do."

We were talking across a pool table about the rash of publicity and how it
had affected the Angels' activities. I was trying to explain to him that the bulk of
the press in this country has such a vested interest in the *status quo* that it can't
afford to do much honest probing at the roots, for fear of what they might find.

"Oh, I don't know," he said. "Of course I don't like to read all this . . .
because it brings the heat down on us, but since we got famous we've had more
rich fags and sex-hungry women come looking for us than we ever had before.
Hell, these days we have more action than we can handle."

Questions

1. *What are the specific characteristics of the Hell's Angels that have led society to define them as deviant? Which of these characteristics are "criminal," and which are "deviant" but not "criminal"?*
2. *Analyze the role of the mass media in the development of deviant definitions and in the development of social control.*

11

What Is Sociology?

Throughout this book, we have looked at the concepts of sociology in an attempt to give some idea of what sociology is. One gains an understanding of a discipline by becoming acquainted with the tools, the techniques, and the terms of that discipline. The concepts and the readings included in this book should give you some feeling for what sociology is all about.

Is it enough, however, merely to be familiar with the concepts of an endeavor? For example, a beginning understanding of the tools and techniques of the garage mechanic may be enlightening, but that understanding won't provide an individual with sufficient skill or experience to fix a car. It is possible that although we have covered a number of the important concepts that sociologists use, you may not be able to go out and solve the problems of the world or even to apply sociology in a meaningful manner. Of course this is only an introductory view of sociology. Additional courses should bring greater knowledge and facility in the use of sociological concepts. In addition, however, there are probably other aspects and characteristics of sociology, aside from its concepts, that would help bring a better understanding of what it is.

A Sociological Perspective

Members of a discipline develop a particular way of looking at the world. They share these views as individuals, although the similarity of their perspectives is most readily seen when a group of people from the same discipline are together. The same thing occurs among engineers, or doctors, or musicians, or sociologists. Becoming a sociologist involves learning the meaning and use of a series of concepts and techniques and acquiring a body of knowledge. Going through this learning—a socialization process—provides one with a particular viewpoint. Members of a discipline share this viewpoint, and it affects the way they think, the way they talk, the way they behave.

There are a number of aspects to this sociological perspective. A major aspect is the tendency to see human behavior in the context of the group. To put it another way, the sociologist understands man's behavior to be a product of his group affiliations. Consequently, in his studies, it is on these group affiliations that the sociologist focuses. For example, let's look at Joe Blow as some of his friends and colleagues might look at him. What stands out to his doctor is Joe's height, weight, pulse rate, blood pressure, and medical history. What his banker sees is his investment portfolio, cash reserves, and loan collateral. His minister may see him as a soul to be saved, a moral state to be improved. His professor may see him as a mind to be molded, a vessel to be filled with knowledge, or an intellect to be challenged. His psychiatrist sees him as an unresolved Oedipus complex with manifestations of latent homosexuality as a result of a mother fixation at an early age. A sociologist looks at Joe Blow and sees a white, middle-class, twenty-one-year-old male who is a member of the Democratic Party, SDS, and the Junior Chamber of Commerce. (Odd . . .)

The sociologist typically is more interested in characteristics of categories and groups than in specific individuals. In Joe's case, the focus would probably be on the characteristics of middle-class whites, of twenty-one-year-old males, or of Democrats and SDSers rather than on Joe as an individual. The sociologist usually studies numbers of people—groups, categories, societies—and their patterns of behavior—norms, roles, and institutions.

Other aspects of the sociological perspective are discussed by Peter Berger in his book *Invitation to Sociology*. Berger feels that there is a "sociological consciousness" having several facets.[1] A *debunking* tendency of sociologists is reflected in their study of things taken for granted. Berger suggests that in analyzing the structure and institutions of societies, it is often necessary to "unmask the pretensions and the propaganda with which men cloak their actions with

---

[1] The discussion in the following paragraphs is drawn from Berger's Chapter 2, "Sociology as a Form of Consciousness." Peter L. Berger, *Invitation to Sociology* (Garden City, N.Y.: Doubleday & Co., 1963).

each other." There is a constant attempt, then, to find the underlying explanations for phenomena instead of just accepting the handy or traditional explanations that people readily give. For example, sociologists would view it as important to put commonsense explanations aside and determine what the real relationship is between narcotics legislation and drug usage, or between use of the death penalty and the homicide rate.

A part of sociology is devoted to the study of the *unrespectable*. Early sociologists were reformers and muckrakers. They believed that sociologists should intervene and attempt to ameliorate problem conditions to ensure social progress. This preoccupation with social problems and the "unrespectable" has abated somewhat today, but its influence in sociology is still strong. We see, for example, a variety of recent studies of "underdogs," deviants, and "outsiders." In addition to several studies of drug users and hippies, books have appeared dealing with shoplifters, pool players, bar behavior, behavior of race track gamblers, prison behavior, death and dying, and on being mentally ill, to mention a few topics.[2]

This is not meant to imply that "respectable" aspects of society are outside the scope of sociology. On the contrary, most sociological study is of this variety. In fact, there has been criticism of late that sociology has become too "establishment," too interested in describing and supporting the *status quo,* and less than it should be, an agent for social change. Without getting involved in that debate, we could conclude that while much of sociology deals with the "respectable," a prominent and growing segment of the discipline deals with the "unrespectable," with problems and/or deviant aspects of society.

Berger suggests that sociologists tend to be *relativists* and *cosmopolitan* in their outlook. Sociologists are involved in studying patterns of human interaction in a variety of cultures under many different conditions. This type of study soon makes it apparent that behavior, ideas, and institutions are relative, relevant to specific cultures and specific locations. The general absence of universals in the social world demands that the social scientist be cosmopolitan in his outlook. It is unacceptable for him to generalize from the local condition or from

---

[2] A short list of recent books on "unrespectable" topics: Lewis Yablonsky, *The Hippie Trip* (New York: Pegasus, 1968); James T. Carey, *The College Drug Scene* (Englewood Cliffs, N.J.: Prentice-Hall, 1968); Mary Cameron, *The Booster and the Snitch* (New York: Free Press, 1964); Ned Polsky, *Hustlers, Beats, and Others* (Chicago: Aldine Publishing Co., 1967); Sherri Cavan, *Liquor License* (Chicago: Aldine Publishing Co., 1966); Marvin B. Scott, *The Racing Game* (Chicago: Aldine Publishing Co., 1968); David Ward and Gene Kassebaum, *Women's Prison* (Chicago: Aldine Publishing Co., 1965); Gresham Sykes, *The Society of Captives* (Princeton, N.J.: Princeton University Press, 1958); Barney Glaser and Anselm Strauss, *Awareness of Dying* and *Time for Dying* (Chicago: Aldine Publishing Co., 1965 and 1968); Thomas Scheff, *Being Mentally Ill* (Chicago: Aldine Publishing Co., 1966); Howard S. Becker, *Outsiders* (New York: Free Press, 1963); *The Other Side*, edited by Howard S. Becker (New York: Free Press, 1964).

the situation immediately around him. He must take a world view, and this becomes part of his sociological consciousness.

The similarities in outlook that are shared by sociologists emerge, to a great extent, as a result of their training. There are, as well, many differences between sociologists. One area of difference is evident when we examine how sociologists look at sociology.

Sociological Perspectives of Sociology

Certain themes or traditions are contained within the discipline of sociology. In combination, these traditions constitute a heritage from which all sociologists draw. A particular sociologist, however, will be influenced more strongly by one tradition or perspective than by others. Just as a doctor specializes in certain aspects of medicine and a lawyer concentrates in certain aspects of law, so the sociologist finds himself specializing in specific areas of sociology (race, social class, or deviant behavior) and following a particular theme or tradition that he feels is most appropriate. In the following paragraphs I want to examine briefly some of the traditions that are part of sociology. These traditions describe varying methods of sociological analysis, and each tradition brings with it a distinct perspective on what sociology is.

Sociology is seen by some as a *pure* science in that its practitioners seek knowledge for knowledge's sake alone, without regard for the possible uses the knowledge may have. The Weberian model suggests that sociology is a science, not a vehicle for social action. In recent years, however, a growing number of sociologists have encouraged the development of an *applied* sociology. In a variety of ways, sociologists are putting their concepts and techniques to practical use. In general, these efforts involve attempts to deal with the problems of society or of individual segments of society: industry, education, labor, government, and the community. Applied sociology is often designed to encourage desired social change or to forestall undesired social change. Applied sociology has been referred to as "action sociology," and those involved are sometimes called "social engineers." Philip Hauser points out that with the proliferation of economic and social planning and the increase in welfare functions of government, the need for sociologists will continue to increase for the performance of both scientific and social engineering tasks.[3]

---

[3] Philip M. Hauser, "On Actionism in the Craft of Sociology," *Sociological Inquiry,* 39, 2 (Spring 1969), pp. 139–147. For more on applied sociology, see *Sociology in Action,* edited by Arthur Shostak (Homewood, Ill.: Dorsey Press, 1966); and *Applied Sociology,* edited by Alvin Gouldner and S. M. Miller (New York: Free Press, 1965).

Some sociologists have a *scientific* perspective. For them, sociology is a social science, and they emphasize the procedures and techniques of science. This sociologist sees himself as a white-coated individual who gains knowledge by applying scientific methods to social phenomena. He is objective, he is detached, he is free of any values or biases that might affect his work. He is, perhaps, a bundle of sensory neurons moving in space, observing and recording the facts of social interaction. Sociologists today are developing sophisticated mathematical models and statistical techniques and using ever-larger computers to aid them in the scientific analysis of human behavior.[4]

The type of scientist I have just described is often called a positivist. He adheres pretty much to the classical view of science as outlined in Chapter 1. His role as scientist is based on the model that has worked so well for those in the physical and biological sciences, and its adoption by sociologists probably reflects the hope that our success may be as great as theirs. At the same time the positivistic model in sociology is criticized by some, and this debate over method has increased in recent years. The criticism has several origins. First, there is the criticism of science in general. There is concern that blind faith in, and uncritical acceptance of, science has led people to ignore the faults of science. Questions are raised about a series of ethical considerations: Shouldn't scientists be responsible for the possible harmful uses of their discoveries? Should scientists tamper with and manipulate people without their knowledge, or even *with* their knowledge? Whom does the scientist represent—himself, science in general, society, or those people (government agencies, large organizations, private concerns) who are paying his research bills? Failure to receive satisfactory answers to these questions has led many to be disillusioned with science.[5]

A second form of criticism of the positivistic model is more specific to sociology. The complaint here is simply that the information we have, especially when gathered by questionnaires and interviews, is not valid, not accurate. Obviously, this is a serious criticism. Derek Phillips states in his book, *Knowledge From What?,* that ninety percent of the data collected by sociologists is done by means of interviews and questionnaires. What sociologists have failed to take into account, he maintains, is that the questionnaire or interview situation is a *social* situation. The responses of the person being studied are affected by the questionnaire, by his response to the interviewer and the interviewer's characteristics (sex, age, race, social class, demeanor, etc.), by the nature of the interaction between the interviewer and interviewed, and by numerous other factors

---

[4] A thorough and interesting discussion of several sociological perspectives, including "abstracted empiricism," is included in C. Wright Mills' excellent book, *The Sociological Imagination* (New York: Oxford University Press, 1959).

[5] A number of works deal with these issues. See, for example, *Ethics, Politics, and Social Research,* edited by Gideon Sjoberg (Cambridge, Mass.: Schenkman, 1967); *Politics of Social Research* by Ralph Beals (Chicago: Aldine, 1968); *The Rise and Fall of Project Camelot* edited by Irving L. Horowitz (Cambridge, Mass.: M.I.T. Press, 1967). There is a discussion of scientific ethics in most methodology texts.

that have been left uncontrolled. The basic problem is that most sociological research is based on people's *reports* of their own behavior rather than on *actual observation* of their behavior. Phillips suggests that the positivistic model in sociology has failed and should be dropped. Sociologists should instead concentrate on participant observation and "hidden" observation techniques. Participant observation, as we suggested earlier, involves the investigator "joining" or living with the subjects he is studying to the extent that he becomes a part of the group. Studies of primitive tribes, delinquent gangs, large organizations (remember Elinor Langer's study of the telephone company, pp. 99–109), and class and ethnic structure of communities as well as many other topics have resulted from this technique. Although less "scientific," participant observation allows study of some events that could not otherwise be studied, and may provide numerous insights that escape the more formal interview and questionnaire methods. Hidden observation refers to making use of records or traces left behind by people (check the nose prints on the glass or the wear on the floor-tile to determine the popularity of a museum exhibit; go to a parking lot and check where the dials on the car radios are tuned to find out the most popular station; etc.) or by actually observing people without letting them know.[6] The key element in both participant and hidden observation is that we *watch* people's behavior rather than *ask* them about it. Concerns about the *accuracy* of what we are doing, then, has led to further disillusionment with some of the scientific aspects of sociology.

These problems as well as other beliefs regarding the most appropriate path to knowledge have led some sociologists to see the discipline not as science but as *social philosophy*. For them, the sociologist is a theorist, perhaps an armchair philosopher who sits by the fire spinning grand generalizations about the nature of mankind. He frequently has remarkable insights about human behavior. However, from the scientist's viewpoint, the social philosopher's statements are often too general and abstract to be put to empirical test. Others see the sociologist-as-social-philosopher as a true scholar rather than a mere scientific technician—he is widely read, a master of many disciplines, and students may gather adoringly at his feet.

Some sociologists have a *humanistic* perspective. For them, the sociologist is interested in and concerned about human welfare, values, and conduct. He wants to improve the lot of man. An ultimate goal for the humanist is the self-realization and full development of the cultivated man. There may occasionally be a tendency for the humanistic and scientific perspectives to be at odds with each other. The humanist is interested in bettering the condition of man and in

---

[6] *Knowledge From What?* by Derek Phillips (Chicago: Rand McNally, 1971). Also see *Analyzing Social Settings* by John Lofland (Belmont, California: Wadsworth, 1971), and *Unobtrusive Measures: Nonreactive Research in the Social Sciences* by Eugene Webb, Donald Campbell, Richard Schwartz, and Lee Sechrest (Chicago: Rand McNally, 1966).

the fullest development of the individual. The objective of science is the gaining of empirical knowledge about the world, without regard for the possible uses of such knowledge. Martindale suggests that humanism is a system of values describing "what ought to be" and modes of conduct designed to secure them; science is the value-free pursuit of knowledge, "of what is," renouncing all concern with what ought to be. It has also been suggested that the scientist is more interested in the *means*—gaining knowledge; the humanist, in the *ends*—improving the lot of man. The humanist may be seen as a moralist; the scientist is seen (usually by the humanist) as amoral, sometimes as immoral.[7]

Is sociology basically concerned with gathering empirical data about man's behavior in a scientific sense or with the study of those conditions that will enable man to realize his fullest potential in a humanistic sense? It is impossible to put all of sociology into one camp or the other. Most sociologists probably operate with a combination of scientific and humanistic viewpoints. Peter Berger expresses the view of many, however, when he argues that sociology must be used for humanity's sake.[8] Social science, like other sciences, can be and sometimes is dehumanizing and even inhuman. It should not be. When sociologists pursue their task with insight, sensitivity, empathy, humility, and a desire to *understand* the human condition, rather than with a cold and humorless scientism, then indeed, the "sociological perspective helps illuminate man's social existence."

What Do Sociologists Do?

Suppose we suggest for a moment that sociology *is* what sociologists *do*. This is not a particularly good way to answer the question "What is sociology?", but it may give us some idea of the career possibilities open to sociologists.

Most sociologists spend most of their time teaching. Opportunities for teaching sociology are found predominantly at the college and university level, but increasing numbers of high schools are adding sociology courses to their curricula. Some sociology courses, especially at the high school level, have more of a practical or "how to do it" focus. These courses might deal with dating, marriage, senior problems, or personal adjustment.

Many sociologists are involved in research, either full-time or in combination with their teaching. Full-time researchers may run their own research agencies, but more often they work for state or federal agencies. They may, for example,

---

[7] This discussion of humanistic and scientific thought follows from Don Martindale's analysis in his *Social Life and Cultural Change* (Princeton, N.J.: Van Nostrand, 1962), pp. 443–462.

[8] See Peter Berger's chapter, "Sociology as a Humanistic Discipline," in *Invitation to Sociology*. Also see R. P. Cuzzort's discussion of Berger in Cuzzort's book, *Humanity and Modern Sociological Thought* (New York: Holt, Rinehart and Winston, 1969), Chapter 10.

be responsible for collecting and analyzing population and census data. They may collect police arrest statistics and analyze and combine these into crime reports. Sociologists, especially at the larger universities, are about equally involved in research and teaching. Often they seek grants to support their research, and this in itself has become big business. Sociologists, like other academicians, are increasingly being criticized for spending more time with their research than with their students. Perhaps this criticism is well founded, but the situation has been created at least in part by the promotion and salary structure of institutions, which rewards professors more for their research and publications than it does for their teaching.

Sociologists work in a number of capacities for a variety of private, state, and federal agencies. Criminologists are hired by institutions (prisons, reformatories) and by departments of correction. Population experts are valuable in a policy-making capacity for a number of agencies. Sociologists act as consultants to cities for recreation programs, city planning, urban renewal, mass transit, etc. The services of specialists in marriage and the family are used by schools, churches, and social agencies, and some sociologists are involved in private marriage counseling. Today, even the with-it social movement will have a resident sociologist.

As a footnote, it might be pointed out that for some reason sociology is becoming increasingly popular today. Possibly this reflects the increasing importance of sociology and social science in a complex world and may indicate a discipline coming of age. Or it may be that people are more conscious than ever of social problems, and for better or worse, sociology is more and more identified as the discipline that deals with social problems. At any rate, it might be argued that the popularity of a discipline is reflected in the extent to which its concepts, terminology, and techniques are adopted by the society at large. This has happened with psychology in the past and is happening to a marked degree with sociology today. There is a tendency to popularize aspects of sociology, and for columnists, novelists, and politicians to talk like sociologists. To a degree, then, sociology today is what *non*-sociologists are doing. . . .

Sociology and You

What good has this time spent in sociology done you? For one thing, with any luck at all you are three or four units closer to that piece of paper that you came to college to collect. Maybe that is enough justification, but possibly something more has occurred. Admittedly it is hard to measure what might have happened. If the subject were typing and you had progressed from two words a minute to eighty, there would be tangible evidence of success. Since the subject is sociology, if you went out and solved eight social problems during summer vacation that might prove that the course had taught something. The problem is, however, that we are not teaching a skill or a technique, but a viewpoint. And it is sometimes difficult to measure the immediate usefulness of a new viewpoint or a new way of looking at things.

After a semester of introductory sociology, members of the class will probably know more about the world they live in. They will certainly know more facts about that world—mainly because they will have stayed up until all hours several nights during the semester frantically trying to sponge up facts for the next day's test. But principally, it seems to me that what they should have discovered from the course is a way of looking at the world and at themselves. As C. Wright Mills commented, the study of sociology may provide you with a self-consciousness.[9] You have a means for evaluating yourself as more than an isolated individual in a sea of humanity. The study of sociology may help you place yourself and history in perspective. You may more accurately identify and evaluate the factors that affect your behavior and the behavior of others. You may become more critical and evaluative of aspects of the world that heretofore you took for granted.

"Who am I?" and "How did I get this way?" are questions that are difficult to answer to anyone's satisfaction. Perhaps a sociological viewpoint will help deal with these questions and perhaps it won't. If the sociological viewpoint only helps to make you more aware of your social environment and some of the forces at work there, it has been worthwhile, for this will provide you with a greater understanding and compassion for others.

[9] Mills, *The Sociological Imagination,* Chapter 1.

Annotated Bibliography

The following books may be helpful for greater understanding of the ideas and concepts presented in this book. All books are available in paperback.

1 Introduction

Bronowski, J., *The Common Sense of Science* (New York: Random House). A short, interesting history of science.

Brown, Robert, *Explanation in Social Science* (Chicago: Aldine, 1963). A detailed, systematic analysis of how social-science research is done.

Chase, Stuart, *The Proper Study of Mankind* (New York: Harper & Row, Publishers, 1956). An analysis of social science: what it attempts to do, its methods of inquiry, and the characteristics of individual social-science disciplines.

Kuhn, Thomas, *The Structure of Scientific Revolutions,* 2nd ed. (Chicago: University of Chicago Press, 1970). Kuhn describes the development of scientific knowledge in terms of revolutions between competing paradigms or viewpoints.

McCain, Garvin, and Erwin Segal, *The Game of Science,* 2nd ed. (Monterey, Calif.: Brooks/Cole Publishing Co., 1973). A very readable description of the characteristics of science and of scientists.

Ravetz, Jerome, *Scientific Knowledge and Its Social Problems* (New York: Oxford University Press, 1971). A thorough evaluation and critique of the scientific establishment.

Sklair, Leslie, *Organized Knowledge* (Bungay England: The Chaucer Press, 1973). Sklair deals with the question of social responsibility in scientific endeavor. He demonstrates that science is the most important basis on which knowledge is organized in the modern world, and he examines the political consequences that science and technology have for societies.

Watson, J. D., *The Double Helix* (New York: Signet). A fascinating account of competition and cooperation among scientists and the process of scientific discovery.

There are numerous short books that deal with social science research methodology. For example, see:

Labovitz, Sanford, and Robert Hagedorn, *Introduction to Social Research* (New York: McGraw-Hill, 1971).

Wallace, Walter, *The Logic of Science in Sociology* (Chicago: Aldine, 1971).

2 Socialization and Self

Aronson, Elliot, *The Social Animal* (San Francisco: W. H. Freeman and Co., 1972). This interesting and well-written book outlines the ideas and theories

345

of the field of social psychology. Aronson defines the field and discusses such topics as conformity, self, and sensitivity-training groups.

Berger, Peter L., and Thomas Luckmann, *The Social Construction of Reality* (Garden City, N.Y.: Doubleday & Co., 1966). This short but influential book covers primary and secondary socialization, social interaction, and society as objective and subjective reality.

Elkin, Frederick, *The Child and Society* (New York: Random House, 1960). Elkin defines socialization, describes its processes and agencies, and analyzes socialization in subcultural patterns and in later life.

Erikson, Erik, *Childhood and Society,* 2nd ed. (New York: W. W. Norton & Co., 1963). A study of the social significance of childhood by one of the leading figures in the field of psychoanalysis and human development.

Goffman, Erving, *The Presentation of Self in Everyday Life* (Garden City, N.Y.: Doubleday & Co., 1959). A very readable, interesting analysis of the self. Goffman uses the language of the theater to describe how each of us presents himself to others and attempts to manipulate the impressions others have of him.

Goffman, Erving, *Stigma* (Englewood Cliffs, N.J.: Prentice-Hall, 1963). Goffman deals with the physically deformed, the ex-mental patient, the drug addict, the prostitute; he analyzes the stigmatized individual's feelings about himself, his relationship to others, and his management of his self-image.

Socialization and development of self can be observed in many biographical and autobiographical works. For example, see:

Frank, Anne, *Anne Frank: The Diary of a Young Girl* (New York: Pocket Books).

Gibson, William, *Miracle Worker* (New York: Alfred A. Knopf, 1957).

Keller, Helen, *The Story of My Life* (New York: Dell).

Malcolm X and Alex Haley, *The Autobiography of Malcolm X* (New York: Grove Press, 1966).

See also descriptions of socialization into occupations. The following come to mind:

Greenwald, Harold, *The Elegant Prostitute* (New York: Ballantine Books, 1970).

Niederhoffer, Arthur, *Behind the Shield* (Garden City, N.Y.: Doubleday & Co., 1967).

Smith, Dennis, *Report from Engine Co. 82* (New York: Pocket Books, 1972).

3 Norms, Roles, Culture

There are numerous anthropological studies of exotic primitive and contemporary cultures. For old standbys, see:

Benedict, Ruth, *Patterns of Culture* (Boston: Houghton Mifflin Co., 1934).

Mead, Margaret, *Sex and Temperament* (New York: William Morrow & Co., 1935).

Riesman, D., N. Glazer, and R. Denney, *The Lonely Crowd* (Garden City, N.Y.: Doubleday & Co., 1953). A study of changing American character that put the terms "inner-directed," "other-directed," and "tradition-directed" into our vocabulary.

Ruesch, Hans, *Top of the World* (New York: Pocket Books, 1951). A novel, closely based on fact, which details the fascinating and unusual culture of the Eskimos.

A number of novelists have offered us a glimpse of cultures of the future:

Heinlein, R. A., *Stranger in a Strange Land* (New York: Medallion, 1968).

Huxley, Aldous, *Brave New World* (New York: Harper & Row, Publishers).

Orwell, George, *1984* (New York: New American Library).

Skinner, B. F., *Walden Two* (New York: Macmillan Co., 1969).

4 Groups, Categories, Aggregations

Blau, Peter, and Marshall Meyer, *Bureaucracy in Modern Society,* 2nd ed. (New York: Random House, 1971). An analysis of what sociologists know about large formal organizations in theory and in practice.

Perrow, Charles, *Organizational Analysis: A Sociological View* (Monterey, Calif.: Brooks/Cole Publishing Co., 1970). An analysis of formal organizations covering such topics as contrasting levels of bureaucratization, the structure and functioning of organizations, the nature of organizational goals and the strategies used to achieve them.

There are several short texts that summarize the research and theoretical knowledge available in the area of small groups:

Mills, Theodore, *The Sociology of Small Groups* (Englewood Cliffs, N.J.: Prentice-Hall, 1967).

Shepard, Clovis, *Small Groups* (San Francisco: Chandler Publishing Co., 1964).

Descriptions of small and primary group interaction appear in numerous works. For example, see:

Liebow, Elliot, *Tally's Corner* (Boston: Little, Brown and Co., 1967).

Whyte, William F., *Street Corner Society* (Chicago: University of Chicago Press, 1943).

A number of books satirize aspects of large bureaucratic organizations:

Parkinson, C. Northcote, *Parkinson's Law* (New York: Ballantine Books, 1964).

Peter, L. J., and R. Hull, *The Peter Principle* (New York: Bantam Books, 1970).

5 Social Differentiation

Blau, Zena Smith, *Old Age in a Changing Society* (New York: New Viewpoints, 1973). A detailed analysis of the problems facing older people in a postindustrial society.

Brown, Claude, *Manchild in the Promised Land* (New York: Signet Books, 1966). An autobiography by a black who made it out of the slums of Harlem. Brown provides an insider's view of the black ghetto that is both brutal and humorous.

Brown, Dee, *Bury My Heart at Wounded Knee* (New York: Bantam/Holt, Rinehart and Winston, 1971). Describes how the American Indian was sacrificed to the doctrine of Manifest Destiny—the idea that whites are the dominant race and therefore destined to rule all of America.

De La Garza, Rudolph, Anthony Kruszewski, and Tomas Arciniega, *Chicanos and Native Americans: The Territorial Minorities* (Englewood Cliffs, N.J.: Prentice-Hall, 1973). A series of readings that examine the diverse social, educational, and governmental problems that affect Chicanos and Native Americans. New solutions are outlined which are urgently needed to avoid continued confrontations and strife.

Frazier, E. Franklin, *Black Bourgeoisie* (New York: The Free Press, 1957). An analysis of the frustrations and insecurities of a new middle class—American Negroes.

Gans, Herbert J., *The Urban Villagers* (New York: Free Press, 1962). A participant observation study of Italian-Americans in Boston's West End.

Greer, Germaine, *The Female Eunuch* (New York: McGraw-Hill/Bantam, 1971). Greer's central thesis is that as wives, employees, mothers, and lovers, women are not only still body and soul in bondage to men, but are deformed by them—made into eunuchs.

Hunter, Floyd, *Community Power Structure* (Garden City, N.Y.: Doubleday & Co., 1963). Hunter studies power as an aspect of stratification; he describes those who make the important decisions in a large Southern city.

Knowles, Louis, and Kenneth Prewitt, eds. *Institutional Racism in America* (Englewood Cliffs, N.J.: Prentice-Hall, 1969). This book reveals how numerous institutions under white control deny blacks a relevant education, a voice in the political process, the right of economic self-determination, just treatment under the law, and decent health care.

Liebow, Elliot, *Tally's Corner* (Boston: Little, Brown and Co., 1967). A participant observation study of lower-class Negro streetcorner men in Washington, D.C.

Morgan, Robin, ed., *Sisternood Is Powerful* (New York: Vintage, 1970). A comprehensive collection of writings from the Women's Liberation Movement, including articles, poems, photographs, and manifestos.

Nava, Julian, *Viva La Raza!* (New York: D. Van Nostrand Co., 1973). An anthology designed to acquaint readers with the history and cultural past of the Mexican-American.

Schnore, Leo F., *Class and Race in Cities and Suburbs* (Chicago: Markham Publishing Co., 1972). A short statistical study comparing city and suburban population characteristics.

Shostak, Arthur, *Blue-Collar Life* (New York: Random House, 1969). An exhaustive study of the blue-collar or working class in America

Silberman, Charles E., *Crisis in Black and White* (New York: Vintage, 1964) Highly acclaimed book which examines the situation of the Negro in America. Silberman disputes the theories of some of the "authorities," and gives special attention to the problem of identification that confronts blacks.

Van Der Slik, Jack, ed., *Black Conflict with White America* (Columbus, Ohio: Merrill Publishing Co., 1970). Articles deal with competition, co-optation, confrontation, combat, and possibilities for the future.

Whyte, William H., Jr., *The Organization Man* (Garden City, N.Y.: Doubleday & Co., 1956). This classic work describes the new life style of Americans—life under the protection of the big organization. According to Whyte, modern Americans find jobs in large organizations that promise security and a high standard of living; in doing so, they give up the hopes and ambitions that dominated earlier generations of Americans.

Many novels use social-class characteristics and life styles as a basic theme:

Marquand, John P., *Point of No Return* (New York: Little, Brown and Co., 1949).

O'Hara, John, almost any work.

Schulberg, Budd, *What Makes Sammy Run?* (New York: Modern Library).

Wilson, Sloan, *Man in the Grey Flannel Suit* (New York: Pocket Books).

6 Institutions

The following books deal with various aspects of the institution of the family:

Billingsley, Andrew, *Black Families in White America* (Englewood Cliffs, N.J.: Prentice-Hall, 1968). An analysis of the history, structure, aspirations, and problems of black families in a white-controlled society.

Cuber, John F., and Peggy B. Harroff, *Sex and the Significant Americans* (Baltimore: Penguin Books, 1965). The authors describe five categories of marital adjustment that they discovered when they interviewed 437 upper-middle-class men and women.

Delora, Joann S. and Jack, eds., *Intimate Life Styles: Marriage and Its Alternatives* (Pacific Palisades, Calif.: Goodyear Publishing Co., 1972). The articles in this book analyze traditional forms of courtship and marriage in the United States along with emerging patterns of interaction involving intimacy and sex. Predictions are made regarding forms which sexual and erotic behavior will take in the future.

Goode, William J., *The Family* (Englewood Cliffs, N.J.: Prentice-Hall, 1964). A theoretical treatment of the family, dealing with mate selection, illegitimacy, family roles, and divorce.

Gordon, Michael, ed., *The Nuclear Family in Crisis: The Search for an Alternative* (New York: Harper & Row, 1972). The articles in this book deal with the family in the kibbutz, the family in socialist and welfare nations, and the current communal movement and group marriage.

Spiro, Melford E., *Children of the Kibbutz* (New York: Schocken Books, 1965). A study of child training and personality on an Israeli kibbutz, where children are raised by the community.

The following books deal with aspects of the institution of religion:

Berger, Peter, *A Rumor of Angels* (New York: Doubleday & Co., 1970). Sociologist Berger attempts to deal with the question of whether theological thinking is possible at all today, and, if it is, in what way.

Hadden, Jeffrey K., *The Gathering Storm in the Churches* (New York: Doubleday & Co., 1970). Hadden describes the growing conflict between clergy and laymen that threatens the traditional role and influence of the church in a modern secular world.

Heenan, Edward, ed., *Mystery, Magic, and Miracle: Religion in a Post-Aquarian Age* (Englewood Cliffs, N.J.: Prentice-Hall, 1973). A chronicle of the varieties of religious experience in the 1970s from "the cabalistic cult of Satanism to the fusion of religion and rock music, from the Americanization of Eastern mysticism to the exuberant exhortations of the Jesus freaks." Heenan analyzes the future of this modern religious revival by means of the elements of mystery, magic, and miracle.

Herberg, Will, *Protestant-Catholic-Jew* (New York: Doubleday & Co., 1960). An interesting analysis of the religions of America.

7 Population and Ecology

Brown, Harrison, and Edward Hutchings, Jr., eds., *Are Our Descendants Doomed?* (New York: Viking Press, 1972). This collection of papers resulted from a conference at Cal Tech and deals with the problems of rapid population growth, the distribution of human population, technological change, economic development, the environment, and the individual desires of human beings.

Ehrlich, Paul, *The Population Bomb* (New York: Ballantine Books, 1968). Biologist Ehrlich describes the crisis of overpopulation that faces us and evaluates our prospects of surviving it.

Petersen, William, *The Politics of Population* (Garden City, N.Y.: Anchor, 1964). A series of essays by a population expert on how population relates to social policy, especially in such fields as social welfare, urban planning, and international migration. Also examines the theories of Malthus, Marx, and Keynes.

Pohlman, Edward, ed., *Population: A Clash of Prophets* (New York: Mentor, 1973). Current readings—mostly from popular sources—on the population question. Includes a section on Third World reactions to population issues.

Stanford, Quentin H., ed., *The World's Population* (New York: Oxford University Press, 1972). Provides world population data, considers the roots of the population crisis, and discusses solutions.

Vidich, Arthur, and Joseph Bensman, *Small Town in Mass Society* (Garden City, N.Y.: Doubleday & Co., 1958). A study of a small rural community striving to maintain its own identity in a mass society.

Warner, Sam Bass, Jr., *The Urban Wilderness* (New York: Harper & Row, 1972). An interesting book describing the historical development of the American city.

Weber, Max, *The City* (New York: The Free Press, 1958). A classic sociological analysis of the development of cities in Western civilization.

Wrong, Dennis, *Population and Society,* 2nd ed. (New York: Random House, 1961). A short basic text dealing with population concepts and variables.

A number of books analyze the problems of the city: urban sprawl, urban renewal, race and class conflict, municipal services, overcrowding, ugliness, mass transit, and so on. The following are among the best:

Banfield, Edward, *The Unheavenly City* (Boston: Little, Brown and Co., 1970).

Downs, Anthony, *Urban Problems and Prospects* (Chicago: Markham Publishing Co., 1970).

Gabree, John, ed., *Surviving the City* (New York: Ballantine Books, 1973).

Gordon, Mitchell, *Sick Cities* (Baltimore: Penguin Books, 1963).

Haar, Charles M., ed., *The End of Innocence: A Suburban Reader* (Glenview, Ill.: Scott, Foresman and Co., 1972).

Jacobs, Jane, *The Death and Life of Great American Cities* (New York: Vintage Books, 1961).

Starr, Roger, *Urban Choices* (Baltimore: Penguin Books, 1966).

8 Social Change and Social Disorganization

Gusfield, Joseph R., ed., *Protest, Reform, and Revolt: A Reader in Social Movements* (New York: John Wiley & Sons, 1970). An excellent source book on all aspects of social movements.

Hoffer, Eric, *The Ordeal of Change* (New York: Harper & Row, Publishers, 1964). An interesting if somewhat one-sided analysis of the causes and consequences of social change by the longshoreman-philosopher.

Hoffer, Eric, *The True Believer* (New York: Harper & Row, 1951). The most famous of Hoffer's books deals with mass movements from the viewpoint of the true believer, the man compelled to join a cause, any cause.

King, C. Wendell, *Social Movements in the United States* (New York: Random House, 1956). A short but thorough analysis of social movements, including their relationships to mass society, their careers, growth factors, and purposes and consequences.

McGee, Reece, *Social Disorganization in America* (San Francisco: Chandler Publishing Co., 1962). McGee analyzes the disorganized individual, the disorganized group, the disorganized organization, and the disorganized society. He sees social disorganization as arising from two conditions: group conflict and anomie. He also provides an excellent short summary of Meadian social psychology.

Moore, Wilbert E., *Social Change* (Englewood Cliffs, N.J.: Prentice-Hall, 1963). A short but comprehensive sociological analysis of social change.

Slater, Philip, *The Pursuit of Loneliness* (Boston: Beacon Press, 1970). Slater focuses on our subservience to technology and the disastrous effect this attitude is having on the quality of life in the United States. He suggests some ways that American society might be changed to avoid even further alienation and disaffection.

Toffler, Alvin, *Future Shock* (New York: Random House/Bantam, 1970). Toffler discusses the social and psychological implications of the technological revolution—the problems of people and groups who are overwhelmed by change in the emerging superindustrial world.

Books making projections about social change of the future include:

Phillips, Bernard S., *Worlds of the Future* (Columbus, Ohio: Merrill Publishing Co., 1972).

Theobald, Robert, *Futures Conditional* (New York: Bobbs-Merrill, 1972).

9 Collective Behavior

Cantril, Hadley, *The Invasion from Mars* (New York: Harper & Row, Publishers, 1940). A Study of the collective, behavior, rumor, mass communication, and panic that resulted from Orson Welles' 1938 radio dramatization of *The War of the Worlds*.

Chaplin, J. P., *Rumor, Fear and the Madness of Crowds* (New York: Ballantine Books, 1959). Chaplin describes in detail eleven instances of mass collective behavior, including examples of mass hysteria, rumor, crowd, mob, and riot behavior. The cases range from the death of Valentino to Martians in New Jersey, from flying saucers to high treason in the State Department.

Hersey, John, *Hiroshima* (New York: Bantam Books, 1959). A journalistic account of the dropping of an atomic bomb. A fascinating and horrifying description of the process and aftermath of a disaster.

Report of the National Advisory Commission on Civil Disorders (New York: Bantam Books, 1968). The report of the Kerner Commission provides a comprehensive analysis of the riots that occurred in the United States during the summer of 1967.

Schultz, Duane, *Panic Behavior* (New York: Random House, 1964). A comprehensive analysis of panic, including a discussion of a number of theories of panic behavior in relation to actual disaster situations.

Skolnick, Jerome, *The Politics of Protest* (New York: Ballantine Books, 1969). The last chapter of this report of the National Commission on the Causes and Prevention of Violence provides an excellent short analysis of collective behavior concepts.

10 · Deviation and Social Control

Becker, Howard S., ed., *The Other Side* (New York: The Free Press, 1964). A series of essays by authors who, like Becker, use the labeling perspective to explain deviant behavior. The essays, which deal with a variety of types of deviant behavior, generally follow the proposition that deviance is a product of group definitions, not a product of something inherent in the act itself.

Clark, Ramsey, *Crime in America* (New York: Pocket Books, 1970). Straightforward and easy-to-read observations on the nature, causes, prevention, and control of crime in America by the former Attorney General.

Erikson, Kai, *Wayward Puritans* (New York: John Wiley, 1966). Erikson applies current theories of deviant behavior to the seventeenth-century Puritans of Massachusetts Bay. Using historical documents, he illustrates how deviant behavior served to define social boundaries and to help keep the social order intact. Crime statistics are analyzed to demonstrate that, even for the Puritans, the number of deviant offenders a community can afford to recognize is likely to remain fairly stable over time.

Rubington, Earl, and Martin Weinberg, *Deviance: The Interactionist Perspective*, 2nd ed. (New York: Macmillan Co., 1973). Readings on the interactionist or labeling perspective with sections on the social deviant, the public regulation of deviance, deviant subcultures, and deviant identity.

Schur, Edwin, *Our Criminal Society* (Englewood Cliffs, N.J.: Prentice-Hall, 1969). A short, readable, comprehensive overview of crime in American society. Schur deals with types and causes of crime, misleading use of crime statistics, and our tendency to create unnecessary crime by over-legislating.

The following selections present good analyses of social control agencies, such as the police and prison systems:

Niederhoffer, Arthur, *Behind the Shield* (Garden City, N.Y.: Doubleday & Co., 1967). Niederhoffer, a former member of the New York City police, describes the profession. He calls special attention to some attitudes—authoritarianism and cynicism—that police officers develop.

Sykes, Gresham M., *The Society of Captives* (New York: Atheneum, 1958). A short but thorough analysis of an American maximum-security prison.

Wambaugh, Joseph, *The New Centurians* (Boston: Little, Brown and Co., 1970). An interesting novel on police work during the time of the Watts riots, written by a Los Angeles police officer.

Wilson, James Q., *Varieties of Police Behavior* (New York: Atheneum, 1970). Wilson studies communities in the United States, identifies the major problems that police agencies face, and describes three styles of police behavior that seem to emerge.

There are numerous good analyses of specific types of criminal and deviant behavior:

Cressey, Donald, *Other People's Money* (Belmont, Calif.: Wadsworth Publishing Co., 1971).

Greenwald, Harold, *The Elegant Prostitute* (New York: Ballantine Books, 1970).

Jackson, Bruce, *Outside the Law· A Thief's Primer* (New Brunswick, N.J.: Transaction Books, 1972).

Maas, Peter, *The Valachi Papers* (New York: Bantam Books, 1968).

Maris, Ronald, *Social Forces in Urban Suicide* (Homewood, Ill.: Dorsey Press, 1969).

Sutherland, Edwin, *White Collar Crime* (New York: Holt, Rinehart and Winston, 1949).

Talese, Gay, *Honor Thy Father* (Greenwich, Conn.: Fawcett Crest, 1971).

Thompson, Hunter, *Hell's Angels* (New York: Ballantine Books, 1966).

Wallace, Samuel, *Skid Row as a Way of Life* (New York: Harper & Row, 1965).

11   What Is Sociology?

Berger, Peter L., *Invitation to Sociology* (Garden City, N.Y.: Doubleday & Co., 1963). For Berger, sociology is a form of consciousness. This consciousness determines how sociologists behave and how they see the world. In describing what sociology is, Berger's focus is the humanistic perspective.

Mills, C. Wright, *The Sociological Imagination* (New York: Grove Press, 1961). Mills provides a searching critique and analysis of what sociology is and what it should be. He challenges the approaches represented by "grand theorists" and "abstracted empiricists" and describes the perspective and approach that he feels best embodies the sociological imagination.

These two books are recent collections of essays that evaluate and criticize sociology from a variety of viewpoints:

Douglas, Jack, ed., *The Relevance of Sociology* (New York: Appleton-Century-Crofts, 1970).

Reynolds, Larry, and Janice Reynolds, eds., *The Sociology of Sociology* (New York: David McKay Co., 1970).

The following two books focus on social research. A number of projects are described. We see the problems sociologists study, the methods they use, the answers they find, and the mistakes they make.

Hammond, Phillip, ed., *Sociologists at Work* (New York: Doubleday & Co., 1967).

Madge, John, *The Origins of Scientific Sociology* (New York: The Free Press, 1962).

Glossary

Acculturation: The process of assimilating, blending in, and taking on the characteristics of another culture.

Achieved status: Position in society that is earned or achieved in some way.

Aggregate: A number of people clustered together in one place.

Amalgamation: Refers to biological (rather than cultural) mixing.

Annihilation: Elimination of one group by another.

Anomie: A state of normlessness; a condition in which the norms and rules governing men's aspirations and moral conduct have disintegrated.

Anticipatory socialization: Occurs when a person adopts the values, behavior, or viewpoints of a group he would like to, but does not yet, belong to.

Ascribed status: Position automatically conferred on the individual through no choice of his own; status he is born with.

Assimilation: Mixing and merging of unlike cultures so that the two groups come to have a common culture.

Bilateral descent: Ancestry is traced through both males and females equally.

Bilocal residence: Married couple lives with the wife's and husband's families, alternating between them.

Bureaucracy (formal organization): An organization in which the activities of some people are systematically planned by other people in order to achieve some special purpose; usually involves such characteristics as division of labor, hierarchy of authority, system of rules, impersonality, and technical efficiency.

Category: A number of people who have a particular characteristic in common.

Centralization: The tendency of people to gather around some central or pivotal point in a city.

Charisma: A quality in an individual that sets him apart from others so that he is viewed as superhuman and capable of exceptional acts.

Church: A large and highly organized religious organization that represents and supports the *status quo,* is respectable, and in which membership is automatic; one is born into a church.

Collective behavior: Spontaneous, unstructured, and unstable group behavior.

Compound family: The family resulting from polygamy; marriages involving multiple spouses—several wives and/or husbands at the same time.

Conjugal family: Family members related by marital ties.

Consanguine family: Family members related by blood ties.

Contraculture: Similar to subculture, but with the idea of opposition to or conflict with the norms and values of the dominant culture. Some customs and norms of the subculture differ from those of the dominant culture; customs and norms of the contraculture conflict with those of the dominant culture.

Criminal behavior: Behavior prohibited by law and subject to formal punishment.

Crowd: A temporary collection of people in close physical contact reacting together to a common stimulus.

Cult: A religious organization that is a small, short-lived, often local group, that is frequently built around a dominant leader. The cult is smaller, less organized, and more transitory than the sect.

Cultural lag: Phenomenon that occurs when related segments of society change at different rates.

Cultural pluralism: A pattern of interaction in which unlike cultures maintain their own identity and yet interact with each other relatively peacefully.

Cultural relativism: Opposite of ethnocentrism: suggests that each culture be judged from its own viewpoint without imposing outside standards of judgment.

Culture: The complex set of learned and shared beliefs, customs, skills, habits, traditions, and knowledge common to the members of a society; the "social heritage" of a society.

Demography: The study of human population, its distribution, composition, and change.

Dependent variable: The "effect" variable; that quantity or aspect of the study whose change the researcher wants to understand.

Deviant behavior: Behavior contrary to generally accepted norms; limits are often established by custom or public opinion, sometimes by law.

Diffusion: The spread of objects or ideas from one society to another or from one group to another within the same society, resulting in changes in society.

Disaster: A situation in which there is a basic disruption of the social context within which individuals and groups function; a radical departure from the pattern of normal expectations.

Discrimination: Actual behavior resulting in unfavorable and unequal treatment of individuals or groups.

Ethnic group: People bound together by cultural ties.

Ethnocentrism: A type of prejudice which maintains that one's own culture's ways are right and other cultures' ways that are different are wrong.

Expulsion: Removal of a group from the territory in which it resides.

Extended family: More than two generations of the same family living together in close association or under the same roof.

Fads: The relatively short-term "obsessions" that members of a society or members of specific groups have toward specific behaviors or objects.

Family of orientation: The family one is born into.

Family of procreation: The family of which one is a parent.

Fashion: Temporary attachment to specific behaviors, styles, or objects; similar to fads but more widespread and of longer duration.

Folkways: Norms that are less obligatory than mores, the "shoulds" of society; sanctions for violation are mild.

Gemeinschaft: Primary, closely-knit society in which relationships are personal and informal and there is a commitment to or identification with the community.

Generalized other: The individual's conception of the sum of the viewpoints and expectations of the social group or community to which he belongs.

Gesellschaft: Secondary society based on contractual arrangements, bargaining, a well-developed division of labor, and on rational thought rather than emotion.

Group: A number of people who have shared or patterned interaction and who feel bound together by a "consciousness of kind" or a "we" feeling.

Horizontal mobility: Movement from one occupation to another within the same social class; also used to refer to spatial or geographical mobility.

Human ecology: The adaptation of people to their physical environment, their location in space.

Hypothesis: A testable statement or proposition used to guide an investigation.

Ideal norm: How a person should behave in a particular situation.

Independent variable: The "cause" variable; that quantity or aspect of the study that seems to produce change in another variable.

Institution: An organized system of social relationships that embodies some common values and procedures and meets some basic needs of society.

Invasion: The penetration of one group or function into an area dominated by another group or function.

Invention: Change introduced through the creation of a new object or idea.

Looking-glass self: Attitudes toward self derived from one's interpretations of how others are evaluating self.

Matriarchal authority: Decisions are made by females.

Matrilineal descent: Ancestry is traced through females.

Matrilocal residence: Married couple lives with the wife's family.

Minority status: People treated as lower in social ranking and subject to domination by other segments of the population.

Mob: A focused, acting crowd, emotionally aroused, intent on taking aggressive action.

Monogamy: Marriage with one person at a time.

Mores: Obligatory norms, the "musts" of society; sanctions are harsh if these are violated.

Neolocal residence: Married couple lives apart from both wife's and husband's families.

Norm: The accepted or required behavior for a person in a particular situation.

Nuclear family: A married couple and their children.

Panic: Non-adaptive or non-rational flight resulting from extreme fear and loss of self-control.

Patriarchal authority: Decisions are made by males.

Patrilineal descent: Ancestry is traced through males.

Patrilocal residence: Married couple lives with the husband's family.

Peer group: Consists of people of relatively the same age, interests, and social position with whom one has reasonably close association and contact.

Polyandry: A form of polygamy in which one woman has several husbands at a time.

Polygamy: Plural marriage; the practice of having more than one husband or wife at a time.

Polygyny: A form of polygamy in which one man has several wives at a time.

Prejudice: Favorable or unfavorable attitudes toward a person or group, not based on actual experience.

Primary group: A group in which contacts between members are intimate, personal, and face-to-face.

Primary socialization: The first socialization an individual undergoes in childhood, through which he becomes a member of society. It ends with the establishment of the "generalized other."

Propaganda: Attempts to influence and change the public's viewpoint on an issue.

Public: A number of people who have an interest in, and difference of opinion about, a common issue.

Race: People related by common descent or heredity; usually identified by hereditary physical features.

Reference groups: Groups that serve as models for our behavior, groups whose perspectives we assume and mold our behavior after.

Reform movement: Seeks modification in certain aspects of society.

Revolutionary movement: Seeks a complete change in the social order.

Riot: A situation in which mob behavior becomes increasingly widespread and destructive.

Role: The behavior of one who occupies a particular status or position in society.

Role conflict: When a person occupies several statuses or positions that have contradictory role requirements.

Role requirements: Norms specifying the expected behavior of persons holding a particular position in society.

Role strain: When there are differing and conflicting expectations regarding one's status or position.

Rumor: Unconfirmed, although not necessarily false, person-to-person communication.

Sample: A selection of a few from a larger universe. The sample may or may not be representative of the whole depending on how it is selected.

Sanction: The punishment one receives for violation of a norm (or the reward granted for compliance with norms).

Secondary group: Group in which contacts between members are more impersonal than in a primary group; interaction is more superficial and probably based on utilitarian goals.

Secondary socialization: Takes over where primary socialization leaves off. Involves internalizing knowledge of new areas and new sectors of life, of special skills and techniques.

Sect: Small religious organization that is less organized than the church, in which membership is voluntary. Members of sects usually show greater depth and fervor in their religious commitment than members of churches.

Segregation: 1) Group conflict context: The setting apart of one group. 2) Ecological context: The clustering together of similar people.

Self: One's awareness of and ideas and attitudes about his own personal and social identity.

Self-fulfilling prophecy: Occurs when a false definition of a situation evokes a new behavior which makes the originally false conception come true.

Sex ratio: Number of males per 100 females.

Significant other: The individual's conception of the viewpoints and expectations of particularly important people (mother, father, older brother, etc.).

Social change: Change in the structure and functioning of the social relationships of a society.

Social control: The processes, planned or unplanned, by which people are made to conform to collective norms.

Social disorganization: The condition resulting when norms and roles break down and customary ways of behaving no longer operate.

Social interaction: The process of being aware of others when we act, of modifying our behavior in accordance with others' responses.

Socialization: The social process whereby one learns the expectations, habits, skills, values, beliefs, and other requirements necessary for effective participation in social groups.

Social movement: A group of people acting with some continuity to promote or to resist a change in their society or group.

Social organization: The "social fabric" of society; the integrated net of norms, roles, cultural values, and beliefs through which people interact with each other, individually and in groups.

Society: A number of people who have lived together long enough to become organized to some degree and who share a common culture.

Statistical norm: How a person actually behaves in a particular situation.

Status: A position in society or in a group.

Status inconsistency: When the factors that determine an individual's rank in society are not consistent with each other—for example, a college-educated carpenter, or a Negro court justice.

Stratification: The division of people in society into layers or ranks. The source of the ranking may be one or a combination of factors: wealth, power, prestige, race, sex, age, religion, and so on.

Subculture: Groups or segments of society that share many of the characteristics of the dominant culture, but that have some of their own specific customs or ways that tend to separate them from the rest of society.

Succession: The complete displacement or removal of an established group; the end product of invasion.

Vertical mobility: Movement up or down the social class ladder.

Index

Abortion, 234, 300
Achieved status, 50
Age:
  and crime, 301
  and stratification, 112
  and U.S. population, 199
Aggregate, defined, 82
Alcoholism, 127, 297–298, 300, 319–323
Allport, Gordon, 129–130
Altruistic suicide, 299
Amalgamation, 129
Amish, 56, 129
Anderson, Barbara, 319
Androcentrism, 247, 250
Annihilation, 128
Anomic suicide, 299
Anomie, 46, 237–238
Anticipatory socialization, 122
Apollonian, 54
Arapesh, 52, 164
Asch, Solomon, 88
Ascribed status, 50
Assimilation, 129
Audience, 261
Authoritarian personality, 124–125
Autokinetic effect, 88
Autosystems, 182–189
Azumi, Koya, 58

Bales, Robert, 85–86
Beals, Ralph, 339
Becker, Howard S., 229, 294, 303, 337
Bell, Daniel, 105
Benedict, Ruth, 54, 178
Bennis, Warren, 93–94
Berelson, Bernard, 207
Berger, Peter, 13, 17, 336–337, 341
Berry, Brewton, 122, 123, 128, 129
Bettelheim, Bruno, 12
Bierstedt, Robert, 49, 163, 230, 231, 236
Bilateral ancestry, 166
Bilocal residence, 166
Birth control, 209
Birth rates, 58–62, 198, 200–201, 207, 209, 210, 224–225, 231
Black Muslims, 252–258

Black Power, 130
Blau, Peter, 90
Bohannan, Laura, 73
Boskoff, Alvin, 229
Bourgeoisie, 115, 171
Bowen, Elenore, 73
Broom, Leonard, 12, 17, 53, 114–115, 174, 238, 259
Brown, Bertram, 127
Brown v. Board of Education, 126
Bureaucracy, 89–94
  characteristics of, 90
  See also Formal organizations

Cameron, Mary, 337
Campbell, Donald, 340
Capital punishment, 267–268
Carey, James T., 337
Category, 111
  defined, 82
  and group, 81–82, 111
Cavan, Ruth S., 56
Cavan, Sherri, 337
Centralization, 206
Charisma, 90–91, 235–236
Charismatic retinue, 90–91
Chavez, Cesar, 128
Chinoy, Ely, 82, 172
Church, 173
Church attendance, 174, 176
Cities:
  and the automobile, 210–211, 215–216
  and crime, 208
  and finances, 217–218
  and government, 213–214, 218–219
  location, 203, 219–220
  and migration to suburbs, 208–209
  and overcrowding, 212–221
  and problems, 210–211, 212–221
  and riots, 262
  and rural life compared, 207–208
  and social class, 204
  and social disorganization, 237
  spatial arrangement and economic competition, 204

Cities (continued)
   spatial arrangement and leisure, 206
   spatial arrangement and race, 204
   spatial arrangement and social class, 204
   spatial arrangement and social inter-action, 204–205
   spatial arrangement and social pathology, 205–206
   typical patterns, 203–204
   See also Population
Clarke, Alfred, 118
Class consciousness, 117, 132–134
Clinard, Marshall, 8, 297
Closed group, 84
Cloward, Richard, 119–120, 302
Cohen, Albert, 56, 119–120, 302
Collective behavior, defined, 259
Consciousness of kind, 82
Contraculture, 55–56
Cooley, Charles H., 15, 16, 20, 38, 44, 84, 91
Courtship and marriage, 178–182
Crime, 120, 127, 208, 298–301, 305, 327
Crowd:
   control of, 261
   defined, 260
   milling, 260
   types, 261
Cuber, John, 82, 117, 171
Cult, 173
Cultural lag, 232
Cultural pluralism, 129
Cultural relativism, 55, 73
Culture, 1, 51–56
   defined, 53
   material, 53
   non-material, 53
   and personality, 54
Cuzzort, R. P., 341

D'Antonio, William, 85, 88
Davis, Kingsley, 12, 114
Davis, Wayne H., 221
Death rates, 198, 201, 209
Decentralization, 206
Definition of the situation, 19
DeFleur, Lois, 85, 88
DeFleur, Melvin, 85, 88
Delinquent subculture, 56
Demographic transition, 209
Demography, 197

Denomination, 173
Dentler, Robert, 88
Deviant behavior:
   and criminal behavior, 299–301
   defined, 293–296
   explanations for, 301–302
   and small groups, 88–89
   and social change, 303
   and socialization, 296
Diffusion, 53, 70, 232
Dionysian, 54
Disaster, 264–265, 285–291
Discrimination:
   and American Indians, 127–129
   and Blacks, 125–127, 146–153
   defined, 124
   in education, 126–128
   explanations for, 125
   in housing, 127–128
   and Jews, 128
   and Mexican-Americans, 127–128
   reactions to, 128–131
   and women, 154–161
Divorce, 169, 207
Dobu, 178–179
Dorn, Dean S., 56
Drug use, 298, 300
Dryfoos, Robert J., Jr., 240
Duncan, Beverly, 204
Duncan, Otis Dudley, 204
Durkheim, Emile, 237–238, 299, 303

Ecclesia, 173
Ecological changes in the U.S., 207–208
Ecological processes, 198, 206–207
   See also Cities, Population
Ego, 15
Egoistic suicide, 299
Ehrlich, Paul, 210
Endogamy, 166
Erikson, Kai, 2, 88, 303
Ethnicity, defined, 124
Ethnocentrism, 55, 73, 77, 170
Exogamy, 166
Expulsion, 128–129

Fad, 264
Family:
   and authority, 167
   and change, 168–170
   compound, 167
   conjugal, 167

Family (continued)
  consanguine, 167
  and courtship and marriage, 165–166,
    183, 186–187
  extended, 167
  functions, 167–168, 183–186
  and instability, 169–170
  nuclear, 167
  of orientation, 167
  and primary relationships, 168–169
  of procreation, 167
  and rules of descent, 166
  and rules of residence, 166
  and socialization, 167
  and women's roles, 168
Fashion, 264
Fava, Sylvia, 204
Felony, 299–300
Finkbine, Sherri, 303
Folkways, 47, 304
Formal organizations, 89–94
  and change, 93–94
  consequences of, 92
  defined, 90
  types, 90–91
Freud, Sigmund, 15, 27, 157–160
Fritz, Charles, 264

Gallup, George, 174, 176, 268
Gambling, 300, 305
Garfinkel, Harold, 46
Gemeinschaft, 91–92, 236
General fertility rate, 200
Gerrard, Nathan L., 189
Gerth, H. H., 90, 113
Gesellschaft, 91–92, 236
Gist, Noel P., 204, 264
Glaser, Barney, 337
Glock, Charles, 171, 173–176
Gockel, Galen, 174
Gordon, Mitchell, 211
Gorman, Benjamin, 85
Gouldner, Alvin, 338
Graham, Billy, 254
Green, Arnold, 232
Griffin, John Howard, 146
Group marriage, 166
Groups:
  defined, 81–82
  and non-groups, 81–83
  types, 83–84

Hall, Calvin, 15
Harlow, Harry, 28
Harrington, Michael, 133
Hauser, Philip, 338
Hedonism, 118–119, 194–195
Heilbroner, Robert, 133
Herberg, Will, 176–177
Hodges, Harold M., Jr., 116–119, 122
Hoffer, Eric, 235
Holdren, John, 210
Hollingshead, August, 116–117
Hopper, Rex, 234
Horizontal group, 84
Horizontal mobility, 120–121
Horowitz, Irving, 339
Horton, Paul, 82, 163, 229, 259
Hoyt, Homer, 204
Hunt, Chester, 82, 163, 229, 259
Huxley, Aldous, 169
Hypothesis, 4

Id, 15
Ideal norms, 47–48
Ideational culture, 236
Immigration, 201
Incest taboo, 167
In-group, 83
Inner-directed, 54
Institutions:
  and change, 164
  defined, 163
Invasion, 207
Invention, 53, 70, 231–232
Involuntary group, 83
Isolates, 11–12

Juries, 89
Juvenile delinquency, 56, 119–120, 301

Kagan, Jerome, 27
Kahl, Joseph, 116–117
Kassebaum, Gene, 337
Keller, Helen, 21
Kenkel, William, 117
Kerner report, 126, 269
Killian, Lewis, 233–234, 236, 259, 261,
  263–264, 266
King, C. Wendell, 233
King, Martin Luther, Jr., 91, 126, 230,
  236
Kinsey, Alfred, 300
Kluckhohn, Clyde, 53
Kohn, Melvin, 119

Kvaraceus, William, 120
Kwakiutl, 54

Landis, Judson R., 5
Langer, Elinor, 88, 99, 340
Language, 18–19
Larsen, Otto, 82
Larson, Richard, 85
Law, 299–300, 304
Leaders, types of, 89
Lee, Harper, 280
Leslie, Gerald, 85
Liebow, Elliot, 95
Life expectancy, 127, 201
Lincoln, C. Eric, 252, 258
Lindzey, Gardner, 15
Linton, Ralph, 70
Lofland, John, 340
Lombroso, Cesare, 302
Looking-glass self, 16
Luckmann, Thomas, 13, 17
Lundberg, George, 82
Lunt, Paul S., 117
Lynd, Helen M., 117
Lynd, Robert S., 117

Malcolm X, 32, 255–256, 258
Malthus, Thomas, 209
Marginal man, 129
Marijuana, 298, 300
Marmor, Judd, 157
Martindale, Don, 341
Marx, Karl, 115, 117, 125, 161, 171,
    230, 236
Mass hysteria, 263
Mass society, 233–234, 266
Matriarchal, 167
Matricentric family, 168
Matrilineal ancestry, 166
Matrilocal residence, 166
Maxon, Bernard, 307–312
Maxwell, Gerald, 7
McMahan, C. T., 61
Mead, George Herbert, 13, 17, 18, 20,
    38, 44
Mead, Margaret, 52, 54, 178, 180
Mental deficiency, 296
Mental illness, 88, 118, 122, 207, 237,
    295–296
Merton, Robert, 19, 264
Meyer, Marshall, 90
Michelson, William, 205–206

Migration, 198, 201–202, 208, 214–215
Milgram, Stanley, 63
Miller, S. M., 338
Miller, Walter, 56, 119–120, 302
Mills, C. Wright, 90, 113–114, 339, 343
Minority status, defined, 122
Misdemeanor, 300
Mob, 261–262, 280–284
Monogamy, 166, 185
Moore, Wilbert, 114
Moreno, J. L., 86
Mores, 47, 304
Morris, Desmond, 211
Muhammad, Elijah, 252–254, 257–258
Mundugumor, 52, 180–181
Murdock, George P., 166

Narcotics, 298
Neolocal residence, 166
Neurosis, 296–297
Niederhoffer, Arthur, 14
Nisbet, Robert, 12, 82, 264
Normlessness, 46
Norms, 58
    defined, 46
    ideal, 47–48
    and laws, 47–48
    statistical, 47–48
Nuclear family, 167

Ogburn, William, 231
Ohlin, Lloyd, 119–120, 302
Open group, 84
Organized crime, 305
Orwell, George, 39
Other-directed, 54
Out-group, 83

Panic, 262–263, 265
Participant observation, 4, 88, 340
Patriarchal, 167
Patrilineal ancestry, 166
Patrilocal residence, 166
Payetter, G. C., 158
Peer group, 54, 84
Permanent group, 84
Personality, 14–15
    and culture, 54
    See also Self, Socialization
Peterson, Warren A., 264
Phillips, Derek, 339–340
Piaget, J., 27–29

Podhoretz, Norman, 132
Police behavior, 14, 269–277
Polling, 266–268
Polsky, Ned, 337
Polyandry, 166
Polygamy, 19, 73, 166
Polygyny, 166
Population:
  and age, 199–200
  and birth rates, 200, 201
  characteristics of U.S., 198–203, 208,
    221–226
  and death rates, 201
  density, 206, 210–211, 214–215, 221–
    226
  explosion, 209–210, 214, 221–226
  problems, 209–211, 221–226
  pyramids, 199–202
  and race, 199, 208
  redistribution, 210
  and religion, 199
  and social planning, 202–203
  world figures, 198, 209
  See also Cities
Power, 113–114
Prejudice:
  defined, 124
  origins of, 124–125
Prestige, 114
Primary group, 84–89, 91–92, 304
  defined, 84
Proletariat, 115
Propaganda, 266–268
Prostitution, 300, 305, 312–318
Psychosis, 297
Public, 265–268
Public opinion, 266–268
Putney, Snell, 182

Race:
  defined, 122–123
  and life expectancy, 201
  and migration, 208
  and population, 199, 208
Racism, 157
Rebelsky, Freda, 29
Reckless, Walter, 120, 301
Reference group, 84
Relative retardation, 30
Religion:
  and church attendance, 174, 176
  defined, 170–171

Religion (continued)
  and diversity of beliefs, 174–175
  and ethnocentrism, 170
  functions of, 171–172, 175–176,
    191–196
  and magic, 172
  membership estimates, 170
  and population, 199
  and science, 172, 175
  and secularization, 176–177
  and social class, 174, 189–196
  and social control, 172
  and socialization, 175
Replacement level, 200, 209
Riesman, David, 54
Riot, 262, 269–277
Role conflict, 50–51
Role requirements, 49
Role strain, 50–51
Roles:
  defined, 49
  and social interaction, 49–50
Rosenhan, D. L., 295
Rumor, 263–264, 270–273, 277–280

Sanctions, 47, 304
Scheff, Thomas, 337
Schrag, Clarence, 82
Schultz, Duane, 263
Schur, Edwin, 300–301
Schwartz, Richard, 340
Science:
  characteristics of, 3–5, 172, 175–176,
    339–341
  criticisms of, 339–341
Scott, Marvin, 337
Secondary group, 85
Sect, 173
Seechrest, Lee, 340
Segregation, 129, 204, 207
Self, 14–19, 39
  defined, 15
  development, 16–19
  and the generalized other, 13, 17
  and "I" and "me", 18
  and language, 18–19
  and significant others, 17
  and social movements, 254–256
  and taking the role of the other, 17
  See also Personality
Self-fulfilling prophecy, 19

Selznick, Philip, 12, 17, 53, 114–115, 174, 238, 259
Sensate culture, 236
Sex ratio, 61, 197–199
Sharp, Lauriston, 244
Sheley, Joseph, 5
Shepard, Clovis, 85, 89
Sherif, Muzafer, 88
Shostak, Arthur, 338
Simon, Julian, 266
Simpson, George, 238, 299
Sjoberg, Gideon, 339
Small groups, 84–89
    and leadership, 89
Smelser, Neil, 90
Social awareness test, 7–8
Social change:
    causes and related factors, 230–231
    consistent patterns, 236
    and cultural change, 229
    defined, 229
    and deviant behavior, 303
    rates, 232, 240–244
    resistance to, 240–244
    and social disorganization, 238–239, 244–251
    and social movements, 233–234
Social class:
    characteristics of classes, 116, 118–120, 132–134, 189–196
    and child training, 119
    and deviant behavior, 119–120, 302
    and fads and fashions, 264
    and juries, 89
    and leisure and recreation, 118
    and mental illness, 118
    number of classes, 115–117
    objectively determined, 117
    and prejudice, 125
    and religion, 174, 189–196
    reputationally determined, 117
    and spatial arrangement, 204
    subjectively determined, 117
    See also Stratification
Social control:
    defined, 303
    internal and external constraints, 304
    mechanisms of, 304
    and primary groups, 304
    and religion, 172
    and socialization, 304

Social disorganization, 237–239
    and cities, 237
    defined, 237
    and social change, 238–239, 244–251
Social interaction, 12
Socialization, 12–14, 21, 32, 84, 154–161, 167–168, 319–323, 336
    agents of, 13
    anticipatory, 14
    defined, 12
    primary, 13, 17
    secondary, 13–14, 17–18
    and social control, 304
Social mobility:
    and caste, 120–121
    consequences of, 121–122
    defined, 120–121
    and prejudice, 125
    process of, 120–121
Social movements, 233–234
    characteristics of, 252–258
    and the charismatic leader, 190, 252–258
    defined, 233
    life history of, 234–235
    revolutionary and reform, 234
    and riots, 269–277
Social organization, defined, 78–79
Social science, 1–2
Society, defined, 53
Sociogram, 86–87
Sociology, 5–7
    applied, 338
    characteristics of, 335–343
    defined, 6
    and the humanistic perspective, 340–341
    and the scientific perspective, 339–340
    as social philosophy, 340
Sociometry, 86–88
Sorokin, Pitirim, 236
Spaulding, John, 238, 299
Spengler, Oswald, 236
Spiegel, John, 285
Spitz, René, 29
Stark, Rodney, 171, 173–176
Statistical norms, 47–48
Status:
    achieved, 50
    ascribed, 50
    defined, 49
Status inconsistency, 114–115

Status symbols, 113, 144–146
Steiner, Gary, 207
Stereotype, 125, 161
Stern, Paula, 154
Stinchcombe, Arthur, 90–91
Strain for consistency, 232
Stratification:
  and age, 112
  and language, 141
  and manners, 132–143
  and power, 113–114
  and prestige, 114
  and race, 112
  and religion, 112
  and sex, 112
  and wealth, 113
  See also Social class
Strauss, Anselm, 337
Subculture, 55–56
Succession, 207
Suicide, 122, 127, 207, 298–300
Sullivan, Daryl, 5
Sumner, William G., 47, 233
Superstition, effects of, 58–62
Superego, 15
Sutherland, Edwin, 302, 305
Sykes, Gresham, 337

Tchambuli, 52
Temporary group, 84
Thomas, W. I., 19
Thomlinson, Ralph, 204, 207, 211
Thompson, Hunter S., 323

Toch, Hans, 89
Toffler, Alvin, 93–94
Tonnies, Ferdinand, 91, 236
Toynbee, Arnold, 236
Tradition-directed, 54
Turner, Ralph, 233–234, 236, 259, 261, 263–264, 266
Tyler, Gus, 212

Vertical group, 84
Vertical mobility, 120–121
Voluntary group, 83

Ward, David, 337
Warner, Lloyd, 116–117
Wattenberg, Ben, 210
Webb, Eugene, 340
Weber, Max, 90–94, 99, 108, 113, 171, 338
White-collar crime, 120, 305
Whyte, William H., Jr., 205
Women, 200, 231
  Freud's viewpoint, 157–160
  and mass media, 159–160
  roles of, 154–161
  and stereotypes, 154–161
Women's liberation movement, 4, 154

Yablonsky, Lewis, 337
Yinger, J. Milton, 56, 173, 178
Yir Yoront, 244–251

Zehring, Robin, 307
Zuni, 54